Greek and the Greeks

Greek and the Greeks

COLLECTED PAPERS
VOLUME I: LANGUAGE, POETRY, DRAMA

K. J. Dover

Basil Blackwell

Copyright © K. J. Dover 1987

First published 1987

Basil Blackwell Ltd
108 Cowley Road, Oxford, OX4 1JF, UK

Basil Blackwell Inc.
432 Park Avenue South, Suite 1503
New York, NY 10016, USA

British Library Cataloguing in Publication Data
Dover, K. J.
Greek and the Greeks: collected papers.
Vol. 1: Language, poetry, drama
1. Civilization, Greek
I. Title
938   DF77
ISBN 0-631-15792-1

Library of Congress Cataloging in Publication Data
Dover, Kenneth James.
Greek and the Greeks.
Bibliography: p.
Includes index.
Contents: v. 1. Language, poetry, drama.
1. Greek philology.   2. Greece—Civilization.
I. Title.
PA27.D73   1987   880′.9   87-15814
ISBN 0-631-15792-1 (U.S.: v. 1)

Typeset in 10 on 11½ pt Baskerville
by Joshua Associates Limited, Oxford
Printed in Great Britain by
TJ Press, Padstow, Cornwall

Contents

Preface

In the course of the last forty years I have written nearly two hundred articles, reviews, addresses, obituaries, chapters in books of composite authorship, contributions to commemorative volumes, broadcast talks and letters to the press. Nearly all, though not quite all this work was intended to contribute something to the study of the language, literature and history of the ancient Greeks. Those contributions have been distributed over some forty journals and books, many of which are not easily accessible to students of Classics in the English-speaking world. When it was suggested to me that all my *scripta minora* should be brought together in one or two volumes, my first inclination was to give precedence to the least accessible items and exclude everything that has appeared in 'main line' periodicals. Having taken a good deal of advice about this, I was persuaded otherwise, and have therefore followed a different principle: to exclude some items written for the general reader, a few articles of which the content and argument were entirely absorbed into books subsequently published, the majority of the reviews, and all items which had nothing to do with Greek.

This volume concerns the Greek language and Greek poetry, including drama. The second volume will concern Greek prose literature, history and society, the transmission of Greek texts and Greek influences on our own culture. It will contain (as this volume does not) a few pieces which have been given as lectures or seminar papers but have not appeared in print.

Short of devoting a year's work solely to the preparation of the two volumes, which would have been an unacceptable interruption of my current programme, I could not undertake to update any item systematically by taking account of controversial issues which have been debated since its publication. In some cases, however, I have a few notes correcting or retracting what I originally wrote, adducing some fresh examples to illustrate an argument, or putting forward some fresh thoughts.

Where transliteration of Greek names is concerned, different periodicals have their own rules. Consequently, the same name will appear in this book in two or more different forms, and I have not attempted to eliminate inconsistency. It should not, after all, cause readers any more trouble than they would encounter if they looked up the articles in the periodicals in which they were originally published. Similar considerations apply to the numeration of fragments, but guidance on alternative numerations is given in section I of the Index.

My thanks for unfailing help and good advice are owed to René Olivieri, who first came up with the idea of the book; to the copy-editor, Graham Eyre; and to Diyan Leake, the senior desk editor.

St Andrews   K. J. D.
April 1987

Acknowledgements

The author and publishers are grateful to the following for permission to reproduce previously published material written by the author.

J. J. Augustin Inc. for 'The Colloquial Stratum in Classical Attic Prose' from *Classical Contributions: Studies in honor of Malcolm Francis McGregor* (1981).

C. H. Beck'sche Verlagsbuchhandlung for review of Bergson, *Zur Stellung des Adjektivs in der älteren griechischen Sprache*, Gnomon xxxiii (1961); review of Thesleff, *Studies in the Styles of Plato*, Gnomon xli (1969); and review of Tarditi's *Archilochus* and Prato's *Tyrtaeus*, Gnomon xliii (1971).

Cambridge Philological Society for 'The Skene in Aristophanes' from *Proceedings of the Cambridge Philological Society*, 192 (1966).

Casa Editrice Licinio Cappelli for 'Notes on Aristophanes' *Acharnians*', Maia N.S. xv (1963).

Edizioni dell'Ateneo S.p.A. for 'The Style of Aristophanes' translated from 'Lo stile di Aristofane', *Quaderni Urbinati di Cultura Classica* ix (1970) and 'Language and Character in Aristophanes' translated from 'Linguaggio e caratteri Aristofanei', *Rivista di Cultura Classica e Medioevale* xviii (1976).

The editors of *Essays in Criticism* for 'The Speakable and Unspeakable', *Essays in Criticism* xxx (1980).

Fondation Hardt for 'The Poetry of Archilochus', *Entretiens de la Fondation Hardt* x (1963).

Dr Rudolf Habelt GmbH for 'ΔE in the Khalkis Decree', *Zeitschrift für Papyrologie und Epigraphik* xxx (1978).

Istituto Nazionale del Dramma Antico for 'The Red Fabric in the *Agamemnon*' translated from 'I tessuti rossi dell *Agamennone*', *Dioniso* xlviii (1977).

Oxford University Press for 'Some Types of Abnormal Word-Order in Attic Comedy', *Classical Quarterly* N.S. xxxv (1985); review of Lasserre and Bonnard's *Archilochus*, *Classical Review* N.S. x (1960); 'Pindar, *Isthmian Odes* 6.4', *Classical Review* N.S. i (1951); 'Pindar, *Olympian Odes* 6.82–6', *Classical Review* N.S. ix (1959); 'Aeschylus, fr. 248 M', *Classical Review* xiv (1964); 'Plato Comicus: *Presbeis* and *Hellas*', *Classical Review* lxiv (1950); review of Taillardat, *Les Images d'Aristophane*, *Classical Review* N.S. xviii (1968); 'Aristophanes, *Knights*

11–20', *Classical Review* N.S. ix (1959); and review of Brook Otis, *Cosmos and Tragedy*, *Notes and Queries* xxx (1980).

The Philological Society for 'The Language of Classical Attic Documentary Inscriptions', *Transactions of the Philological Society* (1981).

Quaderni di Storia for 'Song-Language in Preliterate Cultures', translated with revisions from 'Il linguaggio del canto nelle culture primitive', *Quaderni di Storia* ix (1979).

Society for the Promotion of Hellenic Studies for 'The Portrayal of Moral Evaluation in Greek Poetry', *Journal of Hellenic Studies* ciii (1983); 'Some Neglected Aspects of Agamemnon's Dilemma', *Journal of Hellenic Studies*; and 'The Political Aspect of Aeschylus's *Eumenides*', *Journal of Hellenic Studies* lxxvii (1957).

Every attempt has been made to contact copyright holders, but we apologize for any omissions.

1
Song-Language in Preliterate Cultures

In this paper[1] I shall use the terms 'song' and 'poetry' indifferently, because whatever distinction we make between them in English serves no purpose in relation to the archaic Greek world (about which I shall say something at the end) or the cultures with which this enquiry is concerned. By 'preliterate' cultures I mean those which did not use writing before the era of European colonialism; they are for the most part cultures at a rudimentary technological level, with no social organization on a large scale.

When Maurice Bowra published *Primitive Song* in 1962 he was trying to answer a historical question: what were the general characteristics of poetry at the earliest stage of human development which we can recover through the data at our disposal? Given that in human evolution hunting and gathering preceded agriculture and herding, Bowra studied the songs recorded and translated by anthropologists in the course of their work among peoples which have remained hunters and gatherers down to our own time; in particular the Eskimos, the natives of Tierra del Fuego, the Bushmen of South Africa, the Vedda of Sri Lanka, the so-called 'Negritos' of Malaysia and the Australian aborigines. This procedure is open to the criticism that it does not take sufficient account of the irregularity and unpredictability of cultural and artistic borrowings; for example, the Vedda, although they belong to a stratum of population earlier than the arrival of Indo-European-speaking peoples, now speak Sinhalese, and, just as they were able to discard their original language in favour of that of a more advanced culture, so they could also have taken over new poetic techniques. It is hardly possible to say whether the poetry of hunter-gatherers possesses any positive or negative features which distinguish it from the poetry of primitive cultivators; that would be a question which – if it admitted of an answer at all – would require an immense quantity of data. Nevertheless, as a selective treatment of certain

---

[1] This paper began as the Maurice Bowra Memorial Lecture which I gave in Wadham College, Oxford, in 1977. In 1978 I gave the same lecture in various Italian universities – substituting *Alla mattina appena alzata* for *I Told Every Little Star* – and it was published in *Quaderni di Storia* in 1979. A revised version of the lecture, with the addition of the paragraph about Aristotle's *Poetics*, was given as the Andrew Lang Lecture in St Andrews in 1981.

features of the poetry of some peoples who were culturally and technologically underdeveloped *Primitive Song* was a useful and suggestive book; in particular (and this illustrates the utility of anthropology to the classicist) it raised questions relevant to the function and *persona* of the poet in archaic Greek society.[2] Naturally one cannot solve problems of that kind by 'deductions' founded on universal 'laws' of poetry and society. It is however a fact that the range of possible answers to problems of interpretation raised by Greek poetry is enlarged when we take account of what happens in cultures which have no historical links with the Greeks and show not even the remotest trace of classical influence.

Bowra points out the use of images and allusions in primitive song and draws attention to some of its widespread characteristics, notably refrains and sequences of vowels chosen for their sound,[3] but he has practically nothing to say about the ways in which song is differentiated from speech in phonology, morphology, syntax and vocabulary. More recently Dr Ruth Finnegan has offered some very acute observations on the part played by the language of song in defining the function of the poet in primitive society,[4] but all her examples illustrate images and allusions, ingredients which are apparent in the translated texts. I shall be more concerned with detailed phenomena which cannot be described or illustrated without quoting and analysing the poetic texts in the languages in which they were composed. I am sorry that even today it is still necessary to point out that there are no correlations between the technological progress of a people and the morphological complexity or lexical subtlety of its language; only a few years ago I encountered an eminent hellenist who seriously believed that members of very primitive human societies communicated with one another only by bestial grunts.[5] It is in fact we, the products of a highly technological civilization, accustomed to mathematical formulae, who are reducing verbal communication to incoherent grunts. A people which has not yet discovered metals or invented writing retains its full capacity to use its energy and imagination in discussing the aesthetic merits of hypothetical variants in a verse.[6] Moreover, a lack of subtlety in one artistic area does not imply a similar deficiency in every area; many cultures have invested their quantum of artistic energy, so to speak, in the art of language.

The nature of song-language in preliterate cultures can be most easily comprehended by applying its most characteristic transformations to a popular song in our own language, e.g.

> I told every little star
> How sweet I think you are.
> Why didn't I tell you?

---

[2] Below, 108–15.

[3] The widespread diffusion of these phenomena is established beyond doubt (cf. Welsh 137, 162ff on Eskimo songs), and I shall not refer to it again.

[4] Finnegan 234f.

[5] It was the late Sir Denys Page, but I did not like to disclose that while he was alive.

[6] e.g. the Shoshone of North America (Shimkin 347), and cf. Quain 5 on the Fijians.

The transformations can be classified as follows.

1   Change of vowels, e.g.

I teuld every little stor . . .

2   Abbreviation of words, extension of words, or reduplication of syllables, e.g.

I tetetold ev little star . . .

3   It sometimes happens that a change of this kind presents a form which is recognizable as dialectal or archaic, e.g.

Oi telt every little sterre . . .

4   Substitution of words and phrases drawn from other languages, e.g.

Ich told chaque little star . . .

5   Substitution of words which, so far as the evidence goes, do not belong to other languages, e.g.

Noo told every little remp . . .

In such a case the anthropologist has to discover from the singer, or infer from the analysis of other texts, that in song, though never in the spoken language, 'noo' can mean 'I' and 'remp' 'star'.

In the course of the last hundred years quite a lot of data have been published which are relevant to the relation between spoken language and song-language in various cultures, but we do not as yet have any synthesis offering a comparative study of song-language.[7] For want of anything better, I offer here some provisional observations – necessarily of a dilettante character, because they are founded entirely on other people's field-work. Most of my examples are drawn from the Pacific islands and New Guinea, with some supplementary data from Asia, and the conclusions to which they lead cohere with what I have read about song-language in Africa and America; but I have not studied any collection of texts in African or American languages.

Among studies of the phenomenon in the Pacific (and much has been recorded but not published) three have a particular importance:

---

[7] Fischer's article is full of interesting information on Pacific cultures, but he does not analyse many examples.

1   Five pages of the book by R. H. Codrington, *The Melanesian Languages*. Codrington, a Fellow of Wadham College, Oxford, who dedicated the greater part of his life to missionary work in Melanesia, acquired an intimate knowledge of the language of a small island called Mota (Sugarloaf Island),[8] one of the Banks Islands in the northern New Hebrides. In his book he gives grammatical descriptions of thirty-five languages, with some historical and comparative discussion. Many of these descriptions are only sketches, and they are by no means free of major errors, but they include a detailed grammar of Mota, at the end of which he adds a summary characterization of Mota song-language and the texts of two songs, provided with a literal translation and a succinct linguistic commentary. One of the songs is also given in a language which is closely related to Mota, Motlav, so that the reader can discern without difficulty the differences between spoken Mota, Mota song, spoken Motlav and Motlav song.[9] This handful of data, which to the best of my belief represents the first information ever communicated to Western scholars on song-language in preliterate cultures, was worth, and is still worth, any amount of generalization and theory.

2   The book by G. C. Wheeler, *Mono-Alu Folklore*, published in 1926, contains the texts of seventy stories and nine songs collected in 1908–9 on Treasury Island and Shortland Island, which are situated off the south coast of Bougainville Island in the northern part of the Solomon Islands. Wheeler gives not only a literal translation but also a detailed linguistic commentary, and draws attention to every syllable of difference between spoken and sung language, although he is not always able to disentangle the ingredients of a poetic expression, nor is he always convincing when he offers a tentative explanation of it.

3   More recently, Dr D. C. Laycock published an article[10] on the 'subsidiary languages' of Buin, a Papuan language spoken on Bougainville. Much material had been collected in that region previously and published by Thurnwald,[11] but he had not furnished it with adequate linguistic comment; Laycock, by contrast, systematically investigated the Buin vocabulary, describing and classifying the transformations of spoken language in song and bringing out certain aspects of song-language which had been neglected by earlier scholars, both in Buin and in other languages.

It is assumed, and it is often asserted, that song-language is full of archaisms, and much can be said in justification of this presupposition. Certainly a song has a rhythm and a melody which are in danger of being spoiled if the words are altered to conform with the changes which have occurred in the

---

[8] It seems that the sound transcribed by Codrington as italic *m* is a nasalized *w*; I have ignored the distinction in writing 'Mota' and 'Motlav'.

[9] Codrington 308ff, 321f.

[10] I am grateful to Dr Laycock for sending me a copy of his paper and for his advice on the bibliography of the subject.

[11] Especially the material which he collected in 1912.

spoken language after the composition of the song. There are songs – and this is obvious in our own culture too – which retain their original form when the spoken language has changed; and they make their own archaic language available to the composers of new songs, so that it is not always possible to establish whether a given song is genuinely old or simply archaizing. There are also songs which have a magical or ceremonial function, and when it is believed that the fulfilment of the function depends on precision people try to preserve the words of the song unchanged, even when it is not possible to make them intelligible by translating them into a different register.[12] It can happen that the singer will say to the anthropologist 'This is old language,[13] we don't know now what it means', or 'It was composed a long time ago', or 'It means . . . er . . . Well, it's the beginning[14] of an incantation which . . .', and in cases of that kind it is not unreasonable to believe that in the past it might have been possible to give a more detailed explanation.[15] Where it is believed (as many peoples in the Pacific believe) that the souls of ancestors survive and communicate with the living, it is not easy to distinguish between 'the language of our ancestors', in which one would expect to find some genuine archaisms, and 'the language of the spirits', which differentiates spirits from living people just as human communities are separated by diversity of language.[16] A Mono singer said that the spirits call the porpoise *kuleba*, while humans call it *uriafa*.[17] Homer (to judge from *Il.* xiv 290) would have expressed that by saying *κουλήβην καλέουσι θεοί, ἄνδρες δ' ὀριήφην*.[18] In a preliterate society non-linguistic evidence for the antiquity of a song is not easy to find.[19] On Tikopia the names of poets were transmitted with their songs, and genealogical data suggest that some songs go back to the eighteenth century; possibly some others, whose composers are no longer known, may be older.[20]

Reconstructions made in accordance with the methods of historical linguistics allow us to assign some phenomena of song to the category 'archaic'. In areas where linguistic families are small and numerous all reconstructions are full of uncertainties, but the languages which belong to the immense Austronesian family are a different matter. For example, in the language of

---

[12] Williams 181, in saying that some spells 'have become little more than nonsense syllables', presupposes that verses which at one time were intelligible became corrupted later. I ought not to have said (below, p. 108) that spells are 'handed on without verbal change from one generation to another'.

[13] Malinowski 225 (Trobriand Is.); Welsh 151 (Cherokee).

[14] Evans 48f.

[15] It may well be that not everyone wishes to explain everything to an alien enquirer, and also that many think it discourteous to refuse to offer an explanation of something which is not actually explicable.

[16] Bollig 211; cf. Fischer 1141.

[17] Wheeler 361.

[18] Proclus, in his commentary on Plato's *Timaeus* (32b), cites an Orphic hymn according to which the gods call the moon σελήνη but humans call it μήνη.

[19] Cf. Opie col. 4 on internal and external evidence for the antiquity of a children's song.

[20] Firth 286.

Rotuma (a lonely island over a thousand kilometres distant from Fiji) the spoken language distinguishes semantically between 'complete' and 'incomplete' forms of many words, e.g. *mafa*, *maf*, 'eye'; in the incomplete form there is sometimes metathesis of the final vowel, e.g. *lima*, *liam*, 'five'. In song the complete form prevails;[21] so *mafmea*, 'red eyes' (a species of crab) would be *mafamea* in song. So far as words of Austronesian origin are concerned, it can be shown that the complete form is the older: *mafa* and *lima* are the Proto-Austronesian **mata* and **lima*, and the same is true of *folu*, 'three', and *ono*, 'six' (incomplete forms *fol*, *on*, Proto-Austronesian **təlu*, **ənəm*.[22] The consistent use of complete forms in song has a secondary effect of some interest, because in the spoken language the difference is important: *hosa* means 'the flowers', *hoas* 'flowers', *hosat* 'a flower', and *hoasta* 'the flower', but in song we do not expect to encounter any forms other than *hosa*, 'flowers' or 'the flowers', and *hosata* (a form unknown in speech), 'a flower' or 'the flower'. In such cases, if the hearer wants to understand exactly what is being communicated in a song, he has to attend to the context of each word just as closely as he would if he were listening to a resurrected ancestor using the ancient language in which the incomplete forms had not yet evolved.[23]

Nevertheless, if it were assumed, in the absence of positive evidence to the contrary, that every form characteristic of song in a preliterate culture must necessarily be archaic,[24] this would not do justice to other factors which contribute to determining the language of song. In fact, historical reconstruction leads in different directions. In Mota, for example, 'island' and 'boat' occur in a song quoted by Codrington in the forms *venue* and *ok* respectively. But the spoken language says *vanua* and *aka*, and those forms are Proto-Austronesian (**banuwa* and **vaŋkaŋ*); it is therefore apparent that *venue* and *ok* are innovations, not archaisms. Compare in Tikopia *tomono* (in song)[25] = *tamana* (in speech), 'father' (Proto-Austronesian **ama*, often *tama* in the Pacific), and on Rennell Island *maaa* (in song)[26] = *mata* (in speech), 'eye'. But *ok* is 'boat' in spoken Motlav, and *vono* is 'island' in several languages of the vicinity;[27] thus we have to consider the extent to which foreign forms are imported into song.

A whole song can of course come into a culture through an individual who has learned it in a different ambience, and it can be translated, with varying degrees of fidelity to its original language, by many who do not understand it – that is to say, do not know, whatever meaning they may attach to the words, what the composer meant. This phenomenon is apparent at Waropen (on the

---

[21] Churchward 100f.

[22] Although I have asterisked the forms attributed to Proto-Austronesian, several of them are still in current use, particularly in Indonesia.

[23] I am grateful to Mrs E. K. Inia (Suva, Fiji) for confirming that my interpretation of Churchward is on the right lines; if my actual examples are erroneous in any way, the fault is mine.

[24] The warning of Held 271 has to be heeded.

[25] Firth 290.

[26] Elbert and Monberg 336.

[27] Ray 436.

northern coast of New Guinea), where an imported song can continue in use, after being corrupted, to the point at which it is difficult even for the members of the linguistic community in which it originated to explain its main theme.[28] The phenomenon is not unknown in more sophisticated cultures; not all English people who can sing *Adeste fideles*, *Alouette*, *Frère Jacques* or *Muss ich denn* can translate them, and it is observable that small children are able to learn a song in a foreign language before they know that there are such things as foreign languages. Preliterate communities go two steps beyond that. The first step is exemplified by a song composed by a Mono man who had to go to hospital on Gizo, adjacent to New Georgia, where Roviana is spoken, a language related to Mono but not mutually intelligible with it.[29] In this song, which expresses the melancholy of the sick man in exile, he replaces the Mono words *uligu*, 'my body', and *totogu*, 'my leg', and *maula*, 'pain', by the Roviana words *tiniŋgu*, *neneŋgu* and *sigeti* (*sic*).[30] He also uses phrases drawn from the language of the colonial administration, 'my nephew', 'my grandfather', 'my gran' (*sic*), although he keeps in Mono *kaigu*, 'my brother'. Since the song is the product of the experience of its composer being treated in a British hospital in a region where Roviana is spoken, and since the Roviana words are intimately connected with his physical condition as a patient,[31] their adoption could be compared with the adoption of *hombre*, *señorita* and *sí sí* in an English or American popular song dealing with an imaginary experience in Spain or Mexico. But this hardly suffices to explain the particular phrases of English origin, and it does nothing for the recurrence of *biguuini* (English 'big wind', i.e. 'storm') in another Mono song about a man in a canoe. It looks as if a song can import elements of any other language with which the composer has been in contact, but it has a special tendency to make use of the language which is associated with the power and prestige of higher technological development. Some Alu words have been imported into Buin songs because it is believed that the families to which the Buin chiefs belong originated from Shortland Island; more recently, some English elements have intruded.[32] During the period in which Japan administered the Caroline Islands some Japanese elements entered the language of the love-songs of those islands.[33]

Taste for the exotic, the difficulty of transmitting accurately what no one can translate into another register, the impossibility of an anthropologist's

---

[28] Held 269f.

[29] Wheeler 356f.

[30] It appears from Waterhouse *s.v.* that the Roviana word is *siyiti*.

[31] Wheeler 357 translates *abu era raŋe boŋi ihamoloanita* 'does not (*sc.* the rain) wet us every day?', on the grounds that *raŋe boŋi* is Roviana for 'every day'. But in Waterhouse *raneboŋi* is 'bad weather' (*rane na boŋi* would be 'night and day'), and it is possible that the singer meant 'bad weather does not wet us (*sc.* in the hospital)' – the sequence of thought in the context does not help – using a foreign weather-term (cf. *khamsin* etc.) belonging to the locality to which he is referring.

[32] Thurnwald (1936) 7, 14.

[33] Fischer and Swartz 221f.

acquiring sufficient knowledge of all the languages of the area in which he is working – all this helps to explain why it so often happens that in the published texts whole phrases or verses are designated 'meaningless' or 'musical syllables'.[34] Nevertheless, their presence is relevant to the question of archaism, because in any group of related dialects or languages it is bound to happen that some of them are more archaic than others; that is to say, the current form of a word in a given dialect is identical with the form which was ancestral to the form current in another dialect. For example, the Mono story-tellers and poets ascribe to the Alu dialect certain words in which there is an initial or intervocalic *k* (e.g. *kela*, *boko*)[35] absent from the equivalent words in spoken Mono (*ela*, *boo*). Alu, the dialect once spoken on Shortland Island, is now extinct, replaced by Mono. There is no doubt that in spoken Mono *ela* and *boo* are reflexes of forms **kela*, **boko* in Old Mono (cf. *iana*, 'fish', < **ikana*, Proto-Austronesian **ikan*); but that does not tell us whether *kela* and *boko* exist in Mono song because they once existed in spoken Mono or because they were imported from Alu at a time (down to the middle of the nineteenth century) when Alu was still spoken. One consideration in favour of the latter hypothesis emerges if we turn to the Mota texts.

The most noticeable and consistent difference between spoken Mota and spoken Motlav is that Motlav does not have so many open syllables; for example, 'on his eyes' is *yoro na-mata-na* in Mota but *yor na-mta-n* in Motlav.[36] From this point of view sung Mota has a strong resemblance to spoken Motlav; apart from *ok*, already noted, we find *ar*, 'casuarina tree' (in the spoken language *aru*, and *er* in the Motlav version of the song), and *rere* and *rer*, 'current' (only *rere* in the spoken language). Conversely, in Motlav song we find rather more open syllables than in Motlav speech (so that Motlav song comes a little nearer to Mota speech), because there is a tendency to add the suffix *e*, e.g. *lame*, 'sea' (spoken Motlav *lam*, spoken Mota *lama*, Mota song *lame*), and *turture*, 'stand' (*turtur* in the Mota version of the song, *tur* in Mota speech).[37] Thus when the Motlav text says *na-sri*, 'my bones'[38] – in Mota song *na-sri-k*, in spoken Mota *na-suri-k* – while 'bone' is *hir* in spoken Motlav and *suri*, *sri*, *hir* are all reflexes of Proto-Austronesian **duyi*, 'thorn' generally in Indonesia but 'bone' here and there in its eastern regions[39], it is reasonable to suppose that *-sri-* in the Mota song is not an archaism but a Motlav-like distortion. *Enin*, 'we' in Mota song, and *enaean*, 'we' and *nirman*, 'they' in Motlav song (in spoken Mota 'we' is *inina*, while in spoken Motlav 'we' is *iyed* or *yed* and 'they' *iker* or *ker*), have cognate words in the area, since *inin*, *enin*,

---

[34] Firth 289; Wheeler 254ff, 353ff *passim*.

[35] Wheeler 294, 307.

[36] Codrington 311.

[37] Codrington 322. Cf. the free use of the sound *e* in Hawaiian songs (Elbert 352).

[38] I do not know why the possessive suffix of the first person singular, *k*, is absent in Codrington's text.

[39] Capell 139.

nin, 'we', and *iner*, *ner*, *enir*, *nir*, 'they', are recorded by Codrington in languages of the largest island in the Banks group.[40]

Neither archaism nor borrowing in song-language is satisfactorily explained unless we can at the same time offer some explanation of the fact that there are certain unusual phenomena in song which, according to all the evidence at our disposal, are explicable neither as archaisms nor as importations. The syntax of the possessive pronouns constitutes just such an instance. In Melanesian languages the relation of ownership is expressed in more than one way; the pronoun is affixed directly to a word which means a part of the body or a blood-relation (e.g. 'hand-my', 'brother-my'), but when the ownership is alienable the pronoun is attached to a special substantive in apposition to the noun (e.g. in Mono *sagu numa*, '*sa*-my house' = 'my house', *egu iana*, '*e*-my fish' = 'my fish' = 'the fish which I am going to eat'). Each language exhibits some special developments; for example, in Mono a possessive noun in apposition to a reduplicated verb gives a continuative sense, so that *fefela sagu*, 'cucut *sa*-my' = 'I kept on cutting'. But in song the rules of the spoken language are not always observed. In a Mota song 'my wind', i.e. 'the wind whose blowing I welcome' is *na-lŋi-k*, but in speech it would be necessary to say *no-k o laŋ*, '*no*-my the wind' (*na* and *o* are articles); and in Mono song both possessive nouns, *sa* and *e*, are used with the verb, which may or may not be reduplicated.[41] There is no reason to say that this flexibility in expressing the relation of possession is archaic or that it has been borrowed in Mota and Mono songs from other languages. It seems rather to be a matter of a freedom of linguistic manipulation.

At this point it is useful to offer some tentative explanations of the phenomena which occur in song-language; an entirely comprehensive explanation is not to be expected, but rather an enumeration of the factors which in a given culture are relevant to the development of a song-language.

1   The borrowing of words and phonological or grammatical phenomena from foreign languages exhibits the learning and experience of the composer.[42] That stimulates him in his search for linguistic alternatives if the song is to be sung in public.[43]

2   The use of archaisms not only demonstrates the superior erudition of the composer but also implies an intimacy on his part with ancestral spirits. Sometimes the singer of magical songs is regarded as a spokesman of the spirits,[44] or it may be believed that the text of a song only becomes intelligible

---

[40] Codrington 346, 351.

[41] Wheeler 265, 353.

[42] Thurnwald (1936) 7.

[43] A literate Yabim (New Guinea) wrote a letter in which he used both *ai* and *yau* in the sense 'I' (*ai* is Yabim, *yau* is Tami). His wife was a Tami, but the letter was not addressed to her, nor did the sentence containing *yau* refer to her (Dempwolff 228 n. 1). Possibly he thought a demonstration of knowledge of more than one language appropriate to composition in writing.

[44] Evans 44f; Quain 14, 21.

when the singer has gone into a trance through magical or pharmacological means.[45] A Fijian singer declared that some of the words in his songs, entirely unknown to his audience, were communicated to him by his ancestors while he was in a trance[46] — a claim which he could of course use to justify any invention of words on his part.

3   Professional mystification can be very important to the singer. The greater the power of recall and understanding his art seems to require, the higher his status in the community.[47] There are cultures in which anyone who aspires to become a singer of magical or traditional songs attaches himself as an apprentice to an established singer,[48] and rival schools like to make the process of learning harder for their own pupils rather than easier. The human liking for special intimacies is conducive to the development of esoteric languages for men, women, adolescents, chiefs,[49] secret societies and the like, and languages generated in this way (a phenomenon widely diffused in the Pacific and south-east Asia)[50] become exemplars on which the composers of songs can model their own special diction.

4   It is often believed that the realization of a magical purpose by the control of non-human powers requires special linguistic means.[51] Everyday experience teaches us that, if we use plain language in telling the rain to stop and praying to the gods for wealth, the rain does not stop, nor do we become wealthy. We take to the idea that things might go better if we expressed our imperatives differently, for example in a dead language or a special tone of voice,[52] just as we use a special tool for a difficult operation or a rare and expensive herb to cure a dangerous illness. The more special the means, the more easily we can make excuses when we fail to achieve our end (it is so easy to get a detail wrong) and the more resilient our preconceptions about magic can remain in the face of disappointment (we cannot recognize with complete equanimity how little control we have over our environment). As soon as magical language of any type is differentiated from spoken language, it influences other kinds of speech which have some features in common with magic, even if their function is different. Taboos and inhibitions (e.g. refraining during a hunt from uttering the name of any of the hunters or the ordinary words for the hunted animals)[53] represent another system which can be imitated in song.

[45] Held 270.

[46] Quain 16.

[47] Fischer 1147f.

[48] Bollig 46f; Evans 42f.

[49] Heider lists details of the language of Samoan chiefs.

[50] Cf. Aufinger *passim* and Bollig 211; Aufinger does not give enough explanation of the circumstances in which secret languages are used in Madang.

[51] Held 271: 'the chant has the same object as the ritual, viz. to activate the contact with the sacred world, and for this very reason the poetic language has to be different from that of every day', and 'the obscure and unusual form of the language by itself is an active element in the ritual'. Cf. Malinowski 223ff *passim*.

[52] Malinowski 224.

[53] Laycock 2f.

5   Every artistic genre claims some degree of autonomy, and when particular features have developed in some songs it can happen that those features come to be regarded as appropriate, even *de rigueur*, in all the other kinds of song. The anthropologist Held, who worked at Waropen, found it hard to transcribe songs accurately, but he could not persuade his informants to correct passages which he knew he had reduced to a meaningless sequence of syllables, because they asured him that he had created something better, something more beautiful, more poetic, than the original text.[54] This seems to be a clear example of unintelligibility as a poetic criterion.

6   Freedom to modify on the grounds of function favours also freedom to create forms which are attractive simply as patterns of sound (people might like a sung *o* better than a sung *a*) or which attract by virtue of associations of which neither the singer nor his audience are aware. Modern linguistics, obsessed by the intellectual aspects of communication, has in general chosen to disregard the element of aesthetic choice inherent in human utterance. It is certainly absurd, in discussing sung utterance, to underrate the part played in the determination of its form by aesthetic preference, caprice and experiment, particularly in the light of the evidence that intelligibility is not always of primary importance to the audience.

In both Rotuma and Mota song-language can be called 'systematic' in the sense that in Rotuma it tends to use the complete form of every word and of every ingredient in a compound word, while in Mota song cuts down the words of the spoken language by apocope. The poet encodes in accordance with a simple and comprehensible principle, and the hearer decodes. It seems that in Mota the decoder has to attend to the context more closely than in listening to speech, since (for example) *ar* in song could mean either 'casuarina' (*aru*) or another species (*aro*) of tree.[55]

Song-language in Buin employs a more complicated code.[56] If a common noun or proper name has two syllables, two more are added; if it has three, the number is raised to four by adding one or replacing one by two; if it has four to start with, two of them are replaced by a different two. Thus *tamu*, 'food' > *tamuai*; *atiga*, 'sea' > *atigana*;[57] *mukunu*, 'turtle' > *mukuaka*, *mukukero* or *mukuero*; *Agura* (the name of a river) > *Guranei*; *iritia*, 'hawk' > *irigara*; *kugunia*, 'Venus' > *niakoto*. Eighty-seven suffixes of this kind have been recorded in Buin, and there are about 170 nouns which lose one or two syllables when the poetic suffix is attached to them; naturally, ambiguities are not uncommon, especially with names of persons, villages and rivers. The

---

[54] Held 271; cf. Firth 286.
[55] I may however be mistaken in believing that *aro* would be *ar* in song.
[56] Laycock 5–12.
[57] The suffix *na*, which has several different functions in spoken Mono, occurs so often in Mono songs that Wheeler may be right (360) in calling it a 'song-sound'. The Mono and Buin languages, although in contact, are typologically different and of different origins, since Mono is Austronesian and Buin is Papuan.

system is comparable with that which is used in the language of ritual and narrative myth by the Thulung people of Nepal,[58] where (e.g.) *rep*, 'look', is replaced by *loamiksi toamiksi rep*, 'see-eyes tee-eyes look' (*loas* is 'see' and *miksi* 'eyes'), and to express 'he dried it in the sun' use is made of a periphrasis analogous to 'sun-dry *dəda*-dry make-*so* complete-*so*'. Both Buin and Thulung call to mind the elementary codes sometimes used by a group of children who want to prevent outsiders from understanding what is said within the group; I recall a code of this kind in which *aig* (bearing a stress accent) was inserted before the vowel of every syllable, so that 'Go away!' became 'Gaigo aigawaigay!' – a very crude transformation, but surprisingly efficient, thanks above all to the shift of stress. Such a play-language in fact exists in Buin,[59] where the principle of transformation is simple inversion: *muo > omu*, *amanoko > nokoama*, etc. Trisyllabic words become quadrisyllabic by the reduplication of one of their elements, e.g. *oreu > uuore*. It is hard to say whether this implies influence of song on code or of code on song, but it requires us to add a seventh factor to the six described above: the essentially playful manipulation of language.[60] Such manipulation has affinities on the one hand with the creation of a special language to reinforce the cohesion and exclusiveness of a sect or a class, and on the other hand with the creative variation employed by a poet who indulges his own aesthetic preferences, but is nevertheless distinct from both.

In some cases a play-form in Buin appears to have extended its hold outside its own domain; *piniai*, 'girl', coexists with *aipini*, and (the clearest example) *pororiŋ* (the English word 'florin') goes side by side with *rimporo*[61] in ordinary usage. The same has happened to one common poetic word: *urugito*, 'pig', has largely displaced *uuru*, of which (note its quadrisyllabic structure) it is the poetic transformation.[62] This datum, of limited significance in itself, raises very important questions as soon as it is combined with the observation that song-language absorbs dialectal and foreign phenomena.

First: among the possible determinants of linguistic change in general, ought we not to include the conscious artistic manipulation of words and the importation of forms thus altered into the current vocabulary of the spoken language?

Secondly: what part has been played in the history of linguistic change by borrowing from one dialect into another or one language into another through the medium of poetry?

My categorization of the distinctive features of song-language has been based solely on texts actually recorded in the study of preliterate societies, but it

---

[58] Allen 184ff; I am indebted to Dr Allen for a sight of his monograph and for discussion.
[59] Laycock 14ff.
[60] On the social functions of such games cf. Conklin, and Fischer 1148.
[61] Laycock 16; in Buin the nasal is syllabic.
[62] Laycock 6 n. 20. Thurnwald (1941) 19 calls *urugito* 'archaic', but (1936) n. 7 treats it as an ordinary word.

cannot avoid comparison with what Aristotle says about the language of poetry in chapters 21 and 22 of the *Poetics*. He has a lot to say about metaphor, which I have entirely excluded from my enquiry (one needs to know a language well to judge what is metaphorical and what is not), but he specifies dialectal words, curtailed words, lengthened words and invented words as all appropriate to poetry. Since Classical Greek thinking about language lacked a historical dimension, he is silent on archaism and unaware of the profitable trains of thought which an archaism generates in a modern comparative philologist. His tone is also strongly prescriptive: poetry ought to differ from prose in its language, so that it will be impressive and not 'ordinary or mean', but it ought also to be intelligible; poetry wholly made up of dialectal and unfamiliar words would be 'gibberish' (βαρβαρισμός).

Aristotle's familiarity with Greek epic, lyric and tragedy may possibly have deterred him from wondering how far Homer and Aeschylus achieved, or wanted to achieve, the degree of clarity which he prescribed, and the extent to which Homer, at any rate, might incur the charge of 'gibberish'. That is why it is sometimes helpful to approach Greek poetry without any preconceptions derived from previous acquaintance with it (if that is possible) and with a readiness to ask questions prompted by observation of the poetry of totally alien cultures.

The language of Greek epic exhibits at least one phonological development (the conjugation ὁρόω, ὁράᾳς, ὁράς, etc.) which never belonged to any region of the Greek world at any period of history. It presents, often in the same context, synonymous forms which have to be attributed to the dialects of different regions within the Greek linguistic community. Moreover, it sometimes uses a tense, mood or aspect of a verb in circumstances where, to judge from the semantic distinctions which we can draw in the study of Greek documents,[63] we would have expected some other tense, mood or aspect. All these problems have of course been widely discussed for a long time, but I wonder if the range of data capable of contributing to their explanation has been quite broad enough. This question is marginally 'sociolinguistic' in the sense that it is bound to affect our view of the relationship between the poet and the community for which he composed, and it leads in turn to another question more basic to the history of literary criticism: what were the attitudes of the poet and his audience, at different periods and in different places, to intelligibility?[64]

---

[63] I speak of documents, not of literary texts, because it is desirable that the study of the syntax of the verb should be founded primarily on texts put into writing at an interval of only a few days (or even on occasion minutes) from their composition, and commonly under the very eyes of the composer.

[64] I learn from Dr A. Koopman (University of Natal) that a Zulu reciter of traditional encomia attains (and is expected to attain) extraordinary speed in recitation, and that his performance is accompanied by a lot of whistling and ululation from the audience, so that his words can hardly be heard, let alone understood; the atmosphere of the occasion takes precedence over communication.

BIBLIOGRAPHY

Allen, N. J., *Sketch of Thulung Grammar* (Ithaca, NY, 1973).

Aufinger, A., 'Die Geheimsprachen auf den kleinen Inseln bei Madang in Neuguinea', *Anthropos* xxxvii/xl (1942/5) 629ff.

Bollig, L., *Die Bewohner der Truk-Inseln* (Münster 1927).

Bowra, C. M., *Primitive Song* (London 1962).

Capell, A., *The Linguistic Position of South-Eastern Papua* (Sydney 1943).

Churchward, R. M., *Rotuman Grammar and Dictionary* (Sydney 1940).

Codrington, R. H., *The Melanesian Languages* (Oxford 1885).

Conklin, H. C., 'Linguistic Play in its Cultural Context', *Language* xxxv (1959) 631ff.

Dempwollf, O., 'Beiträge zur Kenntnis der Sprachen von Deutsch-Neuguinea', *Mitteilungen des Seminars für orientalische Sprachen* viii.1 (1905) 182ff.

Dover, K. J., 'The Poetry of Archilochos' [see pp. 97–121 below].

Elbert, S. H., 'Hawaiian Literary Style and Culture', *American Anthropologist* liii (1951) 345ff.

Elbert, S. H., and Monberg, T., *From the Two Canoes: Oral Traditions of Rennell and Bellona Islands* (Honolulu and Copenhagen 1965).

Evans, I. H. N., *The Religion of the Tempasuk Dusuns of North Borneo* (Cambridge 1953).

Finnegan, Ruth, *Oral Poetry* (Cambridge 1977).

Firth, J. R., *We, the Tikopia*, 2nd edn (London 1957).

Fischer, J. L., 'Style Contrasts in Pacific Languages', *Current Trends in Linguistics* viii.2 (1971) 1129ff.

Fischer, J. L., and Swartz, M. J., 'Sociopsychological Aspects of some Trukese and Ponapean Lovesongs', *Journal of American Folklore* lxxiii (1960) 218ff.

Heider, E., 'Die samoanische Häuptlingssprache', *Mitteilungen des Seminars für orientalische Sprachen* xxxiii.1 (1930) 83ff.

Held, G. J., *The Papuas of Waropen*, Engl. tr. (The Hague 1957).

Laycock, D. C., *Sublanguages in Buin*, Papers in New Guinea Linguistics 10 (Canberra 1969).

Malinowski, B., *Coral Gardens and their Magic*, 2nd edn, vol. ii (London 1966).

Opie, Iona and Peter, 'Tradition and Transmission', *Times Literary Supplement* 14 July 1978, 799.

Quain, B. H., *The Flight of the Chiefs: Epic Poetry of Fiji* (New York 1942).

Ray, S. H., *A Comparative Study of the Melanesian Island Languages* (Cambridge 1926).

Shimkin, D. B., 'Wind River Shoshone Literary Forms', in D. Hymes (ed.), *Language in Culture and Society* (New York 1964).

Thurnwald, R., *Forschungen auf den Salomo-Inseln und dem Bismarck-Archipel* vol. i, *Leider und Sagen aus Buin* (Berlin 1912).

——, *Profane Literature of Buin, Solomon Islands*, Yale University Publications in Anthropology 8 (New Haven, Conn., 1936).

——, 'Alte und neue Volkslieder aus Buin', *Zeitschrift für Ethnologie* lxxiii (1941) 12ff.

Waterhouse, J. H. L., *A Roviana and English Dictionary* (Guadalcanar 1928).

Welsh, Andrew, *Roots of Lyric* (Princeton, NJ, 1978).

Wheeler, G. C., *Mono-Alu Folklore* (London 1926).

Williams, F. E., *Orokaiva Magic* (Oxford 1928).

2

The Colloquial Stratum in
Classical Attic Prose

In a modern language the differences between what people say and what they write are quite easily observed and described. In particular, the invention of the tape-recorder has given us access to an ocean of words uttered in a more relaxed way than can usually be achieved in the presence of stenographers. This material can be quantified, analysed and categorized objectively without any reference to the spontaneous reactions which are expressed in praise or blame according to aesthetic (and therefore idiosyncratic) criteria, and without dependence on the selective recollection which is determined by such reactions. We remain free to detest the linguistic habits of those who begin every answer with 'Well, . . .' or every narrative sentence with 'So . . .' or punctuate every explanation with a repeated 'you see' – indeed, we are free to detest everyone's linguistic habits except our own – but the frequency of such phenomena in the transcripts of discussions and interviews makes it senseless to carp at the educational attainments of all those who use them.[1] When we turn to the language of a previous age, the possibility of distinguishing between the spoken and the written language is immensely reduced, and in the case of some cultures may be reduced to nothing. From the past we have only written utterance, and no written utterance can be treated as entirely spontaneous and unconsidered; the act of writing takes time, and therefore gives time, and it entails an awareness, however ill-formed, of a future reader who will receive the message in the sender's absence and therefore without further amplification or explanation by the sender.

An earlier draft of this paper was given in Christ Church, Oxford, as the 1977 Gaisford Lecture, and an earlier version still at the Royal Society of Edinburgh in March 1977.

Reference is made to the following works by author's name only: J. D. Denniston, *The Greek Particles*, 2nd edn (Oxford 1954); P. Kretschmer, *Die griechische Vaseninschriften* (Gütersloh 1894); Mabel Lang, *Graffiti in the Athenian Agora* (Princeton, NJ, 1974); W. Peek, *Inschriften, Ostraka, Fluchtageln* (= *Kerameikos: Ergebnisse der Ausgrabungen* iii; Berlin 1941); P. T. Stevens, *Colloquial Expressions in Euripides* (= *Hermes* Einzelschriften xxxviii [1976]); R. Wünsch, *Defixionum Tabellae Atticae* (= *CIA* Appendix; Berlin 1897).

[1] No one would regard Mr John Freeman or the late Lord Birkett as inarticulate, but a transcript of part of their famous dialogue televized in 1959 (H. Montgomery Hyde, *Norman Birkett* [London 1964] 577ff) reveals eight successive utterances beginning with 'Well, ...'

In the case of classical Attic literature (and no doubt in the case of some other past literatures as well) a further difficulty is created by the fact that, judged by the standards of modern conversation (whether English or Modern Greek), such of it as has been transmitted to us is technically sophisticated and structurally elaborate. Yet we have the strongest reasons to believe that at some other periods in the history of Greek the difference between genres of literature in respect of their distance from speech could be very great indeed. The relation between modern spoken Greek, the poetry of Theodoros Prodromos in the twelfth century AD and the sum total of evidence for ancient Greek enables us to assess the relative distance of Prodromos and his contemporary Anna Komnena from twelfth-century speech and compels us to wonder how far Anna's work was intelligible to those who lacked a literary education. Similarly, the abundance of private letters and documents from Roman Egypt in the early imperial period, considered in relation to earlier literature and modern speech, affords us at least a starting-point for a hypothesis about the linguistic differences between an oration given by Dio of Prusa and the whispered comments of members of his audience; and natural curiosity leads us on to speculation about a Periclean funeral-speech. It is an area of speculation in which ancient writers on style and rhetoric give us no significant assistance, partly because they too are looking back to a past era in ignorance of its conversational idiom, and partly because they do not maintain a distinction between vulgar words for things and words for vulgar things.[2]

Within the ancient evidence available to us there is one clear and important distinction to be drawn. We possess on the one hand much literary portrayal of conversation, composed by skilled writers who wished to be admired for their artistry. We possess on the other hand utterances composed by people who wanted simply to communicate instructions, requests or sentiments. The relation between the former category and actual speech depends on the writers' attitudes to realism and to the function of art. The relation between the latter category and actual speech depends partly on the writers' beliefs about what is functionally efficient or socially acceptable in any given genre of communication,[3] and partly also on the fact that since they read less and write less than the artist the linguistic sources on which they can draw, other than conversation, are more restricted. The distinction is clear enough in modern English. In many people's speech certain words which until recently it was illegal to print are of very frequent occurrence. A novelist portraying conversation may well sow them thickly, but the people who use them freely in speech tend to avoid them in writing messages and letters; conversely, the uneducated often use stilted clichés and formulae in writing which are equally alien to their speech and to that of their more educated contemporaries.

Evidence of the second category from Athens in what I propose to call the

---

[2] Cf. [Long.] *Subl.* 43, with D. A. Russell's comment *ad loc.*

[3] Demetr. *Eloc.* 223–35 lays down rules for the style of letters; rules of that kind tend to have an effect, however fragmentary, at all levels of society.

'central' period, i.e. 430–300 BC, is in short supply;[4] many of the most interesting graffiti and dipinti are earlier or non-Attic or both, and the overwhelming majority of private documents is post-classical and comes from Egypt. Difference of time and place is a factor not to be ignored in dealing with colloquial language. My grandfather would have been surprised by the dentist's exclaiming 'Smashing!' or 'Fantastic!' when he complied with a request to open his mouth a little wider, and a foreigner who heard in Lancashire, 'They wouldn't do well there, wouldn't strawberries', would be mistaken if he adopted this sentence-structure in talking with natives of Surrey.[5] Nevertheless, if a putative colloquial phenomenon in Attic of the central period is found in relevant contexts in another region or period, a tilt is given to the balance of probability in assigning it to the colloquial register. Contrasts between the colloquial and the literary in modern languages also have analogical value, in proportion to the breadth of their distribution in cultures which use languages comparable in structure with Greek and adopt comparable attitudes towards language and literature.[6] Finally, any system of contrasts constructed for Greek merits confidence to the extent to which it resembles a system constructed independently for Latin.

It is time now to review the main types of evidence.

CATEGORY I: LITERARY PORTRAYAL

(A) Attic of the Central Period

1   One thinks first of those portions of Socratic dialogues which introduce or separate passages of sustained exposition and philosophical argument; Demetrios, *Eloc.* 297f (cf. 224 and 226), says of this genre ἐξέπληξαν τῷ τε μιμητικῷ καὶ τῷ ἐναργεῖ. But passages of reported speech in forensic oratory (e.g. Lys. i 16 must not be overlooked, and it is arguable that the great quantity of conversation in Xenophon's *Anabasis* and *Cyropaedia* might be at least as important, for our present limited purpose, as the Socratic material. Assessment of the genuinely colloquial element in it may be helped by reference to the way in which Xenophon on occasion gives dialectal colouring to a reported utterance by a non-Athenian. In *An.* vi 6.34 the Spartan Kleandros says ἀλλὰ ναὶ τὼ σιώ . . . ταχύ τοι ὑμῖν ἀποκρινοῦμαι, using a distinctively Spartan oath (cf. Ar. *Pax* 214, *Lys.* 81, 86, etc.) which recurs in *HG* iv 4.10, where a complete sentence of the Spartan Pasimakhos is given in dialect: ναὶ τὼ σιώ, ὦ 'Αργεῖοι, ψευσεῖ ὑμὲ τὰ σίγμα ταῦτα. Kleandros proceeds to offer

---

[4] I treat 430 BC as the starting-point in order to include as 'central' our earliest extant Attic comedies and prose.

[5] Both examples are genuine and heard by me during 1977. I should add that the dentist is Welsh and my Lancastrian friend an Old Harrovian.

[6] Cf. J. B. Hofmann, *Lateinische Umgangssprache*, 2nd edn (Heidelberg 1936) *passim*, and H. Hermann, *Griechische Forschungen* vol. i (Leipzig and Berlin 1912).

sacrifices in the hope of obtaining divine approval for leadership of the force which Xenophon has offered him, but θυομένῳ . . . οὐκ ἐγίγνετο τὰ ἱερά (6.36). He reports this to Xenophon and the other commanders by saying ἐμοὶ μὲν οὐ τελέθει τὰ ἱερὰ ἐξάγειν. That verb τελέθειν appears as a substitute for the normal Attic γίγνεσθαι in the words of another Spartan, Kheirisophos, at *An.* iii 2.3: δεῖ ἐκ τῶν παρόντων ἄνδρας ἀγαθοὺς τελέθειν; it is a favourite word of Theokritos (e.g. 5.18) and occurs both in Epikharmos (170.17 Kaibel) and a Doric inscription (*Tabulae Heracleenses, DGE* 61.1.111). If a touch of authentic dialect appealed to Xenophon,[7] touches of authentic colloquialism may have appealed to him no less, but perhaps we should not look for more than could fairly be called a touch. After all, Kleandros's Spartan oath in *An.* vi 6.34 introduces not the declaration ἀποκρινίομαι (as we might have hoped from the Spartan sentence in *HG* i 1.23, etc.) but ἀποκρινοῦμαι, a fact which suggests that for Xenophon dialect was a means of achieving occasional dramatic effect; cf. Kebes' Boeotian oath ἴττω Ζεύς in *Phd.* 62a, where Plato adds τῇ αὑτοῦ φωνῇ εἰπών. Serious Greek artists and writers were willing enough to portray what was wicked or frightening, but we should not expect them often to sacrifice elegance and articulateness to realistic portrayal of what they thought clumsy, socially despicable or distractingly quaint.

2 Comic dialogue, although in verse and admitting its own poetic conceits, much sophisticated word-play and much parody of serious poetry, may reasonably be supposed to contain a colloquial element, partly because its subject-matter is so often alien to that of serious literature: domestic, mundane and physiological. It readily uses obscene words, familiar to us from some classes of Category B but excluded from prose (and the occurrence of the verb βινεῖν in *CGFP* 138.8 and 254.1 shows that the distinction between Old and New Comedy in this respect is not absolute). It is surprising, but it seems on present evidence to be a fact, that comedy did not exploit the humorous potentialities of solecism and malapropism in the language of slaves or illiterate citizens. The existence of grammatical deviations which can fairly be called solecisms is attested by archaic dipinti (e.g. δέχε = δέχου, Kretschmer 89 no. 61 [black-figure]) and classical curse-tablets (e.g. καὶ [γ]υνὴν τὴν Ἐργασίωνος, Peek 91–3 no. 3.71f). Yet even the Sausage-seller of *Knights*, whose hold on reading and writing is shaky (188f), speaks as well as anyone else. The conversation of the slaves in *Ra.* 738–813, where we might expect humorous exploitation of linguistic contrast between slaves and masters, is not demonstrably marked by solecism or vulgarity; for example, the idiom μὴ ἀλλὰ πλεῖν ἢ μαίνομαι, 'I'm just crazy about it!' (751), echoes the words of Dionysos himself (103). Foreigners and speakers of dialect are certainly caricatured linguistically, but that is a different matter.[8]

[7] L. Gautier, *La Langue de Xénophon* (Geneva 1911) 22–47, esp. 26–8; J. Wackernagel, *Hellenistica* (Göttingen 1907) 7–11, 29–34.

[8] Dover, *RCCM* xviii (1976) 357–71.

3   In certain circumstances Attic tragedy may make a positive contribution. It is well known that phenomena characteristic of portrayal of conversation in prose or comedy sometimes occur in tragedy (especially in Euripides) at moments when the situation encourages us to think that a character is speaking angrily, rudely or flippantly.[9] That being so, a phenomenon found in a passage of which the emotional tone makes colloquialism appropriate deserves to be considered as possibly colloquial even when more direct evidence is lacking.

(B) Earlier Period: Attic Vases

On some Attick black-figure and (predominantly early) red-figure vases words are shown issuing from the mouths of the people portrayed or elsewhere on the surface but plainly intended by the painter to be associated with the picture. Such words must be classed as artistic portrayal of conversation, not as the direct expression of the painter's sentiments. A black-figure plaque (Athens, National Museum, Acropolis collection 2560) shows a vintage-scene accompanied by ἤδη κανῆ πλέα, then μετὰ κἀγώ (sc. οἴνου πλέως ἔσομαι),[10] followed by κἀγὼ τ[and ἐκφεφορ[. The first utterance reminds us of Ar. Ach. 946 ἤδη καλῶς ἔχει σοι (said when the sycophant has been packed up for export), and the second and third recall Ra. 414–15 ἐγὼ δ᾽ . . . χορεύειν βούλομαι. – κἀγώ γε πρός. Adverbial μετά, however, common enough in Herodotus (μετὰ δέ), is not attested from Attic comedy or prose. On the red-figure pelike (Leningrad 615a, ARV 1594),[11] the sight of the first swallow of spring is greeted by one speaker with the words ἰδοὺ χελιδών, to which a second speaker adds νὴ τὸν Ἡρακλέα. This accords with Ar. Ra. 182f καὶ πλοῖόν γ᾽ ὁρῶ. – νὴ τὸν Ποσειδῶ, κἄστι γ᾽ ὁ Χάρων οὑτοσί, and with the ready use of oaths 'by Herakles' and 'by Poseidon' in comedy, though not in Plato (where Alkibiades' drunken, hectoring μὰ τὸν Ποσειδῶ in Smp. 214d is unique). A black-figure homosexual courting-scene of familiar type (Boston, Museum of Fine Arts 08.30d)[12] contains the sequences of letters αρενμι and ιδορεν (or ιαορεν?). If these are to be interpreted as ἄρρην εἰμί and ἰδοὺ ἄρρην the first utterance is presumably spoken by the youth; the second may possibly reinforce it, but an alternative interpretation is suggested by the comic idiom in which a speaker repeats the word of phrase of the previous speaker and prefaces it with a contemptuous ἰδού, e.g. Ar. Eq. 343f ὅτιὴ λέγειν οἷός τε κἀγώ . . . – ἰδοὺ λέγειν ('Whaddya mean, speak?'). If that idiom was current in the sixth century BC, ἰδοὺ ἄρρην is the vase-painter's cynical comment on the youth who allows himself to be courted;[13] the vase thus

[9]   Stevens 10–18, 23f.
[10]   Kretschmer (90) understands πίομαι, but he interpreted the first utterance as ἤδη κἀνέπιε⟨ν⟩. J. D. Beazley, AJA xxxix (1935) 477f, concurs in πίομαι, although rejecting κἀνέπιεν in favour of κανῆ πλέα.
[11]   Kretschmer 91; E. des Places in Mélanges Bidez (Brussels 1934) 274f.
[12]   Emily Vermeule, Antike Kunst xii (1969) 10f.
[13]   Dover, Greek Homosexuality (London 1978) 146.

combines evidence of category I (B) with evidence of category II (B) 1. The scornful ἰδού is not used in Plato even when characters such as Thrasymakhos and Kallikles are being rude to Socrates; nor is any other kind of ἰδού, except in the words which a certain Leontios, according to *R.* 440a, addressed to his own eyes: ἰδοὺ ὑμῖν, ἔφη, ὦ κακοδαίμονες, ἐμπλήσθητε τοῦ καλοῦ θεάματος (where καλοῦ is sarcastic,[14] κακοδαίμονες is predominantly comic,[15] and ἰδοὺ ὑμῖν has a parallel in Ar. *Ach.* 470 ἰδού σοι, words accompanying the gift demanded in 469 φυλλεῖα δός).[16]

(C) Hellenistic Period

Some Hellenistic poetry, notably Herodas and Theokr. 14 and 15 (cf. parts of 4, 5 and 10), ostensibly portrays the conversation of uneducated people. Theokr. 14.8 παίζεις, ὦγάθ’, ἔχων exemplifies the kind of support to be found in this area for the designation of an Aristophanic and Platonic usage as colloquial; cf. Ar. *Av.* 341, *Lys.* 945 ληρεῖς ἔχων, *Ra.* 202 and 524 οὐ μὴ φλυαρήσεις ἔχων, Pl. *Euthd.* 295c ὅτι ἔχων φλυαρεῖς καὶ ἀρχαιότερος εἶ τοῦ δέοντος, *Grg.* 490e ποῖα ὑποδήματα; φλυαρεῖς ἔχων. It is significant that the last example shows also the scornful ποῖος common in comedy,[17] and *Euthd.* 295c (on which Socrates comments, 'I realized that he was getting annoyed with me'), the dismissive ἀρχαῖος 'not with it', 'square' (e.g. Ar. *V.* 1336 ἀρχαῖα γ’ ὑμῶν, ironic in the mouth of the rejuvenated and outrageous old Philokleon).

(A) Attic of the Central Period

1.   *Private documents.* Most Attic graffiti and dipinti are considerably earlier in date than Aristophanes and will therefore be considered together in (B) 1 below. Some messages incised on potsherds (Lang nos 18, 22, 35, 38) are also early. A fourth-century letter on lead (Wünsch 11f)[18] helps to confirm that the morphological basis of Attic literary prose was identical with that of ordinary communication, but its contribution to our knowledge of colloquialism is questionable. A private contract relating to the sale or loan of a house (Peek 88f, no. 168) is cast, like the depositions interspersed in some Demosthenic speeches, in formal terms and belongs linguistically with (A) 2 below. Curse-tablets, some of which are certainly to be dated well within the central

[14]   Stevens 55; add E., *Md.* 514, Pherekrates fr. 149.
[15]   Stevens 14f.
[16]   The idiom is related to the attachment of a dative pronoun to a demonstrative; e.g. Hdt. v 92. η 4 τοιοῦτο μὲν ὑμῖν ἐστι ἡ τυραννίς.
[17]   Stevens 38f.
[18]   A. Wilhelm, *JOAI* vii (1904) 94–105; W. Crönert, *RhM* lxv (1910) 157f.

period,[19] show a smattering of solecisms (cf. p. 19, above),[20] and some of them even a non-Attic dialectal colouring. Occasional obscenities (Wünsch no. 77b. 1 ψωλή, κύσθος; cf. Ar. *Lys.* 979, 1158) link their language to that of comedy, but the occurrence of καὶ ἔργα [κ]α⟨ὶ⟩ ἔπεα in Wünsch 84b. 2 (cf. ε]πεα in Peek 91–3 no. 3.20) side by side with γλῶτ⟨τ⟩αν (84b. 1, 3) reminds us that in a curse the writer is handling a religious formula to which he might sometimes (and to us, unpredictably) judge poetic forms appropriate. This may account also for μήποτε (alien to Attic prose) rather than μηδέποτε in Wünsch 64.3 καὶ μήπο[τ]ε αὐτὸς εὖ πράττοι, 78.3; cf. the heartfelt curse of Ar. *Pax* 3 καὶ μήποτ' αὐτῆς μᾶζαν ἡδίω φάγοι, where μηδέποτ' would have been permitted by comic metrical practice.

2 *Public documents.* In Ar. *Th.* 431f the woman who has proposed in the 'assembly' of women that Euripides must somehow be destroyed (the substance of her γνώμη is given in 428–31 νῦν οὖν ἐμοὶ ... δοκεῖ ... ὅπως ἀπολεῖται) concludes, ταῦτ' ἐγὼ φανερῶς λέγω, τὰ δ' ἄλλα μετὰ τῆς γραμματέως συγγράψομαι. If this is as close a parody of procedure as the rest of the scene, it seems that what we read in an Attic decree, introduced by ὁ δεῖνα εἶπε, is not the unaided composition of the proposer. Until the 360s the secretary of the assembly was changed for every prytany, so that we have no chance of detecting, in such decrees as remain to us, the individual style of a given secretary, nor of assessing his linguistic competence. Thereafter the possibility becomes less remote, and on the strength of *IG* ii/iii² 110.16 ὅπως ἂν ἐάν του δέηται τυγχάνῃ and 111.17–19 ὅπως δ' ἂν καὶ οἱ ὅρκοι καὶ αἱ συνθῆκαι ἃς συνέθετο Χαβρίας ... ὑπὲρ ... Κείων οὓς κατήγαγον ... κύριαι ὦσι we might attribute to Nikostratos of Pallene, secretary in 363/2, a liking for certain types of hypotactic construction. Yet we must never forget the professional under-secretaries who will have done more than anyone to mould Attic official style. The establishment of formulae in this style was slow and by no means complete even in the fourth century, as we can see by contrasting *IG* ii/iii² 26.9f καὶ ν[υνὶ] καὶ ἐν τῷ προτέρῳ χρόνῳ with 77.14 καὶ νῦν καὶ ἐν τῷ πρόσθεν χρόνῳ, or 107.10f τοὺς] προέδρους οἳ ἂν λάχωσιν προεδρεύειν εἰς τὴν πρώ[την ἐ]κκλησίαν with 128.10 τοὺς μὲν προ[έδρους οἳ ἂν τυγχάνωσι π]ροε[δ]ρεύον[τε]ς [ε]ἰς τὴν πρώτ[η]ν ἐκκ[λησίαν. Nevertheless, it was one of the determinants of the genre from the very first. Such evidence of colloquial language as documentary inscriptions may afford is to be sought in their preservation of (presumably local Attic) forms lost in literature, e.g. *IG* i² 898.1, 900.1, 901.1, ii/iii² 4960.7 δεῦρε = δεῦρο,[21] 1522.30 (*et saepe*) κάτροπτον = κάτοπτρον. It is possible that such forms once existed in Attic literary texts but were purged in transmission; rather as Demosthenes must surely

---

[19] On the dating cf. Wilhelm (above, note 18) 106–21, and L. H. Jeffery, *ABSA* 1 (1955) 74f on material from the Kerameikos.

[20] For an analysis of the linguistic data cf. E. Schwyzer, *NJbb* v.3 (1900) 244–62, and W. Rabehl, 'De Sermone Defixionum Atticarum' (Diss., Berlin 1906).

[21] Cf. A. J. Beattie, *Trans. Philol. Soc.* (1949) 3.

have said and written Κερσεβλέπτης (as in *IG* ii/iii² 126.10, 17, 20) but the manuscripts of his text have Κερσοβλέπτης under the irresistible influence of χερσο- and the predominant pattern of substantival compounds. At phonological and morphological level the stonecutter's language may come through, or at any rate his predilections in spelling (e.g. the indiscriminate initial aspirates of *IG* i² 374).

(B) Earlier Period

1 *Attic graffiti and dipinti.* Graffiti are largely derogatory and make much use of the Aristophanic abusive term καταπύγων (e.g. Lang no. 20), to which we must add the feminine (as yet unattested in literature) καταπύγαινα (*SEG* xiii 32); cf. *IG* i² 921.4f λαικ[ασ]τ[ρια] ~ Ar. *Ach.* 529, 537. By contrast, most dipinti on vases are laudatory, acclaiming someone's beauty. The predicate καλός may be intensified in several ways: simple repetition, καλὸς καλός (Havana, *ARV* 1570); καλὸς ναί (Oxford 333, *ARV* 1602 ~ 26); καλὸς ναίχι (Copenhagen 127, *ARV* 138); καλὸς κάρτα (Compiègne 978, *ABV* 674); καλὸς νὴ Δία (Palermo, *ABV* 675). This handful of expressions turns out, when their history and affinities are explored, to show up the gaps in our evidence and the fragility of inferences. Repetition of an evaluative word and its reinforcement by an oath are echoed in Ar. *Ec.* 213 εὖ γ᾽ εὖ γε νὴ Δί᾽ εὖ γε (representing rapturous applause). Repetition of καλός recurs in Alexandrian erotic poetry:[22] *Anth. Pal.* xii 62.1 καλὰ μὲν καλὰ τέκνα (*sc.* youths) τέκεσθε 130.1 εἶπα ʿκαλὸς καλόςʾ, and cf. [Theokr.] 8.73 καλὸν καλὸν ἦμεν ἔφασκεν. Kallim. *Epigr.* 30.5 reinforces it by ναίχι: σὺ δὲ ναίχι καλὸς καλός (cf. *Epigr.* 53.3). Since ναίχι is also a feature of New Comedy dialogue (Men. *Epitr.* 872f – οὐ σὲ τὴν νύμφην ὁρῶ . . . ; – ναίχι, Sam. 296 ἐμέ τις κέκληκε; – ναίχι – χαῖρε δέσποτα), we should expect to find it in Old Comedy, bridging the gap between archaic dipinti and Hellenistic poetry, but we do not; only the Scythian policeman in *Thesmophoriazusae* uses it (1183 *al.* ναίκι), no doubt because it can be exploited to illustrate his inability to aspirate unvoiced stops. In the Platonic corpus it is only in *Hipparch.* 232a, and it appears once in tragedy (S. *OT* 684 – ἀμφοῖν ἀπ᾽ αὐτοῖν; – ναίχι. – καὶ τίς ἦν λόγος;). It must be said plainly that these passages have nothing in common to distinguish them from the occasions on which ναί is used.[23] If the history of ναίχι is obscure, that of κάρτα is no less so. Commonplace in fifth-century Ionic prose, it is virtually confined in Attic to tragedy; Plato uses it once (*Ti.* 25d πηλοῦ κάρτα βραχέος) and Aristophanes once, in combination with an

---

[22] Cf. also (non-erotic) Pind. *P.* 2.72f.

[23] W. Schulze, *Kleine Schriften* (Göttingen 1934) 706, treats ναίχι as an outright vulgarism. I learn from Professor Morpurgo Davies that Eduard Fraenkel's agreement with Schulze on this matter was by no means as unqualified as might appear from *Due Seminari di Eduard Fraenkel* (Rome 1977) 52. Neither Schulze nor Fraenkel mentions Menander, and though Fraenkel cites the Kallimakhos passages he does not consider that their relation to a tradition of homoerotic formulae.

undoubted colloquialism (cf. p. 21, above), *Av.* 342 τοῦτο μὲν ληρεῖς ἔχων κάρτα. Presumably κάρτα, like adverbial μετά (cf. p. 20, above), belonged to that part of the common Ionic–Attic lexicon which went out of use in Attic in the course of the fifth century;[24] in *Av.* 342 it is virtually an archaism, in *Ti.* 25d quite strongly archaizing.[25]

2 *Non-Attic graffiti and dipinti.* This class is characterized, like its Attic counterpart, by much obscenity, in which some regional variation of vocabulary is noteworthy: οἴφειν 'copulate' (e.g. *IG* xii 3.537) and the noun οἰφόλης (e.g. *SEG* xv 523 [Tenos]) are quite alien to the Attic vocabulary of sex. (Conversely, if βενεοι in *DGE* 412.1 (Elis) is righly interpreted as = βινοίη, it shows that one of the grossest words in Ionic and Attic was permissible in an archaic religious law of the Eleans).

3 *An early Ionic letter.* A letter written on lead and found on the island of Berezan, at the mouth of the Bug,[26] has much of interest to tell us about Ionic, but one feature of its structure is relevant also to early Greek (including Attic) prose literature. The writer says (6–9), 'He protests and says that there is no connection between himself and Matasys. And he says that he is a free man and that there is no connection between himself and Matasys. Whether[27] there is any connection between him (*sc.* Matasys) and Anaxagoras, they themselves know.' Just this kind of repetition occurs in a forensic speech, Lys. i 17: 'I was at once thrown into a turmoil, καὶ πάντα μου εἰς τὴν γνώμην εἰσῄει, καὶ μεστὸς ἦ ὑποψίας, when I thought of how I'd been locked in my room and remembered that the courtyard door and the street door made a noise that night – it had never happened before – and I thought my wife had make-up on; ταῦτά μου πάντα εἰς τὴν γνώμην εἰσῄει, καὶ μεστὸς ἦ ὑποψίας.' Dobree, observing the normal dislike of Attic prose for pure repetition, deleted ταῦτα . . . ὑποψίας, but the Berezan letter simultaneously justifies the retention of the words by modern editors and alerts us to the possibility of deliberate naivety of style in other parts of Lys., i. Comparable repetitiousness in [Xen.] *Resp. Ath.* 2.11f, perhaps an ambitious attempt at rhetorical effect in 11 (where the question ποῖ διαθήσεται ἐὰν μὴ πείσῃ τὸν ἄρχοντα τῆς θαλάσσης is posed twice), but rambling and loquacious in 11 ἐξ αὐτῶν . . . 12 τὸ δὲ τῇ, encourages us to look for a colloquial element in the sentence-structure of early prose in general;[28] cf. (D) and p. 29, below.

---

[24] Cf. Dover in *Wege der Forschungen* cclxv (1975) 127 on θωᾶν and θωά (= p. 226 below).

[25] It is not impossible that Plato wished to offset 'mud' (cf. *Prm.* 130c) by an elevated word; cf. n. 2 above.

[26] J. Chadwick, *PCPS* cxcix (1973) 35–7.

[27] I interpret ματατασνεδετι as Μα[τα]τάσυ⟨ι⟩. ε(ί) δέ τι (Ματά⟨συι. Μα⟩τάσυι δὲ τί Chadwick; Ματάσυι · τί δὲ ed. pr. [Vinogradov]).

[28] On colloquial aspects of the language of the 'Old Oligarch' cf. F. Pfister, *Philologus* lxxiii (1914/16) 558–62.

(C) An Ionic Letter of the Central Period

DGE 736 (*SGDI* iv 865f), from Olbia,[29] is a good companion-piece to the Attic letter mentioned in II (A) 1, and seems to offer an Ionicism familiar from Herodotus:[30] παρὰ ᾿Ατάκους εἰς τὸ οἴκημα· ἦν γὰρ διδῷ· εἰ δὲ μή, παρὰ ᾿Αγάθαρχον κτλ. '(. . .) into the room (hired? borrowed?) from Atakes – if, that is, Atakes allows; otherwise, to Agatharkhos. . . .' Interpretation of other details of the text is controversial; its punctuation, mainly systematic but with one bizarre lapse (3 ὑ·μ[ᾶς]) recalls early Attic public documents.

(D) Private Documents of the Hellenistic Period

Private letters and messages from Ptolemaic and Roman Egypt provide support for the identification of some classical Attic phenomena as colloquial,[31] e.g. *P. Oxy.* 2844 (s.i p.C.) μὴ οὖν ἄλλως ποιήσῃς, a formula of earnest invitation, entreaty or admonition, familiar in Plato (e.g. *Smp.* 173e) and represented in Aristophanes by *Birds* 133.[32] A strikingly vulgar message from the first century AD (*P. Oxy.* 3070) says, εἰ διδῶς (ΗΔΙΔΥϹ) ἡμεῖν τὸ πυγίσαι καὶ καλῶς σοί ἐστι, οὐκέτι οὐ μὴ δείρομέν σε ἐὰν δώσῃς ἡμεῖν τὸ πυγίσαι. The repetition of the protasis is, as it happens, a feature of the earliest prose literature:[33] Anaxagoras B12, 'if it were not on its own but were mixed with something else, it would participate in everything, if it were mixed with something else'; cf. (less blatantly) Diogenes of Apollonia B2, 'if the present components of the universe . . . , if any of them were different from another . . . , they could not in any way be blended . . . nor could any plant . . . come into being, if it were not so constituted as to be the same'.

In II (B) 3 and (D) we have seen a glimmer of affinity between the sentence-structure of non-literary utterance and the sentence-structure of prose literature in its emergent stage or in a deliberately unsophisticated style. The relation between the complex structures of Attic prose and the way people usually talked is crucial to the formation of any clear view of the contrast between the two, and narrative is the genre in which the contrast may be most easily drawn. Consider the sentence with which the narrative opens in Xen. *An.* iv 1.5, a text read by many modern learners of Greek early in their careers: 'When it was about the last watch and there was left of the night enough for them to cross the plain in darkness, then, having broken camp at the passing on of a command, going on their way they arrived at daybreak at the mountain.' In what form did one of Xenophon's soldiers communicate this same datum to his friends or his grandchildren?

[29] A Wilhelm, *JOAI* vii (1904) 94–105; Crönert (above, n. 18), 158–60.
[30] Denniston 67f.
[31] Cf. D. Tabachovitz, *Mus. Helv.* iii (1946) 144–79.
[32] Ed. Fraenkel, *Beobachtungen zu Aristophanes* (Rome 1962) 69f.
[33] D. Fehling, *Die Wiederholungsfiguren und ihr Gebrauch bei den Griechen vor Gorgias* (Berlin 1969) 148f.

In considering possible structures for spoken narrative it is worthwhile to take some examples from cultures which were entirely non-literate until the era of colonialism and compare them with examples from the unlettered stratum of a literate culture.

1 The first example, from the Solomon Islands,[34] illustrates narrative sequence in a language which makes virtually no use either of connectives or of subordinate clauses.

It was nut-time. Her mother, her father, went to the garden. Kanupea went. There she saw Kirikoputu. She called, 'Sister, come on, we will pick nuts, we will gather in.' Kirikoputu said, 'Ah, I have no arms, I have no legs! Now what shall I do?' She said. She refused. 'Oh, sister, I will give you my arms, my legs', said Kanupea. She gave her arms. She gave her legs. They went. They picked.

2 Igorot, a language of the Philippine Islands,[35] makes much use of connectives translatable as 'then' or 'so'.

Then the rice and the crabs are cooked. Then I begin eating. And then comes my companion. Then we eat together, because we are very hungry. Then we start. Then we go to Dagupan, a large town. And then they do not provide for us.

3 A modern folktale from Cyprus[36] mixes connected clauses with asyndeta irregularly.

They reached the boy. The giant dismounted. He takes him. He cut off the head of the boy. And he took the girl and returned back. He took the girl inside. He also went to pasture his horse. The girl recovered from her grief, and took his head, and put it in her bosom, and took up the body, and went. She attached the body there to the head.

4 Each of the two last sequences contains one subordinate clause tacked on to a main clause: 'because we are very hungry' and 'to pasture (νὰ βοσσήσει) his horse'. Spoken narrative can easily accommodate a string of such subordinate clauses,[37] as in this example from a Modern Greek dialect of Asia Minor:[38]

[34] G. C. Wheeler, *Mono-Alu Folklore* (London 1926) 73.

[35] C. W. Seidenadel, *The Language of the Bontoc Igorot* (Chicago 1909) 525.

[36] Brian Newton, *Cypriot Greek* (The Hague/Paris 1972) 167.

[37] In *Eloc.* 10–15 Demetrios might seem to be contrasting a string of this kind with more elaborately planned hypotaxes, but his examples suggest that he has in mind a succession of short main clauses. His §21, on the opening of Pl. *R.*, is more relevant.

[38] R. M. Dawkins, *Modern Greek in Asia Minor* (Cambridge 1916) 284f.

And anger seizes the king. He goes home. He takes his daughter. He leads her to a desert place, and puts here there. He returns to (*vá*) burn it, to (*vá*) kill his daughter and that (*vá*) the ash-seller may not marry her.

5   Spoken narrative may compensate, artistically speaking, for a monotonous simplicity of structure by frequent movement between the past tense and the present (as in 3), and also by rhetorical questions; this development is a positive characteristic of oral delivery, as in the following example from the Dodecanese.[39]

But when he was sixteen, the old man died, and he was unprotected. Who is to look after him? The old woman? – who herself wanted people to look after her! He leaves his books then, and he seeks work, to support his mother and himself. But what work is he to take up? A craft? He needed to learn it first.

6   Many languages in New Guinea have developed a system of participles and 'sentence-medial' tenses,[40] the operation of which is shown by the following examples from Kâte:[41] *mulâ kiopo* 'having spoken, I wept'; *kulâ kiove˙* 'having spoken, he wept'; with change of subject, *mume kiopo* 'when he had spoken, I wept'; *mupe kiove˙* 'when I had spoken, he wept' (different forms are used for other temporal relations between the two actions or events). How this works in narrative is best shown by literal translation:

Later. having seen (*part.*) a kalophyllum tree, climbing (*part.*) up it, he having arrived (*sent.-med. tense*) at the top, straightway having broken off (*part.*), it slinging him away (*sent.-med.*), sailing (*part.*) through the air, having fallen (*part.*) downwards, having pierced (*part.*) a hole in the ground, he having gone down in (*sent.-med.*), fire mounted up (*sent.-final tense*). It burns (*sent.-final*) always.

These specimens of narrative are not in themselves conversation, for they were told by people deliberately transmitting a story, but much conversation is narrative in character, and the specimens illustrate the range of resources in structural types upon which Attic Greek could draw. One of the fundamental differences between speech and writing is that a writer has time to plan ahead and a reader, if he loses the thread, can retrace his steps and pick it up again. We have seen in II (B) 3 and (D) some reason to think that a person unaccustomed to large-scale written composition becomes uneasy when his sentence exceeds a certain modest length and restates what he has already stated. Mere

---

[39] J. Zarriftis (ed.), *Forty-five Stories from the Dodecanese*, tr. R. M. Dawkins (Cambridge 1950) 31.
[40] A. Capell, *A Survey of New Guinea Languages* (Sydney 1969) 82–6.
[41] G. Pilhofer, *Grammatik der Kâte-Sprache in Neuguinea* (Berlin 1933) 35–8, 172.

complexity, as assessed by counting up subordinate clauses and participles, is not so important a difference; the speaker of specimen 4 could, in theory, go on indefinitely adding νά -clauses, one at a time, and start a fresh sentence at any moment of his own choosing, and similarly the Kâte story-teller in specimen 6 never has to look more than a couple of words ahead in deciding whether a participle, sentence-medial tense or sentence-final tense is appropriate.[42] A similar point could be made about some of the giant sentences of Isokrates in which there is an interminable build-up of participial clauses before we come to the main clause (e.g. *Panegr.* 93–5, where the main verb is the ninety-third word, heralded by eleven participles); or again, the composer of an Attic decree sometimes embarks on an ἐπειδή -clause with his eyes fixed on a main verb over the horizon; *IG* ii/iii² 111.27–41 (Nikostratos again, cf. p. 22; the details are given on pp. 37–9 below) contains such a clause of 114 words, containing eight finite verbs, four of them in relative clauses subordinate to the overriding ἐπειδή. More careful planning is actually required for sentences which begin with an element of the main clause, then insert subordinate or participial clauses, and finally reach the rest of the main clause, without which the initial element would be left hanging, e.g. Th. iv 101.3 μετὰ δὲ τὴν μάχην ταύτην κὰι ὁ Δημοσθένης ... ὡς αὐτῷ τότε πλεύσαντι ... οὐ προυχώρησεν, ἔχων ..., ἀπόβασιν ἐποιήσατο κτλ. When Plato portrays a speaker as launched on a sentence of great complexity, he sometimes makes him lose track of the syntax and start afresh, as in *Smp.* 177bc, 182d–183c, 218ab.

Narrative which is predominantly cast in short units tends to develop substantial boundary-markers ('then', 'so', etc.), and one of the most striking differences between narrative in Old Comedy and the narrative speeches of tragedy is the use made by the former of εἶτα, κᾆτα, ἔπειτα and κἄπειτα, which are virtually absent from the latter.[43] Thus we find in the speech of the disguised old man in Ar. *Th.* 481–9 οὗτος ... ἔκνυεν ... κᾀτ᾽ εὐθὺς ἔγνων· εἶτα καταβαίνω ... ὁ δ᾽ ἀνὴρ ἐρωτᾷ ... κᾆθ᾽ ὁ μὲν ἔτριβε ... ἐγὼ δέ ... ἐξῆλθον ... εἴτ᾽ ᾐρειδόμην κτλ. It is agreeable to find exactly the same phenomenon in Lys. i 14, the reported words of a wife whose adultery was remarkably like that of the imaginary wife in *Thesmophoriazusae*: ἔφασκε τὸν λύχνον ἀποσβεσθῆναι τὸν παρὰ τῷ παιδίῳ, εἶτα ἐκ τῶν γειτόνων ἐνάψασθαι. Connective εἶτα figures in some Aristophanic passages where the syntax is anomalous, notably *Ach.* 23f ἀωρίαν ἥκοντες εἶτα δ᾽ ὠστιοῦνται πῶς δοκεῖς (πῶς δοκεῖς has colloquial associations),[44] *Nu.* 409 ὀπτῶν ... κᾆτ᾽ οὐκ ἔσχων, 623f λαχών ... κἄπειθ ... ἀφῃρέθη. Adverbial καί in the construction *ποιήσας καὶ ἀπῄει is virtually unknown, and 'apodotic' δέ in similar circumstances is attested only when the participial clause is

---

[42] In modern Amharic, by contrast, an everyday message may reveal quite elaborate syntactical planning on the part of its composer; cf. E. Ullendorff, *The Challenge of Amharic* (London 1965) 14f.

[43] Dover, *Lysias and the Corpus Lysiacum* (Berkeley, Calif., and Los Angeles 1968) 84f.

[44] Stevens 39.

substantial enough to separate the participle from the verb by several words.[45]
The Aristophanic passages represent a (colloquial?) fusion of (1) *part. εἶτα
verb* with (2) *verb₁ κᾆτα (or εἶτα [δέ]) verb₂*.

It would not be surprising if some of the earliest surviving specimens of
Greek literary narrative showed some affinity with the basically paratactic
structure postulated for speech,[46] and Akousilaos of Argos (*F. Gr. Hist.* 2) F22
does so:

> Καινῆ δέ . . . μίσγεται Ποσειδῶν.
> ἔπειτα (οὐ γὰρ ἦν . . .) ποιεῖ αὐτόν . . . ἄνδρα ἄτρωτον,
>   ἰσχὺν ἔχοντα . . .
> καὶ ὅτε τις αὐτὸν κεντοίη . . . ,
>   ἠλίσκετο . . .
> καὶ γίγνεται βασιλεὺς Λαπιθέων
> καὶ τοῖς κενταύροις πολεμέεσκε.
> ἔπειτα στήσας . . .
>   ἐκέλευεν . . .
>   ]σι δ᾽ οὐκ ἦεν . . .
> καὶ Ζεὺς ἰδών . . .
>   ἀπειλεῖ
> καὶ ἐφορμᾷ . . .
> κἀκεῖνοι αὐτὸν κατακόπτουσιν . . .
> καὶ ἄνωθεν πέτρην ἐπιτιθεῖσιν σῆμα
> καὶ ἀποθνῄσκει.

We value Greek culture mostly for its achievement in the arts and its intellectual confrontation of some enduring problems. Preoccupation with the
way in which Greeks expressed themselves when they were not achieving anything of great worth or exercising their intellects very hard might therefore be
criticized as the product of trendy cant about 'real life'. Yet the relationships
obtaining in any culture between literature and speech, illuminating as they
do the writers' own conceptions of the status and function of literature, ought
to be of concern to historians and literary critics. In the case of the Greeks
there is abundant reason to think that their arts were firmly rooted in the
attitudes and values of ordinary life, and to catch from time to time the sound
of their voices enables us to judge how far, and in what circumstances, a
conceptual relationship between art and life was reinforced by a formal relationship.

---

[45] Denniston 181f and 308f.
[46] S. Trenkner, *Le Style KAI dans le récit attique oral* (Assen 1960) 16–21; S. Lilja, *On the Style of the
Earliest Greek Prose* (Helsinki 1968) 73–100.

ADDITIONAL NOTE

P. 28, on 'build-up' in long written sentences. I originally cited some of Nikostratos's ἐπειδή-clauses here, but have replaced them now by a summary and a reference to Isokrates.

3

The Language of Classical Attic Documentary Inscriptions[1]

1   In *Phdr.* 257a–258c Plato's Socrates argues that the proposer of a decree in council or assembly – the man whose name appears, as subject of εἶπε, at the beginning of the text – is the author of a λόγος and therefore in no position to criticize a forensic consultant such as Lysias for λογογραφία. The words Socrates uses in this connection, συγγράφειν, συγγραφεύς and σύγγραμμα, are the words consistently used in classical Greek of literary composition in prose (e.g. Pl. *Smp.* 177b), setting down a description in writing (e.g. Hdt. iii 103), writing a message (Antiphon v 53) or letter (Dem. xix 316) and drafting the proposals which come from a commission (e.g. *IG* i² 76.3), architect (e.g. ibid. 44.6) and the like. Since there is no association between this word-group and imaginative fiction, but rather the contrary, it is surprising that Phaedrus finds the classification of the politician as συγγραφεύς a novelty and needs to be convinced (as, of course, he is) by Socrates.

Three people could in fact be involved in the production of any Attic decree whose text we read on a stele. The proposer was indispensable; without him, there was nothing to say. The secretary of council and assembly, an elected officer, was responsible for the eventual setting up of the text in public – a decree often assigns him this responsibility explicitly – and it would be surprising if he had no say in the formal presentation of the decree for the assembly's decision. Beside or behind the secretary was the under-secretary (ὑπογραμματεύς), a professional clerk, who was better acquainted than anyone with procedural detail in documentation.

As commonly happens, it is comedy which gives us a glimpse of what went on.[2] In Aristophanes' *Thesmophoriazusae* the women of Athens, assembled for the festival of Thesmophoria, constitute themselves an assembly in order to decide how to rid themselves of Euripides, who is held to have maligned their sex. The parody of real assemblies is close, from the formal prayers and curses

---

[1]   This article is a revised version of a paper read to the Philological Society on 16 February 1979.
[2]   On comedy as evidence for administrative procedures and styles, A. Burckhardt, *Spuren der athenischen Volksrede in der alten Komödie* (Basel 1924) is of fundamental importance; cf. also my *Lysias and the Corpus Lysiacum* (Berkeley, Calif., and Los Angeles 1968) 72–4.

which open the proceedings to the herald's announcement of the council's decision to refer the issue to the assembly. In response to the formal question τίς ἀγορεύειν βούλεται; (379) a woman rises to speak, clears her throat noisily and begins her speech with a disclaimer (384f φιλοτιμίᾳ μὲν οὐδεμιᾷ ... λέξουσ᾽ ἀνέστην) which reminds us of fourth-century forensic speakers' claims that they are not motivated by enmity or personal ambition (e.g. Dem. xxxix 1 οὐδεμιᾷ φιλοπραγμοσύνῃ κτλ.).[3] The upshot of the woman's speech is that Euripides should be destroyed 'by poison or *some* means or other', and she ends (431f),

> ταῦτα μὲν φανερῶς λέγω.
> τὰ δ᾽ ἄλλα μετὰ τῆς γραμματέως συγγράψομαι.

'That is what I am saying before you all. The rest I will get written down with the secretary.'

A distinction of meaning between the active συγγράφειν and the middle συγγράφεσθαι can be discerned throughout the classical period.[4] The active verb takes as its object something which is wholly composed by the person who is the subject. The middle verb is used of copying down someone else's utterance (e.g. an oracle, Hdt. i 47.1, 48.1) and of agreeing or subscribing to a treaty or contract (e.g. Th. v 41.3, Xen. *Eq.* 2.2, Isoc. *Panath.* 158, Dem. xxxv 1). The distinction is neatly illustrated by Isoc. *Trap.* 20 ~ 30: the speaker describes how 'we' put in writing (συγγράψαντες) the agreement they had reached in discussion, but then, in speaking of his own relationship to the document, he uses the middle (πρὶν μὲν συγγράψασθαι τὸ γραμματεῖον ... ἠπίστησα κτλ. and τοιοῦτον ἔλεγχον κατ᾽ ἐμαυτοῦ συνεγραψάμην).[5]

There are four instances of which the interpretation is disputable. In one of these, *IG* i² 310.181]ρχ[]]ιο[|. συγ[|μενοι[. στα]| θμον το[, the preceding lines are lost and have so far defied supplementation.[6] Demosthenes' use of the middle in xix 176 πρῶτον μὲν ἐγὼ συγγραψάμενος καὶ καταστήσας ἐμαυτὸν ὑπεύθυνον μαρτυρήσω, εἶτα τῶν ἄλλων πρέσβεων ἕκαστον καλῶ καὶ δυοῖν θάτερον ἢ μαρτυρεῖν ἢ ἐξόμνυσθαι ἀναγκάσω is explicable on the hypothesis that Demosthenes wishes to suggest that he has copied down what was admitted or disclosed to him by others (cf. his reference in 175 to what he was told by Derkylos and his own slave). Pl. *Euthd.* 272a 'they are better able than anyone to win the kind of battle that is fought in the courts and to teach

[3] On attitudes to φιλοτιμία cf. my *Greek Popular Morality in the Time of Plato and Aristotle* (Oxford 1974) 230–4.

[4] LSJ *s.v.* συγγράφειν IV does not draw any distinction of meaning in the case of Ar. *Th.* 432 and Pl. *Grg.* 451c.

[5] The active voice in the contrast between speech and writing might also be justified by comparing Hdt. viii 135.3 τὰ λεγόμενα (*sc.* in Carian) ... γράφειν ἐς αὐτήν (*sc.* τὴν δέλτον) ... συγγραψάμενον δὲ οἴχεσθαι κτλ. ; but in the simple verb γράφειν the semantic differences between active and middle are by no means the same as in συγγράφειν.

[6] I follow the text given by J. Johnson, *Am. Journ. Arch.* xxxv (1931) 31–43, correcting *IG* i²; cf. the photograph in B. D. Meritt, *Athenian Financial Documents* (Ann Arbor, Mich., 1932) 21.

another λέγειν τε καὶ συγγράφεσθαι λόγους οἵους εἰς τὰ δικαστήρια᾽ is a case in which we might for a moment have expected συγγράφειν – but not if the λογογράφος was regarded more as consultant for a client than script-writer for an actor.[7] The fourth passage deserving remark is Pl. *Grg.* 451c, where the formula τὰ μὲν ἄλλα καθάπερ κτλ. (familiar to us as introducing a 'rider' in a decree) is treated as characteristic of οἱ ἐν τῷ δήμῳ συγγραφόμενοι, 'those who get (proposals) composed in the assembly'. There is no sign here of the argument used in the *Phaedrus*, which was indeed devised in order to make a paradoxical point, but there is perfect accord with Aristophanes' speaker at the Thesmophoria and with what the facts of Athenian procedure would have led us to expect.

2   That classical Athens had a 'chancellery style' in the sense that certain formulae were trated as the 'right way' of saying something in a decree, draft or report, is adequately demonstrated by Plato's recognition of τὰ μὲν ἄλλα καθάπερ κτλ. as possessing just that character.[7] Even a cursory look through Meisterhans's *Grammatik der attischen Inschriften* reveals a numnber of phonological, morphological and syntactical features which differentiate the language of Attic documentary inscriptions from the language of Attic prose literature of the same period. One of these features, the consistent use of -ττ- in preference to the -σσ- found in Antiphon, Thucydides, tragedy and Ionic, is shared by documentary inscriptions (from the archaic period onwards) with comedy, graffiti and uneducated *defixiones*.[9] It could be said that within the totality of Attic utterance -σσ- is stylistically 'marked', and -ττ- eschewed in literature as 'parochial', documentary language thus aligned with the vernacular. This issue is unfortunately obscured by uncertainty on how far we are dealing with alternative sounds or with alternative ways of spelling the same sound. Moreover, some phenomena attested in inscriptions may originally have been in prose literature but 'ironed out' in transmission. This certainly happened to proper names: *IG* ii² 126 reveals that the Thracian ruler so often mentioned in Dem. xxiii was called Κερσεβλέπτης, but in the manuscripts of Demosthenes he is always Κερσοβλέπτης (the analogy of 'Chersonese' proved invincible); and the name Διειτρέφης survives corruption to Διϊ- or Διο- only in Palatinus 252 (Διε-) at Th. iv 53.1. The chances that δεῦρε, normal in fifth-century boundary-stones, would escape alteration to δεῦρο at an early stage of transmission (*if* it ever stood in a literary text) could not be rated high.

---

[7] I have argued on other grounds for a consultant–client relationship, and thus for some degree of joint composition, in *Lysias and the Corpus Lysiacum*, 148–74.

[8] B. Rosenkranz, *IF* xlviii (1930) 131f postulates a 'Kanzleisprache, die der Entwicklung der lebenden Sprache nur langsam nachfolgt', and implicitly identifies prose literature with 'die Sprache des taglichen Lebens'.

[9] E.g. γλῶτ(τ)αν, W. Peek, *Kerameikos* iii (1941) no. 3.29. Ibid. no. 2.5f πράσ(σ)ει seems to point the other way, but the Attic *defixiones* sometimes contain elements of poetic language designed to give magical potency (e.g. ἔπεα, μήποτε).

The case is quite different with the first declension dative plural endings -ασι and -ησι, exhibited in documentary inscriptions down to about 420 but unknown to prose literature. If Antiphon, Thucydides and the 'Old Oligarch' had used these forms, it is hard to explain why transmission of the text in the fourth century should have removed them systematically, while leaving -σσ-, -ρσ- and ξυν- intact. Fortunately, we do not need speculative explanations, for the internal evidence of the inscriptions answers the question: the rapidity and completeness of the change from -ασι and -ησι to -αις in the neighbour-hood of 420 point to a conscious decision and agreement, of a kind which plays no part in the evolution of literary or vernacular language.[10] Moreover, the occasion intrusion of Ionic -ησι in *IG* i² 6 (2 δραχμεῖσ[ιν, 51 [ἐπ]όπτεισιν, 69f τεῖσι) suggests that even in the early part of the fifth century -ησι and -ησι were equally alien to the stonecutter's language (or the secretary's?). *IG* i² 94 (418/17), the swansong of the old dative plurals, presents a mixture in line 10, χιλίαισι δραχμεσι (cf. 76.20), and in line 20, μυρίεσι δραχμεσιν, creates a form which is neither Attic nor Ionic.

An archaic element in documentary language, deliberately retained and no less deliberately discarded, is thus proved. The hypothesis that there was a conscious intention about 420 to reduce such archaic elements receives support from the history of the comparatives ὀλείζων and ἐλάττων: the first datable appearance of ὀλείζων is in 485/4 (*IG* i² 4.18f) and its last in 418/17 (94.33), while ἐλάττων first appears in 73.8 and – together with ὀλείζων (line 8)[11] – in 76.6, 7, both decrees being datable to the neighbourhood of 420. If Wilamowitz was right in introducing ὀλείζων into Attic literature by emend-ing μείζους to ὀλείζους in [Xen.] *Ath.* 2.1 (and if Heinrich's μείους is wrong; the sense required is 'smaller in number'), the change in documentary lan-guage was perhaps in step with the change in literary language. On the other hand, -αται and -ατο in the third personal plural of some middle-passive perfects and pluperfects disappear from inscriptions first; the last instances are in *IG* i² 57 (428/7), but there are a few in Thucydides, and Xen. *An.* iv 8.5 has ἀντιτετάχαται.

If there was in fact a systematic attempt to modernize documentary lan-guage in the decade 430–20, it was only partially successful. ἵνα, 'in order that', puts in a brief appearance as a rival to ὅπως (ἄν) in 425/4 (*IG* i² 63.41, 46) and 421/0 (81.12) – cf. *SEG* x 58.21, datable *c.* 430 – but thereafter the exclusive rights of ὅπως (ἄν) are reasserted. The transition from a dative object with ἐπαινεῖν, unexampled in Attic literature, to an accusative object (often attested in Attic poetry and prose alike from the fifth century onwards) was effected over a twenty-year period. The accusative first appears in 423 (*IG* i² 70.7f), but the dative endures until 405/4 (*IG* ii² 1.7); both cases are used in 410/09 (*IG* i² 108.6, 39, ii² 142.5, dative; i² 110.6, accusative), and the two

---

[10] The history of -οισι vs. -οις is less tidy, but comparable.

[11] Stylistic variation (cf. the end of section 4 below) may possibly have determined the choice of ὀλείζων after two instances of ἐλάττων in close succession.

decrees of 403/2 which are included in *IG* ii² 1 have the accusative (47, 64). In the fourth century the accusative is universal. A *prima facie* exception to that generalization is a decree in Ionic script, *IG* ii² 60, which has (4–8) Ξανθι[...]ρει ὡς ὄντι ἀνδρὶ ἀγ[αθῶι ...] ... ἐπαινέσαι. It is however virtually certain that this document (like ii² 142) is a reissue of a fifth-century decree,[12] Charias (archon 415/14) being the most likely candidate for the six-letter archon in the prescript, so that there is no linguistic anomaly here.

One thing at least is certain: documentary language never became strong enough to exclude intrusions from literature and the vernacular. Even apparently fixed formulae were not immune from alteration. καὶ νῦν καὶ ἐν τῶι πρόσθεν χρόνωι, first attested for sure in 423 (*IG* i² 70.7), remains the norm in the first half of the fourth century (e.g. *IG* ii² 77.14, 96.9f, 206.11f), looking as if it has come to stay. Yet ii² 26.10f sports καὶ ν[υνὶ] καὶ ἐν τῶι προτέρωι χρόνωι. In 348 comes another variant, καὶ νῦ]ν καὶ ἐν τῶι ἔμπροσθεν χρόνωι (ii² 207.5ff), which gains some ground, but room is still left for experiment: 347.14f (in 331) κα]ὶ νῦν καὶ ἐν τῶι παρ[εληλυθό]τι χρόνωι, 400.10 (*c.* 320) καὶ ἐν] τῶι πρόσθεν χρ[όνωι καὶ νῦν ...], 401.5f (*c.* 320) ἔν τ[ε τ]ῶι ἔμπροσθεν χρόνωι καὶ νῦν.

The imperative form καθελόντωσαν in a decree of 352 (*IG* ii² 204.47f; contrast 34f κατενεν[κόν]των, 42 ἀνεν[εγ]κ[ό]ντω[ν]) anticipates by fifty years the general change from -όντων, -άντων to -έτωσαν, -άτωσαν in Attic documents at the end of the century (μισθωσάντωσαν in *IG* ii² 1241.52, of 300/299, is, like καθελόντωσαν, a transitional form). That -σαν could be kept at bay so long advertises the strength of documentary style; that it could intrude once, the weakness.

It must be emphasized that the phenomena mentioned in this section are selected as illustrative. A comprehensive account of all the relevant phenomena, including variation of mood and word order, would complicate the picture but would not change its essential structure.

3   Because absolutely uniform documentary style was never achieved and personal choice never excluded, there exists a theoretical possibility of identifying, here and there, an individual style. If, for example, several decrees proposed by the same speaker during the terms of office of different secretaries are positively characterized, we have identified that speaker's style. There are, however, only a few Athenians who are known to have proposed more than one of the surviving decrees; the texts being fragmentary, it often happens that the name of the proposer is lost and the legible content of his decree exiguous in any case. Positive characteristics common to two or more decrees proposed by different speakers during the term of office of the same secretary could be treated as betraying the hand either of that secretary or of his under-secretary. Down to the 360s the secretary was changed every prytany, so that ten

[12] Cf. M. B. Walbank, *Athenian Proxenies of the Fifth Century B.C.* (Sarasota, Fla. 1979), no. 63. (I owe the reference to Dr D. M. Lewis; the decree is now *IG* i³ 177.)

different secretaries held office in the course of one conciliar year. Hence the survival of two or more decrees, of that period, on which the same secretary could have collaborated is very rare. If we had several decrees which belonged to the same year but were all proposed by different speakers and all bore the names of different secretaries, and if they were all differentiated from decrees of other years by common positive characteristics, then in those circumstances (and only in those circumstances) we could say something about the style of the unknown man who was under-secretary in that year; no one was allowed to serve as under-secretary to the same office more than once (Lys. xxx 29), so that features characteristic of decrees of more than one year can never be attributed to a single under-secretary. After the term of office of the secretary was extended to a year (363/2 is the earliest year for which that is demonstrable), the possibility that two or more decrees proposed by different speakers during the term of office of the same secretary would survive to our time was increased. Simultaneously the possibility of our differentiating between secretary and under-secretary was extinguished, since their tenures were coterminous. If the material available to us were a hundred times greater than it actually is, enquiries of this kind could be pursued in detail, and they would form a basis for generalizations about the respective roles of proposer and secretary (or under-secretary) in forming the text of a decree. As it is, the material is only enough to afford us a few hints; but these hints are worth taking.

Utter in the presence of a historian the words 'two decrees proposed by the same man', and the historian is likely to think at once of the 'Kallias decrees', *IG* i² 91 + 92 (Meiggs and Lewis, *Greek Historical Inscriptions* no. 58). A promising case, at first glance: the texts are substantial, and the first of the two is very well preserved. Since, however, they were proposed not only by the same man during the office of the same secretary, but actually on the same day (unless the fact that the ἐπιστάτης at the time of the first decree was Eupeithes and at the second]υπ[ε]ιθες is a wild coincidence), they cannot be used to differentiate in any way between proposer and secretary. Moreover, although further scrutiny may disclose features which differentiate the two decrees jointly from other documents of the same period, the feature which catches the eye is confined to the first of the two: a certain liking for the perfective aspect, and for its expression in periphrastic form, viz.

A 3f   ἐπειδέ . . . τὰ τρισχίλια τάλαντα ἀνενένεκται ἐς πόλιν
A 4   ἡὰ ἐφσέφιστο
A 5f   ἁ ἐς ἀπόδοσίν ἐστιν . . . ἐφσεφισμ[έ]να
A 11f   καὶ ἐάμ π[ο ἀλ]λοθι ἦι γεγραμμένα
A 30   ἐπειδὰν δὲ ἀποδεδομένα ἐι . . . [τὰ χρ]έματα

I use the imprecise phrase 'a certain liking' deliberately, because I doubt whether ἐπειδή . . . ἀνηνέχθη presented itself as a serious alternative in A 3f. In A 11f ἐάν . . . γραφθῆι is certainly not an alternative to ἐάν . . . ἦι γεγραμμένα (it would not mean the same at all), but εἴ που ἄλλοθι γέγραπται is, to judge from *IG* i² 39.54 καὶ εἴ τοι δέδοται . . . ἀτέλεια, 116.10f εἴ το χρέματα ἐδεδέμε[ντο and καὶ εἴ τις ἄλλος οἶδεν in the Kallias decree itself (A 13). An alternative to ἐψήφιστο in A 4 is indicated by *IG* i² 110.40]δ ἐφσεφ[ί]σθε Ἀπολλ[οδόροι and 39.42 καθάπερ Ἐρετριεῦσι ἐφσεφίσατο ho δῆμος; an alternative to ἐστιν . . . ἐψηφισμένα in A 5f by *IG* i² 108.43 καθhάπερ ἐφσέφισται Σερμυλιεῦσι and 154.12f κ[αθάπερ Ἀθηναίοις ἐφ]σέφισται; and an alternative to A 30 ἐπειδὰν δὲ ἀποδεδομένα ἦι by A 7 ἐπειδὰν πραθεῖ, A 10f ἐπει[δὰν] ἀποδῶσιν, *IG* i² 75.26 ἐπ]ειδὰν δὲ πραθεῖ, 76.16 ἐπειδὰν δὲ ἐγλεχθεῖ, and a further half-dozen examples of ἐπειδάν + aorist subjunctive in the fifth century.

These data in themselves do not amount to much of a characterization of the style of the first Kallias decree, but they are the *kind* of thing it is worth looking for. The fourth century has a more impressive example to offer. The secretary of 363/2 was a certain Nikostratos of Pallene, and three substantial and well-preserved decrees (*IG* ii² 109–11) survive from that year; the proposer of 110 was Satyros, of 111 Aristophon, and of 109 a man with an eight-letter name. Both 110 and 111 contain an example of the deferment of the finite verb of a subordinate clause to a position after an inserted clause,[13] viz.

110.16f ὅπως ἄν, ἐάν του δέηται, τυγχά[νηι]
111.17–19 ὅπως δ'[ἄ]ν κ[αὶ] οἱ ὅρκοι καὶ αἱ συνθῆκαι, ἃς συνέθετο Χαβρίας ὁ στ[ρ]ατηγὸς κα[ὶ] ὤμοσε Κείοις ὑπὲρ Ἀθηναίων καὶ Κείων, ὃς κα[τή]γαγον [Ἀ]θηναῖοι, κύριαι ὦσι

Contrast:

47.25f (script and spelling point to the early fourth century) ὅπως ἄν τά τε προθύματα θύηται ἃ ἐξηγε(ῖ)ται Εὐθύ[δ]η[μ]ος
96.10f (of 375) ὅπως δ'] ἂν πραχθῆ[ι] ὧν δέονται
141.1–4 (of *c.* 367) ὅπως ὡς κάλλιστα πορευθήσονται οἱ πρέσβεις ὡς βασιλέα, οὓς ὁ δῆμος ἔπεμψεν

It is not wholly surprising that 111.27–42 is the most formidably complex sentence so far to be found in classical Athenian decrees. Its framework is 'since (ἐπειδή) . . ., let them be exiled . . .', and in this respect it resembles commendatory decrees of the type 'since So-and-so is a benefactor of Athens, let him be commended . . .' (first attested in the mid fifth century, *IG* i² 28 and 31).

---

[13] Cf. a mid-fifth-century document from Halikarnassos, Meiggs and Lewis no. 32.42–5 τούτωι ἐλεύθερον ἔναι, ὃς ἄν . . . , κατόπερ . . . , ἐπικαλεῖν.

ἐπειδὴ δὲ   Ἰουλιητῶν   οἱ
Since   (SUBJECT) those of the men of Iulis who

παραβάντες τὸς ὅρκος καὶ τὰς συνθήκας
(*a*) violated the oaths and the treaty

καὶ   πολεμήσαντες ἐναντία τῶι δήμωι τῶι Ἀθηναίων
and   (*b*) fought against the people of Athens

καὶ Κε[ί]οις καὶ τοῖς ἄλλοις συμμάχοις
and the Keans and the other allies

καὶ   θανάτο αὐτῶν καταγνωσθέντος
and   (*c*) sentence of death having been passed against them,

κατελθόντ[ε]ς ἐς Κέω
returned to Keos

τάς τε στήλας ἐξέβαλο[ν]
(PREDICATE) (*a*) removed the stelae,

ἐ[ν αἷ]ς ἦσαν ἀναγεγραμ[μ]έναι
on which were inscribed

αἱ συνθῆκαι πρὸς Ἀθηναίος καὶ τὰ ὀνόματα
the treaty with Athens and the names

τῶν παραβάντων τὸς ὅρκος καὶ τὰς συνθήκας,
of those who had violated the oaths and the treaty,

καὶ   τὸς φίλος τὸς Ἀθηναίων,
and   (*b*) the friends of Athens,

ὃς κατήγαγεν ὁ δῆμος,
whom the assembly restored,

τὸς μὲν ἀπέκτειναν,
(1) in some cases they killed,

τῶν δὲ   θάνατον κατέγνωσαν
and   (2) in other cases they (A) condemned them to death

καὶ   τὰς ὀ[σ]ίας ἐδήμευσαν
and (B) confiscated their property,

παρὰ τὸς ὅρκος καὶ τὰς συνθήας,
contrary to the oaths and the treaty,

Σατυρίδο καὶ Τιμοξένο καὶ Μιλτιάδο,
namely, Satyrides and Timoxenos and Miltiades,

ὅτι   κατηγόρον   Ἀντιπά[τ]ρο,
because those men were accusers of Antipatros,

ὅτε ἡ βολὴ ἡ Ἀθηναίων κατέγνω αὐτὸ θάνατον,
when the Athenian council condemned him to death,

ἀποκτ[εί]ναντος τὸν πρόξενον τὸν
᾿Αθηναίων ᾿Α[.]αισίωνα,
because he had killed the Athenian proxenos,
A[ ]aision,

(I) παρὰ [τ]ὰ ψηφίσματα τὸ δήμο τὸ ᾿Αθηναίων
contrary to the decrees of the Athenian
assembly,

κ[α]ὶ   παρα[βά]ντα [14] τὸς ὅρκος καὶ τὰς συνθήκας,
and (II) had violated the oaths and the treaty,

φεύγειν αὐτὸς Κέω καὶ ᾿Αθήνας κτλ.
(MAIN CLAUSE) let them be exiled from Keos and Athens, etc.

It is not the mere length of the ἐπειδή-clause which is remarkable, for a chain of items connected by 'and' or 'or' is a long-standing phenomenon in Greek documents (e.g. *IG* i² 103, of 412/11, and the early fifth-century imprecations from Teos [Meiggs and Lewis no. 30],[15] but the fact that κατέγνωσαν in line 35 is the first point at which the clause *could* stop; τε precludes a stop at ἐξέβαλον, and μέν similarly precludes it at ἀπέκτειναν. In this respect the elaborate hypotactic construction of the decree differentiates it from the enormous sentences of Isokrates (e.g. *Panegr.* 93f), in which the rules of syntax would normally permit clause-end at any one of several points at an early stage. If the proposer Aristophon was Aristophon of Azenia, he was an active and experienced public speaker, and we might attribute the ambition composition to him; the peculiarity of lines 16f, however, in combination with 111.17–19 suggests that Nikostratos may have had more to do with it.

4   I have suggested elsewhere[16] that the rich and versatile vocabulary of Antiphon and Thucydides was not an autonomous development of a literary and intellectual tradition; its growth was stimulated by the example of technology and administration. A run through the index of *sermo Atticus* in *IG* i² yields an extraordinary crop of agent-nouns in -της, abstracts in -σις, neuter nouns in -μα, adjectives in -ικός and -τος and in alpha privative with -τος.[17] Some in this last category are technical, e.g. ἀκατάξεστος and ἀρράβδωτος (both in the Erechtheum accounts), while others are administrative, e.g.

---

[14] A slip for παραβάντος. Cf. Meiggs and Lewis no. 38 (Selinus, fifth century) 7–10 ἐν χρυσέο[ι] ἐλά[σ]αντα[ς] . . . καθθέμεν τὸ Διὸ[ς . . (.)] γράψαντες (*sic*) κτλ.

[15] *SEG* x 114 (*IG* i² 103), a commendatory decree of 421/0, begins with a long ἐπειδή-clause, but the verbs therein are co-ordinated by τε and καί. *IG* xii (1) 1032.1–20 (Karpathos, s. IV ex.) is more complex, involving some participial clauses.

[16] In *Wege der Forschung* cclxxv (*Aristophanes und die alte Komödie*) 131f (= p. 229 below).

[17] It seems to me that when λευκωτής, λιθοπριστής and λογιστής are not to be found among the c.1700 entries in the index of G. Redard, *Les Noms grecs en -της, -τις* (Paris 1949), nor ληξιαρχικός and λιθουργικός in the index of P. Chantraine, *Études sur le vocabulaire grec* (Paris 1956), 75 pages of which are devoted to -ικός, something has gone wrong with our approach to the history of fifth-century Attic.

ἀπρόσκλητος (39.10) and ἀχορήγητος (187.4). A passage of Aristophanes, *V.* 725f ἵν᾽ ὁ κῆρυξ φησί ᾽τίς ἀψήφιστος; ἀνιστάσθω᾽ may fairly be judged, on this analogy, to offer us a genuine formula rather than a poet's invention.

New material gives us new words; φυσητής, 'bellows-man', in *SEG* x 394, a fifth-century *defixio*, belongs to a category whose magnitude cannot be ignored by the critic who wants to 'place', within the history of Greek style, such passages as Th. i 70.3f οἱ μὲν καὶ παρὰ δύναμιν τολμηταὶ καὶ παρὰ γνώμην κινδυνευταί . . . ἄοκνοι πρὸς ὑμᾶς μελλητὰς καὶ ἀποδημηταὶ πρὸς ἐνδημοτάτους. Thucydides has an exceptional fondness for abstracts in -σις, of which he uses 224, nearly twice as many as in the whole of Xenophon. In this fondness he was anticipated by the composer of a decree of the Attic deme Sypalettioi no later than the mid fifth century, *IG* i² 189.6–8 λέξεως[18] [πέρ]ι ἒ δόσεος ἀλ(λ)ά[χσε]ος πέρι. The variety of expression imparted by the use of an abstract noun in (e.g.) Isoc. *Trap.* 16 ἔγνωσαν δὲ Πασίων᾽ ἐμοὶ παραδοῦναι τὸν παῖδα . . . περὶ μὲν τῆς παραδόσεως οὐκ ἤθελεν αὐτοῖς πείθεσθαι is matched by (e.g.) *IG* i² 94.5 μισθῶσαι τὸ τέμενος . . . 14f ὁπ[ό]σεν δ᾽ ἂν ἄλφει[19] μίσ[θ]οσιν τὸ τέμενος.

To make this observation is not (I hope) to derogate from the magnitude of the achievement of the poets in the centuries preceding the earliest surviving Greek prose literature. It was their inventiveness, more than anything, which made the Greeks responsive and sensitive to language as an art-form. It is only necessary to remember *also* that the need for public written utterance in the fields of technology, law, administration and politics made its own contribution to the παιδεία of the Athenians, and that interaction between different genres of utterance was continuous. In so far as the predilections of proposer, secretary and under-secretary had opportunities for expression within the constraints of documentary language, we might expect to find in a document an occasional metaphor[20] or other evidence of sensitivity to style. *SEG* x 98 (*IG* i² 154) 13f κ[αὶ ἐὰν βλαβῶσι, τὲν βλάβε]ν ἰᾶσθαι δ[ιπλῆν presents a usage which does not occur in any passages of the orators concerning βλάβη (note Dem. xxi 43 διπλοῦν. . . τὸ βλάβος κελεύουσιν ἐκτίνειν, and, in another connection, xxiv 15 χρήματα ἐκτίνειν διπλᾶ, 83 τὰ μὲν διπλᾶ . . . γίγνεται τῶν ὀφλημάτων, 198 διπλᾶ πράττονται), but surfaces in Pl. *Lg.* 933e μεχριπερ ἂν ἰάσηται τὸ βλαβέν: a figure of speech which occurred independently to the composer of *SEG* x 98 and to Plato, or an ingredient of the traditional language of Attic law? Again, when we read in the Phaselis decree of *c.* 460, *IG* i² 16, 15–19, ἐὰν δέ τ[ις ἄλλη τῶ]ν ἀρχῶν δέξηται δ[ίκην κατὰ] Φασηλιτῶν τινος [........, ε]ἰ μὲν καταδικάσ[.., ἡ καταδίκ]η ἄκυρος ἔστω, and the sense required of]ι μὲν καταδικάο[is in fact ἐὰν μὲν καταδικάσηι,[21] are we to say (1) that εἰ + sub-

---

[18] I.e. λήξεως, with omega despite the following δόσεος.

[19] ἀλφάνειν happens not to occur in Attic prose (despite several references in the orators, e.g. Is. ii 34, to money raised by sale); but, though in epic and Euripides, it is not specifically poetic, for it is attested in colloquial contexts in comedy (Ar. fr. 324, Eup. fr. 258).

[20] ᾽ῥ[υ]θμέσει᾽ in *SEG* x 142.8 was a false reading; cf. E. W. Handley, *BICS* 23 (1976) 58.

[21] H. T. Wade-Gery, *Essays in Greek History* (Oxford 1958) 182, translates as if we had ἐὰν

junctive (εἰ καταδικάσηι) was acceptable in Attic prose usage as late as 460, or (2) that εἰ + future (εἰ καταδικάσει) was a normal alternative to εἰ + subjunctive, without the undertone of conjecture, hope, fear or threat which is detectable in the literary examples? Or are we to postulate a readiness on the part of the composer either to 'stretch' εἰ + future semantically or to adopt a poetic construction, εἰ + subjunctive, for the sake of stylistic variation (cf. n. 11 above), avoiding ἐὰν . . . δέξηται . . . ἐὰν καταδικάσηι? We are dealing here with suspicions and possibilities, not demonstrations, but with suspicions which must be voiced and tested repeatedly if the history of Attic Greek is to be understood.

καταδικάσηι and (181n.) betrays some uneasiness about the syntax, but does not consider the possibility of εἰ . . . καταδικάσ[ηι.

4

ΔE in the Khalkis Decree

IG i² 39 (Meiggs and Lewis no. 52) 52–6: τὸς δ/ὲ χςένōς τὸς ἐν Χαλκίδι, hόсοι οἰκôντες / μὲ τελôσιν ᾿Αθέναζε, καὶ εἴ τōι δέδοται h/υπὸ τô δέμō τô ᾿Αθέναιôν ἀτέλεια, τὸ δὲ ἄ/λλōς τελêν ἐς Χαλκίδα κτλ.

In *ZPE* xxv (1977) 279 n. 11 S. R. Slings comments, 'It is uncertain whether *ΔE* is δέ or δή; both particles can be used in apodosi, though δή more frequently so than δέ (cf. Denniston, *Greek Particles* 2nd edn [Oxford 1954] 177ff; 224f). No particle is present with οἱ λοιποί in Hdt. ii 77.5 and Th. v 10.10 and this passage, too, would have been better without it.' However, the lively and dramatic particle δή is alien to the usage of Attic documentary inscriptions after the introduction of *H* = ē and is never a demonstrably correct interpretation of *ΔE* before that time, whereas δέ accompanies 'the rest' after a word-group introduced by 'except' in Hdt iv 189.1, vii 95.2, Pl. *Lg.* 824a, 873e (all cited by Denniston 181) and in a passage of Thucydides which Denniston does not mention, vii 33.2: σχεδὸν γάρ τι ἤδη πᾶσα ἡ Σικελία πλὴν ᾿Ακραγαντίνων (οὗτοι δ᾿ οὐδὲ μεθ᾿ ἑτέρων ἦσαν) οἱ δ᾿ ἄλλοι ἐπὶ τοὺς ᾿Αθηναίους . . . ἐβοήθουν. This kind of δέ is not, strictly speaking, resumptive (Denniston 182–5), nor is it wholly akin to the commoner types of apodotic δέ. The contrast between part and whole which it points is interestingly reversed in Pl. *Smp.* 220b καί ποτε ὄντος πάγου οἵου δεινοτάτου, καὶ πάντων . . . οὐκ ἐξιόντων . . . οὗτος δ᾿ . . . ἐξῄει κτλ. (cited by Denniston 182, but omitting all between πάγου and οὗτος, an omission which obscures the point).

5

Some Types of Abnormal Word-Order in Attic Comedy

It is not difficult to identify the characteristic features of Attic comedy, or of any period of its history, in respect of vocabulary, and not unduly laborious to extend this characterization to morphemes. The word-indexes and concordances now available for the whole of Attic literature enable us to differentiate with some assurance between comedy and the body of 'control' texts which is constituted by tragedy, prose and inscriptions.[1] Syntactical characterization, however, presents a problem of a different kind, especially when the questions in which we are interested concern word-order. Given the importance of context as a determinant of word-order in Greek, word-indexes can help us only to hunt down the occurrences of specified members of some chosen category of words, and concordances, in which the context is not merely limited but arbitrarily limited, can be positively misleading if used by themselves. The sheer bulk of the control texts makes a thoroughgoing, systematic attempt to identify characteristic features of word-order in comedy an unattractive

CAF = Kock's *Comicorum Atticorum Fragmenta*; *CGFP* = *Comicorum Graecorum Fragmenta in Papyris Reperta*, ed. C. Austin (Berlin 1973); *PCG* = *Poetae Comici Graeci*, ed. R. Kassel and C. Austin, vol. iv (Berlin 1983); *TrGF* = *Tragicorum Graecorum Fragmenta*, ed. (i) B. Snell, (ii) R. Kannicht and B. Snell, (iv) S. Radt (Göttingen 1971, 1981, 1977). Comic fragments are cited from *CAF* unless otherwise indicated; fragments of Sophocles, minor tragedians and tragic *adespota* from *TrGF*; of Aeschylus, from Mette; and of Euripides, from Nauck with Snell's (1964) supplement. The following books are cited by author's name only: J. Blomqvist, *Greek Particles in Hellenistic Prose* (Lund 1969); J. D. Denniston, *The Greek Particles*, 2nd edn (Oxford 1954); K. J. Dover, *Greek Word Order*, 2nd edn (Cambridge 1968); H. Thesleff, *Studies on Intensification in Early and Classical Greek* (Helsinki 1954); J. Werres, 'Die Beteuerungsformeln in der attischen Komödie' (Diss., Bonn 1936). I am indebted to the University Librarian of Bonn for a copy of Werres' work; and even more indebted to the anonymous referee who criticized the first version of my article and compelled me to reconsider some points of classification and exposition.

[1] Control is crucial; there is no point in listing features found in one genre unless it can be shown that they do not occur with equal frequency in all genres. For example, the title of J. W. Poultney's article, 'Studies in the Syntax of Attic Comedy', *AJPh* 84 (1963) 359ff, raises hopes which the article itself disappoints, because specifically comic features are not distinguished from shared features.

prospect, when there can be no confidence at the outset that comedy will turn out to differ in such respects from other genres.

There may be more profit in nibbling at the question from starting-points indicated by passages in which a common word strikes us, in the light of our knowledge of Greek, as abnormally placed. A reader does not have to be deeply learned to recognize that such Thucydides, Plato and Euripides as he has read has not prepared him for (e.g.) Philemon fr. 136 οὐκ εὐψυχία / τοῦτ᾽ ἔσθ᾽ ὃ ποιεῖς νῦν γάρ, ἀλλ᾽ ἀνανδρία. It can be verified by sampling that post-ponement of γάρ and δέ is more frequent in comedy, as a percentage of its total stock of γάρ and δέ, than in tragedy and prose. To validate the suspicion that some of the postponements of γάρ and δέ in comedy are without parallel elsewhere entails reading the rest of Attic literature attentively. Denniston did just that, and it is unlikely that anything of importance in the placing of par-ticles escaped his notice;[2] Blomqvist has extended the enquiry into much of Aristotle, Theophrastus and Hellenistic historical and scientific writing. Here at least is a phenomenon which is not only distinctively comic but extends its hold on comedy, in the course of the fourth century BC, before our very eyes. The phenomenon has not escaped attention, but very little consideration has been given to its literary and sociolinguistic implications. Wilamowitz treated it, together with other kinds of hyperbaton, as 'offenbar keine poetische Freiheit': as a feature, in fact, of 'die lebendige Rede', which orders words according to the feeling of the moment.[3] I hesitate, however, to accept this explanation of phenomena which are signally absent from those passages of Greek literature in which we have grounds for thinking that the writer is deliberately reproducing the idioms and patterns of colloquial language in order to give an impression of uninhibited conversation or lively emotion.[4] Postponed γάρ and δέ sound to me more like the inversion of verb and object which was once normal in serious English poetry but is now the hallmark of old-fashioned pantomime, doggerel epitaphs, Christmas cards and occasional verse in provincial newspapers. I would not seriously set my intuition against the judgement of Wilamowitz were it not that his 'offenbar' was quite un-justified by the evidence available to him and it turns out from systematic investigation (see section V, below) that, so far as δέ is concerned, 'keine poetische Freiheit', though not absolutely irreconcilable with the evidence, is not easily reconciled with it.

---

[2] He did not claim to have listed every instance of every comparatively rare phenomenon; in particular, his list of examples of postponed γάρ in Middle Comedy (97) is selective, and he is a little perfunctory on the comic postponement of δέ (188); Blomqvist (115–17) picks up a handful of (unremarkable) prose examples ignored by Denniston. Nevertheless, it seemed to me, when I went through Denniston's marked texts and annotations after his death, that he was extremely unlikely to have missed any really striking placing of a connecting particle in classical prose or the major dramatists.

[3] *Menander, Das Schiedsgericht* (Berlin 1925) 156.

[4] Cf. my article 'The Colloquial Stratum in Classical Attic Prose', *Classical Contributions. Studies in Honor of Malcolm Francis McGregor* (Locust Valley, N.Y. 1981) 15–25 (= pp. 16–30 above).

We know that the language of comedy includes elements both of colloquial vulgarity and of high poetic diction, and it is natural to think of it as analogous to a culinary recipe.[5] Any given recipe contains ingredients no one of which is unique, because each is found in other recipes, and the uniqueness of the recipe itself lies in the specific combination of ingredients and in their ratios and treatment. If, however, there is an actual ingredient in comic language which does not occur in the recipes of other genres and appears to have been generated by an autonomous development within comedy, this has a bearing on the acceptability of conventions in the relationship between comic poet and audience – that is to say, on the relationship between 'on stage' and 'in real life'.

I propose in this paper to examine three phenomena and to reserve the starkest of the three, the postponement of γάρ and δέ, to the end. The other two, selected on the basis of one passage of Aristophanes which seemed to me odd enough to justify further enquiry, are beset by interesting uncertainties, and whether either of them contains an element truly peculiar to comedy – as I am inclined to think both of them do – is a question to which not everyone will give the same answer.

In Ar. *Pl.* 234, when Khremylos has urged the god Wealth to come into his house, Wealth replies, ἀλλ' ἄχθομαι μὲν εἰσιὼν νὴ τοὺς θεοὺς / εἰς οἰκίαν ἑκάστοτ' ἀλλοτρίαν πάνυ. ἀλλοτρίαν πάνυ cannot here mean 'completely alien (*sc.* to me)', i.e. 'totally uncongenial'; apart from the fact that ἀλλότριος, especially qualifying οἰκία, would normally be taken to mean 'someone else's' (cf. *V.* 1020, 1022, *Th.* 795, *Ra.* 1048, *Ec.* 642), Wealth has been given no reason at all to suppose that Khremylos's house is peculiarly uncongenial. He goes on, in fact, to explain (237–44) that accepting invitations has in the past landed him in trouble for a variety of reasons; and Khremylos replies that this time it will be different, for Wealth has not yet met a μέτριος householder. What word, then, does πάνυ intensify? Is it ἄχθομαι at the beginning of 234?[6] Or does it somehow reinforce the whole couplet? In either case, it seems to be functioning in a way which differentiates it from the familiar πάνυ immediately preceding or immediately following the intensified word. Moreover, its function seems to be duplicated by νὴ τοὺς θεούς, and that oath itself has an unfamiliar location, separated by two 'mobile' words (see below), ἄχθομαι and εἰσιών, from the nearest preceding major pause. The passage thus suggests a double line of enquiry as *prima facie* worth pursuing: the comic poets' placing of oaths, and their placing of the very common intensifier πάνυ (to which we may append consideration of another common intensifier, σφόδρα).

The questions posed by γάρ, δέ and oaths are framed in terms of the distance of these words from the last preceding pause, and distance from the next following pause is relevant to my questions about πάνυ and σφόδρα. A

---

[5] Cf. my article 'Der Stil des Aristophanes', *Wege der Forschung* 265 (1975) 124–43 (= pp. 224–36 below).

[6] So Σ[θ] *ad loc.* and Thesleff 58.

working definition of 'pause' is therefore needed. I treat a full stop, colon, dash or mark of interrogation in a modern printed text[7] as a *prima facie* indication of 'major pause' (symbol '‖'), and within this category I use the symbol '⦀' to mean 'change of speaker'.[8] There will inevitably be some exceptional cases requiring individual assessment. It is also hard to know whether a citation from a lost comedy begins or ends with a change of speaker, and sometimes impossible to locate change in a fragmentary text; where there is room for doubt, I use an asterisk. By 'minor pause' (symbol '|') I mean the boundary between a main clause and a subordinate clause, either way round; this again is a *prima facie* classification, and some instances (e.g. an indicative clause introduced by ὥστε) may call for consideration. 'Minimal pause' (symbol ' : ') is the boundary of a colon within a clause; colometry is a subjective business much of the time, and when instances to which I refer cannot easily be subsumed under simple formulae I shall quote the words.[9]

Quantifying distance from pause is not simply a matter of counting words. Word-indexes which classify the instances of (e.g.) γάρ as *tertio loco, quarto loco*, etc., are admirable time-savers but insufficiently refined, because we need to know the nature and function of the words occupying the preceding *loci*.[10] πρῶτον μὲν γάρ, ἐν ἀριστερᾷ δέ, δὶς βιῶναι γάρ (Men. *Theoph.* fr. 1) and χρηστὸν ἄνθρωπον δέ (Antiphanes fr. 205.3) all exhibit the connecting particle *tertio loco*, but the first two examples differ from the other two: μέν is a postpositive and ἐν a prepositive, whereas in the examples from Menander and Antiphanes both the words preceding the particle are 'mobile', i.e. words which, unlike prepositives and postpositives, can occur anywhere in a clause.[11] The distinction between prepositives (symbol '*p*'), postpositives (symbol '*q*') and mobiles (symbol '*M*') is fundamental to all discussion of Greek word-order. Some negatives (e.g. οὔτε and μηδέ) are *p*, others (e.g. οὐδέν and μηκέτι) are *M*, and I shall use the symbol '*neg*' for all of them, so that 'except *neg*' must be understood with '*p*' and '*M*'. The bracketing of a symbol is a concise means of making a statement about a pair of set of patterns; for instance, any statement about ‖ (|) (*neg.*) *M* is a statement about all the patterns ⦀ *neg M*, ‖ *neg M*, ⦀ *M* and ‖ *M*. I shall not, however, trouble to

---

[7] Including instances where modern editors print a comma but a respectable case could be made for stronger punctuation.

[8] Quoted words contained within narrative are treated as beginning and ending with change of speaker; a few cases of formal change in drama, where an interruption is ignored (e.g. Ar. *Av.* 1148; cf. Werres 34), are not treated as change.

[9] The fundamental treatment of colometry is in Eduard Fraenkel, 'Kolon und Satz', *NGG* Ph.-hist. Kl. 1932, 197–213 and 319–54 (= *Kleine Beiträge* [Rome 1964] i 73–130, with additional notes). The second part, which takes as its starting-point J. Wackernagel, 'Ueber ein Gesetz der indogermanischen Wortstellung', *IF* i (1892) 333ff (= *Kleine Schriften* [Göttingen 1953] 1ff), is particularly important for our present purposes.

[10] Emphasized by Fraenkel (yet still widely ignored) in a footnote to his note on A. *Ag.* 222. Cf. Blomqvist 113ff.

[11] Dover 12–14. In this paper I treat 'prepositional' ἐντός, πάροιθε, χάριν and the like as *p* or *q*, according to their position.

write '(*p*)' or '(*q*)'; the presence or absence of *p* and *q* will be treated as irrelevant.

There are analogies between the ordering of *M* and *q* and the ordering of two *M*s when one of them is a 'nucleus' (symbol '*N*') communicating information-content which could not have been inferred from the context and the other is a 'concomitant' (symbol '*C*') which could have been inferred.[12] There is more than one kind of *C*. In modern colloquial English, for example, the same utterance may elicit from three different hearers the responses 'I think that's right', 'That's right' and 'Right.' The one-word answer consists of a single *N*, and the alternative answers wrap it up in words which are not indispensable for the communication of the message. Much the same is true of Greek; words meaning 'be', 'think', 'seem', anaphoric demonstratives, and personal pronouns which do not seem to be antithetical, are very commonly *C*. So are words meaning 'must' or 'ought', where their sense could be adequately (even if ungrammatically) communicated by the infinitive alone, given the context. Of course, in 'I think that's right', any of the words 'I', 'think' and 'that' can be stressed in English in order to imply antithesis between the speaker and others, between opinion and certainty, or between the referent of 'that' and alternatives of which the speaker is conscious. Implicit antithesis is just as common in Greek, and often positively signalled by word-order or particles such as γε – fortunately; we can only imagine variations of volume of sound in Greek. When an anaphoric demonstrative implies no antithesis and could be translated as 'it' or omitted altogether, e.g. Ar. *Lys.* 949 ποήσω ταῦτα νὴ τὴν Ἄρτεμιν,[13] it is plainly *C*, whereas a demonstrative designed to alert the hearer to an important point not yet uttered, e.g. ibid. 486 καὶ μὴν αὐτῶν τοῦτ' ἐπιθυμῶ ... πυθέσθαι, ὅτι βουλόμεναι κτλ., has a different character. A second type of *C* is a word whose information-content can be assessed in the light of the preceding context but not so easily, if at all, out of context. For example, in Ar. *Lys.* 777 σαφής γ' ὁ χρησμὸς νὴ Δία, the words σαφής γ' are *N q* and the words ὁ χρησμός are *p C*, because Lysistrata said in 768 'Here is the oracle', a woman asked her to recite it, she has now done so, and 777 is the woman's reaction to it; cf. *Eq.* 1188 ὡς ἡδὺς ὦ Ζεῦ, where the masculine gender, metrically protected, shows that 'the wine you are giving me' is understood from the previous line. Vocatives (unless they are elaborated or otherwise show by their form that they carry an affective charge) mostly belong to the second type of *C*, since we learn from the preceding context who is addressing whom. A vocative addressed by the speaker to a third party would be a different matter, if it were ever unheralded; in drama it cannot be unheralded, since the speaker turns.

---

[12] Dover 32–41.

[13] On the formulae ταῦτα ποήσω, ἔσται τάδε, etc., see Fraenkel, *Beobachtungen zu Aristophanes* (Rome 1962) 79ff. Since ταῦτα and ποιήσω can occur in either order (with *Lys.* 949 contrast ibid. 506 and *Ra.* 1515), and the verb can be omitted (e.g. *V.* 142), it looks as if the *N/C* relationship within the formula can vary from one instance to another.

There are inevitably cases which hover on the borderline between the two types, and thereby remind us that the criteria of difference between those types, though adequate much of the time, do not always stand up to rigorous scrutiny. These are cases in which an M is predictable – in varying degrees – from the immediately preceding word or phrase, taking into account – again, in varying degrees – the situation in which the words are uttered. A case could be made for treating in this way δήσω in Ar. *Eq.* 705 ἐν τῷ ξύλῳ δήσω σε (what else but δεῖν does one do to someone ἐν τῷ ξύλῳ?) and τῶν ὄντων in Lys. vii 4 δημευθέντων τῶν ὄντων (what else but ὄντα is subject to δημεύειν?), together with μελήσει in *Th.* 240 ‖ ἐμοὶ μελήσει, ἐμπεσών in Men. *Sam.* 565 εἰς τοιαύτην ἐμπεσών . . . ταραχήν, etc.

There is however another way of looking at ἐν τῷ ξύλῳ δήσω σε and the like. *M M* demands treatment as a single unit (symbol '[*M M*]') when it is a very familiar phrase, e.g. εὖ εἰδέναι, νοῦν ἔχειν, ὀλίγῳ ὕστερον, κακῶς ἀπόλοιο. This principle accounts for quite a number of instances of *M M γάρ* and *M M δέ* in Attic prose, and with them we can group an adjective or adverb accompanied by an intensifier (e.g. πολύ πλείονες), polyptota such as μόνος μόνῳ and substantives qualified by numerals (e.g. ἓξ μῆνες). In some of the familiar phrases one component carries heavier information-content than the other, as is apparent from the fact that προσέχειν can be used in the sense προσέχειν τὸν νοῦν. At a far remove from [*M M*] are instances which might be mistaken for [*M M*] if we encountered them only as isolated phrases, divorced from their context, but in fact carry a considerable weight of information-content in each of their ingredients; in Antiphanes fr. 205.3, for example (see above), χρηστὸν ἄνθρωπον does not mean '*good* person' (*N C*) or 'good *person*' (*C N*), for the scarcity of good people (*N N*) is being contrasted with the abundance of (good or bad) peacocks.

II. OATHS

Oaths are characteristic of the dialogue of comedy and of Plato and Xenophon. They are uncommon in tragedy, and E. *Andr.* 934 μὰ τὴν ἄνασσαν is the only tragic approximation to the banal oaths of conversation, the other examples being multiple or elaborated (A. *Ag.* 1432; S. *El.* 626, 881, frr. 140.1, 957; E. *Hp.* 307, *Md.* 395, 1059, *Ion* 1528, *Ph.* 1006, *IA* 739, 948f, *Rh.* 827). Satyr-plays, as we would expect, tend towards comic usage: S. *Ichn.* (*TrGF*) 118; E. *Cy.* 9, 154, 265, 555, 560, 586; Lykophron *Menedemos* 2.3. Banal oaths appear also in dipinti on vases, e.g. Leningrad 615 (Beazley, *ARV*, 1594) νὴ τὸν Ἡρακλέα ('By God, so it is!') and a black-figure cup in Palermo (Beazley, *ABV*, 675) Θέογνις καλὸς νὴ Δία. In these circumstances it is not surprising that the oath is uncommon in continuous exposition, and when it occurs it has the effect of infusing sudden warmth into the relation between writer and reader, e.g. Xen. *Lac.* 14.1 τοῦτο μὰ Δί' οὐκ ἂν ἔτι θρασέως εἴποιμι; in Epicurus 31.11.5 (Arrighetti) ὦ Μητρόδωρε prepares the way for ἀλλὰ μὰ Δία τῶν καθ᾽ ἕκαστα κτλ. It is noticeable that while the orators sometimes use oaths in this way they are particularly inclined to use them in quoting hypothetical utterances (e.g. Dem. xxi 222), answering rehtorical questions (e.g. Is. iii 25) or postulating objections and comments, especially in the well-known ἀλλὰ νὴ Δία formula.[14]

On my reckoning[15] there are 850 oaths in extant comedy and 800 in the prose corpus used as a control, viz. Plato (excluding *Ax.* and the like), Xenophon (plus *Cyn.*) and the orators. Some 60 per cent (*c.* 550) of all those in comedy and nearly 80 per cent (614) of those in prose either follow a pause immediately or are separated from it only by *neg, p* or *q*, not by *M*. [16] Using the symbol 'Δ' for 'oath', I subsume all those instances under the formula ‖ (|) (*neg*) Δ, ignoring – as in other formulae, in default of special reasons – *p* and *q*. | (*neg*) Δ adds fewer than 40, mostly in the orators, and if the instances involving the connecting relative ($\delta\varsigma$ = 'and he...'), ἐπεί = γάρ and ὥστε = οὖν are reclassified as ‖ (*neg*) Δ the total comes down to 30. I count 52 examples of ⁚ (*neg*) Δ, again with a predominance of prose. Connective καί ('and, moreover,...'), ἤ ('or, indeed,...') and οὔτε ('nor, indeed,...') account for 19 (Ar. *Av.* 574, *Ra.* 863, Men. *Asp.* 201, *Dis* 95, fr. 683.2, *Adesp.* (*CAF*) 166.1, Philemon frr. 90.4, 98.4, Dem. xi 18, xix 52, 215, xxi 3, Pl. *Grg.* 482b, 483e, 513b, 527c, *Lys.* 211e, Xen. *Ap.* 20, *HG* i 7.21); to these I would add 6 examples from Demosthenes, where *p* Δ introduces a second finite verb in a subordinate clause (xxiii 194) or a second participle (xlii 7) or participle-equivalent (ἑκών, xlviii 2) or infinitive (xli 12, lv 26), plus *verb* ἤτοι Δ *object*$_1$ ἤ *object*$_2$ in xxv 51.[17] The formula '*x* (and/but) *neg* Δ *y*' covers 12 (Ar. *Nu.* 344, 1066, *Av.* 1237, Dem. viii 28, xix 212, xxi 25, xxii 33, xxiii 48, Din. i 40, Is. xi 35 bis, Xen. *Cyr.* vi 1.14); '*neg* Δ *x* but *y*' covers 6 (Dem. xiv 38, xxiv 28, xxv 41, lii 14, Lys. vi 38, Pl. *Ap.* 17b); and there are 4 examples of *neg* repeated and reinforced by Δ (Ar. *V.* 26, *Ra.* 28, *Pl.* 551, Men. *Kolax* fr. 2.4). To these I would add passages in which Δ is separated from a major pause only by a vocative (Ar. *V.* 1404, Men. *Dysk.* 666) or an exclamation (Ar. *V.* 310, *Av.* 194, *Lys.* 836, *Pl.* 359), Pl. *Smp.* 219c εὖ γὰρ ἴστε, Δ and Dem. lvii 42 τῷ μὲν εἰς ἐμ᾽ ἥκοντι κινδύνῳ νῦν ⁚ μὰ τὸν Δί᾽ οὐχὶ συμφέρον πρᾶγμα (an antithetical δέ-clause comes later).

---

[14] There is also a tendency for an oath to occur when any reference is made to the hypothetical thought or speech of others, e.g. Dem. viii 7 πλὴν εἰ τοῦτο λέγουσι νὴ Δί᾽, ὡς κτλ.

[15] The reservation is required not just by arithmetical incompetence on my part but by the number of doubtful and variant readings (mostly in comedy), the gradations of assurance about restoration of fragmentary comic texts, and my suspicion that in making notes over a long period I was not wholly consistent in my admission or exclusion of Platonic works of questionable authenticity. I have left out of account 'real' oaths uttered in response to a command 'Swear...', citations which consist wholly of oaths without context, and two dozen oaths which are themselves quite clear in fragmentary texts but do not reveal with sufficient clarity their position in the clause. Each multiple oath is treated as one example. Dem. xviii 208 is unique and unclassifiable.

[16] Cf. Werres 31.

[17] Antiphanes fr. 159.7 μετά γε νὴ Δία / τοὺς μητραγυρτοῦντας can be treated as ⁚ *p q* Δ if Kock is right in printing the whole passage without change of speaker; but the more persuasive division of the passage between speakers in Kaibel's Athenaeus (226d) points to ‖ *p q* Δ.

I turn now to passages in which a single M intervenes between pause and Δ.[18] The totals for comedy (c. 160) and prose (157) are very close, but they do not favour all types of $M\,\Delta$ equally. In prose, 91 of the examples occur in answers to questions; Plato favours the form 'Is x the case?' '$x\,\Delta$', Xenophon and the orators 'Wh-/how . . . ?' '$x\,\Delta$', and Xenophon has a particular liking for 'x or y?' '$x\,\Delta$' (or '$y\,\Delta$'). In comedy, on the other hand, only 32 of the examples are answers to questions, the remainder being comment, intervention, applause, threat or intensified assertion in continuous utterance. Comedy and prose together produce 22 examples of | (neg.) $M\,\Delta$, among which we must classify Ar. Pl. 234 (see above).[19] I count 20 examples of ⋮ $M\,\Delta$, namely Philemon fr. 213.13 (καὶ M), Diphilos fr. 32.25 (ἢ M), Pl. Ap. 35d (ἄλλως τε μέντοι); Philetairos fr. 4.3 and Philiskos CGFP 215.12 (neg M); Ar. Av. 661 and Men. Asp. 399 (exclamations); Men. Sam. 283 and Sik. 117 (vocatives); Ar. V. 133, Ec. 155, Adesp. (CAF) fr. 421.3, Philemon fr. 101.1, Xen. Cyr. ii 2.2 (all . . . M μὲν ⋮ $M\,\Delta$); Ar. Pl. 165, Xen. Oec. 3.8 (both antithetical M δὲ ⋮ $M\,\Delta$); and finally, Aiskhines iii 172 καὶ γαμεῖ γυναῖκα ⋮ πλουσίαν μὲν νὴ Δία κτλ., Dem. xxiv 126 ἀλλὰ Μελάνωπος ⋮ δεινόν ἐστιν εἰ κτλ., liv 36 ἡ δ᾽ ἀπ᾽ αὐτῶν ἑτοιμότης ⋮ οὐδ᾽ ἂν εἰπεῖν μὰ τοὺς θεοὺς δυναίμην ⋮ ὅση κτλ., and lv 17 τίς ἂν ὑμῶν ⋮ εἴτ᾽ ἐν ἀγρῷ νὴ Δί᾽ εἴτ᾽ ἐν ἄστει . . . δέξαιτ᾽ ἄν;[20]

It is at the next degree of separation of Δ from preceding ‖ (|), i.e. ‖ (|) (neg) $M\,M\,\Delta$, that prose and comedy begin to part company, and it becomes worth while to distinguish between the different functions of M_2 in relation of M_1. In the classified list which follows I symbolize verse-end by '/', indicate pause when it immediately follows Δ, and put an asterisk at the end of a citation, where ‖ (|) is probable but not demonstrable. I include in each class not only the examples which satisfy the criterion of that class but also those which both satisfy the criterion and include features characteristic of one or more of the preceding classes.

Class 1: $M\,M = \mathcal{N}\,C$, where C is 'clutter'. C = 'be': Ar. Av. 1433, Th. 858 / ‖, Ra. 947, Ec. 761 ‖, Pl. 337; Men. Dysk. 320, Epitr. 400 / ‖, Georg. 34 / ‖, Sam. 686 |; Adesp. (CGFP) 255.8 ‖, Alexis fr. 163.1 / ‖, Ameipsias fr. 19.1, Antiphanes fr. 124.15 /*; Dem. xxxvi 61. C = unstressed or anaphoric pronoun: Ar. Lys. 949 / ‖, 1147; Men. Mis. 176; Antiphon (Thalheim) fr. 70. C = 'think' or 'seem': Ar. Lys. 81 / ‖, Pl. 380 /; Men. Perik. 302 ‖; Dem. xx 151 |, Pl. Phdr. 228b |, Xen. M. i 5.5; add Dem. x 20 καὶ Φίλιππον δ᾽ αὐτὸν ⋮ οὐδὲν ἂν ἀλλ᾽ οἶμαι μὰ τοὺς θεοὺς εὔξασθαι. C = vocative: Ar. Pax 979 ‖, Pl. 366 / ‖; Men.

---

[18] In many, as in many of the category ⋮ $p\,\Delta$, one can see the force of Werres' assertion (6, 30, 32, 37f) that a banal oath by Zeus is in effect a particle. Cf. also W. Blaszczak, 'Götteranrufung und Beteuerung. Untersuchungen zu volkstümlichen Ausdrucksformen in der griechischen Literatur' (Diss., Breslau 1932) 7f, 13.

[19] Xen. Cyr. ii 3.23 ὁποσάκις γε, ἔφη, καὶ δειπνοποιούμεθα νὴ Δία is formally $p\,q$, ἔφη, $p\,M\,\Delta$, but one may hesitate to treat so massive a relative as p.

[20] Cf. Dem. xxv 51, mentioned above.

Sik. 156f‖; Dem. xxi 2. In Ar. *Lys.* 983 κᾶρυξ ἐγὼν ὦ κυρσάνιε ναὶ τοὺς θεούς / the pronoun, answering 'What are you?', is *C.* I treat Men. fr. 171.1 ἐγὼ μὲν ἤδη μοι δοκῶ νὴ τοὺς θεούς / as *N q C q C* Δ.²¹ With initial *neg*: Ar. *Eq.* 843 οὐκ, ὦγαθοί, ταῦτ᾽ ἐστί πω ταύτῃ μὰ τὸν Ποσειδῶ / ‖; Men. fr. 85 οὐκ ἔστιν ἐκτεὺς τοῦτο μὰ τὸν Ἀσκληπιόν /*; Philemon fr. 72.1 οὐκ ἔστιν οὔτε ζωγράφος μὰ τοὺς θεούς / :.²²

Class 2: *M M = N C*, where *C* can be inferred from the preceding context. Ar. *Lys.* 777 σαφής γ᾽ ὁ χρησμὸς νὴ Δία ‖, 942 οὐχ ἡδὺ τὸ μύρον νὴ τὸν Ἀπόλλω τουτογί /|; Men. *Epitr.* 358 δεινή γ᾽ ἡ [κρίσις] / νὴ τὸν Δία τὸν Σωτῆρα, *Sam.* 272 σύνοιδα γὰρ τῷ μειρακίῳ νὴ τοὺς θεούς / καὶ κοσμίῳ. . . ὄντι; Dem. viii 7 πλὴν εἰ τοῦτο (prospective) λέγουσι νὴ Δία |, xxv 77 ὧν ὁ πατήρ τι πεποίηκε νὴ Δία ‖.

Class 3: *M M = [M M]*. Familiar phrases: Ar. *Nu.* 817 / ‖| (οὐκ εὖ φρονεῖς), *Av.* 1371 /‖| (νοῦν ἄρ᾽ ἕξεις), *Ra.* 1481‖ (εὖ λέγεις), *Ec.* 433 /‖| (νοῦν γὰρ εἶχον); Men. *Asp.* 238 / | (κακὸς κακῶ)ς ἀπόλοιο), *Dysk.* 544 / ‖ (οὐκ ἔχω λέγειν), *Sam.* 715 ‖| (οὐκ οἶδ᾽ ἔγωγε); Dem. xxi 109 (ποιήσας δεινά). One *M* intensifies the other: Ar. *Nu.* 1098; Men. *Sam.* 442 /; Eupolis fr. 74.2 /*; Is. v 61; add Pl. *Ap.* 39c τιμωρίαν ὑμῖν ἥξειν . . . : πολὺ χαλεπωτέραν νὴ Δία. One *M* a numeral: Ar. *Nu.* 483 / ‖. Repetition: Ar. *Ec.* 213.

Class 4 consists of all the instances which occupy an intermediate position between classes 2 and 5 or 3 and 5; each of them may appear to many readers, as they do to me intermittently, to belong in class 2 or 3 or 5, but there is much room for doubt and change of mind over their allocation. Ar. *Ach.* 779 πάλιν τυ ἀποισῶ ναὶ τὸν Ἑρμᾶν οἴκαδις, *Eq.* 705 ἐν τῷ ξύλῳ δήσω σε νὴ τὸν οὐρανόν / ‖, *Av.* 24 οὐ ταὐτὰ κρώζει μὰ Δία, *Lys.* 521 ὀρθῶς γε λέγων νὴ Δί᾽ ἐκεῖνος, *Th.* 240 ἐμοὶ μελήσει νὴ Δία; Men. *Dysk.* 629 καλά γ᾽ ἐπόησε νὴ τὸν οὐρανόν / ‖, *Ph.* 44 τἀληθῆ λέγω νὴ τοὺς θεούς / ‖, *Sam.* 515 καὶ πέπηγα τῷ κακῷ νὴ τοὺς θεούς / ‖|, 565 οὐδεπώποτ᾽ εἰς τοιαύτην ἐμπεσὼν νὴ τοὺς θεούς / οἶδα ταραχήν; Alexis fr. 195.2 ἐπιπονώτερον / ⟨ἔργον add. Porson⟩ μὰ τὸν Διόνυσον οὐκ εἴληφ᾽ ἐγώ, Diphilos fr. 43.28 ἀπὸ συμβολῶν συνάγοντα νὴ Δία, Eupolis (*CGFP*) frr. 74.1 ἀνόσια πάσχω ταῦτα ναὶ μὰ τὰς Νύμφας / ‖|, 95.170]οἰσυουργῷ γ᾽ ἀνδρὶ νὴ τὸν Διοκλέα /*, Heniokhos fr. 4.1 πρὸς ἐμαυτὸν ἐνθυμούμενος νὴ τοὺς θεούς /|, Philippides, fr. 5.4 ᾽καλοί γε᾽ φησίν ᾽οἱ νεφροὶ / νὴ τὴν φίλην Δήμητρα᾽ ‖; Pl. *Euthd.* 305c ἀλλ᾽ ἐπαΐειν αὐτόν φασι περὶ τοῦ πράγματος νὴ τὸν Δία : (*prima facie p N q C = q p p C* Δ and therefore class 1, but in the context φασί is not unimportant), Xen. *Oec.* 11.25 τὸν ἥττω λόγον, ὦ Σώκρατες, οὐ μὰ τὸν Δί᾽ οὐ δύναμαι κρείττω ποιεῖν.

Class 5: *M M = N N*. Ar. *Eq.* 409 οὗτοι μ᾽ ὑπερβαλεῖσθ᾽ ἀναιδείᾳ μὰ τὸν Ποσειδῶ / ‖, 812 πεποιηκότα πλείονα χρηστὰ / νὴ τὴν Δήμητρα Θεμιστοκλέους πολλῷ, 1163 ἀλλ᾽ ἢ μεγάλως εὐδαιμονήσω τήμερον / ὑπὸ τῶν ἐραστῶν νὴ Δί᾽‖, *Nu.* 516 κατερῶ πρὸς ὑμᾶς ἐλευθέρως τἀληθῆ νὴ τὸν Διόνυσον κτλ., ²³

---

²¹ I treat unstressed temporal adverbs as *C.*
²² Perhaps minimal pause should be placed after οὐκ ἔστιν; cf. Dem. xxv 51, lv 17.
²³ This oath, however, is not banal but elaborated at length.

V. 426 τοῦτο μέντοι (demonstrative stressed) δεινὸν ἤδη[24] νὴ Δία |, *Av.* 386 μᾶλλον εἰρήνην ἄγουσι νὴ Δία |, *Lys.* 34 βέλτιστα τοίνυν μηκέτ᾽ εἶναι (= 'exist') νὴ Δία / ‖, 206 καὶ μὴν ποτόδδει γ᾽ ἀδὺ ναὶ τὸν Κάστορα / ‖, 486 καὶ μὴν αὐτῶν τοῦτ᾽ (prospective) ἐπιθυμῶ νὴ τὸν Δία κτλ., 731 ἀλλ᾽ ἤξω ταχέως νὴ τὼ θεώ / |, 1174 ἐγὼ δὲ κοπραγωγὴν γα πρῴ ναὶ τὼ σιώ / ‖, *Ec.* 779 ἀλλὰ λαμβάνειν / ἡμᾶς μόνον δεῖ νὴ Δία ‖, 831 ἃς ἐγὼ φυλάξομαι / νὴ τὸν Ποσειδῶ |, 998 καὶ γὰρ ἐγὼ σὲ (*sc.* οἶδα) νὴ Δία / ‖, *Pl.* 715 ὀπὰς γὰρ εἶχεν οὐκ ὀλίγας μὰ τὸν Δία / ‖, 1006 καὶ μὴν πρὸ τοῦ γ᾽ ὀσημέραι νὴ τὼ θεὼ / ... ἐβάδιζεν, 1028 ἀναγκάσαι δίκαιόν ἐστι νὴ Δία / ⫶, 1043 πολιὰ γεγένησαι ταχύ γε νὴ τὸν οὐρανόν / ‖; Men. *Dysk.* 147f οὐ πάνυ φιλάνθρωπον β[λέπειν μ]οι φαίνεται / μὰ τὸν Δία ‖, 160 νῦν δ᾽ οὐ βιωτόν ἐστι μὰ τὸν Ἀσκληπιόν / ‖, 162 παρ᾽ αὐτὴν τὴν ὁδὸν γὰρ νὴ Δία /, 639 εἰσὶν ('really exist') θεοὶ μὰ τὸν Διόνυσον,[25] 658f ἡδέως / ἴδοιμ᾽ ἄν, ἄνδρες, νὴ τὸν Ἀπόλλω τουτονί / ‖, 877f ἔσται μέγα κακὸν πάλιν [τί σοι] / νὴ τὼ θεώ ⫶, *Epitr.* 951 αὖ]τη μ᾽ [ἔπε]ισε νὴ τὸν Ἀπόλλω[, *Mis.* 284f ὠμότητος ἐκτόπου / ἀμφοῖν ἀπανθρώπου τε νὴ τὸν ἥλιον / ‖, *Perik.* 339 ἀκοῦσαι τὰ παρὰ σοῦ γε νὴ Δία / ‖, 361f χαλεπὰ ταῦτα παντελῶς / τὰ πράγματ᾽ ἐστὶ νὴ τὸν Ἀπόλλω, 504f οὐκ οἶδ᾽ ὅτι / λέγω μὰ τὴν Δήμητρα, *Sam.* 422 οὐδ᾽ ἂν ἐπὶ πολλῷ γενέσθαι τὸ γεγονὸς μὰ τοὺς θεοὺς / πρᾶγμ᾽ ἐδεξάμην, *Sik.* 114 νῦν δοκεῖ (stressed) μοι νὴ Δία / ‖, frr. 127.3 χωρίον κεκτημένος κάλλιστον εἶ νὴ τὸν Δία /, 215.5 ῥῆμά τι / ἐφθέγξατ᾽ οὐδὲν ἐμφερὲς μὰ τὸν Δία / τῷ ᾽γνῶθι σαυτόν'; *Adesp.* (*CGFP*) 240.35 οὐ νῦν (stressed?) ἐπιτηδείως ἔχει μὰ τὸν Δία / ⫶, 244.221 [ἐπέ]ρχεται δ[ὲ πο]λλάκις νὴ τοὺς θεούς / |, Alexis frr. 62.4 ἀποβεβαμμένας / εἰς οὐχὶ ταὐτὸν μὰ Δία τὴν αὐτὴν μύρον, 123.3 οὐδ᾽ εἰ γάλα λαγῷ / εἶχον μὰ τὴν Γῆν, 144.1 στρουθὶς ἀκαρὴς νὴ Δί᾽ ἐγένου (Kaibel: νὴ Δί᾽ εἶ cod. Ath.) ‖, Antiphanes fr. 122.3 ἀκολουθεῖν ἔρις / ἐν τῷ Λυκείῳ μετὰ σοφιστῶν νὴ Δία / λεπτῶν, Dionysios fr. 2.1 σφόδρα μοι κεχάρισαι, Σιμία, νὴ τοὺς θεούς / |, Euboulos (Hunter) frr. 60.2 ἀλλ᾽ ἠκούσαμεν / καὶ τοῦτο (prospective) νὴ τὴν Ἑστίαν, 126.4 ⟨οὐ μετρίως (Kaibel)⟩ πέπωκ᾽ ἐγὼ / μὰ ⟨τὸν (Meineke)⟩ Δία τὸν Μενδαῖον, Eupolis fr. 252.4 κρόκης / πέντε στατῆρας εἶχε ναὶ μὰ τὸν Δία / ‖, Nikostratos fr. 24.1 Κηφισόδωρον οὐ κακῶς μὰ τὸν Δία / ... φασὶ κτλ., Pherekrates fr. 69.3 γλισχρόν γε μοῦστὶ τὸ σίαλον ναὶ τὼ θεώ / ‖, Philemon fr. 114.1 ὡς εὐφυὲς ζῷον κοχλίας νὴ τὸν θεόν / ‖, Theophilos fr. 2.4 οὐδ᾽ ἂν Αὐτοκλῆς / οὕτω μὰ τὴν Γῆν εὐρύθμως. Xen. *Cyr.* i 4.27 προσελθεῖν γάρ σοι, ἔφη, ἀεὶ βουλόμενος ναὶ μὰ τοὺς θεοὺς | ᾐσχυνόμην, *Smp.* 4.27 αὐτὸν δὲ σέ, ἔφη, ἐγὼ εἶδον ναὶ μὰ τὸν Ἀπόλλω |, Dem. iv 49 ἐγὼ δ᾽ οἶμαι (stressed) μέν, ὦ ἄνδρες Ἀθηναῖοι, νὴ τοὺς θεοὺς ἐκεῖνον μεθύειν, viii 17 κρινοῦμεν Διοπείθη νὴ Δία ‖,[26] xxi 205 οὐχ οὕτω τούτῳ χαρίσασθαι μὰ τοὺς θεοὺς βουλόμενοι, xxxvii 16 καὶ τοῦτον οὐδ᾽ ὁτιοῦν ἀδικῶν νὴ τοὺς θεούς |.

---

[24] Cf. n. 21.

[25] On positive μά see Sandbach's note on *Dysk.* 151.

[26] A good example of unitary *M M* created by the sense of the context, not an established phrase. The words are an answer to a question, and the question is not 'What shall we do to Diopeithes?' or 'Whom shall we put on trial?' but 'What shall we do then?'

Given the number of oaths in comedy and in prose, the fact that there are 105 examples of two or more M between pause and Δ in comedy (of which 58 can be 'demoted' to classes 1–4)[27] would lead us to expect 98 in prose; but there are only 20, of which all but 6 belong to classes 1–4. Against 10 comic examples (all quoted above) in which no fewer than four M intervene we cannot set any prose examples except Xen. *Smp.* 4.27 and Dem. iv 49, and they are unimpressive by comparison with (e.g.) Antiphanes fr. 122.3.

III. πάνυ

Thesleff has made a systematic analysis of the function of πάνυ,[28] listing all the words which it intensifies in classical literature (the words are classified first by part of speech and within each part of speech by alphabetical order), marking instances where it comes after the intensified word and discussing some examples in which other words intervene; but he does not discuss the nature of the intervening words (except δοκεῖν) or set out the data which show the extent of the differences between comedy and prose.

I symbolize πάνυ by 'π' and the intensified word by '$M\pi$'.

πάνυ is rare in tragedy, found only[29] in A. *Pe.* 926, *Ag.* 1456, *Ch.* 861; S. *OC* 144; Theodektas F 6.2. Satyr-plays have it: A. fr. 464 II 26 (*Diktyoulkoi*); S. *Ichn.* (*TrGF*) 105, 345; E. *Cy.* 646 (the only instance in Euripides). A very high proportion of its occurrences in Plato and Xenophon are accounted for by the elliptical formulae of assent πάνυ γε and πάνυ μὲν οὖν, and these occur sporadically in comedy also (e.g. Ar. *Eq.* 971, *Pl.* 97). They contribute nothing of interest to the linguistic differentiation of comedy; nor does πάνυ qualifying a substantive phrase with the article (e.g. Ar. *V.* 1181), or the type of elliptical πάνυ found in (e.g.) Pl. *Meno* 94e ἐν ἄλλῃ πόλει ῥᾷόν ἐστιν κακῶς ποιεῖν ἀνθρώπους ἢ εὖ, ἐν τῇδε δὲ καὶ πάνυ.

When πάνυ and a negative occur in the same clause or colon the order is normally *neg π*, but it is often hard to choose, in translating, between 'not altogether' (πάνυ intensifying the adjective, adverb or verb) and 'not at all' (πάνυ intensifying the negative). English often substitutes a diffident 'not very easy' for 'quite impossible', a patronizing or sarcastic 'not very difficult' for 'ridiculously easy', or a courteous 'not obviously' for 'obviously not'. Many passages of Plato suggest that Greek had similar subtleties,[30] and when meiosis is an

---

[27] In Men. *Epitr.* 878 ὑπομαίνεθ᾽ οὗτος (deictic)· νὴ τὸν Ἀπόλλω μαίνεται the oath intensifies the following word (which discards the restraint of ὑπο-), not the preceding words.

[28] Thesleff 56–80.

[29] In S. *Ph.* 650 ὥστε πραΰνειν πόνου, the reading πονου, formerly attributed only to some *recentiores*, is now known to have been the original reading of Ven. gr. 468 (R. D. Dawe, *Studies on the Text of Sophocles* [Leiden 1973–8] iii 55). πάνυ, the reading imported by a corrector and shared by the other manuscripts, was long ago assailed and emended, first by Reiske and later by Meineke and Hense, all of whom had a keen ear for the difference between tragic and comic tone. In *TrGF* ii.152 Kannicht and Snell rightly discard as comic a passage designated τραγικόν by Stobaeus (iv 41.51) and printed as *Adesp.* fr. 547 by Nauck.

[30] Thesleff 77.

accepted convention the sense of the context is not always helpful. Hence Simmias's words in Pl. *Phd.* 64b οὐ πάνυ γέ με νυνδὴ γελασείοντα elicit translations such as 'not much inclined to laugh', superficially an understatement on the part of a man visiting a dear friend in the death-cell. Where it is very important that there should be no misunderstanding, an unusual order may be adopted, e.g. Antiphon vi 29 εἰ μὲν πάνυ μὴ παρεγένοντο μάρτυρες ('no witnesses at all' is demanded by the argument) and Xen. *Eq.* 3.8 οὐ μέντοι τὸν μὴ καλῶς πάνυ ταῦτα ποιῶντα ἀποδοκιμαστέον ('not in every respect well', implying 'but well in some or most respects', as the argument requires), or additional words may remove ambiguity, e.g. πάντων and πάντα in Pl. *Smp.* 178a (where a statement that Aristodemos remembered nothing at all of the symposium would be an unpromising start). In general, however, doubt about the reference of πάνυ in a negative clause is frequent enough, both in prose and in comedy, to make unprofitable any attempt to isolate *neg* π M_π from the total of *neg* π M.[31]

The two significant areas of difference between comedy and prose in respect of πάνυ are: first its location in positive clauses before or after M_π; and secondly, the nature of the intervening words in cases of $M_\pi \ldots \pi$.

We have no option but to treat π M_π and M_π π as constituting a stylistic choice,[32] in the light of Pl. *Tht.* 180a ἀλλ᾿ εὖ πάνυ φυλάττουσι τὸ μηδὲν ... ἐᾶν, 203b ὥστε πάνυ εὖ ἔχει τὸ λέγεσθαι, Aiskhines i 98 σαφῶς πάνυ καὶ διαρρήδην ... μαρτυροῦντας, 129 πάνυ σαφῶς φράζων. If we set aside (for subsequent examination) cases in which there is doubt whether the M adjacent to π or some remoter M is to be identified as M_π, the ratio π M_π:M_π π in positive clauses in comedy is 59:88. The references are:

π M_π: Ar. *Ach.* 2, 993, *Eq.* 23, 1134, *Nu.* 324, 429, *V.* 585, 627, 1165, *Av.* 573, 1328, 1458, *Lys.* 73, 620, 1035, 1219, *Ra.* 65, 195, 512, 1056, 1236, *Ec.* 54, *Pl.* 25, 389, 503, 745, 1092, fr. 125; Men. *Asp.* 316 /, *Dis* 95, *Dysk.* 104 /, 567, *Fab. Inc.* 53, *Georg.* 61, *Kith.* 53, *Perik.* 318, 490, 1006,[33] *Sam.* 378 /; *Adesp.* (Demiańczuk) 29, Alexis frr. 57.2 /, 172.4, 183.1, Anaxandrides fr. 57.1 /, Antiphanes frr. 45.1, 54.12, 97, 179.4, 271.2, Dromon fr. 1.2 /, Eupolis frr. 292.2, 311.1, Hermippos fr. 63.8, Kratinos (*PCG*) fr. 133, Nikon fr. 1.1, Nikostratos fr. 4.4, Philemon fr. 88.8, Plato Com. fr. 46.2, Theopompos Com. fr. 40.1.

M_π π: Ar. *Arch.* 381 /, *Nu.* 212 / |||, 216 / |||, 484 / ||, 485 / |||, *V.* 16 /, 104 / |, 803 / |, 980, /, 1176 / ||, *Pax* 55 / ||, 198/ ||, 727 /, 822 / ||, 895 / ⦂, 1173 / |, 1228 / |||, *Av.* 819 |||, 1349, *Lys.* 164 /, 566 |||, 612 /, 864 / ||, 924 / |||, 1118 / |, *Th.* 259 / |||, 916 |||, *Ra.* 26 / |||, 166 / |||, 563, 615 / ||, 760 / |||, 1123 / ||, *Ec.* 52 /, 290, *Pl.* 57 / |||, 122 / |||, 377 /, 698 /, 709 / ||, 800; Men. *Asp.* 78 /, 307 / ||, *Dysk.* 4 / ||, 195 / ||,[34] *Epitr.* 488 / ⦂, 894 /, 911 /, *Georg.* 48 / |||, *Her.* 38 / ⦂, *Kith.* fr. 5.1 /, *Mis.*

---

[31] The negative status of εἰ μή, 'unless', is variable, and interrogative οὐ (e.g. Eupolis fr. 311.1) commonly introduces a positive command. Examples of these categories will be included.

[32] I mean by this term a pair or set of alternatives ('style markers'; cf. *Gnomon* 41 [1969] 636f [= p. 73 below]) available to writers at a given time and place.

[33] Everyone prints πάνυ σοῦ φιλῶ, but I prefer enclitic σου here.

[34] κακ[ῶς πάνυ] Kassel; cf. Sandbach's n. *ad. loc.*

275 / ‖‖, *Perik.* 541 / ‖, 710 /, *Perinth.* 5 /, *Sam.* 263 / |, 364 / |, 639 /, *Sik.* 215 /, 356 / ‖‖, frr. 20.1 /, 129 /*; Alexis frr. 19.2 / ‖‖, 163.2 / ‖‖, 189.1 /, 270.2 / ⋮, Anaxandrides fr. 9.6 /*, Anaxilas, frr. 34.1 / |, 37 /*, Antiphanes frr. 52.6, 208.2 /, 242.1 / ⋮, Epikrates fr. 1.1 /, Euboulos (Hunter) frr. 30.2 /, 82.2 /, Eupolis fr. 148 /*, Heniokhos fr. 4.4 / ⋮, Krates (*PCG*) fr. 30 /*, Kratinos (*PCG*) fr. 163, Nikomakhos frr. 1.1 / ⋮, 1.12 / |, Pherekrates frr. 39.2 / ‖, 141.3 /*, Philetairos fr. 4.2 / ⋮, Theopompos Com. fr. 14.3, Timokles fr. 21.2 / |, Xenarkhos frr. 7.10 / ‖, 8.4 /.

In the major prose authors the ratio $\pi\ M_\pi : M_\pi\ \pi$ is strikingly different: in Thucydides, 26:1 (the sole example of $M_\pi\ \pi$ is viii 89.2, σπουδῇ πάνυ ‖, in a sentence which multiple corruption has tangled beyond repair); in Xenophon, 150:6 (*An.* i 9.27, *Cyr.* v 1.4, *HG* vii 4.37, *M.* iii 5.26, *Oec.* 11.1, 12.16 ⋮); in Plato, approximately[35] 260: 18 (*Ap.* 21b, *Cra.* 402a, 418a, 421c, *Cri.* 45 b ‖, *Euthd.* 300d, 302b, *Grg.* 450d |, *Hp. Ma.* 290e, 298e, *Iohn* 533e, *Mnx.* 235a, *Prm.* 129e, *Phdr.* 252b ⋮, *Prt.* 337c, 342a ⋮, *R.* 605c, *Tht.* 180a). Only in the orators do we find a less uneven ratio, 56:23; the examples of $M_\pi(q)\ \pi$ are: Aiskhines i 2, 31, 42, 92 *bis*, 98 ⋮, Dem. viii 68, xvii 5, xviii 130, xix 96 ‖ (ἄτοπον μέν . . . ἀληθὲς δὲ πάνυ),[36] xx 123 ⋮, xxi 44, xxiv 140, xxx 2, 36, xliii 10, 53 *bis*, xlviii 5, lii 21, lvi 1, Is. vi 34, Isoc. xii 199. Note the comparative infrequency of pause immediately after πάνυ in prose.

π . . . M_π is quite common in prose and comedy alike, and the intervening words can be classified in the same way as those intervening between pause and Δ, but some additional classes will be needed.

Class 1. 'Be': Krates (*PCG*) fr. 43.1. Enclitic φάναι: Dem. v 15. Unstressed pronouns: Eupolis fr. 159.9, Men. *Ph.* 48, Andoc. ii 22, Xen. *Cyr.* v 1.17. Vocatives: Men. *Her.* 39. Vocative and anaphoric pronoun: Xen. *Cyr.* v 3.3 πάνυ, ἔφη, ὦ Κῦρε, τοῦτο ποιήσωμεν. 'Must' and 'ought': Ar. *Av.* 479, Lys. vi 45, Xen. *Cyr.* iii 1.15 (it is hard on occasion to distinguish between 'we should fortify the place very strongly' and 'it is absolutely necessary to fortify the place'). 'Think' and 'seem' are especially common between π and M_π,[37] and here again there are uncertainties in interpretation: 'I am absolutely sure you're wrong' or 'I think you're absolutely wrong'? Unstressed adverbs and adverbial phrases: Pl. *Grg.* 521c (ἴσως), Xen. *An.* vi 8.18 (ἤδη), *Eq. Mag.* 7.7 (ὡς τὸ εἰκός), Isoc. xv 320 (ἔτι).

Class 2. Pl. *Lg.* 697c πάνυ μὲν οὖν εἰρήσθω σαφῶς, *Tht.* 144c Εὐφρονίου. . . καὶ πάνυ γε, ὦ φίλε, ἀνδρὸς οἷον καὶ σὺ τοῦτον διηγῇ καὶ ἄλλως εὐδοκίμου.

Class 3. Phrases: Xen. *Hi.* 9.1 πάνυ πρὸς ἔχθραν ἄγειν . . . πάνυ διὰ χαρίτων εἶναι.

Class 4. Ar. *Ra.* 1461 πάνυ γε μέλη θαυμαστά (sarcastic), which picks up κάλλιστα μέλη from 1455 and thus approximates to class 2. Pl. *R.* 538c εἰ μὴ ('unless') πάνυ εἴη φύσει ἐπιεικής has a touch of class 3.

---

[35] Cf. n. 15.
[36] There is an obvious affinity between this usage and 'absolute' πάνυ.
[37] Thesleff 60f.

Class 5. Men. *Asp.* 189f πάνυ μοι δοκεῖ / τὸ ῥῆμα τοῦτ' εἶναί τι μεμεριμνη-μένον / τὸ 'γνῶθι σαυτόν', *Epitr.* 932 πάνυ κακῶς ἔχω σφόδρα (πάνυ in-tensifies σφόδρα),[38] *Georg.* fr. 1.2 κἂν πάνυ λέγῃ δίκαια (the context forbids demotion of λέγῃ to C-status), fr. 361 πάνυ γάρ ἐστι τῇ φύσει / ⟨x –⟩ φιλάνθρωπον τὸ παιδάριον σφόδρα (πάνυ intensifies σφόδρα); Alexis fr. 135.3 ἔπειτ' ἀναγνώσει πάνυ γε διασκοπῶν / ἀπὸ τῶν ἐπιγραμμάτων ἀτρέμα τε καὶ σχολῇ (it looks remarkably as if πάνυ intensifies ἀτρέμα), Timokles fr. 21.5 καὶ παριόντα Φείδιππον πάνυ / τὸν Χαιρεφίλου πόρρωθεν ἀπιδὼν τὸν παχὺν / ἐπόππυσ' (πόρρωθεν is the nearest candidate), Xen. *Hi.* 2.1 ἀλλὰ ταῦτα μὲν : πάνυ ἔμοιγε μικρὰ δοκεῖ εἶναι, *Oec.* 7.3 τά γε ἐν τῇ οἰκίᾳ μου : πάνυ καὶ αὐτὴ ἡ γυνή ἐστιν ἱκανὴ διοικεῖν, 15.10 οἴομαι δ', ἔφη, καὶ πάνυ καὶ λεληθέναι πολλά σε, 16.7 καὶ πάνυ τοίνυν τοῖς ἐμπείροις γεωργίας ὁρῶ αὐτοὺς τὰ πλεῖστα κατὰ ταὐτὰ ἀποφαινομένους περὶ τῆς ἀγαθῆς γῆς.

Class 5A, in which πάνυ intensifies a C from which it is separated by *N*. Ar. *Ec.* 806 πάνυ γ' ἂν οὖν 'Αντισθένης / αὗτ' εἰσενέγκοι, *Pl.* 565 (the same sarcastic idiom); Xen. *Cyr.* i 6.39 μηχανὰς ἃς καὶ πάνυ ἐπὶ τοῖς μικροῖς θηρίοις ἐμηχανῶ, Pl. *R.* 510d πάνυ μὲν οὖν, ἔφη, τοῦτό γε οἶδα, *Tht.* 203a πάνυ μὲν οὖν καὶ ἐμοὶ φαίνεται (in *Lg.* 676b πάνυ μὲν οὖν τοῦτό γε C is omitted altogether).

Class 5B is best exemplified by Ar. *Ach.* 362 πάνυ γὰρ ἔμεγε πόθος ὅτι φρονεῖς ἔχει and *Ec.* 954 πάνυ γάρ τις ἔρως με δονεῖ τῶνδε τῶν σῶν βοστρύχων. A formal rule to the effect that πάνυ can intensify adjectives, adverbs and verbs, but not nouns, would require us to say that πάνυ there intensifies ἔχει and δονεῖ respectively, but that would not ring true; does it not intensify πόθος... ἔχει in the first case and ἔρως με δονεῖ in the second?[39] The formal rule looks even more implausible if applied to Pl. *Phdr.* 238c πάνυ μὲν οὖν, ὦ Σώκρατες, παρὰ τὸ εἰωθὸς εὐροιά τις σε εἴληφεν, where there is a loud echo of the affirmative formula πάνυ μὲν οὖν, 'Yes, indeed!'; and the oath-like character of initial πάνυ is nicely brought out by comparison of Dem. xxv 13 πάνυ δ', ὦ ἄνδρες 'Αθηναῖοι, μετὰ πάσης οἰκειότητος ἐρῶ τἀληθῆ πρὸς ὑμᾶς with Ar. *Nu.* 516 κατερῶ πρὸς ὑμᾶς ἐλευθέρως τἀληθῆ νὴ τὸν Διόνυσον κτλ. πάνυ seems to me to fulfil this function, in varying degrees, in Ar. *Pl.* 1195, Pl. *Ap.* 17c, *Euthd.* 274d ('Yes, do, I beg you, ... both ... and ...'), *Plt.* 264c (also 'both ... and ...'), *Phd.* 68c, *Phlb.* 45b, *Sph.* 216c, *Tht.* 159d, Xen. *Oec.* 7.15.

On Pl. *R.* 529a πάνυ ποιεῖν κάτω βλέπειν and Th. viii 56.4 μὴ πάνυ φωραθῇ ἀδύνατος ὤν I vacillate.[40]

Instances of $M_\pi M \pi$ can be classified in the same way as $\pi M M_\pi$, according to the information-content of the intervening *M*.

---

[38] There is room for doubt; cf. Thesleff 107f.

[39] Cf. Thesleff 60 n. 1, where this interpretation of *Ec.* 954 is treated as 'possible'.

[40] Thesleff (60) takes πάνυ with φωραθῇ.

Class 1. Unstressed pronouns: Men. fr. 98.3, Aiskhines i 25 (both also with 'be'); 'think' and 'seem': Ar. *Th.* 233 / ‖' ἔτι: Isoc. xv 320; ἔχων = 'with': Ar. *Lys.* 278.

Class 2. Ar. *Ra.* 137 ἐπὶ λίμνην μεγάλην ἥξεις πάνυ /.

Class 3. Familiar phrases: Ar. *Eq.* 1064 (προσέχειν τὸν νοῦν) / ‖, *An.* 1629 (εὖ λέγειν) / ‖; Men. *Asp.* 125 (χρηστὸς τῷ τρόπῳ) / ∶, *Georg.* 52 (κακῶς ἔσχεν) / ‖; Xenarkhos fr. 7.8 (θεοῖσιν ἐχθρὸς ἄνθρωπος) /; Pl. *Hi. Ma.* 282e (ἐν ὀλίγῳ χρόνῳ), Dem. liv 1 (πολὺν χρόνον).

Class 4. Ar. *Pl.* 198 εὖ τοι λέγειν ἔμοιγε φαίνεσθον πάνυ / ‖; Eupolis fr. 229 ἔχω γὰρ ἐπιτήδειον ἄνδρ᾽ αὐτῇ πάνυ /*; Pl. *Euthd.* 305d σοφοὶ δὲ ἡγοῦνται εἶναι πάνυ (ἡγοῦνται carries some weight here).

Class 5. Ar. *Pl.* 235 (section I, above), 994 πολὺ μεθέστηκεν πάνυ / ‖; Men. fr. 336.6 κακῶς ὁ δεσπότης βεβούλευται πάνυ / ‖; Pl. Com. fr. 166.2 βουλεύειν ὀλίγου ᾿λαχες πάνυ / ‖, Philetairos fr. 7.6 περίεργόν ἐστιν ἀποκεῖσθαι πάνυ / ἕωλον ἔνδον ἀργύριον; Lys. xix 16 πολλὴν ἐξὸν πάνυ προῖκα λαβεῖν. This last is the only example I can find in prose, and it has the additional peculiarity of scanning as an anapaestic dimeter.

IV. σφόδρα

The functions of σφόδρα[41] are similar to those of πάνυ, except that it occurs much less frequently with a negative and only rarely as a formula of assent. In positive clauses in which it intensifies an adjacent *M* comedy has a certain preference for putting the intensified *M* ('$M_σ$') first and σφόδρα ('σ') second. The examples are these:

σ $M_σ$: Ar. *Ach.* 71, *Eq.* 1288, *Nu.* 135, *V.* 152, *Av.* 592, *Lys.* 56, *Th.* 93, 1123, *Ra.* 41, *Pl.* 571, 1016, frr. 150.1, 165; Men. *Dysk.* 284, 688, 718, 733, *Epitr.* 489 /, 889 /, 1081 /, 1127, *Georg.* fr. 2.4, *Perinth.* fr. 8.2, *Sik.* 128, *Theoph.* fr. 1.14 /, frr. 61.3, 250.8, 416.6, 480.1, 519.1, 620.10; Amphis fr. 14.7, Antiphanes frr. 34.5 /, 124.15, Demetrios fr. 4.1, Diphilos fr. 38.6, Epinikos fr. 1.4, Eupolis frr. 45, 117.2, 244.2 /, Straton (*CGFP*) 219.17 (v.l.). This is the only pattern attested in tragedy (S. *Aj.* 150, *El.* 1053, Adesp. F700.26) and satyr-drama (Akhaios F11.2); there is no σφόδρα in Aeschylus and Euripides.

$M_σ$ σ: Ar. *Ach.* 257 /, 371 / |, 1059 / |, *V.* 1355 / ‖, 1428 / ‖, *Th.* 466 /, 613 / ‖, *Ec.* 357 / ‖; Men. *Asp.* 48 / ‖, 149 / |, *Dis.* 57 /*, *Dysk.* 105 / ∶, 680 / ‖, *Epitr.* 922 /, *Kolax* fr. 4.2 /*, *Perik.* 126 / |, *Sam.* 621 / |, *Sik.* 14 / |, 126, 399 ∶, frr. 173 /*, 198.3 /, 287.1, 509.1 /, 543.8, 754.6 /*, 800.2 /*, Adesp. (*CAF*) fr. 606, Alexis frr. 270.3 / ∶, 282.2 / |, Amphis fr. 37.3, Antiphanes frr. 55.18 / ‖, 56.1 / |, 68.8 /, 140.3 / ‖, 328.1, Arkhedikos fr. 3.9 / ‖, Baton fr. 7.1, Dionysios fr. 3.7,

[41] Thesleff 92–111; his treatment of σφόδρα follows the same plan as his treatment of πάνυ (section III above).

Diphilos fr. 64.1 / ‖, Euboulos (Hunter) fr. 23a, Krobylos (*PCG*) fr. 7.1, Niko-
stratos fr. 8.1 ‖, Pherekrates fr. 13.2 / | (lyric), Philemon frr. 75.4 /, 108.2 /,
Philiskos fr. 3, Sotades fr. 1.8 / ‖, 1.20 / ‖, 1.26 / ‖, Straton (*CGFP*) 219.18 / ‖.

To these we should add the examples in which σφόδρα is strengthened (as
often in σ $M_σ$ in the orators) by οὕτως or the equivalent: Ar. *Av.* 508, *Ra.* 54
(πῶς οἴει) / ‖‖, *Pl.* 1101 (οὑτωσί) / ‖‖, Men. *Epitr.* 528 (ὡς) / ‖, *Kol.* 9 /*.

Leaving aside one or two examples of which the interpretation is doubtful,
the ratio in comedy is thus 41:56. The corresponding ratio in prose is approximately 185:30. Of those 30, 7 (all in Plato) have some degree of pause after
σφόδρα: *Cra.* 428e ⁞, *Hi. Mi.* 372d ‖, *Lys.* 211b |, *Phd.* 83b ⁞, *R.* 331a ‖, *Tht.*
194e ⁞, *Ti.* 62c ⁞.

σ M $M_σ$ is actually commoner in prose than in comedy, with 73 examples
against 13; those 5 of the comic examples which demand classification as σ N
$N_σ$ are Ar. *Eq.* 714, Antiphanes frr. 26.17, 240a.1, Dionysios fr. 6.1, Euboulos
(Hunter) fr. 39.1. As with πάνυ, σφόδρα at the beginning of a sentence seems
on occasion to impart an oath-like affirmative charge to the whole sentence,
e.g. Lys. xii 63 καίτοι σφόδρ᾽ ἂν αὐτὸν οἶμαι μετὰ Θεμιστοκλέους πολιτευό-
μενον προσποιεῖσθαι πράττειν κτλ., Pl. *Prt.* 327d ἢ σφόδρα ἐν τοῖς τοιούτοις
ἀνθρώποις γενόμενος, ὥσπερ ..., ἀγαπήσαις ἂν ... καὶ ἀνολοφύραι᾽ ἂν
κτλ.

And again, as with πάνυ, the ratio is decisively reversed in $M_σ$ M σ, since
comedy has 29 examples of that, prose only 5, namely:

Class 1. 'Be': Ar. fr. 108.3 /*; Men. *Fab. Inc.* 41 /. Unstressed pronouns: Pl.
Lg. 629c, 679b. 'Think': Men. *Asp.* 295 ⁞, fr. 451.1 / ‖. 'Must': Pl. Com. fr.
47.1.

Class 2. Ar. *Pl.* 25 εὔνους γάρ ὢν σοι πυνθάνομαι πάνυ σφόδρα / ‖‖; Men.
Sik. 360 ἀγαθὸς ἄνθρωπος σφόδρα / ‖‖, fr. 361.2 φιλάνθρωπον τὸ παιδάριον
σφόδρα /*.

Class 3. Men. *Epitr.* 932 (κακῶς ἔχω) / |; Pl. *Smp.* 212e μεθύοντα ἄνδρα
πάνυ σφόδρα.

Class 4. Ar. *Pl.* 645 φιλεῖς δὲ δρῶσ᾽ αὐτὸ σφόδρα / ‖; Men. *Dysk.* 6
ἀπάνθρωπός τις ἄνθρωπος σφόδρα /; Th. viii 109.1 διαβεβλῆσθαί τε
νομίσας αὐτοῖς σφόδρα, Pl. *Hi. Mi.* 365d δυνατοὺς ἔγωγε (*sc. λέγω*) καὶ
μάλα σφόδρα ⁞.

Class 5. Ar. *Ach.* 509 μισῶ μὲν Λακεδαιμονίους σφόδρα / ‖, *Ra.* 88
ἐπιτριβομένου τὸν ὦμον οὑτωσὶ σφόδρα / ‖‖, *Pl.* 745 ἐγὼ δ᾽ ἐπῄνουν τὸν θεὸν
(not *C*) πάνυ σφόδρα / |; Men. *Dysk.* 526 ἐξαίρων ἄνω / σφόδρα τὴν
δίκελλαν, 628 ὁ χαλεπὸς γέρων σφόδρα /, 674 ἔτυπτε τὸ στῆθος σφόδρα / ‖,
Sam. 34 συνθλάσας τὸ σημεῖον σφόδρα /, fr. 545.1 καλὸν οἱ νόμοι σφόδρ᾽
εἰσίν ‖, Antiphanes fr. 159.1 εἶτ᾽ οὐ σοφοὶ δῆτ᾽ εἰσὶν οἱ Σκύφαι σφόδρα / |.
Hegesippos fr. 1.29 πολλοὺς ἐγὼ σφόδρ᾽ οἶδα (ἐγώ probably N, given the
preceding ἀγνοεῖς πρὸς ὃν λαλεῖς), Pl. Com. fr. 190.1 φείδεσθε τοὐλαίου
σφόδρα ‖, Timokles (*CGFP*), 222(b).4 διότι τηρεῖν δεῖ παρόντος τοῦδε τὰ

σκεύη σφόδρα / ‖; and possibly Men. *Her.* 78]πάθος ἡ γνώμη σφό[δρα /, but the immediate context is obscure. I can find no examples in prose.

v. δέ

δέ is normally separated from major pause by *p* (*p*), *M* or *p* (*p*) *M*, and on occasion by *neg* (*p*) *M*.[42] Separation by more than one *M* is abnormal. In sections II–IV we have seen comedy and prose aligned against tragedy, in so far as they use oaths, πάνυ and σφόδρα abundantly, and all three phenomena are rare in tragedy. Now we have an opportunity to see tragedy and comedy aligned against prose in the use of words abundant in all three genres. Classification in terms of N and C will be adopted as in sections II–IV, but some additional categories will be required.

Class 1. 'Be': A. *Eu.* 176, 615, *Se.* 1024, *Su.* 914 (δ' transp. Porson); Men. *Sik.* 161, *Theoph.* fr. dub. 18; Anaxandrides fr. 9.6, Philemon (*CGFP*) 206.7; Pl. *Phlb.* 50a (v.l.). Unstressed pronouns: A. *Ag.* 1320, E. fr. 776.1; Men. *Dysk.* 24; Antiphanes fr. 159.2. ἔχων: E. *Ion* 1187. ἤδη: Xen. *Eq.* 11.8 (v.l.).

Class 1A/2A is a new class, comprising instances in which not M_2 but M_1 is C. E. fr. 382.6 ταύτας διείργει δέ; Men. *Mis.* 173 βαδιοῦμ᾽εἴσω δέ, 269 ταῦτα θαυμάσαιμι δ᾽ ἄν, *Sam.* 260 εἰποῦσ᾽ ἐκείνη δέ, *Sik.* 239f ἀκούσατε / καὶ τἀμὰ δέ; Antiphanes fr. 196.8 οὗτοι κεκραγότες δέ. Possibly also Men. *Sik.* 416]ἄνθρωπον ἐλπίσαντα δέ. In Alexandros fr. 6 ἦσαν ἄνθρωποι ⟨δὲ add. Meineke⟩ πέντε, δέ comes after a C C 'run-up'.

Class 2. Antiphanes fr. 154.4 ὡς θᾶττον ἡ παῖς δέ, Philippides fr. 15.4 αὐτὸν ('oneself') μάχεσθαι δέ; Pl. *Lg.* 805b εὖ διελθόντος δέ.

Class 3. Familiar phrases: E. *Ion* 731 ἃ μὴ γένοιτο δέ, *IA* 1006 ψεύδη λέγων δέ; Ar. *Pax* 1311 εὖ ποιεῖς δέ; Men. *Perik.* 356 ἀκαρὲς δέω δέ; Diphilos fr. 60.9 θεοῖς ἐχθρὰν δέ; Aiskhines iii 164 (v.l.) αὐτίκα μάλα δέ, Dem. vi 18, x 13 εὖ φρονεῖν δέ, viii 9 δεινὰ ποιοῦσι δέ, Pl. *Lg.* 721b τῇ καὶ τῇ δέ. Repetition: E. *Hel.* 331, 370; Ar. *Av.* 856. Polyptota: A. *Eu.* 530, S. *Aj.* 522, *Ph.* 959, E. *Su.* 614, fr. 296.2, Dem. xxx 22. Intensifiers: A. *Ch.* 879, *Pe.* 729; Men. *Dysk.* 532f. (+ 'be'), fr. 215.2 (+ 'be'); Alexis frr. 16.3, 118.4, 172.4, Anaxippos fr. 1.44, Antiphanes fr. 218.4 ἐὰν σαπροὺς κομιδῇ δέ (*sc.* πωλῇ). Numerals: Pl. *Alc.* I 121e, Dem. xxiii 167, xxvii 9, 63, Isoc. xix 24.

Class 4. Ar. *Pax* 186 ποδαπὸς τὸ γένος δέ; Men. *Asp.* 78 συναγαγὼν πάντας δέ; *Adesp.* (*CGFP*) 289(a).2 ἐπὶ ταῖς θύραις ἔξω δέ; Lys. vii 4 δημευθέντων τῶν ὄντων δέ.

I insert at this pont a new class, 4A, which is of considerable importance in connection with particles but had little or none in the phenomena discussed earlier. It consists of (i) substantive and adjective in agreement and (ii) substantive and dependent genitive.

---

[42] Cf. Denniston 185–7, 189. I treat instances such as Ar. *Ra.* 1007 ἵνα μὴ φάσκῃ δέ as involving only one M.

Class 4A (i). A. *Ag.* 278, 606, 1277, 1664, *Ch.* 839, *Eu.* 21, 197, 281, 965, *Pe.* 446, 793, *Se.* 546, 599, 1010, *Su.* 998, frr. 17.59, 64, 125.25, S. *Aj.* 169 (δ' add. Dawes), E. *Andr.* 617, *Hp.* 835, *Ion.* 261, *Or.* 88, 610, *Su.* 783, fr. 163.1; Ar. *Ach.* 80, *Th.* 746; Men. *Mis.* 297, frr. 24.2, 333.15; *Adesp.* (*CAF*) 383.2, (*CGFP*) 256.17, Alexis frr. 141.6, 253.3, Anaxilas fr. 22.10, 22, Antiphanes frr. 52.4, 205.3, Euphron fr. 9.1, Philemon fr. 170.1, Xenarkhos fr. 8.4; [Pl.] *Amat.* 135c ἄκρον ἀρχιτέκτονα δέ.

(ii) A. *Ag.* 963, 1291, *Ch.* 266, *Eu.* 19, *Pe.* 818, *Se.* 199, *Su.* 786; *Adesp.* (*CAF*) 523, Alexis fr. 110.4, Philippides fr. 6.2.

Antiphanes fr. 52.7 ξουθῆς μελίσσης νάμασιν δέ combines (i) and (ii).

Class 5. A. *Ag.* 296 σθένουσα λαμπὰς δέ, 653 ἐν νυκτὶ δυσκύμαντα δέ, 745 παρακλίνασ' ἐπέκρανεν δέ, *Ch.* 519 τὰ δῶρα μείω δέ, 761 ἐγὼ διπλᾶς δέ, *Eu.* 68 ὕπνῳ πεσοῦσαι δέ, 620 βουλῇ πιφαύσκω δέ, *Pe.* 330 πολλῶν παρόντων δέ, 719 πεζὸς ἢ ναύτης δέ, 729 ὧδε παμπήδην δέ, 749 θνητὸς ὢν θεῶν δὲ (v.l.) πάντων ᾤετο ... κρατήσειν, *Se.* 41 αὐτὸς κατόπτης δέ, fr. 343.38 κλύουσ' ἐμοῦ δέ, S. *OT* 1282 ὁ πρὶν παλαιὸς δ' ὄλβος, frr. 210d ἀρετῆς βέβαιαι δ' εἰσὶν αἱ κτήσεις μόναι,[43] 738.2 πᾶς προσκυνεῖ δέ, E. *El.* 928 ἄμφω πονηρὼ δ' ὄντε, fr. 413.4 γαστρὸς κρατεῖν δέ, *Adesp.* (*TrGF*) 515a.3f παιδεύματα / προσλαμβάνειν δέ; Ar. *Ra.* 344 φλογὶ φέγγεται δέ; Men. *Asp.* 203f τὰ τῶν ἐλευθέρων αὐτοὶ δὲ πράττετε, *Dysk.* 10 προσηγόρευκε πρότερος δέ, 297 ἕτερον κύριον δ' αὐτῆς ποεῖ, 419 πάλιν αἴρου δέ, *Mis.* 278f πηνίκα / ἔθεντο δέ, *Perik.* 542 τὸν Δᾶον εἰσπέμπω δέ, *Sam.* 340 τί τὸ πάθος δέ, Pap. Didot I 32f μέχρι πόσου τὴν (δὲ Weil) τῆς τύχης, πάτερ, δέ (σὺ Weil) λήψει πεῖραν, frr. 416.7 σεμνότερα τούτων ἕτερα ⟨δ' add. Porson⟩, 644.3 πάντες εἰς σὲ δὲ / ἐλθεῖν, *Adesp.* (*CGFP*) 306(a).3 τἀργύριον ἀνθρώπου δέ (sc. βάσανός ἐστι), Alexis fr. 274.8 ὃς ἂν εἰς ἑτέραν ληφθῇ δέ, Antiphanes fr. 251.1 ἐγὼ γυναικὶ δέ, Apollodoros Karystios[44] fr. 27.2 γυναιξὶ διαφέρειν οἴει δέ τι, Aristophon (*PCG*) fr. 5.7 κονδύλους πλάττειν δέ, Damoxenos fr. 2.25 τίς παρακολουθεῖ δέ, Diphilos fr. 80.4 ὁ λαβρώνιος χρυσῶν δέ, παῖδες, εἴκοσι, Philemon frr. 28.11 ἀεὶ τὸ λυπεῖσθαι δέ, 79.3 ἕτεραι διώκουσιν δέ, Theophilos fr. 6.3 τὸ πεῖσμ' ἀπορρήξασα ⟨δέ add. Musurus⟩ /.

It will be observed that δέ sometimes overruns the minor pause which divides a participial from a finite clause (e.g. A. *Ag.* 745); but in A. *Pe* 749f (where Döderlein proposed δὲ θεῶν ἀ- for θεῶν δέ) the first three words have the flavour of an established poetic phrase; cf. A. *PV* 733 θνητῇ θεός / χρῄζων μιγῆναι. Overrun of the minimal pause[45] which marks off an initial *N* in

---

[43] This puzzling one-line citation (and the puzzle is in no way removed by Naber's μόνης for μόναι) appears to contrast ἀρετή with something else. It is conceivable that the passage is spoken by a cynical character, that the previous line or lines decried the lasting value of ἀρετή (as opposed to κτήσεις), and that an excerptor transformed the sentiment by putting the pause before ἀρετῆς instead of after it. Wilamowitz suggested (cf. Radt *ad loc.*) that the excerptor invented ἀρετῆς. Cf. the radical and unscrupulous transformation of Ar. *Nu.* 412–19 in Diog. Laert. ii 27.

[44] 'Apollod. Gel.' in Denniston 188 n. 1.

[45] For the colometric principle involved here cfr. Fraenkel (n. 9 above) 329ff.

explicit (e.g. A. *Pe.* 719) or implicit (e.g. Men. *Asp.* 203) contrast is more remarkable; note especially the form $A_1 \mu \grave{\epsilon} \nu : B_1 \| B_2 : A_2 \delta \acute{\epsilon}$ in *Adesp.* (*CGFP*) 306(a).3, and compare the examples of $A_1 \mu \grave{\epsilon} \nu : B_1 \gamma \acute{\alpha} \varrho \| A_2 \delta \grave{\epsilon} : B_2$ given below.

VI. γάϱ

The normal rules governing the position of γάϱ are comparable, though not identical, with those governing δέ.[46] Abnormality lies in the separation of γάϱ from major pause by two or more *M*s. As with δέ, analogies to comic usage are more readily found in tragedy than in prose; but unlike δέ, γάϱ in post-Aristophanic comedy is much more often and much more widely separated from pause than in tragedy. The classification of types follows the pattern used for δέ.

Class 1. 'Be': Ar. *Pl.* 1188, Men. *Asp.* 160f, *Dysk.* 332, 945, *Epitr.* fr. 2, *Mis.* 172, *Perik.* 508, *Sik.* 352, *Adesp.* (*CGFP*) 301 col. iii 2, Alexis fr. 21.1, Arkhippos (*PCG*) fr. 6.6, Diphilos fr. 60.3, Pherekrates fr. 155.1, Timokles fr. 14.3; Dem. xxiii 136 (v.l.). Enclitic φάναι: Men. *Epitr.* 304. Unstressed pronouns: E. *Rh.* 17 τί σὺ γάϱ; Men. *Asp.* 268 (given the context, ἐγώ seems to be *C*), 286f, *Sam.* 56, fr. 614.5, *Adesp.* (*CAF*) fr. 124, (*CGFP*) 253.11. ἔχειν: Men. *Dysk.* 379, *Adesp.* (*CGFP*) 272.13, Xenarkhos fr. 13.1. λαβών: Apollodoros Karystios fr. 24.3. 'Must', 'ought': Damoxenos fr. 2.16 τοῦτο (prospective) δεῖ γάϱ, Philetairos fr. 7.1 τί δεῖ γάϱ. Temporal adverbs: Men. *Dysk.* 382 οἷς ἀποτρέπεις νυνὶ γάϱ. Add (with *neg*) Men. fr. 298.1 οὐχὶ παρακληθέντας ὑμᾶς δεῖ γάϱ.

Class 2. S. *OC* 837 πόλει μάχη γάϱ; *Adesp.* (*CAF*) 372.2 οὐ τοῖς φίλοις θύω γάϱ, Philemon fr. 136.2 οὐκ εὐψυχία / τοῦτ᾿ ἔσθ᾿ ὃ ποιεῖς νῦν γάϱ, ἀλλ᾿ ἀνανδρία.

Class 1A/2A. A. *Ag.* 222 βροτοὺς θρασύνει γάϱ (unless it can be argued that Aeschylus intends here implicit contrast between mortals and immortals), E. *Ba.* 477 τὸν θεὸν ὁρᾶν γάϱ, fr. 1063.1 δεῖ πυνθάνεσθαι γάϱ σε, Men. *Mis.* 264 οὐκέτι / τὸ τοιοῦτον εἰκάζειν γάϱ, Ph. 89 ἐρῶν παύσει γάϱ, *Theoph.* 25 εἰ θεοφορεῖται ταῖς ἀληθείαισι γάϱ, Alexis fr. 213.4 μέλλοντα δειπνίζειν ⟨γὰϱ add. Meineke⟩, Antiphanes fr. 163.4 οὗ μὲν ἦμεν ἄρτι γάϱ, Philemon fr. 106.2 διὰ λύπην καὶ μανία γάϱ γίνεται, Philetairos fr. 18.2 τούτοις ἐν ῞Αιδου γάϱ, Sophilos fr. 4.4 κωμάσαι / πρὸς τὴν Ταναγρικὴν δεῖ γάϱ (*C ρ ρ N C* γάϱ). The run-up to *N* γάϱ is longer in Men. fr. 323.1 πεποιήκατ᾿ ἔργον οὐχ ἑταίϱων γάϱ and Philemon fr. 28.10 οὐκ εἰς ἡμέραν χειμάζομαι μίαν γάϱ. Alexis fr. 163.3 τραγήματ᾿ αἰσθάνομαι γὰϱ ὅτι νομίζεται / τοῖς νυμφίοις . . . παρέχειν is *C C* γὰϱ *ρ C ρ N*. . . . I find it hard to assess the weight of information-content on ἔχω in S. *Tr.* 338 τούτων ἔχω γὰϱ †πάντ᾿ ἐπιστήμην ἐγώ.

---

[46] Denniston 95ff. On such examples as E. *Or.* 314 κἂν μὴ νοῇς γάϱ see n. 38 above.

Class 3. Familiar phrases: Ar. *V.* 814 αὐτοῦ μένων γάρ; Men. *Epitr.* 953f
τῆς γαμετῆς γυναικός ἐστί σου / [τέκνον] γάρ, 1070f οὕτω τί μοι ἀγαθὸν
γένοιτο (formula), Σωφρόνη γάρ; *Adesp.* (*CAF*) 154.1 ἀμορφότατος τὴν ὄψιν
εἰμὶ γάρ, 564 αὐτὸς αὐτοῦ ⟨γάρ add. Haupt⟩, Alexis fr. 156.4 κακῶς λέγειν
γάρ, Diphilos fr. 43.14 ἡδέως ποιεῖ γάρ; Pl. *Phd.* 60d εὖ οἶδα γάρ, *Sph.* 255e
ἓν ἕκαστον γάρ. Repetition: S. *Aj.* 867; and cf. E. *El.* 492 ἄλεκτρ᾽ ἄνυμφα
γάρ. Polyptota: A. *PV* 29, S. *Aj.* 522, E. *Ion* 690, *Tr.* 621; Men. *Sam.* 140.
Intensifiers: Men. *Dysk.* 438, *Georg.* fr. 2.4, *Perik.* 471; *Adesp.* (*CGFP*) 257.69,
Alexis fr. 200.4, Amphis fr. 37.3, Antiphanes fr. 147.3, Dromon fr. 1.3.
Numerals: S. *Ant.* 141.

Class 4. Ar. *Lys.* 489 διὰ τἀργύριον πολεμοῦμεν γάρ, *Pl.* 146 ἅπαντα τῷ
πλουτεῖν γάρ; Men. *Asp.* 288 ἔρωτι περιπεσὼν γάρ, *Mis.* 301 τοὔνομα λέγει
γάρ, *Perik.* 496 ποῖ φέρει γάρ, fr. 951.16 αὐτὴ π]ρὸς αὐτὴν συνεθέμην γάρ.

Class 4A (i). A. fr. 273.4 παντ]ὸς (Pfeiffer) κακοῦ γάρ, E. *Alc.* 715, *Andr.*
764, *IA* 122, *Or.* 1244, *Adesp.* (*CAF*) 406.1, Amphis fr. 39.1, Anaxandrides fr.
52.3, Anaxilas fr. 22.11, Euboulos (Hunter) fr. 14.3, Pherekrates fr. 108.23,
Dem. lix 55 (v.l.). Two examples are extended: Athenion (*PCG*) fr. 1.4f τοῦ
θηριώδους καὶ παρασπόνδου βίου / ἡμᾶς γὰρ ἀπολύσασα, Diphilos fr.
102.1 ἀνδρὸς φίλου καὶ συγγενοῦς γάρ. Add one apposition: Ar. *Pl.* 1189 ὁ
Ζεὺς ὁ σωτὴρ γάρ.

(ii) A. fr. 279 μόνος θεῶν γάρ, Ar. *Av.* 1546 μόνον θεῶν γάρ, Men. *Epitr.*
440, *Sik.* 187, *Adesp.* (*CGFP*) 257.49 τοῦ βίου τί γάρ, Antiphanes fr. 243.1,
Philemon fr. 207.

Class 5. S. *Ph.* 1450f δδ᾽ (deictic) ἐπείγει γὰρ καιρὸς καὶ πλοῦς,[47] E. *HF*
1126 ἀρκεῖ σιωπῇ γάρ, *IA* 1560 σιγῇ παρέξω γάρ, Ar. *Eq.* 32 ἐτεὸν ἡγεῖ γάρ,
Av. 342 πῶς κλαύσει γάρ, 1545 ἀεί ποτ᾽ ἀνθρώποις γάρ (ἀνθρώποις is not
C; Prometheus is speaking), Men. *Asp.* 71 τετάρτην ἡμέραν / ἐρριμμέναι γὰρ
ἦσαν, 138f τοὺς ἑξακοσίους / χρυσοῦς ἀκούσας οὑτοσὶ γάρ, *Dysk.* 67f εἰς
πάντα τὸν λοιπὸν χρόνον / μνείαν γάρ, 376 τὴν αἱμασιὰν ἐποικοδομήσω
γάρ, 692f οὐκέτι / ὑμῖν ἐνοχλήσει τὸν ἐπίλοιπον γὰ[ρ χρόνον] / Κνήμων,
Epitr. 364 ἐν ταύτῃ περιφέρεις γάρ, 853f κλαυμυρίζεται, τάλαν, πάλαι γάρ,
869f σὲ / ὁρῶ γάρ, fr. 10 ἐλευθέρῳ τὸ καταγελᾶσθαι ⟨γάρ add. Hense⟩, *Kith.*
fr. 4.1 τὸ μηθὲν ἀδικεῖν ἐκμαθεῖν γάρ, *Perik.* 359f κακοδαίμον᾽ οὕτω
δεσπότην οὐδ᾽ ἐνύπνιον / ἰδὼν γὰρ οἶδα, *Perinth.* 13f τὸν μὲν ἀπράγμονα /
καὶ κοῦφον ἐξαπατᾶν γάρ, *Sam.* 43f ἀγρυπνίαν / [ὁ θ]όρυβος αὐτῶν ἐνεπόει
γάρ μοι τινά, 45 ἐπὶ τὸ τέγος κήπους γάρ, 636 μᾶλλον εἰς τὰ λοιπὰ γάρ, *Sik.*
241 ἀφεῖται τοῦ φόβου γάρ, *Theoph.* fr. 1 δὶς βιῶναι γάρ, frr. 8.1 πρὸς
ἅπαντα δειλὸν ὁ πένης ἐστὶ γάρ, 13 θεός ἐστι τοῖς χρηστοῖς ἀεὶ / ὁ νοῦς γάρ,
59.5f νῦν ἀλήθινον / εἰς πέλαγος αὐτὸν ἐμβαλεῖς γάρ, 97.3 ὑποδούμενος τὸν
ἱμάντα ⟨γάρ add. Meineke⟩, 133.1 ἐγὼ μετ᾽ ἄριστον γάρ, 150.1 τοῖς ἀναι-
δέσιν βοηθεῖ γὰρ λόγοις, 397.2 διαφέρει τῷ μαγείρῳ τοῦτο γάρ, 631.1

---

[47] The manuscripts have καιρὸς καὶ πλοῦς δδ᾽ ἐπείγει γάρ, which Jebb, Pearson and Denniston
all accepted. Webster found it difficult, and favoured the rather awkward repunctuation proposed
by Cavallin. Dawe finds it incredible, as I do too, and adopts Burges' simple transposition.

πολλοὺς δι᾽ ἀνάγκην γάρ, *Adesp.* (*CAF*) 379.1 μέγ᾽ εἰς πόθον γάρ, (*CGFP*)
253.3 ἐμὲ μὲν ᾠάδιον / ἔσται μεταθέσθαι γάρ, 256.3 μέ[χρι τινὸς] τῶν ἐνθαδὶ
γάρ, 256.26 [τὴ]ν μὲν φυλακὴν ὁρῶ γάρ, 292.3 τῶν σῶν ἐγὼ γάρ, Alexis frr.
7.1 ἐγὼ δέδωκα γάρ, 36.1 ὁ δεσπότης οὑμὸς περὶ λόγους γάρ ποτε, 135.2
βυβλίον ἐντεῦθεν ὅτι βούλει προσελθὼν γὰρ λαβέ, 261.8 ἅπαντ᾽ ἐνῆν τἀκεῖ
γάρ, 263.4 οὗ μήτε πράττεται τέλος μηδεὶς γὰρ ὑμᾶς, Amphis fr. 30.8
ἅπαντες ἀνδροφόνοι γάρ εἰσιν (ἅπαντες is stressed, I think), Anaxandrides
fr. 55.1 ὅστις λόγους παρακαταθήκην γὰρ λαβὼν / ἐξεῖπεν, Anaxippos fr. 3.5
ἀβάτους ποεῖν γάρ, Antiphanes frr. 26.22 ἐπὶ τὸ τάριχός ἐστιν ὡρμηκυῖα
γάρ, 174.4 συνάψαι βούλομαι γάρ, 202.7 ἐάσας τἆλλα γάρ, 212.6f αἱ μὲν
ἄλλαι τοὔνομα / βλάπτουσι τοῖς τρόποις γάρ, 214.1 λευκὸς Ἀφροδίτης εἰμὶ
γὰρ περίστερος, 235.4 ἀμφότερα μηνύει γάρ, 261.8 ταῖς εὐτελείαις οἱ θεοὶ
χαίρουσι γάρ, Dionysios fr. 2.3 τὸν μάγειρον εἰδέναι / πολὺ δεῖ γάρ, 2.22
πάντα μὲν λήψει σχεδὸν / ἀεὶ γάρ, *Dubia* (*CGFP*) 350.42]Αἰγεὺς λιπὼν γὰρ
η[, Euphron fr. 10.4 οὐδεὶς εἶχέ σοι / κωβιὸς ὅλως γὰρ ἧπαρ, Eupolis
(*CGFP*) 95.151 ἦ μὴν ἐγώ σε σκέψομαι γάρ, Krobylos (*PCG*) fr. 4.2f τὴν
ἀσωτίαν / ᾽ὑγρότητα᾽ γὰρ νῦν προσαγορεύουσίν τινες, Nikostratos fr. 24.3
ἱκανῶς κεχόρτασμαι γάρ (possibly *N C*), Philemon frr. 56.2 μετέχειν ἀνάγκη
τῶν κακῶν γάρ, 60.2 τοὺς ἐν τῇ πόλει / μάρτυρας ἔχω γάρ, 123.3 καινὰ
ῥήματα πεπορισμένος γάρ ἐστιν, 162.1 ἐνταῦθ᾽ ἀνὴρ γάρ, 171.1 ἐλαφρὸν τὸ
γένος γάρ (*N C* ?), Pl. Com. fr. 166/7.2 Ὑπερβόλῳ βουλῆς γάρ, ἄνδρες,
ἐπέλαχον, Timokles fr. 14.5 ταρίχους εὐπόρως γὰρ τυγχάνει / ἔχουσα,
Xenarkhos fr. 4.13 αὐταὶ βιάζονται γάρ. I can find no examples in prose.

γάρ overruns minimal pause[48] in a famous line of Aristophanes, *Ra.* 1434 ὁ
μὲν : σοφῶς γὰρ εἶπεν, ‖ ὁ δ᾽ ἕτερος : σαφῶς; cf. Alexis fr. 278.4 ὁ μὲν :
δάκνει γάρ, ‖ ὁ δέ : . . . ποεῖ, Amphis fr. 1.3 ἡ μὲν : νόμῳ γαρ . . . , ‖ ἡ δ᾽ :
οἶδεν, Philemon fr. 79.17 οἱ μὲν : ἥρπασάν τι γάρ, ‖ οἱ δ᾽ : οὐδέν (contrast
Ar. *Ra.* 72 οἱ μὲν γὰρ : οὐκέτ᾽ εἰσίν, ‖ οἱ δ᾽ ὄντες : κακοί, Laon fr. 2.2 ὁ μὲν
γὰρ : χρηστός, ‖ ἡ δ᾽ : ἐφίμερος). It may be that since 'the one' or 'some' in
an antithetical pair could be omitted altogether (e.g. Xen. *HG* i 2.14 ᾤχοντο
εἰς Δεκέλειαν, οἱ δ᾽ εἰς Μέγαρα)[49] it could be felt as a run-up to the predicate.
Note, however, that in Men. *Epitr.* 568 ταχέως | ἐὰν γὰρ εὑρεθῇ . . . , |
λήψεται the particle overruns a stronger pause.

VII. SUMMARY AND CONCLUSIONS

On the analogy of the colloquial register in some modern languages, where
narrative and argument may be punctuated by oaths and exclamations
(sometimes obscene or blasphemous) in order to maintain a high affective

---

[48] Cf. n. 45.
[49] Denniston 166.

level and compel the hearer's attention,[50] it is reasonable to postulate that Attic conversation also was punctuated by oaths, that this ingredient in comic language was drawn from life, and that the comparative frequency of $\|(|) M M (M) \Delta$ in comedy is sufficiently explained thereby. There are obvious affinities between some passages of comedy, relaxed conversation in Plato and Xenophon, and the forceful, man-to-man tone which Demosthenes sometimes adopts to such good effect (e.g. xxi 209). Compare, for instance, Ar. *V.* 133f ἔστιν δ᾽ ὄνομα ⋮ τῷ μὲν γέροντι ⋮ Φιλοκλέων / ναὶ μὰ Δία, τῷ δ᾽ υἱεῖ κτλ., where the oath is a response to imagined incredulity,[51] and Xen. *Smp.* 4.27 αὐτὸν δὲ σέ, ἔφη, ἐγὼ εἶδον ναὶ μὰ τὸν Ἀπόλλω, ὅτε κτλ. ('Oh, yes, I did!').

It is also important that the commonest oaths fit, in most of their forms, the end of an iambic trimeter: (ναὶ) μὰ τὸν Δία, νὴ (τὸν) Δία, νὴ τοὺς θεούς, μὰ τοὺς θεούς. Add that in Aristophanic dialogue (by contrast with Menander) over half the iambic trimeters end with major pause, and half the remainder with minor pause, and we can see why Δ / established itself early as a distinctive comic pattern. Out of 105 examples of $M M (M) \Delta$ cited from comedy in section II above, 59 have the oath at verse-end.

In the case of πάνυ, which was almost exclusively Attic[52] and – to judge from its great rarity in tragedy[53] – felt by Athenian poets to be prosaic, we lack evidence on its functions in the colloquial register; it may or may not have served as affective punctuation. In prose, we have to reckon with the fact that πM_π and $M_\pi \pi$ constituted a genuine stylistic choice (cf. n. 32) as far back as the evidence will take us, since the two earliest instances in prose are [Xen.] *Ath.* 2.3 πάνυ διὰ χρείαν and ibid. 3.5 πολλὰ ἔτι πάνυ. The oath, as treated by the comic poets on the basis of colloquial usage, is bound to have served as a model for πάνυ, exerting an influence which pulled πάνυ to the end of the verse, but there was also a powerful metrical constraint. As a dibrach ending in a vowel which could not be elided or enter into crasis, πάνυ was especially appropriate for verse-end.[54] That in itself was enough both to establish $M_\pi \pi$ as the dominant pattern in comedy and to promote $M_\pi \ldots \pi$. Out of the total of 104 examples of $M_\pi (\ldots) \pi$ in comedy, 93 have πάνυ at verse-end, which makes $M_\pi (\ldots) \pi$ / one of the hallmarks of comic style. $M_\pi \ldots \pi$ does not occur in prose in association with any other feature identified as colloquial,

[50] Cf. the archaic 'Damme!', and at a coarser level (I heard this from a Lancashire soldier), 'All on a sudden he turns left. He did that! Eh, fucking hell! And I couldn't stop. Eh, fuck me! . . .' etc.

[51] Werres 13.

[52] Xenophanes (*IEG*) Bl. 18 is the only pre-Aeschylean example. Instances in Democritus are attributable to Attic influence on Ionic.

[53] Theodektas fr. 6.2 ἰσόμετροι πάνυ / has a thoroughly comic ring, and I do not think it irrelevant that the speaker of the passage is an illiterate rustic.

[54] On the relevance of metrical constraints to word-order cf. E. Hofmann, *Ausdrucksverstärkung* (= *Z. Vgl. Spr.* Ergänzungsheft ix, 1930) 145ff. Bertha Ellis Booth, 'The Collocation of the Adverbs of Degree in Roman Comedy and Cato' (Diss., Chicago 1923) explains the placing of *magis*, *maxume* and *satis* at verse-end primarily in metrical terms (esp. 31ff, 43ff, 59, 79ff) and comparable phenomena in prose as poetic influence (e.g. 48) or – vaguely and unsatisfactorily – as 'stylistic'. I am indebted to Dr Elaine Fantham for a copy of Booth's work.

but it should be noted that Aiskhines and Demosthenes are much fonder of M_π π than other prose authors. In some cases one can see that the order M_π π avoids a succession of short syllables (e.g. Dem. xviii 130, liv 1) or hiatus (e.g. Dem. xxx 36) or both (e.g. Dem. xliii 10), but there are other cases in which it has the opposite effect (e.g. Dem. xxiv 140, xliii 53). The possibility of comic influence on oratorical language cannot be dismissed out of hand. It is also possible that someone will find positive determinants which will explain all the cases of M_π π in prose.

σφόδρα, which, like πάνυ, is peculiarly Attic,[55] is metrically more tractable than πάνυ, since it can be elided; even so, out of the 80 comic examples of M_σ (...) σ no less than 58 have σφόδρα at verse-end, and of those 58 there are 22 at major pause, 8 at presumed major pause and 9 at minor pause. The comic treatment of σφόδρα is thus comparable with the treatment of πάνυ, and Timokles (*CGFP*) 222(b).4 τηρεῖν ... σφόδρα is in fact the closest analogy we have to Ar. *Pl.* 234f ἄχθομαι ... πάνυ.

δέ and γάρ are a different matter, and in some significant respects different from each other. Postponement of δέ is especially prominent in Aeschylus (45 examples, including a few in which the text is suspect)[56] and then abundant in fourth-century comedy. It is much less common in Euripides (18 examples), rare in Sophocles (6) and Aristophanes (6),[57] and virtually limited in prose to the categories which I labelled 1–3. There is as yet no evidence to associate postponement of δέ with colloquial language; on the contrary, it seems to have begun as a feature of poetic language[58] and to have been taken up and exploited by fourth-century comedy. If, in addition to being Aeschylean, it was colloquial in the fourth century, what happened to it afterwards? Except for such an isolated and inexplicable case as Diod. xx 85.1 (v.l.!) – in a military narrative – it is not a feature of the Koine at literary, documentary or subliterate level.[59]

Postponement of γάρ was no doubt encouraged by postponement of δέ, but it is not itself notably poetic (20 examples in tragedy, of which only three come in my class 5). One can see how it could possibly have developed in the spoken language of the fourth century, extending the function of γάρ as an explanatory particle (rather on the lines of γε) in a way which makes it comparable with the English 'you see' in (e.g.) 'He didn't dare pick it up. He hurt his back last year, you see.' For an extension of this kind we may compare the

---

[55] The only example in Ionic Greek is Hdt. ix 17.1, in an oddly self-contradictory sentence: ἐμήδιζον γὰρ δὴ σφόδρα καὶ οὗτοι, οὐκ ἑκόντες ἀλλ᾿ ὑπ᾿ ἀναγκαίης.

[56] There is however no example in *Prometheus*. *Su.* 791 would be class 5 if the text were sound, but Johansen and Whittle (n. *ad. loc.*) make a strong case for Burgard's deletion of δ᾿; cf. Fraenkel's n. on *Ag.* 653.

[57] My figures for Sophocles and Aristophanes *may* be a little too low.

[58] Xenophanes (*IEG*) Bl.17 is doubtful; see West's punctuation *ad loc.*, retaining the plural ὕβρεις.

[59] For this negative generalization I rely on Blomqvist 120f, on the lack of examples of postponement in Mayser and Blass–Debrunner, and (more positively) on Mauersberger's *Polybios-Lexikon*.

current extension of the English genitive affix in (I heard both examples a year or two ago) 'Then the girl whose place she was taking's mother turned up' and 'The man that Christopher liked's Introduction is much better.' Moreover, postponed γάρ appears in a segment of conversation constructed in indirect speech by Theophrastus in *Char.* 8.9 τὸ πρᾶγμα βοᾶσθαι γάρ (*p* C N γάρ). Again we must ask: what happened to it afterwards? A couple of cases in Theophrastus's botanical works (*CP* iii 11.3 and *HP* iv 6.1) could be a reflex of the influence of comedy on literary language at Athens.[60] The influence was plainly short-lived, since it did not affect the Koine.[61]

It is not hard to see why serious poetry in the fifth century and earlier should have experimented occasionally with the postponement of δέ and γάρ: treatment of $M M q$ as a valid alternative to $M q M$ is metrically very convenient. No poet, however, could afford to use common words in a bizarre, un-Greek way merely to save himself time and trouble in constructing a verse. Linguistic innovation is normally analogical, proceeding by extension from a starting-point already there, and the most obvious starting-point for postponement of δέ and γάρ is constituted by my class 3. This consideration provides comic postponement with a pedigree, but does not deny it individuality. The remarkable scale and frequency with which comedy exploited a phenomenon which tragedy used with restraint and prose hardly at all gives comic postponement the right to be regarded as a quite distinctive artificial feature of comedy.

---

[60] Cf. Blomqvist 121.

[61] Cf. n. 59. Peek, *GVI* i 104, reads ἀνέστασαν γινάμενοι τόδε γάρ in a Hellenistic epitaph (Argos, s. i a.C.); the first editor (Vollgraff) read nothing after -νοι. Composers of epitaphs, struggling to produce verse, not always very successfully, are apt to employ abnormal language which tells us nothing about the prose or colloquial usage of their time.

6

Review of Bergson,
Zur Stellung des Adjektivs

Leif Bergson, *Zur Stellung des Adjektivs in der älteren griechischen Prosa. Die Motive der Voran- bzw. Nachstellung in ihren Hauptzügen*, Acta Universitatis Stockholmiensis: Studia graeca Stockholmiensia 1 (Almqvist u. Wiksell, Stockholm 1960) 173 pp.

This book is the first systematic investigation of the circumstances in which the attributive adjective without the article precedes or follows the noun in classical Greek prose. Its essential argument is that the 'determinative' adjective follows the noun unless contrasted explicitly or implicitly with another determinative, while the 'qualificative' adjective precedes the noun unless the noun is contrasted explicitly or implicitly with another noun. This basic practice undergoes substantial variations according to the genre, period or author, as the relevant statistics show (pp. 157ff), and the exceptions to it are largely explicable by reference to the crystallization of formulae and to the operation of various logical and rhetorical principles.

The most important of these logical principles is the distinction between what I have elsewhere called 'concomitant' and 'nuclear' elements (*Greek Word Order*, 2nd edn [Cambridge 1968] 40ff). Bergson deals with this distinction explicitly in a brief section (pp. 124ff) on 'Bekanntes' and 'Unbekanntes', but exemplification of the principle is to be found throughout his book (e.g. p. 35, Pl. *Grg.* 452e; p. 111, Xen. *An.* vii 4.14). The concept 'contrast', so important to his general argument, is only a special case of it, and many instances in which he attributes the position of the adjective to the fact that it states something surprising can be subsumed under it.

P. 37: in Hdt. iv 95.4 κατάγαιον οἴκημα ἐποιέετο there is a contrast with κατασκευάσασθαι ἀνδρεῶνα in 95.3, οἴκημα ἐποιέετο thus becoming concomitant. P. 38: in Th. iv 87.6 ἄρξαι πρῶτοι ἐλευθερίας καὶ ἀΐδιον δόξαν καταθέσθαι the relation between 'first' and 'for ever thereafter' is important. P. 41: in Hdt. i 80.2 ἱππάδα στολὴν ἐνεσταλμένους we have just been told that the men were mounted on camels. *Contra*, p. 33: in Xen. *Cyr.* ii 3.15 νῦν γὰρ ἄνδρες εἰλημμένοι εἰσὶν ἐν δημοτικῇ ἀγωνίᾳ, ἄνδρες does not mean 'die vornehmeren Herren', but is simply soldiers' language for 'they', cf. Th. v 10.5; vi 34.9, etc.

Apart from concomitants which are 'given' in terms of the logical context, there is a further group of concomitant nouns which are superfluous in that the termination of the adjective says all that needs be said. Bergson points this out (p. 52) in connection with πρὸς βορῆν ἄνεμον, ἐν ἀλλοτρίᾳ γῇ, and other expressions in which the noun is sometimes omitted, but we may include in the same category νεώτερα ἔργα (p. 55) and many other instances in which the noun is ἄνδρες, ἄνθρωποι, πράγματα, etc.

Among formal principles, the most important is the generation of fixed adjective–noun phrases, e.g. θείᾳ μοίρᾳ, μέγα μέρος. Many of these are dealt with individually (e.g. pp. 131ff), but, rather surprisingly, nothing is said of the influence of these formulae, e.g. the extent to which the orders μέγα + noun and adjective + μέρος are determined by the familiarity of μέγα μέρος. Bergson perhaps underrates the irrational and mechanical aspects of language.

The fullness with which Bergson quotes the contexts of his examples, his caution in the use of the term 'emphasis' (e.g. pp. 67, 87, 91, 96, 101), his awareness of the limitations of all attempts to explain the word order of a dead language (e.g. pp. 9ff, 128, 136), and his invariably pertinent recourse to translation in order to bring out the nuances of a passage (e.g. p. 72), combine to make a book which is scholarly, sensitive and judicious. It is not, however, a definitive study of the problem, for it is marred, in conception and in detail, by one radical inadequacy: the continual isolation of the noun–adjective complex from its formal context. If an instance of a noun (x) and an adjective (y) is embodied in a word-group of the form $axyb$, the layout of the group as a whole must always be counted among the possible determinants of the order xy.

P. 76: in Hdt. i 183.2 ἔξω δὲ τοῦ νηοῦ βωμός ἐστι χρύσεος· ἔστι δὲ καὶ ἄλλος βωμὸς μέγας κτλ. it is true that the translation 'ein anderer Altar, ein größerer' represents the order of communication, but the position of μέγας is determined not by its having 'the same defining character as χρύσεος' but by the weight put upon ἄλλος and by the concomitant character of βωμός. P. 93: in Xen. *M.* ii 1.33 ὦ παῖ τοκέων ἀγαθῶν Ἡράκλεις ~ Pl. *Lg.* 772e ὦ παῖ, τοίνυν φῶμεν ἀγαθῶν πατέρων φύντι, παῖ and ἀγαθῶν are nuclear, τοκέων and τοίνυν φῶμεν concomitant. P. 126: in Hdt. vi 27.1 φιλέει δέ κως προσημαίνειν . . . καὶ γάρ Χίοισι πρὸ τούτων σημήια μεγάλα ἐγένετο the nuclei are Χίοισι and μεγάλα so that the whole clause καὶ . . . ἐγένετο is divided into two groups and the division falls between σημήια and μεγάλα.

The most important consequence of the analysis of word-groups is the devaluation of traditional semasiological categories. Bergson rightly emphasizes the difficulty of drawing a firm distinction between 'attributive' and 'predicative' (pp. 52 n. 1, 62ff), but shows few misgivings in his use of the most elusive term of all, 'appositive' (e.g. pp. 59 n. 1, 76ff). These terms are essentially relative, in that they serve to classify Greek instances according to the constructions needed in German or English to clarify the point of the Greek, and although such classification has its uses it does less than justice to the elasticity of the order of communication in Greek. The same considerations apply to the terms 'determinative' and 'qualificative'; Bergson is well aware of the problems of classification which can arise in many cases (e.g. p. 49), but he does not observe that it is possible for a noun to 'determine' an adjective, e.g. (p. 92) Pl. *R.* 391d μηδ' ἐῶμεν λέγειν ὡς Θησεύς ... Πειρίθους τε ... ὥρμησαν οὕτως ἐπὶ δεινὰς ἁρπαγάς. In order to answer the question 'why does this word come at this point in this group?' we should ask not 'what part of speech is it?' but (1) 'what element of the sense of the whole group does it communicate, and what is the order of communication in the group?' and (2) 'what are the formal affinities of the group with familiar types of group?' By insisting on limiting the syntactical roles of each morphological category we obscure the facts that (e.g.) Καρίῃ γλώσσῃ and ὀρθῷ λόγῳ play adverbial roles, the adjectival termination plus the whole noun being in effect an adverbial termination, or that in the type ἀνήρ + adjective the point of ἀνήρ is often best represented not by 'a man ...' or 'a man who ...' but by 'by nationality ...' or 'by nature ...' or 'who was ...'.

P. 39: in Th. iii 19.1 ἐξέπεμψαν ... ἀργυρολόγους ναῦς δώδεκα the point is 'they sent ... a force to collect money, twelve ships ...'. P. 40: in Pl. *Ap.* 27b ἵππους μὲν οὐ νομίζει, ἱππικὰ δὲ πράγματα the essential antithesis is between -ους and -ικά (cf. *Greek Word Order*, 51f) and there is no question of 'Anknüpfung'. P. 126: Hdt. viii 36.1 ἐς πᾶσαν ἀρρωδίην ἀπίκατο· ἐν δείματι δὲ μεγάλῳ κατεστεῶτες ἐμαντεύοντο is certainly a case of 'Anknüpfung'; μεγάλῳ is 'nuclear' and ἐν δείματι is best compared to the Herodotean use of a participle to give the sense 'thereupon' or 'therefore'.

7

Review of Guiraud,
La Phrase nominale

Charles Guiraud, *La Phrase nominale en grec d'Homère à Euripide*, Études et Commentaires xlii (Klincksieck, Paris 1962) 337 pp.

In Greek 'A B' and 'A is/are B' appear to be semantically indifferent alternatives and to differ – with increasing sharpness – only in respect of the speaker's attitude to subject, hearer, and circumstances. Guiraud's book explores the history of these alternatives in epic, Theognis, tragedy and Herodotus, and shows by abundant evidence that there is no simple and consistent evolution (pp. 124, 225, 233, 329 are especially interesting in this connection). It is a pity that Herodotus is the only prose author included in the survey, that he is consistently treated (e.g. pp. 83, 109f, 121, 185) as if he were earlier in date than Attic tragedy as a whole, and that no allowance is made for the very high proportion of archaic literature which is lost (e.g. pp. 97, 158, on alleged influences on Herodotus).

Guiraud's primary distinction is semantic, between (1) 'vérités générales', in which the formulation 'A B' constitutes the 'phrase nominale authentique', while the presence of the copula 'particularise et actualise l'énoncé' (p. 60), and (2) all other propositions. His second criterion of distinction is grammatical, and his third is again semantic, between (1) 'appréciations particulières', an 'annexe' of general truths, and (2) 'descriptions et renseignements', in which the copula is appropriate and its absence demands explanation, if possible, in semantic terms. It will be clear from this somewhat over-simplified summary that he has set himself serious problems of classification and interpretation. Every reader will find occasion to dispute subtleties of tone which Guiraud professes to catch in the numerous passages which he quotes and translates (e.g. E. *El.* 245, p. 153; A. *Se.* 226, p. 172). We are told too often that a speaker 'is insisting that what he says is really true', or that what appears a straightforward generalization is actually 'attached to the particular', or that this 'appreciation' is 'a reminder of something well known' whereas another is 'an argument meant to convince'; and some of these interpretations are mere verbiage, e.g. p. 298 on E. *El.* 1182: 'le rapprochement de αἰτία et de ἐγώ énonce le fait fondamental, "ma responsabilité"'.

Nevertheless, it would be a mistake to dismiss this book as one more circular argument generated by a characteristically French reluctance to acknowledge the power of mechanical irrationality in language. For one thing, however many of Guiraud's interpretations we may dispute as subjective and leading into circularity, there remain many passages where interpretation in conformity with his thesis supports a translation which is dramatically and rhetorically superior (e.g. pp. 92f, on the difference between *PV* 500 and *Eu*. 480). Secondly, Guiraud goes out of his way to draw our attention to pairs or sets of passages which go against his thesis, e.g. pp. 56–8, on *E* 406f ~ *Y* 264ff; p. 73, on Theognis 41 ~ 1082a; p. 141, on Her. iii 108 ~ v 27. Thirdly, he recognizes many other determinants, including:

1 Mechanical analogy, formulae, and the influence of familiar expressions; pp. 60, 81f, 118, 120, 124f, 215, 242, 306.
2 Metrical convenience; pp. 65, 72, 124f, 158, 180.
3 Speed and economy of expression; pp. 65, 76f, 105f (but it is wrong to speak [p. 129] as if poems inscribed on graves aimed above all at economy).
4 Individual preference; pp. 73f, 138, 227 (Pindar), 87 (Herodotus), 300 (Theognis).
5 Rules of genre; pp. 79, 84 (tragic lyric), 88, 153 (oracles), 158 (gnomic poetry).
6 Liking for variety; pp. 76f, 83.
7 Indifference and arbitrariness; pp. 70, 72, 79, 83, 150, 188.

These determinants are to some extent played down. Examples which can be held to illustrate semantic determination in conformity with Guiraud's thesis are 'satisfactory' or 'favourable', those which cannot are 'unfortunate' – although sometimes 'the situation is not as serious as it looks' (p. 122) – and semantic explanation is sometimes forced where some other determinant seems plainly at work (e.g. p. 212, on ἢ θέμις [ἐστί]). Moreover, the admission of so many determinants and the inclusion of 'convenience' and 'indifference' among them necessarily raise the question: if 'A B' and 'A is B' differ in *meaning*, so that to choose one is to exclude the meaning of the other, may not indifferent choice convey to the hearer a meaning which is not intended? The answer suggested by Guiraud's data is that the semantic determinant can be detected, by *study*, in one author but not in another; it is not necessarily a phenomenon of the language shared by composer and hearer but a mental habit of the composer, a phenomenon of the language which he has created regardless of complete intelligibility to the average hearer.

In suggesting that Guiraud has weighted the scales too heavily in favour of the rational, I am thinking of the fact that when alternative formulations of the same utterance are open to an author his choice is determined by his total linguistic experience up to that moment, and this experience is not classified by his memory in grammarian's categories but in shapes and sizes and sounds. For example, as soon as I read (p. 175) *Tr. πολλοὶ γὰρ οἷς εἴρηκας*,

Ag. 916 μακρὰν γὰρ ἐξέτεινας came into my mind; the reason is obvious enough – the two utterances share the sense 'for you have spoken', the notion of quantity, and the form $--$ γὰρ $-\cup-$ ας, the fifth and sixth syllables having an *e*-sound – and so, I suggest, is the implication for the mechanism of language. Guiraud's comparative insensitivity to such mechanisms is illustrated by his indifference to the gulf that lies between initial ἔστι and postpositive ἐστι, his treatment of πάρα/πάρεστι on the same basis as zero/ἐστι (pp. 197, 204, 220), and occasional over-insistence on the distinction between parts of speech and syntactical categories (e.g. p. 131, on S. *Tr.* 62f, and p. 155, on E. *Phoen.* 438). He has nevertheless given us a remarkably full and useful treatment of a phenomenon which no historian of the Greek language can afford to neglect.

Misprints are rather numerous, though very few are misleading; on p. 119 τοι is omitted from Hes. *Sc.* 447, and on p. 72, line 31, 'verbaux' should be 'non-verbaux'.

8

Review of Thesleff,
Studies in the Style of Plato

Holger Thesleff, *Studies in the Styles of Plato*, Acta Philosophica Fennica xx (Societas Philosophica Fennica [Akat. Kirjak. in Komm.], Helsinki 1967) 192 pp.

How many styles are there in Greek? The nature of the question is most clearly indicated by constructing a hypothetical situation immeasurably simpler than reality. Imagine that we possess, instead of the Greek literature which is extant, only five passages, and that we are able to distinguish only one stylistic choice, at morphemic level, comprising two mutually exclusive style markers which we will call X and Y. Imagine now that of our five passages the first contains a single example of X, the second a single example of Y, the third two of X, the fourth two of Y, and the fifth one of each. It will then be possible to distinguish five styles:

Style I	Marker: X	Passage 1
		Passage 5, part i
Style II	Marker: Y	Passage 2
		Passage 5, part ii
Style III	Markers: (a) X	Passage 3
	(b) Consistency	
Style IV	Markers: (a) Y	Passage 4
	(b) Consistency	
Style V	Marker: Inconsistency	Passage 5, whole

Clearly, if we had two further passages (6 and 7) each of which contained many examples of both X and Y, it might be possible to enlarge and to modify our lists of styles. Thus, if 6 and 7 contained respectively XYXYXY and XYYXYXXXY, we should have some new markers and new styles, thus:

Style VI	Marker: regular alternation	Passage 6
		Passage 7, part ii (YXYX)
Style VII	Marker: random alternation	Passage 7, part iii (XXY)
		Passage 7, whole

In the light of that we should have to demote style V to the status of 'potentially VI or VII'.

Four important consequences follow:

1 One and the same marker can be an ingredient of more than one style.
2 A single pair of markers can generate more than two styles, if patterns of distribution are taken into account. Hence the number of styles can be greater not only than the number of choices but even than the number of markers.
3 The style of a passage containing several instances of markers can be a 'realization' of the styles of passages containing fewer.
4 A passage as a whole can be characterized by markers which do not necessarily characterize all its parts; indeed, it could have a marker – e.g. a constant rate of change from the wholly colloquial to the wholly poetic and thence back to the wholly colloquial – which did not characterize any of its parts. The number of styles could not be restricted by dividing each extract into minimum units and allocating each unit to style I or style II, because the question 'And what is the style of the passage as a whole?' imposes itself and must be answered. Plato's *Symposium* is an obvious example of a work which as a whole does not have the styles of its parts; yet it has a style, by contrast with *Phaedo* and *Gorgias*.

Thesleff's book is founded on the explicit recognition of the first and fourth of these principles, and the caution with which he expresses himself implies recognition of the third; he takes no account of the second, which in fact is important for the stylistic characterization of Greek (or other) authors.

His starting-point (cf. pp. 78f and 171) seems to have been observation of the fact that different parts of Plato's work make different stylistic impressions on modern readers who are well acquainted with Greek. This is entirely natural and reasonable. Stylistics, like any branch of Classical studies, is an attempt to answer a set of questions; the scholar asks no questions until his curiosity is aroused; and our curiosity is most commonly aroused when we are 'struck' by something. Although Thesleff speaks (p. 28) of stylistic 'classes' or 'standards' to which Plato conforms, his actual procedure is founded on contrasts within Plato, not on stylistic theory independent of Plato. He distinguishes ten Platonic styles, to some of which he attaches novel names, e.g. 'pathetic' – a term which unfortunately is no longer associated in modern English with imagery, poetry and solemnity – and 'onkos'. The classification is not founded on a tabulation of the relative frequency of combinations of markers; there is, I think, a practicable way of achieving that by computerization, but hardly otherwise (Thesleff speaks [p. 28] of 'a few typical style markers', but their number is in fact very large indeed). Thesleff pays attention rather to community of content and of dramatic purpose between passages in which the same markers occur, and to community of character and of dramatic role (pp. 159–64) between participants in the dialogues. He accordingly offers a broad classification of types of dialogue-structure (pp. 33–62) before proceeding to stylistic description, and later (pp. 95–158) works through the *Republic* and the major divisions of other dialogues in order to relate style to structural type, philosophical purpose and dramatic characterization.

It is important to remember that his classificatory terms are primarily internal to Plato. When he speaks of 'historical style', for example, he does not imply that every marker assigned to that style is specially characteristic of Thucydides and Xenophon; the name applies to a certain Platonic style which shares *some* markers with the work of the historians. The name is determined by the nature of the Platonic passages in which the style appears. Yet I cannot help feeling that at the present stage of stylistic studies it would have been wiser to use neutral terms for the conjunctions of markers observable in Plato. There is a great danger that the use of terms as 'rhetorical' and 'historical' may lead to inclusions and exclusions on such a scale as to reduce significantly the value of any list of markers. The question which has to be asked with reference to every instance of a phenomenon which is a putative marker is simply this: what were the *associations* of this phenomenon, for author and audience, at *that* time and in *that* place? This question can be answered only by observing the distribution of the phenomenon in extant Greek down to that time; but it must be remembered that association is often not with genres but with individuals, occasions and types of non-literary activity.

Thesleff's catalogue of generic phenomena (pp. 81–5) is neither long enough nor refined enough. 'Expansion', 'weight' and 'variation' (p. 79) are genera which admit (and indeed demand) very extensive subdivision. On word order, I cannot agree (for the reasons expounded in *Greek Word Order*, 1960) with the approach implied in Thesleff's footnote (p. 85 n. 4) 'by "expressive word-order" I mean a change of the logical order for the sake of emphasis'.

The catalogue of words (pp. 86–94) is open to criticisms which I will indicate *exempli gratia* by discussion of the 27 words beginning with α.

1 I agree, subject to trivial reservations, with Thesleff's treatment and classification of 8 of these words: ἀδαμάντινος, ἀκμή, ἀκούω, ἅμα, ἀμήχανος, ἀναμνηστός, ἀνήρ, ἀπατεών.

2 7 words of wide distribution do not seem to me to be markers at all. Can it be demonstrated that they represent choice between alternatives? ἀγαπάω, ἀγαπητός, ἀκριβής, ἄνω (καὶ) κάτω, ἄξιος c. inf., ἄρδην, ἄτοπος.

3 ἄγαλμα is an ordinary word for 'statue', in documentary inscriptions as well as in literature. Since statues are a familiar part of Greek life, the 'contextual probability' of ἄγαλμα (to borrow Enkqvist's expression) is never so low as to deserve remark.

4 ἀγέλη, assigned to 'onkos' style, is an idiosyncratic metaphor of which Plato was fond (from *Republic* onwards). Almost every writer has his favourite words and images, and in such cases the appropriate label is 'Platonic', 'Herodotean', etc.

5 ἀγράμματος, ἀνήκεστος (both 'onkos') and ἄστρωτος ('mythic narrative')
should not be treated as individual words but as realizations of α- -τος,
which, as a look through the indexes of Diels–Kranz and *IG* i² shows,
achieved a firm hold in the fifth century on scientific and philosophical
exposition, architecture and sculpture (e.g. ἄθετος, ἀρράβδωτος), and law,
administration and finance (e.g. ἄτακτος, ἀχορήγητος – and cf. Ar. *V.* 752f
ὁ κῆρυξ φησί· τίς ἀψήφιστος;). ἀδέσποτος ('ceremonious style') should be
similarly regarded, despite the different origin of its τ.

6 ἀκλεής, ἀτεχνῶς and αὐτίκα (in the sense 'for example') are words of which
the chronological distribution is as important as the generic.

7 ἀμφιλαφής, used of a spreading plane-tree in *Phdr.* 230b and of palm-trees
in Hdt. iv 172.1, is probably a 'technical term' (or better, 'vox propria'). The
same may be true of ἄρνυμαι when its object is μισθός, and of ἄοπλος.

Thesleff's explanation of his position in regard to problems of Platonic
chronology and authenticity calls for a few comments.

P. 13 n. 4: 'Plato cannot really be expected to have written two Hippiases.'
Why not? A tragic poet sometimes wrote two plays about the same hero, and a
comic poet two plays with the same title. P. 20, n. 3: 'Is it possible that Plato
should have risked such a voyage (*sc.* to Sicily) before the (*sc.* Corinthian) war
was over?' It is more than 'possible'; hostile interception was a normal and
accepted risk of travel. P. 23 n. 1: The argument that Eukleides and Terpsion
must have been dead before Plato wrote *Theaetetus* begs the question.

9

The Portrayal of Moral
Evaluation in Greek Poetry

Anyone who has read my book *Greek Popular Morality in the Time of Plato and Aristotle* (Oxford 1974) (hereafter '*GPM*') and has also read Professor A. W. H. Adkins's book *Merit and Responsibility* (Oxford 1960) ('*M&R*')[1] will have noticed that the two books differ substantially in their approach to the history of Greek moral values and in some of the conclusions which they reach. Adkins's critical review of *GPM*, entitled 'Problems in Greek Popular Morality', *CPh* lxxiii (1978) 143–58 ('*Problems*'), explains very clearly why he finds *GPM* in many respects inadequate or misleading, and it has greatly helped me to understand my own disquiet at the influence exercised by the presuppositions, methods and conclusions of *M&R*. My purpose in this paper is not to offer a review of *M&R* twenty years too late, nor to attempt a rebuttal, point by point, of the criticisms of *GPM* contained in *Problems*,[2] but to examine one major issue: how should the portrayal of moral evaluation on the tragic stage or in epic narrative be used as evidence for the history of Greek moral values?

A very important proposition is stated in *M&R* 127: 'A drama is a practical work; it involves action. People appear on the stage and behave as they do in real life.' With this proposition I agree, subject to three provisos, of which one limits its application and two amplify it. The limiting proviso is obvious. No one, I imagine, would contend that people on stage always and necessarily 'behave as they do in real life', for they sometimes behave in a demonic way which is rare in life, and they commonly organize, intellectualize and articulate the expression of their emotions unrealistically. Since, however, there are passages which become wholly intelligible on the hypothesis that the poet is aiming at realistic portrayal, that hypothesis deserves to be considered as a possible explanation of any passage. The amplifications of Adkins' proposition are more important. First, there is no reason to confine the proposition

---

[1] I refer also to *Moral and Political Values in Ancient Greece* (London 1972) ('*MPV*') and 'Homeric Values and Homeric Society', *JHS* xci (1971) 1–14 ('*HV*').

[2] I find I disagree with Adkins's interpretation of practically all the individual passages mentioned in *Problems*; an important exception is his correction of my oversight in discussing Xen. *HG* ii 4.40f (*GPM* 67, *Problems* 154).

to drama, excluding epic narrative, the other main genre of Greek representational poetry. Secondly, there is also no reason to exclude linguistic behaviour from the category 'behaviour'. A word is indeed 'a tool with uses' (*MPV* 4); its uses are heterogeneous, and one of them is the shaping of the personal relationship between speaker and hearer.

What are the distinctive features of linguistic behaviour in respect of moral evaluation? The answer offered by *M&R* seems to be made up of four ingredients.

(I) 'Any word of general commendation will, in any society, be applied not at random but to persons or events possessing certain characteristics' (*M&R* 5). It is conceded (ibid.) that evaluative language 'possesses another element – whose nature it is unnecessary to discuss here – which is peculiar to itself', a concession which leaves open the possibility that this 'peculiar element' may seem to some of us the most important.

(II) Some evaluative words are so 'powerful' (e. g. *M&R* 156, 173, 186, 254, 268, 282) that they can not only 'restrain' violent or oppressive action (e.g. *M&R* 39, *HV* 4)[3] but even 'end an argument' (e.g. *M&R* 184f).

(III) The utterance of an evaluative word can also constitute the 'solution' of a 'problem' (e.g. *M&R* 152, 175, 185).

(IV) To judge from the number of well-known passages which have a bearing on the history of Greek morality but are not mentioned in *M&R*, Adkins's argument seems to presuppose that only the presence of one of the limited number of words which he classifies as commendatory or disapproving identifies an utterance as morally evaluative.

I propose to argue that (I) is quite inadequate as a statement about evaluative utterance; that (II) is true only in certain senses which contribute nothing to the argument of *M&R*; that (III) is untrue; and that (IV) imposes a crippling constraint on investigation of the history of values.[4]

With regard to (I), it may be agreed without more ado that evaluative words are not applied 'at random' – we are, after all, concerned with a form of interactive behaviour which merits the label 'language' – but 'possessing certain characteristics' is not the only alternative. Philosophers have had a great deal to say about the difference between evaluative and non-evaluative language, but one does not need to be a philosopher to observe the most striking differ-

---

[3] A. A. Long, 'Morals and Values in Homer', *JHS* xc (1970) 121–39, contains much valuable criticism of *M&R*. At one point (127) Long refers to 'the poverty of Homeric restraints upon the *agathos*'. Adkins (*HV* 9) says 'I take it that "restraints upon" means "sufficiently powerful ethical language to restrain".' *M&R* 152, 210, 254 furnish other examples of the transformation of moral issues into linguistic terms.

[4] Hugh Lloyd-Jones, *The Justice of Zeus* (Berkeley, Calif., Los Angeles and London 1971) 6 lays proper emphasis on *Il.* xvi 384–92 (Zeus sends heavy rain when he is angered by the 'crooked judgments' of men), a passage not mentioned in *M&R*. See below for other instances.

ence. If I say 'There's a cat in my garden', the chances are that you will believe that there is a cat in my garden. If I add 'It's a horrible cat', you are more likely simply to 'register' the addition than to believe or disbelieve it, aware that the cat may possess characteristics which you too would call 'horrible' but may perhaps not. I have disclosed something about my own emotional attitude to the cat, but nothing for sure about the cat, nor even anything for sure about the characteristics which I think I discern in it. The more general a term of commendation or disapproval, the less the things to which it is applied have in common. What is common to many speech-events containing the attribution or predication of a general evaluative term is the disclosure of a favourable or unfavourable reaction on the part of the speaker. At the same time there are circumstances in which the precise grounds of the reaction are understood, e.g. when the predication of 'good' in English communicates the fact that meat has not begun to decompose or that a baby does not cry at night.[5] In other circumstances, the information-content of an evaluative word is zero, as when a union describes its pay-claim as 'just' and the employer describes his offer as 'fair' and 'reasonable'. In others again, a speaker uses an evaluative word not to disclose or express a reaction of his own but simply because it is the most familiar evaluation in his own ambience. He may speak ironically or conventionally; and often the hearer does not know whether or not the evaluation contained in the speaker's words is shared by the speaker himself. In all cases we have to interpret evaluative language as contributing something to the construction of a relationship between speaker and hearer.

For example, *Od.* xv 323f, where the term ἀγαθοί is contrasted with 'inferiors' and denotes the socially dominant class, is of considerable importance to Adkins's argument (*M&R* 32f) about the 'world-view' implicit in Homeric terms of evaluation:

> δαιτρεῦσαί τε καὶ ὀπτῆσαι καὶ οἰνοχοῆσαι,
> οἷά τε τοῖς ἀγαθοῖσι παραδρώωσι χέρηες.

However, Odysseus is speaking here in the role of a labourer looking for work, anxious to serve and to please, and his ingratiating evaluation of himself among χέρηες and of his potential employers as ἀγαθοί suits the role very well. He is not making a considered sociological statement, but conveying an impression of his own attitude, and the passage does not justify insistence on interpretation of ἀγαθός as social in other contexts. *Od.* xvii 322f exemplifies a quite different function of evaluation. Eumaios, commenting sadly on the neglect of the old dog by the slave-women of the household, says that servants

---

[5] *Problems* 153 points out that 'such usages do not abolish the possibility that there exists a usage of "good" where the class is no narrower than "human being"'. True, but in what circumstances do we hear the word 'good' so used? Rarely, if ever, in my experience, outside discussions concerned with ethical theory; and is nothing to be learned from that fact?

do not do ἐναίσιμα when there is no master to compel them, and he ends with the *gnome*

> ἥμισυ γάρ τ᾽ ἀρετῆς ἀποαίνυται εὐρύοπα Ζεὺς
> ἀνέρος, εὖτ᾽ ἄν μιν κατὰ δούλιον ἦμαρ ἕλῃσιν.

Pl. *Lg.* 777a, quoting the passage, writes τε νόου for τ᾽ ἀρετῆς.[6] Adkins (*M&R* 83 n. 28), while accepting τ᾽ ἀρετῆς as the earlier text, 'cannot agree . . . that *arete* here makes any real sense'; 'in view of the very different qualities expected from men and women in Homer, the loss of *arete* has very different implications in men and in women, and the transitions in thought are thus difficult'. But there is no difficulty if we suppose that Eumaios's *gnome* proceeds from the reflection that enslavement diminishes in anyone, of either sex and any age, the capacity to behave in ways which elicit approval and admiration.

These considerations have a bearing on the interpretation of the expression ἀγαθός περ ἐών, which occurs six times in the *Iliad*, viz.

(a) i 131f (Agamemnon to Achilles)

> μὴ δὴ οὕτως ἀγαθός περ ἐών, θεοείκελ᾽ Ἀχιλλεῦ,
> κλέπτε νόῳ.

(b) i 275 (Nestor to Agamemnon)

> μήτε σὺ τόνδ᾽ ἀγαθός περ ἐὼν ἀποαίρεο κούρην.

(c) ix 626f (Ajax to Odysseus)

> ἀπαγγεῖλαι δὲ τάχιστα
> χρὴ μῦθον Δαναοῖσι καὶ οὐκ ἀγαθόν περ ἐόντα.

(d) xv 185f (Poseidon to Iris, about Zeus)

> ὢ πόποι, ἦ ῥ᾽ ἀγαθός περ ἐὼν ὑπέροπλον ἔειπεν,
> εἴ μ᾽ ὁμότιμον ἐόντα βίῃ ἀέκοντα καθέξει.

(e) xix 155f (Odysseus to Achilles)

> μὴ δὴ οὕτως ἀγαθός περ ἐών, θεοείκελ᾽ Ἀχιλλεῦ,
> νήστιας ὄτρυνε προτὶ Ἴλιον υἷας Ἀχαιῶν.

---

[6] Cf. J. Labarbe, *L'Homère de Platon* (Liège 1949) 249–54 and G. Lohse, *Helikon* v (1965) 289–91. Their discussions, however, take insufficient account of the fact that *Lg.* 776c–778a concerns the treatment of slaves by their masters, a matter to which the antithesis between brutal conditioning and rational persuasion is highly relevant. νόου suits the context in Plato better than ἀρετῆς; indeed, after the admission in 776d that some slaves have proved themselves κρείττους πρὸς ἀρετήν than brothers and sons, citation of the Homeric passage in the form in which our Homer texts have it would have been irrational.

(f)   xxiv 53 (Apollo to the gods, about Achilles)

μὴ ἀγαθῷ περ ἐόντι νεμεσσηθέωμέν οἱ ἡμεῖς.

Adkins discusses (a), (b) and (f) in *M&R* 37f and (d) in *HV* 13. He argues in the case of (b) that 'an *agathos* might well do this' (*sc.* seize Briseis) 'without ceasing to be an *agathos*, and indeed derives a claim to do it from the fact that he is an *agathos*', and in the case of (f) 'The gods do not approve of Achilles' action' (*sic*; some of them do) 'but clearly the fact that he is *agathos* gives him a strong claim against gods and men to be allowed to do it'. Adkins alludes to (a), without quoting it, and says that Agamemnon 'complains of Achilles' claims *qua* warrior and hence *agathos*' but 'has no higher standards to which he can appeal'. We are encouraged to infer that Achilles as 'an *agathos*' has a 'claim' to be deceitful. But does Agamemnon really not intend to evoke any sympathetic indignation from the assembled Greeks? If it is possible to contrast a 'good *agathos*' with a 'bad *agathos*' – and Adkins recognizes that it is, in saying 'the gods do not approve' of Achilles' treatment of Hektor's corpse – then a criterion of evaluation, not necessarily 'higher' or 'lower' than social and military deference, but certainly in conflict with it, is operative.

In five of the six passages cited above the point of ἀγαθός περ ἐών is incompatibility between normally evoking a favourable evaluation (from the speaker, among others) and on the occasion of the utterance doing or proposing to do something which evokes an unfavourable evaluation from the same speaker. The conciliatory tone of (b) and (e) is clear.[7] (a), though it leads on rapidly to open expression of hostility, is courteous, even flattering, as θεοείκελε shows (and if θεοείκελε is ironic, so might ἀγαθός be); both (a) and (d) have something in common with the angry 'With respect, Sir, . . .' which one may hear at a committee meeting. Apollo in (f), trying to win over the gods,[8] implies that, while their evaluation of Achilles is normally favourable, in this instance Achilles may incur a displeasure in conflict with that evaluation. The point of (c) is the exact converse: incompatibility between the unwelcome character of news and promptitude in transmitting it. (c) is the only one of the six passages in which the objective ground of the evaluation can be stated; in the other five the explicit recognition of the person addressed or spoken about as ἀγαθός serves to define the speaker's standpoint and

---

[7] Martin Hoffmann, 'Die ethische Terminologie bei Homer, Hesiod und den alten Elegikern und Iambographen' i, 'Homer' (Diss., Tübingen 1914) 74–8, though he anticipates Adkins in his view of the conduct expected of someone valued as ἀγαθός, concedes (76) that in *Il.* i 275 the phrase ἀγαθός περ ἐών tones down ('mildert') Nestor's admonition. In this connection, Adkins's question (*HV* 13) 'Why does Poseidon say that Iris's words are κατὰ μοῖραν and αἴσιμα?' is answered by Poseidon's own words in 207: she has shown forbearance and diplomatic skill in sudggesting he might reconsider his answer to Zeus.

[8] The question posed in *HV* 11, 'Now why does Hera take this very different view?' is answered by xxiv 25–30. For the reason given there, she wishes to cause the gods not to restrain Achilles, and she judges that the best way to do that is to try to implant in them a feeling which may swamp the feeling evoked by Apollo.

construct a certain relationship between him and his hearer(s). Many of us have heard (e.g.) 'I am sure Mr X would be an excellent chairman, but . . .' uttered by a speaker who was convinced that Mr X would be a very bad chairman; and, if it is objected that it is frivolous and misleading to compare Greek gods and heroes with modern committee-members, I must reply that I am comparing modern conventions which in some circumstances govern the expression of very strong feelings with the portrayal of the expression of strong feelings by an ancient poet who was patently sensitive to social convention.

The importance of interpreting an evaluation in terms of the function of the entire utterance which contains it is illustrated by certain passages concerning the suitors in the *Odyssey*. In *Od.* xxiii 121f Odysseus tells Telemachos,

> ἡμεῖς δ' ἕρμα πόληος ἀπέκταμεν, οἳ μέγ' ἄριστοι
> κούρων εἰν Ἰθάκῃ,

and in xxiv 429 Eupeithes, father of Antinoos, inciting the kinsmen of the suitors to vengeance, says that Odysseus has slain Κεφαλλήνων ὄχ' ἀρίστους. Medon and Halitherses attempt to persuade them not to seek vengeance (439–62), the former on prudential grounds and the latter on moral grounds (epic poets, like dramatists, attach some importance to symmetry and eschew the portrayal of two speakers making the same point). *M&R* 243 n. 24 says, 'Stress the crimes of the suitors as they will, [they] can do nothing to outbid Eupeithes' evaluation of the matter.' The terminology of games ('outbid'; cf. on 'trumping' below) distracts the reader from the essential point. Eupeithes is a bereaved father; naturally he wants revenge, he wants to persuade others to join him in seeking revenge, and therefore he speaks of the dead suitors as good men and of their killing as a crime. In xxiii 121f Odysseus is deeply apprehensive about the consequence of his victory: the killing of even one man who has no followers causes the murderers to flee into exile, 'and *we* have killed the bulwark of the city . . .'. When we want to assess a danger on the principle of 'the worst case' and to impress on someone else its magnitude and the urgency of providing against it, we not uncommonly look at the situation through the eyes of those from whom the danger threatens. In a different context, Odysseus denies the ἀρετή of the suitors, xviii 383: provoked by the insults of Eurymachos, Odysseus tells him,

> καί πού τις δοκέεις μέγας ἔμμεναι ἠδὲ κραταιός,
> οὕνεκα πὰρ παύροισι καὶ οὐκ ἀγαθοῖσιν ὁμιλεῖς.

παύροισι rhetorically plays down the number of the suitors (in other contexts the number seems formidably large to Odysseus) to emphasize the point, 'a big fish in a little pond', and however we translate ἀγαθοῖσιν here and ἄριστοι in xxiii 121 we are left with the fact, since ἄριστος is unquestionably the superlative of ἀγαθός, that contradictory evaluations of the same people are elicited from the same speaker by different moods and purposes.

When Halitherses is trying to dissuade the kinsmen of the suitors from seeking revenge, he tells them (xxiv 455–7)

> ὑμετέρῃ κακότητι, φίλοι, τάδε ἔργα γένοντο·
> οὐ γὰρ ἐμοὶ πείθεσθ', οὐ Μέντορι ποιμένι λαῶν,
> ὑμετέρους παῖδας καταπαυέμεν ἀφροσυνάων.

We are rightly reminded in *M&R* 30 that κακός and κακότης are the antonyms of ἀγαθός and ἀρετή. The implication of the passage is that the kinsmen were κακοί because they did not prevent the suitors from committing the acts which Halitherses regards as reasons for not avenging the suitors' death. In view of Adkins's statements (*M&R* 57 n. 2) that '*kakos* and *kakotes* in Homer normally decry failure' and 'Homer knows only one sense of *kakotes*', it may be that he regards 'your failure' as an adequate translation of ὑμετέρῃ κακότητι in xxiv 455. However, 'failure (to . . .)' is ambiguous in English, covering both an unsuccessful attempt and the absence of an attempt. The former is irrelevant here; in Halitherses' view, the κακότης of the kinsmen lay in their rejection of – or indifference to – his advice, not in the collapse of any earnest attempts at restraint on their part (he himself is the one who has 'failed' in that sense), nor in the calamity which is now the end-product of their rejection of advice.

In *Od.* xxi, when the disguised Odysseus has asked if he may try the great bow, Antinoos threatens him (288–310). Penelope reproaches Antinoos, saying (312f) that it is not καλόν or δίκαιον to abuse her son's guest. Eurymachos explains that if by chance the beggar can draw the bow when the suitors cannot they will be regarded as inferior and suffer ἐλέγχεα (323–9). Penelope replies that men who, like the suitors, dishonour the house of an ἀνὴρ ἀριστεύς by their behaviour cannot in any case expect to be εὐκλεής; why then do they treat failure to draw the bow as ἐλέγχεα (331–3)? She implies that their behaviour merits such great reproach that by comparison the matter of the bow is trivial and irrelevant. Adkins says (*M&R* 39) that such an implied use of the word ἔλεγχος is 'impossible'; 'she (or rather the poet) attempts a use of language, a "persuasive definition", which, if accepted, would effectively restrain the suitors.[9] The definition cannot succeed.' There is certainly one sense in which Penelope 'cannot succeed' in filling the suitors with effective remorse: if she did, the rest of the *Odyssey* would be a flop; the story, after all, is about the triumph of a hero in disguise, against heavy odds, over offenders who did not repent and therefore could not, without spoiling the story, be portrayed as 'accepting' *any* reproach, whatever words were cast at them. But the somewhat hyperbolic description[10] of Penelope's use of the

---

9 An example of a persuasive definition may be found (as remarked in *Problems* 155) in *GPM* 43, where I am trying to persuade the reader to define a certain term in a certain way. What have come to be called 'persuasive definitions' in common practice are not definitions but applications.

10 Cf. Long (n. 3) 126 n. 16.

word ἔλεγχος as 'impossible' presumably means that Penelope is mistaken if she thinks the behaviour of the suitors likely to incur adverse evaluation from anyone other than those materially affected by it (e.g. Odysseus, Telemachos, Eumaios) or committed (as Athena is) to support of Odysseus. But what evaluation of such behaviour does the poet expect from his hearers? Does nothing in it merit our reproach, indignation or contempt except the suitors' imprudence in assuming that Odysseus was dead and their inability to save their own lives? And how is the 'impossibility' of ἔλεγχος to be reconciled with Halitherses' attitude in xxiv 455?

Curiously enough, 'cannot', which in this connection provokes objection, in another connection demands the assent which we give to a banal truism. In *Il.* viii 137–56 Nestor advises Diomedes to retreat; Diomedes says that he is intolerably distressed by the thought that Hektor will boast that Diomedes has fled from him in fear; and Nestor assures him that if Hektor says any such thing, the Trojans and the widows of Trojans killed by Diomedes will know better. Adkins comments (*M&R* 49) that 'Nestor cannot say, "Don't worry. It isn't true"', from which he deduces that 'facts are of much less importance than appearances'. Certainly Nestor cannot usefully or relevantly say 'Don't worry. It isn't true', because Diomedes already knows it isn't true, and what 'worries' him is his reputation. 'Don't worry. It isn't true' would be a fatuous reply, not only in archaic Greece, but nowadays too, or at any time and place; *Il.* viii 137–56 therefore tells us nothing whatever about any distinctive features of early Greek morality.

Consideration of the 'effectiveness' of Penelope's words has brought us into the area of what I have listed as Adkins's principle (II), the treatment of certain words as intrinsically 'powerful'. For a given individual, there may well be words which he is inclined to use only when strongly moved and words which, when they are used of him by others, particularly gratify him (e.g. 'elegant', 'professional') or anger him (e.g. 'disingenuous', 'fat'). In this sense of 'power', each of us has his private hierarchy of words. It so happens that within twelve months I have heard ' . . . is an absolute shit' predicated (i) by A of B, (ii) by C of D and (iii) by E of F. The forthright word could fairly claim to be among the most 'powerful' (and least ambiguous) expressions of moral disapproval in modern spoken English; I myself would not use it with a second-person subject, for fear of being struck or damaging a relationship irreparably. The intended information-content was different in each case, and the application of the same predicate to the three subjects B, D and F was not determined by their possession of what a third party could perceive to be common characteristics. (i) was more or less jocular; A communicated the opinion that B, whom in fact he likes and respects (they are both senior military commanders), is a strict disciplinarian, and in order to communicate this he spoke (using ''s', while C and E used 'is') from the standpoint of someone adversely affected by B's insistence on discipline. (ii) and (iii) were far from jocular. C's evaluation of D was generated by his conviction that D had acted in a ruthlessly selfish manner contrary to the interests of the institution which it is C's job to serve, and E's evaluation of F by firm evidence that F is untruthful and unreliable. C is an irascible man who has ready recourse to strong and vulgar language, but E had never before, in my long acquaintance with him, voiced an uncharitable judgement or expressed himself intemperately; hence for me as hearer the moral impact of (iii) was far greater than that of (i) or (ii). The communication of information, with incidental revelation of the speaker's own standpoint, was a more important determinant of (i) than of (ii) or (iii). The intention to influence the hearer was prominent in (ii), negligible in (i) and subordinate in (iii). The main function of utterance in (ii) and (iii) was to alleviate the physical discomfort created in the speaker by anger.[11] The power of the term 'absolute shit' to affect my own evaluation of B, D and F was derived from my knowledge of the character and practice of the speaker in each case and from my understanding of the purpose of the utterance in its whol context.

My intention in citing these examples is not to labour the point, familiar to everyone, that the way one talks on a particular occasion depends in part on one's social and personal relations with the hearer (this consideration is most obviously relevant to the interpretation of comic and Platonic dialogue, and even sometimes to its textual criticism, e.g. Pl. *Grg.* 497a). What I deduce from the examples is that if we are to talk about the power of words in the interactions portrayed by poets we must start from careful observation of how words are actually used in the interactions of our daily lives. Neither Greek nor English is a game played under rules which define certain words as trumps. Suppose, in the examples cited, that I had contended that B is a kindly and lenient man, that D is notably altruistic, and that F is invariably truthful. The contrary evaluations made by A, C and E might well have *started* an argument, but are there any circumstances in which they could have *ended* an argument, and, if so, how? What does end an argument? I stop[12] arguing with someone (i) when I judge it very unlikely that he will change his mind; or (ii) when he betrays emotion and I fear his hostility or would be sorry to impair friendship with him; or (iii) when he is someone whose judgement and sensitivity I respect so highly that my confidence is shaken by the bare fact of his disagreement and I need to think further; or (iv) when I am struck by second thoughts for some other reason; or (v) when I get bored with the argument; or, of course, (vi) an argument may end when one of us has convinced the other by reasoning that the particular instance about which we are arguing exemplifies a general rule on which we agree. The overt evaluative signals used by my opponent – language, silences, hesitations, facial expressions, slight bodily movements – may bring about (ii) and may have a bearing on (i)

---

[11] This is what I meant by my reference in *GPM* 50 to 'finding the right words' and to 'the expressive aspect of the utterance'. *Problems* 149, to my surprise, takes 'expressive' to mean 'descriptive'.

[12] With reference to a stylistic habit which has on at least one occasion given rise to uncertainty (*Problems* 149), it should be said that Dover borrows from Locke the use of the first-person singular pronoun, with present, future and conditional tenses, in a generalizing sense.

and (iii), but not on (iv) or (v). They may help to stimulate effort towards (vi), but cannot of themselves accomplish it, because what matters in (vi) is the movement of our thought about the situation under discussion, not any particular signals in which we expose our thought.

Let us turn now to three of the examples in which Adkins discerns 'trumping power' in words; all three concern the killing of Agamemnon by Klytaimestra or her killing by Orestes.

(a) S. *El.* 558–60 (*M&R* 156, cf. 185). Klytaimestra has argued (516–51, esp. 528, 538, 550f) that her killing of Agamemnon was justified retaliation for the sacrifice of Iphigeneia. Elektra retorts,

> τίς ἂν
> τούτου λόγος γένοιτ' ἂν αἰσχίων ἔτι
> εἴτ' οὖν δικαίως εἴτε μή;

Adkins comments, 'To say that an action is *aischron* is to play the ace of trumps; to justify performing it, one cannot press the claim that it is *dikaion*, for this is of less importance, but must maintain that it is in fact not *aischron* after all.' Why then, after 'playing the ace of trumps', does Elektra go on to argue (i) 560–79, that the killing of Agamemnon was not in fact justifiable retaliation, (ii) 580–3, that by giving precedence to the principle of retaliation Klytaimestra is imprudently endangering her own future, (iii) 584–94, that Klytaimestra's marrying Aigisthos and driving out her own children is behaviour going beyond anything which could be represented as justifiable retaliation, and after (iv) 595–605, an expression of hatred and of self-pity, declare (v) 605–9, 616–21, that her own behaviour is indeed αἰσχρός and ἀναιδής but forced upon her? Why does the chorus-leader (610f) remark on Elektra's vehemence but admit to bewilderment over the rights and wrongs of the argument? And why is Klytaimestra, so far from being silenced by Elektra's 'ace', moved to voluble anger? That last question, at any rate, is answered easily enough. Depicting two enemies in irreconcilable conflict (the irreconcilability is a datum of the legend) Sophokles has constructed an ἀγών of familiar type, comprising one long speech on either side. He has represented Elektra as trying to hurt Klytaimestra as much as possible, to which end, as we should expect, she treats Klytaimestra's action as both ἄδικος and αἰσχρός. It would have been an aesthetic error to make the first speaker embark on a systematic refutation of the second speaker's rebuttal of the first speaker's case.

(b) E. *Or.* 194 (*M&R* 185). Elektra's despairing utterance (191–3)

> ἐξέθυσ' ὁ Φοῖβος ἡμᾶς
> μέλεον ἀπόφονον αἷμα δοὺς
> πατροφόνου ματρός.

provokes from the chorus the comment δίκᾳ μέν, to which Elektra retorts

καλῶς δ᾽ οὖ and goes on to apostrophize her mother. Adkins says, 'Naturally
. . . this settles the matter, for there is no higher term of value to invoke.' But
for whom is anything 'settled' by the words καλῶς δ᾽ οὖ? Persistence by the
chorus in maintaining that Apollo's verdict was just would spoil the symmetry
within the kommos, so we cannot expect to hear more than three syllables
from them at this point. A simple 'No, *not* justly!' from Elektra would be
ψυχρόν. We already know (28, 162–5) what she thinks about the 'justice' of
Apollo's verdict, and when the chorus still assert that it was just, what can she
do but brush that aside and express, by one of the most general of all evaluative adverbs, her reaction to the limitless suffering, rejection and mortal
danger into which she and Orestes have now been cast? (It is worth recalling
in this connection that the chorus in E. *El.* recognize the matricide both as
just [1169, 1189] and also as no more ὅσιος than Klytaimestra's own crime
[1203f ~ 1170]; many an act can be looked at with conflicting emotions which
find expression in conflicting evaluations.)

   (c) E. *El.* 1051–4 (*M&R* 185). After Klytaimestra's speech of self-exculpa-
tion (1011–50), ending with the challenge to Elektra

> λέγ᾽ εἴ τι χρῄζεις κἀντίθες παρρησίᾳ,
> ὅπως τέθνηκε σὸς πατὴρ οὐκ ἐνδίκως,

the chorus-leader says,

> δίκαι᾽ ἔλεξας, ἡ δίκη δ᾽ αἰσχρῶς ἔχει.
> γυναῖκα γὰρ χρὴ πάντα συγχωρεῖν πόσει, κτλ.

'The judgment, and the result', says Adkins, 'are the same' (*sc.* as in E. *Or.*
194?): 'the argument goes no further'. What argument? The issue is between
Klytaimestra and Elektra, and that argument goes a great deal further, for
Elektra delivers a long riposte (1060–96), ending by picking up Klytaimestra's
ἐνδίκως:

> εἰ γὰρ δίκαι᾽ ἐκεῖνα, καὶ τάδ᾽ ἔνδικα.

Each participant in the conflict, that is to say, claims to be making a just case,
but to Elektra, as in (a) and (b) above, cool assessment of justice is not what
matters. It is common for a chorus-leader present during such a conflict to act
as 'moderator'. Sometimes he or she expresses carefully-worded impartial
approval (e.g. S. *Ant.* 681f, 724f) or disapproval (e.g. S. *Aj.* 1091f, 1118f, *OT*
404–7), sometimes outright partiality, particularly when the fate of the chorus
is part of the story (e.g. E. *Su.* 463f, 511f, *Tro.* 966–8), but in any event neither
participant in the conflict turns it into a three-cornered fight by rebuttal of the
chorus-leader's comment. In the present case the chorus-leader sides with
Elektra, expressing a preference for a conventional, submissive attitude which
would have prevented the tearing-apart of the House of Atreus.

I say 'preference' deliberately, and 'the chorus-leader' and 'Elektra' rather than 'Euripides' no less deliberately, in order to introduce discussion of Adkins's principle (III), neatly exemplified in his view that passages (a)–(c) 'express the solution of the two poets to the problem set by the crime within the family'. It is perfectly true that for a member of the audience properly engaged by what is set before him the question 'Ought Klytaimestra to have killed Agamemnon? Ought Orestes to have killed Klytaimestra? What would I have done in their position?' fully merit the dignity of the term 'problem', but each of the utterances quoted in (a)–(c), so far from meriting the dignity of 'solution', simply discloses one of the ingredients which constitute the problem. In any case, treatment of a selected utterance by one character in a play as the poet's own voice, without regard for the function of that utterance by that character in that situation, is a throwback to the attempt by a certain Hygiainon (Arist. *Rhet.* 1416a28–35) to persuade a jury that the author of *Hp.* 612 could not be trusted. At one point (*M&R* 151 n. 18, on A. *Su.* 228–31) Adkins seems to be affirming Hygiainon's Law: 'Aeschylus himself presumably believed in a post-mortem judgment since, unlike the court-poet Pindar, he had no incentive to produce beliefs which were not his own.' But this is worse than uncritical; it is anti-critical. The composition of fiction is no mean incentive to 'produce' beliefs which are not one's own, and it would be sensible to work on the assumption that the dramatist, imitating reality, made people say the kind of thing that people say.

One kind of thing is a generalization which (in common with its denial) can be supported by examples and is elicited by emotional reaction to an example or by perception of its usefulness as a way of bringing about a desired situation. Unverifiable religious statements are a related genre. Two passages of Homer, bearing upon moral responsibility, require comment in this connection.

(a) *Il.* iii 164 (Priam to Helen)

οὔ τί μοι αἰτίη ἐσσί, θεοί νύ μοι αἴτιοί εἰσιν.

So-long as it is believed that *some* events are determined by the gods, the belief is available for use by anyone who wishes to represent a *particular* event as so determined. He may, for example, wish, out of kindliness or courtesy, to relieve someone else of guilt or self-reproach. Helen is filled with self-reproach in *Il.* iii, and Priam's gentle forbearance towards her[13] is a motif which recurs in xxiv 770. The passage does not tell us what the poet, or any actual person, thought about the culpability of Helen, still less what he thought about divine responsibility in general.

(b) In *Od.* i 32–4 Zeus, speaking to the gods about the fate of Aigisthos, says,

---

[13] Cf. Albin Lesky, 'Göttliche und menschliche Motivation im homerischen Epos', *Sitz. Heidelberg* 1961.4, 40.

ὦ πόποι, οἷον δή νυ θεοὺς βροτοὶ αἰτιόωνται·
ἐξ ἡμέων γάρ φασι κάκ' ἔμμεναι· οἱ δὲ καὶ αὐτοὶ
σφῇσιν ἀτασθαλίῃσιν ὑπὲρ μόρον ἄλγε' ἔχουσιν.

Adkins (*M&R* 24) describes Zeus's words as a 'violent response' to *Il.* iii 164 and as 'a comment by the poet himself on a contemporary belief'. He rightly observes that as a universal statement Zeus's 'response' appears to be refuted by the obstacles which Poseidon is putting in the way of Odysseus's return. He tries to solve this contradiction by suggesting that Zeus is speaking only of those κακά which proceed ultimately from the wrong decisions of mortals, i.e. κακά of the type exemplified by the case of Aigisthos, described in 33–43. I cannot deny the possibility that the poet may have intended his hearers, who will have taken κακά in 33 as a reference to unwelcome happenings in general, to revise their interpretation of the line after hearing 35–43, but there is a simpler explanation. The essential data are: people believed that some calamities were caused by gods; they also recognized that some were not; and they knew that there is no sure way of deciding whether or not a given calamity has been caused by a god, given that a god can even distort a mortals' thinking and feeling. To these fundamentals must be added a most unusual feature of the case of Aigisthos.[14] Unlike the sinner who chooses to blame the gods in retrospect for his sin (and is sometimes right), Aigisthos had actually received in advance from Hermes a perfectly explicit warning of the danger he would face if he killed Agamemnon. This fact makes the exasperation of Zeus pardonable; he speaks under the stress of emotion, for his opening words, ὦ πόποι οἷον κτλ., are an exclamation. When exasperated, we exaggerate, saying (e.g.) 'You never wipe your feet!' rather than 'You sometimes forget to wipe your feet', and Zeus's (untrue) generalization illustrates normal behaviour.

A comparable situation is portrayed in *Il.* xxii 490–500, where Andromache, cast into extreme grief and despair by Hektor's death, foresees that if their baby son survives he will endure hardship as an orphan: he will be dependent on the compassion of his dead father's comrades even for a meagre drink, and some other boy whose father is alive will insult him and push him away from the feast. We have no firm evidence for the actual treatment of orphans in early Greece, though we can see what Hesiod preached: *Op.* 330 classifies offences against orphans with maltreatment of suppliants and guests, abuse of one's parents and adultery with one's sister-in-law. Andromache's words are poor evidence. Obviously an orphan, in Greece as elsewhere, was a potential victim of neglect by adults and bullying by another child; and any woman in Andromache's situation is likely to foresee, in the most vivid and concrete terms, continuous and unrelieved realization of all

---

[14] W. Jaeger, *Scripta Minora* (Rome 1960) 322 has some interesting remarks on this exceptional feature of the case of Aigisthos.

the worst possibilities. The passage is realistic dramatic portrayal of a despairing imagination at work, not a social worker's report.[15]

One does not need to ask how a widow in Andromache's position in the archaic Greek world would have evaluated the character and behaviour of a man who went out of his way to be kind and helpful to her orphaned son. It is however legitimate curiosity to ask how other people, not bound to her by kinship or any special obligations, would have evaluated such conduct, and also to ask what Greek words the widow would have used in thanking the man to his face or praising him in his absence. It is, of course, possible that she would not have used the commendatory words which are studied in *M&R*. None of those words is used in *Od.* ii 229–41, where Mentor bitterly reproaches the people of Ithake for their ingratitude in allowing the suitors to appropriate the wealth of a kindly king (cf. Athena in v 8ff). That passage might well be among the first to come into the head of anyone considering the history of morality in the Greek world, because the question it raises are so important.[16] Why is ingratitude treated as meriting reproach? Is ingratitude towards a kindly king worse than disloyalty to a king who asserts a 'claim' to act 'as an *agathos*'? By what criteria do subjects evaluate their rulers? Yet another passage, this time from Aeschylus, raises, without using words translatable as 'good', 'bad', 'admirable', 'shameful', or the like, a moral question of peculiar importance and interest (except, apparently, to commentators on Aeschylus), *Ag.* 950–3. Agamemnon tells Klytaimestra to treat Kassandra kindly:

> τὸν κρατοῦντα μαλθακῶς
> θεὸς πρόσωθεν εὐμενῶς προσδέρκεται.
> ἑκὼν γὰρ οὐδεὶς δουλίῳ χρῆται ζυγῷ.

Since it is in Agamemnon's interest to utter a generalization which, if believed, would tend to the advantage of his concubine, the passage does not tell us what Aeschylus himself thought about ὁ μαλθακῶς κρατῶν. Nor does it tell us whether we are intended by the poet to regard Agamemnon as a man in whom kindly behaviour towards slaves was a firm principle or as a hypocrite who moralizes to his own advantage, for those two alternatives are not exhaustive; he may be a man who, like many of us, is easily induced by perception of advantage or disadvantage to voice a belief which is held by some people and *might* be true. The only thing unambiguously shown by the passage is that the generalization was *available* in 458 BC, and this provokes questions. *Why* should the gods look with favour on a conqueror who behaves nicely to his captives? Is it an eccentric whim on the part of the gods, which we

---

[15] Yet M. L. West comments on Hes. *Op.* 330 'Another uncommon item. An orphan has to go begging . . . ; see *Il.* 22.490–9', and W. den Boer, *Private Morality in Greece and Rome* (Leiden 1979) 38, even turns Andromache's vision into a statement of accomplished fact: 'The little Astyanax was banished from the circle of his friends . . .'.

[16] Cf. Long (n. 3) 123 n. 8, and J. de Romilly, *La Douceur dans la pensée grecque* (Paris 1979) 16f, 20f.

are prudent to humour, or has a religious sanction been created for a mode of behaviour approved by mortals? *Why* is the fact that no one chooses to be a captive slave a *reason* for treating such a slave nicely? And how are our answers to these questions to be integrated with all our other evidence for Greek values in the time of Aeschylus?

Enquiry into the values apparently underlying favourable and unfavourable responses to events which have a moral aspect is a much larger task than scrutiny of passages which contain a common evaluative word, and it seems to me that the narrow focus of *M&R* – narrowed even further by casual treatment of *Il.* i 131 and omission of (e.g.) *Od.* xxiv 445 – has resulted in a wholly unconvincing picture of Greek morality. Granted that it is not practicable to be consistent in translating evaluative words from one language into another (and this is so even when the two languages concerned are both modern and Western), Adkins's insistence on keeping Greek terms in Greek tempts him on occasion, by importing those terms into the description of situations,[17] to make what is actually familiar and intelligible sound alien and mysterious. For example, *M&R* 238 says, 'Odysseus, having killed the suitors for the sake of his *arete*, because it would be *aischron* not to do so ...'. I have always assumed that Odysseus killed the suitors for exactly the reasons for which I would have sought to kill them if I had been Odysseus: they had conspired against my son, pestered my wife and consumed my possessions.[18] It is obscurantist to imply that Odysseus said to himself, 'My God, I must do something about my *arete*!'

Adkins's enquiry into the history of Greek moral values was promoted (*M&R* 1f) by his observation that in the philosophical writings of Plato and Aristotle comparatively little attention is paid to the problem of moral responsibility, a problem of considerable interest to modern philosophers. He rightly seeks to explain the difference by reference to the moral values and presuppositions which Plato and Aristotle inherited from the culture into which they were born. It may be that it is his philosophical starting-point which predisposes him to treat pre-Platonic non-philosophical writers as if they were struggling towards the analysis, definition and classification of virtues; and, conversely, to treat our own morality as the produce of modern philosophy (in particular, of Kantian philosophy; cf. *M&R* 2, 253).

[17] E.g. *M&R* 183 (on Agamemnon's quarrel with Achilles), 231 and 259 (on Socrates) and *MPV* 55 (on Solon). In *MPV* 141 the translation of Th. vi 39.1 φύλακας μὲν ἀρίστους εἶναι ... βουλεῦσαι δ' ἂν βέλτιστα ... κρῖναι δ' ἂν ... ἄριστα as 'most *agathoi* guardians ... best counsellors ... best judges' might just conceivably be defended by arguing that 'be ἄριστος' does not have quite the same connotations as 'do ἄριστα' (cf. *GPM* 70f on καλῶς ~ καλός), but I do not know how many people would be convinced by such a defence. (I am grateful to Ms Cynthia Farrar for drawing my attention to the example.)

[18] R. Pfeiffer, *Ausgewählte Schriften* (Munich 1960) 17, sees the killing of the suitors as something which the archaic Greek world regarded as 'natural' but which 'das rechtliche Denken' of a later age was not so likely to accept. True, but it is feeling, not thought, which is the point at issue in *M&R* 238.

The notion that our society lacked a moral ingredient until Kant fed it in should not be allowed to pass without scrutiny. I am not thinking simply of the fact that out of those few people who actually study moral philosophy not all find the doctrine of the Categorical Imperative appealing at the time and hardly any recall five years later what it says. A fact of far greater significance is the continuity and wide diffusion of general moral rules which have some degree of superficial affinity with the Categorical Imperative but are much older than Kant. 'Do as you would be done by' is Christian (Mt 7.12) and pre-Christian;[19] it is most commonly treated, especially in the upbringing of small children, as a rule of self-regarding prudence. The unconditional claim of duty (to the law of God)[20] is also Christian, foreshadowed by the pagan gods' unwillingness to tolerate violation of the rights of suppliants.[21] 'How would *you* like it if . . . ?' is neither prudential nor religious, but an appeal to the imagination and human solidarity; cf. *GPM* 268–72.

As for moral responsibility, Kant's attempt at metaphysical level to reconcile freedom of the will with causal determination can fairly be called 'a hopeless failure, as has often been pointed out',[22] and his statement (*Critique of Pure Reason* B 582f) 'although we believe the action to be thus determined, we none the less blame the agent' is false, because we don't.[23] The question, 'Was this person free to abstain from that action?' is a question which understandably interests philosophers and theologians,[24] and courts of law often have to pretend that it is answerable,[25] but in most circumstances we ask a different question, '*How difficult* was it for this person to abstain from that action?' The answer is commonly determined by our relations with the person whose action we are judging and by the function of the judgement in its practical context. An individual tends to excuse himself (not surprisingly, since he knows how the forces acting on him were experienced, which no one else can know) and those to whom he is bound by affection and loyalty (not unreasonably, for people can be expected to try to divert hostility away from their own ambience). Conversely, he seeks reasons for denying merit to an adversary. The key words are 'I/he/etc. never had a chance' and 'Well, it's easy for you/him/etc.!' In Greek literature, where the possibility of direct intervention by deities in human kinds is accepted, the conflict between Hecuba and Helen in E. *Tro.* 914–1032 is paradigmatic (cf. *M&R* 124–7). This conflict is not a seminar on responsibility but περὶ ψυχῆς ἀγών. Nor did the arguments in it

[19]   See Albrecht Dihle, *Die goldene Regel* (Göttingen 1962) esp. 96 and 101.

[20]   Keith Ward, *The Development of Kant's View of Ethics* (Oxford 1972) 167, remarks that Kant produced 'a deeply religious ethics expressed in a radically humanistic terminology'.

[21]   Cf. Hdt. i 159.4, discussed by John Gould, *JHS* xciii (1973) 83f.

[22]   R. C. S. Walker, *Kant* (London 1978) 148.

[23]   This is the kind of thing I had in mind when I expressed reservations (*GPM* 7) about philosophers' assertions about what 'we' say, think or feel.

[24]   The idea of 'self-damnation' is important to many Christians; cf. *JHS* xciii (1973) 58, on modern attitudes to Agamemnon's dilemma.

[25]   Punishment without 'blame' is not unknown, and a judicial sentence has several determinants other than the judge's assessment of the defendant's responsibility.

have to wait for the sophistic age, for the same notions operate in epic. Note in particular *Il.* i 178 and 290f, where Agamemnon decries Achilles' pre-eminent strength and skill in battle as a gift of the gods and therefore not adequate grounds for a high evaluation of Achilles. When Homer portrays Agamemnon in *Il.* xix 85–138 as blaming his treatment of Achilles on distortion of his wits by an external (superhuman) force, and no one contests or comments on the excuse, we recognize a familiar situation: if we are glad to see a quarrel settled, we do not hark back to its origin and dispute the terms in which face is saved, whether we believe them or not[26] (key-words: 'Something came over me', 'I can't think what made me do it' and 'I wasn't myself at the time').

It may well be thought that the picture I have given of ancient and modern morality is cynical and 'reductionist' in the sense that it reduces morality to politics. I will compound the offence by declaring my conviction that the contrasts commonly drawn between ancient and modern morality lose their appeal when we turn our attention critically to the values implicit in the resolution of everyday dilemmas, and in ordinary conversation, interviews, advertising and press reports of proceedings in local government and the magistrates' courts. My 'reduction', however, does not touch moral philosophy, which is legitimately and interestingly concerned to investigate the relation between morality and reason.[27] According to his definition of morality, the philosopher must abstract the moral aspect or ingredient from actions which will not necessarily seem to the agent to admit of dissection, and he is likely to distinguish, in the case of any word of commendation or disapproval, between its 'moral sense' and 'non-moral senses'. Such a distinction is not as easy as it might seem even in the case of ἀγαθός, as we see from Pl. *R.* 379a–c. Plato there makes an argument turn on the inclusion of a good person (in this case, God) in the category of ἀγαθά. Beginning with the premise that God is ἀγαθός, Socrates asserts (a) οὐδὲν τῶν ἀγαθῶν βλαβερόν, (b) what is not βλαβερόν does not βλάπτειν, (c) what does not βλάπτειν does not κακὸν ποιεῖν, (d) what does not κακὸν ποιεῖν cannot be κακοῦ αἴτιον, (e) ὠφέλιμον τὸ ἀγαθόν and so (f) αἴτιον εὐπραγίας; therefore (g) τὸ ἀγαθόν is not πάντων αἴτιον but κακῶν ἀναίτιον; therefore (h) God, since he is ἀγαθός, cannot be πάντων αἴτιος.

Plato is not playing tricks with us here. He is aware (indeed, the awareness is fundamental to his metaphysics) of the affinity between our response to a person who is κακῶν ἀναίτιος and our response to nourishing food or fertile land; and aware, I think, that *as an experience* a response which even the most refined analysis would allow to be moral may be indistinguishable from an

---

[26] I find myself in essential agreement with Lesky (n. 13) 41f on Agamemnon's admissions and apologies, but where Lesky speaks of 'two sides of the same coin' I would prefer to speak of two coins which have the same nominal value but are acceptable social tender in different circumstances. Cf. also Lloyd-Jones (n. 4) 14f.

[27] The immensity of the gulf between the logic of morality and the experience of morality may be glimpsed in A. N. Prior, *Papers on Time and Tense* (Oxford 1958) 51–8.

aesthetic reaction. Sloppy table manners can create more implacable enmities than pride or callousness; if we cause the death of a bird by accident, a pretty bird that sings is a more grievous burden on our conscience than an ugly bird that croaks; and 'nauseating' as a term of moral disapproval is not just a metaphor.[28] The determinants of the moral values of an individual or a society are remarkably heterogeneous. That is why I stressed in *GPM* (e.g. 1–4, 46f) the inconsistent, incoherent and unsystematic nature of Greek (or any other) popular morality. In criticizing me for this Adkins (*Problems* 147f)[29] points out that 'a functional structure may exist in the absence of rational design' and that the grammar of a language is an example of systems which 'exhibit coherent structures in the absence of grammarians' (etc.) 'to design them'. I welcome this analogy, but employ it differently. The generalizations ('rules') which constitute a descriptive grammar of a language include some of very wide application, but a great number each one of which applies to a single word or to a group of words definable only by enumeration. Few rules cohere in the sense that one is predictable from another or explicable in the light of others. During the continuous process of change which characterizes a living language, rules contract and extend their domains, some perish and others are born. The determinants of linguistic change, as of morality, are heterogeneous. The rules are not at any moment coherent or systematic to the extent which we expect of the product of deliberate, rational planning and deduction, and in speaking of human behaviour that is the standard of coherence and system which I apply. A comparable lack of coherence and system is apparent in moral, legal and religious codes; fervent adherence to the Fifth Commandment is not only logically comparible with total rejection of the Second, but compatible in practice, as much of human history shows.

In the work of ancient philosophers the distinction between moralizing (i.e. telling us how we ought to behave) and moral philosophy (i.e. telling us how we ought to think about morality if we wish to avoid logical error) is harder to discern than in modern philosophical works, because the 'evangelical' ingredient in ancient philosophy is greater. This has a bearing on the question posed in the opening sentence of *Problems* (143), 'Do moral philosophers affect the values of nonphilosophers . . . ?', and affects explanation of any changes which might be discerned in Greek morality during a given period. Moral change is most spectacularly determined by technological change; a new 'can' generates a tempting 'ought' and its consequences provoke a reflective 'ought not'. Less spectacularly, any completed action demonstrates a 'can' by virtue of being completed and so takes its place in the range of possible models available to any subsequent agent. That the utterances of philosophers might cause moral change is implied by Ar. *Ra.* 1491–9 (in conjunction with 905–

---

[28] I invite the reader to consider the reaction of his own stomach to the comment made in *M&R* 237 on the Athenians under the Thirty Tyrants: 'The democracy squealed, as democracies will; but it is difficult to see what cause it had for complaint.'

[29] Cf. also Gould, *CR* xxviii (1978) 287. The statement in *Problems* 148 about my view of the 'structure' of popular morality is incorrect, despite the verisimilitude imparted by inverted commas.

1098), fr. 376, Telekleides frr. 39f. We can understand why comic poets should say this, but we are not obliged to believe them. There is, however, no reason *a priori* why a dramatist should not exploit an idea which he has taken directly from a philosopher: that is to say, from the moralizing element, intelligible and memorable without sustained intellectual effort on the part of the hearer or reader, in the work of someone whose distinctive contribution to ethics is rigorous argument not so easily understood and remembered. Equally, there is no reason why an idea expressed by an intellectual should not be widely disseminated (*nescit vox missa reverti*) and generate an innovation at popular level.[30] The difficulty, for the historian of literature or of morality, is to decide when, if ever, that has actually happened. It will not do simply to treat the grumbles of characters in comedy or the polemic of intellectuals hostile to rhetoric (*Problems* 146) as evidence that Athenian forensic speakers actually used persuasive sophistical arguments which subverted popular values. Even in academic life I have heard perfectly clear expositions described as 'sophistical', 'laboured' or a 'rigmarole' by people who resented the conclusions to which the exposition pointed, and it is to be expected that old men in comedy will complain about 'clever' young men. In any case, the rhetorician did not teach his pupils how to override the jury's values but (like a modern barrister) how to exploit those values.

Moreover, a reflex of philosophical moralizing is hardly to be distinguished from a reflex of didactic poetry, proverbs or oracular maxims – any of which may itself be the ancestor of a moralizing passage in a philosophical work – or of a simple but penetrating idea suggested by a certain conjunction of circumstances and articulated by a political or forensic speaker or even a participant in a conversation. On Adkins's own premisses Theognis 147f

ἐν δὲ δικαιοσύνῃ συλλήβδην πᾶσ' ἀρετή 'στιν,
πᾶς δέ τ' ἀνὴρ ἀγαθός, Κύρνε, δίκαιος ἐών·

is a landmark in the history of Greek moral thinking: 'suddenly . . . we find . . . the amazing couplet'. Now, the authors of the *Theognidea* exercise, as a rule competently and on occasion excellently, σοφία in the sense which the word had in their day, but they are not 'philosophers', and I doubt whether we should class them as 'intellectuals', if we define[31] an intellectual as a person who enjoys (as many artists and creative writers do not) analytical investigation. It is not in the least necessary (*pace M&R* 79) to imagine that Theognis 147f is the product of deep reflection. A didactic poet may be, so to speak, a character in the drama of his own life, and the couplet sounds like the cry of someone who thinks he has suffered intolerable injustice at the hands of a self-

---

[30] *Problems* 144 confuses the classification popular/sectional/idiosyncratic with the antithesis traditional/innovative. *Problems* 145 debits me with an 'apparent' reason for citing (*GPM* 10–13) references to philosophy in the orators which is not the same as the reason I actually gave *ad loc.*
[31] Cf. n. 9 above.

satisfied and generally admired adversary. Hesiod could have voiced the same sentiment at the time when he was composing parts of *Works and Days*;[32] so could the Penelope of *Od.* xxi 312ff in the mood of the moment.

Adkins remarks (*Problems* 156 n. 6) that I 'like modern parallels'. I do indeed, and grow daily fonder of them, in the confident belief that they help to remind us that the few Greeks whom we know through surviving literature are only samples drawn from a poulation whose days were as fully occupied by action and speech as ours. In part ii, ch. 2 of *Piccolo Mondo Antico* Fogazzaro makes Luisa utter a perceptive and unconventional view on why people believe in immortality, heaven and hell. I do not know whether Fogazzaro had any literary or philosophical 'source' for this view but I do recall hearing it expressed, less neatly but with no less conviction, by a semi-literate Italian countrywoman. Perhaps her words were a reflex, through many intermediaries over an eighty-year period, of Luisa's, but it is equally possible that they occurred independently to her and to Fogazzaro; possible, too, that Fogazzaro himself was drawing upon the rebellious ideas which surface from time to time in an ambience dominated by orthodox preaching. There is a certain analogy between such a case and Hecuba's subordination of the divine world to νόμος in E. *Hec.* 798–805 or the deadly criticism of majority rule attributed to the youthful Alkibiades in Xen. *M.* i 2.45. Neither of those two arguments would have been appropriate or welcome in a speech delivered to a mass jury, and it would be contrary to the available evidence to assign either of them to the broad stream of 'popular morality'; yet neither need be attributed to a cultural and intellectual stratum above the level of ordinary, intelligent speculation.

---

[32] Cf. J. P. Vernant, *Mythe et pensée chez les Grecs* (Paris 1974) chs 1–2, and Lloyd-Jones (n. 4) 32f, 35f. The cursory treatment of Hesiod in *M&R* 70–3 concludes rather simply that 'Homeric society' and 'Hesiodic society' are different societies. It would have been more interesting to consider the extent to which 'Homeric' and 'Hesiodic' evaluations could be uttered not only in the same society but even by the same individual in different circumstances.

10

The Poetry of Archilochos

The fragments of Archilochos present us with a remarkable variety of metrical form. Two forms, the sequence of elegiac distichs and the sequence of iambic trimeters, were destined to a longer and more illustrious life than the remainder. Their functions were increasingly differentiated during the Classical period, and it is natural for us, viewing Archilochos from the standpoint of later times, to think of him as a composer in at least two quite different genres: on the one hand, elegiacs, and on the other, that group of forms to which I shall consistently refer as a whole by the Greek word ἴαμβοι (though I retain the English adjectives 'iambic' and 'trochaic' in their usual restricted sense). This impression, howver, may be mistaken. The rhythmical affinities of the elegica distich are, of course, with the dactylic hexameter; but architecturally it has affinities with the many different epodic distichs employed by Archilochos – and, indeed, with the so-called ἀσυνάρτητα – in so far as it consists of a longer verse followed by a shorter one.[1] Linguistically, differentiation between elegiacs and ἴαμβοι is neither clear nor significant.[2] Both of them, like archaic epitaphs and dedicatory poems, give an epic colouring to a predominantly vernacular phonology and morphology;[3] and the colouring in elegiacs is stronger, since many epic phenomena, metrically intractable in most forms of ἴαμβοι, are welcome in elegiacs. Both of them – and this is true of archaic elegiacs in general,[4] and of verse inscriptions, irrespective of metre – eschew the particles and combinations of particles which are characteristic of epic and highly convenient in dactylic rhythm: νυ, ῥα, ἀλλά τε, γάρ τε, δέ τε, καί τε and μέν τε, all of which are prominent in the hexameters of the later philosophical poets, Xenophanes (frr. 13D.3, 20D), Parmenides and Empedokles.

[1] Cf. H. Fränkel, *Dichtung und Philosophie des frühen Griechentums* (Munich 1962) 168 n. 44.
[2] Cf. Fränkel 168.
[3] Cf. O. Hoffmann, *Die griechischen Dialekte* vol. iii (Göttingen 1898) 182ff; the epic colouring is less in Archilochos and Kallinos than in their successors.
[4] Cf. A. Fick, *NJA* i (1898) 509. ἐπε[ί ῥ’]ἐ[ν]εδέξατο is presented by Diehl[3] in Mimnermos fr. 12(A).1; ἐπείτ’? In Solon fr. 3D.33 καὶ θαμά is interpreted by Bergk (but not by Diehl) as καί θ’ ἄμα.

When we turn from form to content and ethos we observe that Archilochos's elegiacs, like his ἴαμβοι, may be ostensibly addressed to individuals. The gnomic character explicit in the elegiac frr. 7D (κήδεα μὲν στονόεντα κτλ.) and 9D (Αἰσιμίδη κτλ.) and implicit in 10D.3f (οὔτε τι γὰρ κλαίων κτλ.) is prominent also in the trochaic frr. 58D (τοῖς θεοῖς ἰθεῖα πάντα κτλ.), 64D (οὔ τις αἰδοῖος μετ᾽ ἀστῶν κτλ.), 67aD (θυμέ, θύμ᾽, κτλ.) and 68D (τοῖος ἀνθρώποισι θυμός κτλ.).[5] The moral tone of all these fragments can be summarized as a shrug of the shoulders, a gesture of resignation which contains at the same time an assurance of self-sufficiency. The gesture of resignation is not, however, a gesture of modesty; with the boast of the elegiac fr. 1D (εἰμὶ δ᾽ ἐγὼ κτλ.) we may compare the trochaic fr. 66D (ἐν δ᾽ ἐπίσταμαι μέγα κτλ.) and the powerful lines in one of the new iambic fragments, 35LB.7ff (ἐς τοῦτο δὴ τοι τῆς ἀνολβείης δοκ[έω] / ἥκειν; κτλ.). Flippancy is the keynote of the elegiac fr. 6D (ἀσπίδι μὲν Σαΐων τις κτλ.), and the vigorous exhortation to drunkenness in 5aD.6ff (ἀλλ᾽ ἄγε σὺν κώθωνι κτλ.) is matched in the ἴαμβοι by lively anticipations (frr. 69D and 72D) and descriptions (frr. 28D, 34D, 102D) of sexual indulgence. The grim joke of the elegiac fr. 4D (ξείνια δυσμενέσιν λυγρὰ χαριζόμενοι) appears to recur in the new trochaic fr. 114LB.5ff, where ξεινίων φειδοίατ[ο is found in the same context as σ]υμβαλόντε[ς, ἀθρόοι γενοίμεθα and τεύχεσιν πεφρ[αγμένοι. Fr. 2D (ἐν δορὶ κτλ.) is a polished conceit in which, ὥς᾽ ἐμαυτὸν πείθω, at least three separate jokes lie in ambush for the hearer. Fr. 15D (συκῆ πετραίη), though outwardly decorous in phraseology, is none the less a clever joke about a prostitute.[6] Every note which is struck in the elegiac fragments is struck also in the ἴαμβοι.[7] The reverse is not true; we do not encounter in the elegiacs the ferocity or the undisguised obscenity of the ἴαμβοι; but since the elegiac fragments amount to less than forty intelligible lines in all, representing at the most fourteen poems and possibly as few as eight, the completeness of their coincidence in ethos with the ἴαμβοι is more significant than the incompleteness of the reverse process.

I propose now to investigate the extent to which the hypothesis that for Archilochos there was no generic difference between elegiacs and ἴαμβοι accords with the history of both genres in the archaic period as a whole.

---

[5] Cf. M. Treu (ed.), *Archilochos* (Munich 1959) 164, 166ff.

[6] Cf. E. Riess, *Classical Weekly* 1943/4, 179, and Treu 195. More than one indecent interpretation is possible. Σ Arat. 1009 says, καὶ παρ᾽ Ἀρχιλόχῳ ἡ ὑφ᾽ ἡδονῆς σαλευομένη κορώνη ὥσπερ κηρύλος πέτρης ἐπὶ προβλῆτος ἀπτερύσσετο (fr. 49D, with Wilamowitz's ὥστε for ὥσπερ). This resembles an extract from an ornithologist's notebook, if κορώνη was really a bird: but if she was a person, it is in keeping with frr. 28D and 102D. I suspect that κορώνη must be added to Archilochos's numerous terms for 'prostitute'; in fr. 49D the girl, ὑφ᾽ ἡδονῆς σαλευομένη (cf. ἀμφισαλευομένης, *Anth. Pal.* v 55, 6; Hor. *Sat.* ii 7. 50), 'was, as it were, a κηρύλος shuffling its wings . . .'. Thus in fr. 15D Pasiphile is compared to a host who can entertain lavishly because of the herds and flocks which he βόσκει; cf. the classical πορνοβοσκός.

[7] Cf. A. Hauvette, *Archiloque* (Paris 1905) 245ff; the insistence of F. Della Corte, *RF* lxviii (1940) 93, that the ethos of elegiacs and ἴαμβοι is fundamentally different seems coloured by the later history of the genres.

Something of value may be learnt from the relevant metrical termonology; but not, I fear, in LSJ, where the principal articles on metrical terms are characterized by the highest degree of confusion and error.[8] Comparatively few of the terms used by the Hellenistic metricians are attested in extant Greek Literature before the end of the fourth century BC, and where they occur the context rarely permits us to say exactly what they mean.

The word ἴαμβος first occurs in fr. 20D of Archilochos, καί μ(οι) οὔτ' ἰάμβων οὔτε τερπωλέων μέλει, in which, according to Tzetzes, he is 'speaking to those who urge him to write' when he is overcome with grief at his kinsman's death. Whether Archilochos means by ἴαμβοι his poetry as a whole, irrespective of its metrical form, or one category of his poetry only, we do not know; three different interpretations of οὔτ' ἰάμβων οὔτε τερπωλέων are possible,[9] and both meanings of ἴαμβοι would be reconcilable with each of the three. Aristotle (Rhet. 1418b 28ff) used ἴαμβος to denote a poem of Archilochos composed of iambic trimeters and also to denote one composed of trochaic tetrameters. If, therefore, a poem was called ἴαμβος in the fourth century BC by virtue of its form, the minimum denotation of the word at that time was 'a poem in iambic or trochaic rhythm'. This would be consistent with Herodotos's statement (i 12.2) that Archilochos spoke of Gyges ἐν ἰάμβῳ τριμέτρῳ i.e. 'in a trimetric ἴαμβος', 'in an ἴαμβος composed of trimeters' (cf. i 47.2 ἐν ἑξαμέτρῳ τόνῳ). It is also consistent with Ar. Ra. 661, where Dionysos quotes an iambic trimeter which he describes as coming from 'an ἴαμβος of Hipponax'. Clearly iambic rhythm came to be regarded as the characteristic rhythm of ἴαμβοι, for in Pl. R. 400b (where Socrates is referring to the technical terminology of Damon) and Arist. Rhet. 1408b 33 ἴαμβος is the name not of a kind of poem but of a kind of rhythm, and in both passages is distinguished from τροχαῖος. The derived word ἰαμβεῖον, which first occurs in Kritias fr. 2D.4 and Ar. Ra. 1133, 1204, denotes in all three passages an iambic trimeter. Naturally we cannot know for certain whether Kritias and Aristophanes would have applied it also to trochaic tetrameter. Damon would certainly not have done so; nor would Aristotle, for in speaking of the dialogue of drama (Poet. 1449a 21, Rhet. 1408b 35) he distinguishes between the ἰαμβεῖον and the τετράμετρον.

Whereas it was natural to discuss ἴαμβος before ἰαμβεῖον, in the case of the pair ἔλεγος/ἐλεγεῖον it is necessary to reverse the process. The neuter noun ἐλεγεῖον first occurs in Pherekrates (fr. 153K.7), Kritias (fr. 2D.3), Thucydides (i 132.2f) and the poem composed by Ion of Samos for the dedication of Lysander at Delphi. Neither of the meanings 'verse inscription' or 'dedicatory poem' is reconcilable with Pherekrates and Kritias, and the meaning 'epitaph' is not reconcilable with any of them. The meaning 'elegiac distich' suits

---

[8] There are some excellent remarks by U. Bahntje, 'Quaestiones Archilocheae' (Diss., Göttingen 1900) 23ff.

[9] 'Neither ἴαμβοι (as creative work) nor relaxation', 'neither ἴαμβοι (as expression of bitterness and enmity) nor enjoyment', and 'neither ἴαμβοι nor any other enjoyment'.

Kritias and Thucydides, and also Pherekrates, who used the plural to denote discontinuous verses cited from a poem (Theognis 467ff) which was composed in elegiacs (cf. also Pl. *Meno* 95d), but does not suit Ion, who denotes by ἐλεγεῖον a poem of two distichs; and the meaning 'poem in elegiacs' does not suit Pherekrates. The most plausible hypothesis is that ἐλεγεῖον in the fifth century BC normally meant 'elegiac distich', and that Ion used it with reference to a poem of two distichs because that poem was serving a purpose very often served by a single distich. Thus ἐλεγεῖον, like ἰαμβεῖον, was a unit characteristic of a kind of poem called ἴαμβος, it follows that at some time and place in the Greek world before Pherekrates there existed a kind of poem called ἔλεγος, and that the elegiac metre was, or became, characteristic of it.[10]

The word ἔλεγος is first attested in the dedication of a Echembrotos the Arkadian, cited by Pausanias x 7.4[11] and dated by him to the first Pythiad. This poem, although it distinguishes ἔλεγοι from μέλη, does not tell us what they were. Since the musician and poet Sakadas of Argos, associated with Echembrotos by Pausanias on the strength of the Pythian records, is also described in *De musica* (8) as ποιητὴς μελῶν τε καὶ ἐλεγείων μεμελοποιημένων and (9) as leader of a school of elegiac poets, it seems that an association between the generic term ἔλεγος and the elegiac metre existed in the Peloponnese in the sixth century BC. This is not to say that every Peloponnesian ἔλεγος had always been composed in the elegiac metre, or that every poem in elegiacs would have been called ἔλεγος by the Peloponnesians. Nor does it imply that the word ἔλεγος was known to Archilochos and his Ionian contemporaries. It is noteworthy that in Attic tragedy ἔλεγος first appears in Euripides, who uses it five times; it is absent from Aischylos and Sophokles, despite the great range of their vocabulary for all kinds of vocal and musical utterance. In four of these five Euripidean instances the word refers to a lament; but in two of them (*Hel.* 185, *IT* 146) its accompaniment by the adjective ἄλυρος suggests that Euripides thought of it as normally – that is to say, in circumstances which do not call for lamentation – accompanied by the lyre.[12] In the fifth passage (*Hypsipyle* 62 Page) Ἀσιάδ᾽ ἔλεγον ἰήιον denotes the music which Orpheus played on his lyre to enable the crew of the Argo to row in time.[13] This points to something different from the ἔλεγοι of Echembrotos and the elegiacs of Sakadas, which were threnodic in character and accompanied by the flute.[14] The semantic history of ἔλεγος and ἐλεγεῖον thus seems

[10] The feminine noun ἐλεγεία, 'poem composed of elegiac distichs', first occurs in Arist. *Ath.* 5.2. Kallimachos refers to his own elegiac poems as ἔλεγοι (fr. 7Pf.13); that is the earliest certain example of an equation ἔλεγοι = ἐλεγεῖαι.

[11] The dedicatory poem defies restoration as elegiacs, but Pausanias is clearly quoting, not paraphrasing, and I assume that the essentials μέλεα καὶ ἐλέγους are authentic.

[12] Cf. M. Platnauer on *IT* 146.

[13] It is Ἀσιάς because it is played on the lyre (cf. E. *Cy.* 443, where Ἀσιάδος ... κιθάρας is associated with merrymaking) and ἰήιος perhaps because of the association between rowing and rhythmic cries (cf. ἰήιον ... Παιᾶνα in A. *Ag.* 146).

[14] Cf. D. L. Page in *Greek Poetry and Life* (Oxford 1936) 206ff on threnodic and aulodic elegiacs in the Peloponnese and the ancestry of the elegiac passage E. *Andr.* 103ff. K. Zacher, *Ph.* NS xi

to be one in which arbitrary choice and historical accident have played their familiar role in semantics; there were ἔλεγοι, of which some were threnodic and aulodic, of which some, again, were in the elegiac metre; and that is how and why the elegiac distich acquired the name by which it was known universally from the fifth century BC onwards.

This survey of terminology offers no grounds for doubting the conclusion which I drew from the community of ethos between the elegiacs and ἴαμβοι of Archilochos: no grounds for believing that he regarded them as different genres. It also leaves open the possibility that he used the word ἴαμβοι with reference to all the forms of poem which he composed, their common characteristic being not their metre or language but the type of occasion for which they were composed – their 'social context', in fact. It has, however, raised another question: since an association between the elegiac metre and threnodic poetry existed in the Peloponnese at least as early as the beginning of the sixth century BC, are we to suppose that the elegiac metre was employed from prehistoric and preliterate times independently in both Ionia and the mainland, or that it was imported from one to the other? And, if it was imported, who imported it to whom?

A decisive answer to this question is indicated by the fact that the language of Tyrtaios[15] is derived not primarily or directly from epic but from the Ionic vernacular.[16]

I base this statement in the first instance on two phenomena in Tyrtaios's adaptation (fr. 7D.21ff) of the theme represented also in X 66ff, where Priam envisages his own fate. The point I am making is, strictly speaking, independent of the problem of the chronological relation between these two passages;[17] on that, I confine myself to an affirmation of agreement with Wilamowitz[18] to the extent of saying that the passage of Tyrtaios is a transmutation into elegiacs of a passage which already existed in hexameters.[19] Be that as it may, where Homer (71) has νέῳ δέ τε πάντ' ἐπέοικεν Tyrtaios (27f) has νέοισι δὲ

(1898) 8ff, in pursuance of a fallacious inference that elegiacs must always have been the characteristic metrical form of the threnodic ἔλεγος, combined with a persuasive argument that the origin of the word ἔλεγος is to be sought in a cry like the Germanic welaga, posits an original refrain Ϝηλεγε Ϝηλεγε Ϝη. It might just as well have been ελεγελεγελεγει.

[15] My argument assumes the authenticity of the fragments of Tyrtaios, since (a) I see no force in the contrary arguments, many of which, in any case, were offered before the publication of the papyrus (fr. 1D.50ff) which refers to the tribal army, (b) in their preference for ⌣‿⌣ over ‿| and for ⌣‿‿ over ‿| the fragments agree with early elegy in general but disagree with the elegiacs of Xenophanes and Kritias, and (c) in spirit and style they are archaic (cf. Jäger, SPA W 1932, 537ff, and E. Römisch, Studien zur älteren griechischen Elegie [Frankfurt 1933] 70ff).

[16] Cf. O. Hoffmann and A. Debrunner, Geschichte der griechischen Sprache i³ (Berlin 1953) 75.

[17] On this much-discussed problem cf. O. von Weber, 'Die Beziehungen zwischen Homer und den älteren griechischen Lyrikern' (Diss., Bonn 1955) 35ff.

[18] Die Ilias und Homer (Berlin 1920) 95f n. 1; cf. C. Rothe, Jb. d. philol. Vereins zu Berlin xxxiii (1907) 302.

[19] There are, of course, other passages in elegiac poets (e.g. Theognis 389–92) which make a similar impression, but for which no actual hexametric original can be suggested.

πάντ᾽ ἐπέοικεν, followed by ὄφρ᾽ ἐρατῆς ἥβης ἀγλαὸν ἄνθος ἔχῃ. To understand 'a young man' as subject of ἔχῃ,[20] or to take ἄνθος as subject[21] and
understand 'them' as object, is linguistically possible,[22] but neither is smooth
or natural. All awkwardness could have been avoided if Tyrtaios had availed
himself fully of epic diction and said νέῳ δέ τε; but, like all the early elegists
and the composers of verse inscriptions, he eschewed those combinations of
particles which are characteristic of epic and distinguish it from drama and
prose.[23] Now, in the previous line (26) he says αἰσχρὰ τά γ᾽ ὀφθαλμοῖς καὶ
νεμεσητὸν ἰδεῖν. Again we have a syntactical inconcinnity avoidable[24] by
simply observing initial digamma in ἰδεῖν and saying νεμεσητά. Tyrtaios
would have found the digamma of ἰδεῖν observed often enough in epic; and
his Lakonian audience observed it in their own speech; why then did he strike
an alien note by dropping it? In fact, he normally drops it. πίονα ἔργα (fr.
4D.7) is a Homeric phrase and ὄβριμα ἔργα (fr. 8D.27) is of familiar epic type;
περὶ ᾗ πατρίδι, a certain emendation in fr. 6D.2, accords with the general
poetic observance of digamma in the possessive ὅς. Elsewhere, observance of
digamma could be restored by emendation in three passages (fr. 1D.46, 6.8,
8.15), but there remain seven passages in which it could not (fr. 3aD.1, 3b.1,[25]
3b.2, 4.4, 6.9, 8.7, 9.19). In this respect Tyrtaios's principle is that of the Ionian
elegiac poets, but it is conspicuously at variance with that of all the archaic
verse inscriptions, which, whatever their metre and whatever the degree of
epic phraseology they adopt, observe digamma in regions where the vernacular observed it and omit it in regions where the vernacular omitted it.[26] Among
the verse inscriptions particular mention should be made of a sixth century
stele from the sanctuary of Athena Chalkioikos at Sparta, which contains
either a hymn or a long dedication;[27] beginning Παλ(λ)ὰς Ἀθαναία
θύ[γατερ Διός (?), it exhibits at one point].τα Ϝιδε(ί)ν, with digamma
written and metrically observed.

I do not believe that non-observance of digamma in Tyrtaios can be
explained by the fact that to a Lakonian what might appear especially remarkable in epic would be not the general presence of digamma but its occasional
absence, so that he would regard its non-observance as epic colouring; this

---

[20] Cf. passages cited by Diehl[3] *ad loc.*

[21] Cf. LSJ *s.v.* ἔχω (A).A.I.8.

[22] Cf. Kühner–Gerth, *Gr. Gr.* i 87. Theognis 381f provides a parallel shift from pural to singular, and so does Archilochos fr. 58D.4f if Friedländer's emendation κείνοισ᾽ is right.

[23] Cf. p. 97 n. 3 above.

[24] The 'natural' way of making a point like that of 21ff may be seen in Pl. *Lg.* 879c, where we
may suspect that Tyrtaios was not far from Plato's mind: αἰκίαν οὖν περὶ πρεσβύτερον ἐν πόλει
γενομένην ὑπὸ νεωτέρου ἰδεῖν αἰσχρὸν καὶ θεομισές· ἔοικεν δὲ νέῳ παντὶ ὑπὸ γέροντος πληγέντι
ῥᾳθύμως ὀργὴν ὑποφέρειν κτλ.

[25] Πυθωνόθεν οἴκαδ᾽ is hardly susceptible of emendation; cf. *Maia* NS xv (1963) 19f (= pp. 300–1
below).

[26] Cf. B. Kock, 'De Epigrammatum Graecorum Dialectis' (Diss., Göttingen 1910), and
Hoffmann–Debrunner 79f.

[27] A. M. Woodward, *ABSA* xxix (1927/8) 45ff; *SEG* xi 652; L. H. Jeffery, *The Local Scripts of
Archaic Greece* (Oxford 1961) 192, 199.

explanation might suffice if Tyrtaios were an isolated phenomenon, but it does not account for the situation in Ionic elegy or verse-inscriptions. Nor do I believe that a satisfactory explanation is afforded by acceptance of the story that Tyrtaios was not a Lakonian but an Athenian. This story is first found in Plato (*Lg.* 629a), and since it illustrates the theme of community of interest between Sparta and Athens which is so prominent throughout the first part of *Laws* (cf. 642b–d) I am by no means persuaded that it antedates the fourth century BC. It is evident from Strabo's discussion (362) that there was nothing in the matter of Tyrtaios's own poems to justify the story.[28] It should also be observed, first, that not everyone agreed with Plato, since Tyrtaios in the Suda is 'Lakonian or Milesian', and, secondly, that Tyrtaios was not the only eminent figure of archaic times to be awarded a posthumous and gratuitous Athenian nationality in the fourth century. Ephoros (fr. 137J) did the same for Thukles, the founder of the first Greek colony in Sicily, and produced a story to explain how an Athenian came to be leading an expedition of Chalkideans and Naxians; Hellanikos (fr. 82J) and Thucydides (vi 3.1), however, plainly regarded Thukles as a Chalkidean.

If Tyrtaios in composing elegiac poetry for a Lakonian audience adopted a poetic form long familiar in the Peloponnese and brought it into conformity with Homeric epic by adoption of Ionic eta and elements of epic phraseology, his persistent non-observance of digamma is not intelligible. If, however, he adopted a poetic form which existed only in the Ionic vernacular, his decision to conform with the most conspicuous phonological features of that vernacular, while also drawing upon epic material and phraseology, calls for no further justification.

Adoption of the hypothesis that the elegiac distich was an Ionic poetic form, and that it was brought into the Peloponnese by, or in the time of, Tyrtaios makes it difficult to accept both the statement by Herakleides Ponticus (fr. 157 Wehrli), summarized in *De musica* 3, that elegiac poetry was composed by Klonas and the statement of *De musica* 5 that Klonas was earlier than Archilochos. Rejection of part, or even the whole, of this complex of statements attached to so shadowy a figure as Klonas does no violence to my conscience.[29]

Tyrtaios's poetry is hortatory in character, and the gnomic and narrative elements in it are plainly subservient. Between his ethos and that of Archilochos there is at first sight a great gap. This gap is half bridged by Kallinos, the contemporary[30] of Archilochos, who composed at least one hortatory

[28] Strabo's positive deduction of Tyrtaios's Spartan nationality was, of course, fallacious (cf. Schmid–Stählin, *Gesch. d. gr. Lit.* i.1 385 n. 2); it is the absence of any contrary indication which is important.

[20] Klonas is associated with Terpander, and is thus closer to historical reality than – for example – Olympos; but the Suda calls even Olympos ('pupil of Marsyas . . . before the Trojan War') ποιητὴς μελῶν καὶ ἐλεγείων.

[30] Strabo's reason (647) for dating Kallinos *before* Archilochos, in which he is followed by (e.g.) Schmid–Stählin i. 1 357, and Lesky, *Gesch. d. gr. Lit.* 111, was trivial; the evidence of Lydian and

poem in elegiacs, from which our only extensive citation (fr. 1D) is drawn. The other half of the bridge is furnished by the ἴαμβοι of Archilochos, in which a hortatory element is clearly discernible: frr. 52D (ὦ λιπερνῆτες πολῖται κτλ.), 74D (μηδεὶς ἔθ᾽ ὑμέων εἰσορῶν θαυμαζέτω), 127LB (πάντ᾽ [εὐφρ]ονες γένεσθε [. . .] . . . συμβα[λεῖ]ν δ᾽ ἴωμεν ἔντεα) and perhaps 114LB.7 (ἀθρόοι γενοίμεθα).

Thus Tyrtaios did not inherit a tradition of hortatory elegiacs;[31] he took one element out of the many which existed in Ionian poetry, and by exploiting its possibilities created a new genre. There was nothing inevitable about this; had there been no Tyrtaios, another individual might have developed a different element of Ionian poetry in quite another direction. An instructive parallel is provided by the circumstances in which elegiacs supplanted hexameters as the metrical form regarded as appropriate for epitaphs. Down to the middle of the sixth century BC all extant verse inscriptions – epitaphs, dedications and graffiti alike – are, with two exceptions,[32] in dactylic hexameters. One exception is the iambic graffito preceding the hexameters on the Ischia cup.[33] The other is the syllables]γαλης αντι φιλημ[on a dinos from the Heraion at Samos dating from the second half of the seventh century;[34] presumably με] γάλης ἀντὶ φιλημ[οσύνης, a phrase which would fit into an elegiac pentameter but not into a dactylic hexameter. Then, within the period 560–540, both the elegiac distich and the iambic trimeter appear simultaneously in both epitaphs and dedications.[35] The dominance of the hexameter collapses;

Assyrian chronology (cf. H. Kaletsch, *Historia* vii [1958] 1ff) proves no more than that both poets were active in the middle of the seventh century BC. I see no reason to date any poem of Tyrtaios earlier than 640. His statement (fr. 4D) that Messenia was conquered by πατέρων ἡμετέρων πατέρες in the reign of Theopompos is perfectly valid if made eighty years after the conquest; it would be exaggeration, or imprecision, only if the interval approached a hundred years; and it is not Tyrtaios's purpose to give us chronological information.

[31] F. Dümmler, *Ph.* liii (1894) 201ff, argued that the original function of elegiac poetry was that of the war-dance ('patriotische Ekstase'); but he conceived the problem in the wrong terms.

[32] I exclude from consideration the elegiac dedication (fr. 17D) and epitaph (fr. 16D) attributed to Archilochos in the *Anthology*; the attribution is to be treated with greatest caution, considering the irresponsibility with which verse inscriptions were assigned to famous names (cf. M. Boas, *De epigrammatis Simonideis* [Groningen 1905] 32ff, Wilamowitz, *Sappho and Simonides* [Berlin 1913] 192ff, F. Jacoby, *Hesperia*, xiv [1945] 196 n. 138), and in any case I am concerned here only with verses actually extant on stone. A dedication from Perachora, presented in *SEG* xi 224 as the vestiges of an elegiac distich and dated there 'c. 750ᵃ', makes much better sense when interpreted (Jeffery 122ff) as a hexameter, and the date should probably be brought down by a hundred years.

[33] *SEG* xiv 604.

[34] Jeffery 328 and pl. 63 no. 1.

[35] The earliest specimens in each category are (I give Jeffery's dates; J₁ refers to *The Local Scripts*, J₂ to *ABSA* (vii [1962] 115ff): (a) Elegiac epitaphs: grave of Chairedemos, Attica, *c.* 560? (*SEG* iii 55 = Peek, *GVI* i 159 = J₁ pl. 3 no. 20 = J₂ 118); grave of Tettichos, Attica, *c.* 560–550? (*IG* i² 976 = *GVI* i 1266 = J₁ pl. 3 no. 19 = J₂ 133); (b) Elegiac dedications: dedication of Aristis, Nemea, *c.* 560? (*SEG* xi 290 = J₁ pl. 24 no. 5); dedication of Exoides, Kephellenia, *c.* 550–525? (*IG* 9.1 649 = J₁ pl. 45 no. 5); (c) Iambic epitaphs: grave of Archias and his sister, Attica, *c.* 540? (*SEG* x 452ᵃ = *GVI* i 74 = J₁ pl. 4 no. 31 = J₂ 139l); (d) Iambic dedications: dedication of Alkmeonides, Attic, from Ptoion in Beotia, *c.* 550 (*IG* i² 472 = J₁ pl. 3 no. 25).

elegiacs and iambics contend briefly for the succession,[36] and the elegiacs win decisively; from the third quarter of the sixth century onwards they are the favoured metrical form of epitaphs and dedications alike, a new genre created by a change in fashion of which we cannot expect to know the cause.

Let us now turn back from the threshold of the Classical age to Archilochos himself.

Any critical assessment of a poet necessarily involves an assessment of his originality. This is a practicable undertaking when the work of a poet's precursors in his own genres is available; but the extant Greek poetry of earlier date than Archilochos is the poetry of Homer and Hesiod. With *Works and Days*, which, like so many poems of Archilochos, is ostensibly addressed to a named individual, Archilochean poetry has a limited community of content and ethos. The animal fable, regarded in antiquity as a speciality of Archilochos, is represented by one impressive example in *Works and Days* (202ff). The gnomic element predominant in *Works and Days* is, as we have seen, conspicuous in Archilochos; there are autobiographical elements in both *Works and Days* and *Theogony*, and *Works and Days* gives very free expression to Hesiod's own emotional attitudes. Yet the vaster scale of the Hesiodic poems amounts in itself to a fundamental difference of genre, and the flippancy, wit, scurrility and blatant eroticism of Archilochos are profoundly out of tune with Hesiod's earnestness.

Archilochos's difference from Hesiod is trivial by comparison with his difference from Homer. His spirit and ethos have often been described as a conscious rejection of the Homeric ideal,[37] and this interpretation appears to have good support in fr. 60D (οὐ φιλέω μέγαν στρατηγὸν κτλ.)[38] and 6D (ἀσπίδι μὲν Σαΐων τις κτλ.). The Homeric hero is capable of fear, but not of flippancy on the subject of his fear. The Homeric hero, again, makes handsome provision for his own sexual satisfaction, but he does not writhe under the lash of unrequited passion,[39] as Archilochos appears to do in frr. 104D (δύστηνος ἔγκειμαι πόθῳ κτλ.) and 112D (τοῖος γὰρ φιλότητος ἔρως κτλ.).[40] The sexual phraseology of epic is circumscribed and decorous; Archilochos's is neither.[41]

Historians and critics of literature are telling the truth when they say that

---

[36] It should be noted that among the verse inscriptions tentatively assigned on epigraphic and archaeological grounds to the decade 550–540 elegiacs predominate; and from the fact that Chairedemos's name, so apt to iambics, is incongruously placed in an elegiac distich it might be inferred that the composer of his epitaph regarded elegiacs as more appropriate than iambics.

[37] Lesky 104f; Fränkel 151f, 167; B. Snell, *Die Entdeckung des Geistes*, 3rd edn (Hamburg 1955) 89; Treu, *Von Homer zur Lyrik* (Munich 1955) 266. For reasons given above (p. 103 n. 30) I do not think that it is legitimate to speak (with Fränkel 155 n. 18) of a deliberate rejection of the martial ideal which inspired Tyrtaios.

[38] Treu, *Von Homer zur Lyrik* 71, 78, notes a change from the Homeric *Sehweise* in this fragment; cf. Snell 89.

[39] Cf. Snell 92f.

[40] Bonnard's translation of fr. 245LB assumes, perhaps wrongly, that the poet is speaking of himself.

[41] A new fragment (134LB) presents us with an earthy Aristophanic word: γυναῖ]κα βινέων[.

Archilochos introduces us to a new world.[42] If, however, they assume that what is new to us, because of the great gaps in our knowledge of antiquity, was also new to Archilochos's contemporaries, they go somewhat beyond the positive evidence and fail to do justice to some anthropological considerations which are not without evidential force.

Given the chronological order Homer–Hesiod–Archilochos and the fact that Hesiod falls between Homer and Archilochos in genre and ethos, two alternative hypotheses are rivals for our adherence. One is that between the early eighth century and the middle of the seventh the values and ideals of Greek society changed, and that Homer, Hesiod and Archilochos represent successive stages in the spiritual development of the Greek people.[43] This hypothesis can take a firm stand on the solid fact that the structure of Greek society in the eighth and seventh centuries did undergo important changes, notably in the physical expansion of the Greek world, the enlargement of its contacts with other cultures, the development of wealth in forms other than booty and land, and the increasing demand of the citizen body within each community for a share in political power.[44]

The alternative hypothesis would regard Hesiod and Archilochos as two different personalities through whom, shortly after the introduction of writing, poetic genres of long standing found expression at a very high artistic level. These two poets would represent the substratum upon which a highly specialized development of epic poetry had been superimposed. Homer and Archilochos would represent the obverse and reverse of the same coin; there would be no point of contact between them, and therefore no field of conflict. So it might be said tht Archilochos expressed the feelings of men as they really were; Homer described the actions, thoughts and speech of a race of imaginary heroes, ἀνδρῶν ἡρώων θεῖον γένος, οἳ καλέονται ἡμίθεοι, creatures of superhuman ferocity and extravagance. One may reject a view of one's ancestors by talking about *them*, but it is not so easy to reject a view of them by talking about one's own day. The coexistence of Homeric and Archilochean poetry is, after all, less striking than the coexistence of Attic ἐπιτάφιοι with *Acharnians*.[45] The very nature of epic poetry demanded professional rhapsodes and the creation of a highly conventional language, and didactic poetry made similar demands in so far as it rivalled epic in scale, whereas the maker of short songs was naturally always an amateur. The rhapsodes, their imagination committed to a heroic world, not only elaborated a special language (which, of course, influenced their concepts, as language does) but filled in the details of this world with a conventional ethos and theology; the extent to which a professional reciter–composer may adopt a conventional *Sehweise*

---

[42] Snell 87f; R. Pfeiffer, *Ausgewählte Schriften* (Munich 1960) 43.

[43] Cf. Pfeiffer 46.

[44] Cf. Snell 116. This view is developed to extreme lengths by Bonnard, xxx ff, xliv f, lvi; and it influences his interpretation of some of the fragments, e.g. 9D (Αἰσιμίδη κτλ), which really says no more than 35LB.3f (φάτιν μὲν τὴν πρὸς ἀνθρώπω[ν κακὴν] / μὴ τετραμήνης μηδέν).

[45] Cf. O. Seel in *Festschrift Franz Dornseiff* (Leipzig 1953) 311.

and project himself into a different culture is a problem which deserves further study by comparativists and not *a priori* generalizations.[46] The amateur poet, by contrast, expressed feelings and beliefs in terms familiar to contemporary society.

The second hypothesis must, I think, concede one point: the simple fact that when Archilochos, as a young member of a distinguished family on the island of Paros in the seventh century, grew up to find himself a poet of genius, he did not compose epic narrative or heroic catalogues or didactic poetry; he composed songs. We are bound to wonder whether he would have done that if he had been born a hundred years earlier; and, idle though such speculation may seem, we would be wise to leave open the possibility that it was changes in Greek society during the early seventh century which had made the song artistically respectable. But then we must ask another question of a less speculative nature: what were Greek songs like a hundred or two hundred years before Archilochos? Song is a phenomenon of every human culture without exception, however primitive; therefore there *were* Greek songs before Archilochos. I am reluctant to use as evidence those remnants of Greek folksong and cult-song which have survived in citation, for none of them is necessarily of the degree of antiquity which we are seeking; in a culture which produces and values poetry of high quality, subliterate poetry tends to become subliterary and derivative.[47] We need to draw our evidence from the songs of modern preliterate cultures. If we find that the same characteristics recur in many different parts of the world, in cultures so diverse that they have little in common except an ignorance of writing, we shall be tempted to attribute these characteristics to the preliterate songs of the Greeks;[48] and if we find some of them present also in the fragments of Archilochos himself and of other archaic Greek poets, we shall not be rational if we do not yield to the temptation. Before I embark on this part of my enquiry, let me say firmly and clearly that I am well aware that the Ionians of the seventh century BC were immeasurably more civilized (in any sense of the word which deserves serious consideration) than any of the cultures to which I shall shortly refer. They were, however, not yet generally accustomed to the use of writing, and for that reason I shall draw my comparative material from cultures in which the possibility of writing has simply not been envisaged. I want to give a picture of the preliterate in its purest form.

---

[46] On the development of special characteristics in epic cf. C. M. Bowra, *Heroic Poetry* (London 1952) esp. chs 2–4. A trivial but striking example is provided by a Dayak epic (which 'if it were given in full, would take nearly a whole night to sing') mentioned by H. M. and N. Chadwick, *The Growth of Literature* (Cambridge 1940) iii 480f: 'a long house which a bird could only just fly through in a day'; cf. γ 321f.

[47] Cf. the manner in which popular music and the background music of films echo the idiom of the concert-hall of fifty years ago.

[48] The preliterate foundations of Archilochean poetry are acknowledged by Snell 84, Lesky 101, 105, and A. R. Burn, *The Lyric Age of Greece* (London 1960) 159. A valuable survey of the general characteristics of preliterate poetry is given by C. M. Bowra, *Primitive Song* (London 1962), from which many of my examples are drawn.

A high proportion of songs in preliterate cultures can be described both as 'traditional' and as 'practical'; that is to say, they are spells, charms or hymns, handed on without verbal change from one generation to another, and regarded and used as furthering or completing some action or process. In more advanced cultures work-songs retain an affinity with this genre; an obvious Greek example is ἄλει μύλα ἄλει, in which the singer feels subconsciously, as her primitive ancestor believed more explicitly, that she speeds the work of the handmill, as one speeds an animal or person, by giving it verbal encouragement. But people do not sing only when they are trying to hasten the end of necessary work, propitiate a god, bring game to the net, ruin an enemy, or enchant a lover; they also sing while they are waiting, travelling, entertaining friends, or dancing on an occasion which does not demand traditional ritual utterance; and it is with these categories of song – song as self-expression, not song as magic[49] – that I am concerned.

The general characteristics of preliterate song may be summarized as follows:

1 It very commonly expresses an emotional reaction to an event. This reaction may be fear, shame, rage or despair; the singer may boast; he may lament his rejection in love or deplore his own sexual inadequacy; he may also commiserate with himself or reproach and ridicule himself, his soul or guardian spirit, or other people.

2 The event to which the song is a reaction may be treated as past, so that the song is a narrative; more often, the event is treated as present at the time of singing.

3 Not surprisingly, the song may be addressed to a person, or category of people, whom the composer would often have occasion to address in ordinary life. It is, after all, normal for us to express our emotional reactions in speech to others, and this characteristic of normal utterance is carried over into song.

4 The emotion expressed in the song is not necessarily that of the composer; he may adopt the personality and standpoint of another person – individual or generic – or, indeed, of two other people in succession or alternately.

5 The event which evokes the emotion is most commonly actual, but may be wholly or in part imaginary.

---

[49] The distinction is not always a sharp one, and its validity might be questioned by the school of linguistic pragmatism of which B. Malinowski, *Coral Gardens and their Magic* (London 1935) ii 4ff, 45ff, is the most persuasive exponent. It is, however, a distinction drawn easily enough for practical purposes in many cultures. Cf. M. Vanoverbergh, *Anthropos* lv (1960) 464, on those songs of the Isneg people of Luzon which 'could be sung at any time', and R. F. Fortune, *Sorcerers of Dobu* (London 1932) 251: 'Every Dobuan is a song-maker. Any interesting event calls forth a number of songs. . . . The song-maker is proud of his creation, proud of its originality. . . . The song-maker must give his permission before his song is used for the dance. Later on it may gain currency in far-away places, for the songs are sung everywhere, on canoes and about the land, after they have been danced to.'

6 Accurate generalization about obscenity in preliterate song is not easy, since there is reason to believe that some modern observers have been inhibited in their selection of specimen songs. It is, however, clear that sexual relationships form the context of a very high proportion of preliterate song,[50] and precise physical reference is normal, though the language in which such reference is made is oblique and symbolic.[51]

7 The song may refer to animals, birds or insects, either as possessing personalities of their own, or as constituent elements in an event with strong emotional associations, or as symbolic of actual persons or categories of people. The sung fable, in which the conversation or interaction of two animals is related, is a special aspect of this general phenomenon.[52]

I offer now a selection of examples, each of which illustrates at least one of the characteristics which I have summarized.

1 From the Solomon Islands.[53] A man called Fagalafuna grew frightened when the canoe in which he was sailing came into very rough water. Another member of the crew afterwards composed a song which began 'Fagalafuna, your body shivers with fright.' The song contains the words 'you, a kindly person, rock the canoe for me', using a verb which in the spoken language is used of a spirit communicating with the living by moving an inanimate object; I take it that this treatment of Fagalafuna as a spirit is sarcastic. At the end of the song we have 'I yearn for . . .' and this is repeated with a variety of persons as its object; it is not clear to me whether the speaker is here describing his own emotions or shifting to what he imagines to have been the standpoint of Fagalafuna in the rough sea.

2 From New Guinea.[54] A song taunting a man called Seduna, who lives on the island of Sanaroa, for making too much fuss when his wife was taken away to another island, contains the words 'Embark and come to sea, Sanaroa mothers. Wishing to marry, they wail, and you, Seduna, wail.' Not all these words describe an actual situation; they are a way of saying two things: (a) 'the women of Sanaroa wish that they could go and find new husbands, like Seduna's wife', and (b) 'Seduna is no better than a woman'.

3 Also from New Guinea.[55] A song beginning 'I go hillwards to the home of the dead' was composed with reference to a person who had recently died. The first person singular represents the dead man, not the composer of the song.

[50] Cf. Fortune, *loc. cit.*

[51] Cf. Vanoverbergh 468; note especially the song on 481ff.

[52] On the fable and other types of animal story cf. K. Meuli, *Herkunft und Wesen der Fabel* (Basel 1954).

[53] G. C. Wheeler, *Mono-Alu Folklore* (London 1926) 257.

[54] Fortune 302.

[55] Fortune 257.

4 From Hawaii.[56] A song beginning 'O my land of rustling trees!' and con-
tinuing in the first person throughout is intended to represent the emotions
of a shark at Pearl Harbour homesick for the coast off which it was reared.
5 From the Vedda people of Ceylon.[57] A mother sang to her children during a
thunderstorm a song which includes the words 'See, brother, thunder and
lightning coming from seaward; it is getting bad; my body is losing strength.'
'Two princes' appear in the song; it is not clear to me how much of it is
addressed to them and how much addressed by one of them to the other.
6 From the Andaman Islands.[58] In a song beginning 'Thou art sad at heart'
the singer expresses his emotions towards a past event by addressing himself
as he was at that time.
7 From the South African Bushmen. A cat is imagined as the person uttering
the song, and she reports what a lynx said of her. Another Bushman song
tells a story about a beetle and a mouse; and there are Eskimo songs which
represent a dialogue between a raven and a gull or between a blowfly and a
waterbeetle.[59]

The characteristics which I have summarized and illustrated are so conspicuous in Archilochus that citation is superfluous – I am sure that many
fragments have come into your kinds already – and they may be thought adequate evidence for the hypothesis that although Archilochos's poems were
more lucid, rational and formally polished than any of my specimens, he drew
his inspiration from poetic genres which had existed among the Greeks from
time immemorial. But we cannot let the matter rest there. Anthropological
data have a value which is both cautionary and suggestive; sometimes they
curb the assurance with which we interpret the fragments of archaic poetry,
and at other times they prompt positive interpretations which might not have
occurred to us without their aid.

There are four aspects of preliterate song which must affect our interpretation of the fragments of Archilochos. The first three have already been mentioned: that short songs express feelings, that the feelings which a song
expresses are not necessarily those of its composer, and that the event or situations which is the object of the feelings expressed is not necessarily actual.
The fourth and most important aspect of preliterate songs is that they are
composed in comparatively small communities where everyone knows everyone else's business. The majority of the specimens would be unintelligible to
us without the helpful explanations provided by the anthropologists who
recorded them and knew the circumstances in which they were composed. If
we had to treat them as isolated fragments, we should constantly misunderstand their point.

---

[56] Chadwick iii 351.
[57] Bowra, *Primitive Song* 67.
[58] Ibid. 102.
[59] Ibid. 159, 162ff.

The significance of the fact that songs express feelings is simply that, whereas we are entitled to demand consistency of belief from a philosophical poet (subject always to the acknowledgement that change of mind is the hallmark of rationality) and consistency of standpoint from the author of a big work which exhibits a distinct architectural design, we cannot expect to find consistency of feeling in a poet who does not even profess to be a systematic thinker. Propositions about the supernatural and generalizations about fate or the nature of human life may be identical in form with informative communications on the weather or the price of fish, but the purpose which they serve, on the lips of most of those who utter them, is the expression of emotional attitudes. When Archilochos says (fr. 7D.5ff) 'for ills that cannot be healed the gods have created endurance as remedy', or (fr. 64D.1f) 'when a man has died his fellow-citizens grant him neither respect nor good repute', his words are not in any serious sense contributions to theology or sociology, but the kind of thing we all say to relieve our feelings even when different situations, only a short time before, have evoked the opposite feelings. This consideration sets a limit to our reconstruction of a poet's system of beliefs.[60] Even so, we could plausibly reconstruct some elements of his biography from the predominant and recurrent notes struck in his work, were it not for those other aspects of preliterate song which I have briefly mentioned and must now discuss more fully: the assumed personality and the imaginary situation.

The *locus classicus* is that passage of *Rhetoric* (1418b 23ff) in which Aristotle says that when it would be an error of taste for a man to speak *in propria persona* he may represent another as speaking for him, 'as Isokrates does in *Philippus* and the *Antidosis*, and as Archilochos does in criticizing others' (καὶ ὡς Ἀρχίλοχος ψέγει); 'for he represents a father as speaking about his daughter[61] in the ἴαμβος "χρημάτων ἄελπτον οὐδέν ἐστιν οὐδ᾽ ἀπώμοτον"' (fr. 74D) 'and Charon the carpenter in the ἴαμβος of which the beginning is "οὔ μοι τὰ Γύγεω"' (fr. 22D). On this passage several observations must be made.

Aristotle tells us explicitly that οὔ μοι τὰ Γύγεω were the opening words of a poem. He does not say this of χρημάτων ἄελπτον κτλ., but it is nevertheless highly probable; the poem as a whole he regards as an example of ψόγος, but neither the line which he quotes nor the eight following lines (provided by Stobaios) are in themselves ψόγος, nor are they about anyone's daughter, being in fact about an eclipse of the sun and the attitude of mind which that

---

[60] This must be remembered also in the interpretation of narrative and drama. Pfeiffer 49f notes a moral and theological difference between *T* 96ff and α 32ff; but this difference is in no way evidence for a change in Greek ideas; it is the difference between a man excusing his own actions and the gods regarding a man's actions. Cf. A. *Ag.* 1500–12.

[61] I.e. 'a man who is the father of a daughter speaking about his daughter'; πατέρα τινά would be doubtful Greek, since πατήρ is one term of a two-term relation, as Plato observes in *Smp.* 199d. Alternative interpretations, neither of which seems to me attractive, are: 'Archilochos's father speaking about Archilochos's daughter' and 'Archilochos's father speaking about Archilochos's father's daughter'. Nor does the identification of the father and daughter as Lykambes and Neobule seem to me persuasive; these two people figured elsewhere in Archilochos's work, but there is never a shortage of fathers and daughters (cf. Arist. *Meteor.* 356b πρὸς τὸν πορθμέα).

event may properly engender. Had Aristotle wished to select from a poem whose purpose was ψόγος a passage which actually ψέγει, he would surely have made a better choice than the verse χρημάτων ἄελπτον κτλ. I therefore assume that he means not 'in that well-known ἴαμβος, when he says χρημάτων ἄελπτον κτλ.' but 'in the ἴαμβος "χρημάτων ἄελπτον κτλ.'", i.e. 'the ἴαμβος of which the opening words are χρημάτων ἄελπτον κτλ.' In two poems of Archilochos, therefore, the opening words represented the utterance of someone other than the poet himself, and in neither case is the hearer warned that this will be so. An interesting parallel is provided by fr. 10LP of Alkaios, ἔμε δείλαν ἔμε παίσαν κακοτάτων πεδέχοισαν. The poet is not speaking in propria persona, since the words agreeing with ἐμέ are feminine; but we know both from the papyrus text and from Hephaistion that this verse was the beginning of a poem.[62] Anakreon fr. 40P (= PMG 385), ἐκ ποταμοῦ 'πανέρχομαι πάντα φέρουσα λαμπρά, where the first person is feminine, may also be the opening line of a poem, since it is quoted as a specimen verse by Hephaistion.[63] How did Aristotle know that the imagined speaker of χρημάτων ἄελπτον κτλ. was the father of a daughter, and that of οὔ μοι τὰ Γύγεω κτλ. Charon the carpenter? The analogy of the second epode of Horace,[64] where we learn in line 67 that fenerator Alfius has been expressing his feelings to us from the beginning, has naturally suggested that somewhere towards the end of οὔ μοι τὰ Γύγεω κτλ. there occurred some such words as 'thus spoke Charon the carpenter'.[65] I am not so sure of this. There are, after all, many ways in Greek by which a speaker may tell us his own name – by boasting, prayer, imprecation, and other forms of solemn and emotional utterance, or by reporting, or half-reporting, what others have said or may say to him or about him.[66] The possibility that Charon named himself appears to me to have at least equal status with the alternative possibility that Horace in Epode 2 is imitating an Archilochean procedure, especially since the disliked and despised profession of Alfius and the ending of Horace's poem strike a note of irony which I cannot see anyway of importing into any reconstruction of Archilochos's poem. As for χρημάτων ἄελπτον κτλ., the possibility that the father who is the imagined speaker neither named himself nor was named by the poet appears to me more probable; for if he was named, why does Aristotle not name him too?

Now, since in preliterate cultures the person whose emotions are expressed in a song is commonly identified not by any words of the song itself but by the community's knowledge of the entire context of the song, it would not surprise me if some of the poems of Archilochos and of other early Greek poets were of this kind. Indeed, it would surprise me more if they were not. I

---

[62] Cf. Wilamowitz, Sappho und Simonides 305 n. 2, and Page, Sappho and Alcaeus (Oxford 1955) 291ff.

[63] I am not quite sure that it is not quoted as a variant ch ia . . . occurring among ch ch . . . .

[64] Cf. Eduard Fraenkel, Horace (Oxford 1957) 59f.

[65] Hence fr. 19LB.

[66] E.g. A 240, Pl. Euthphr. 4e–5a, Ap. 23c, 26e, Ar. Th. 77.

am not shaken in this view by Horace. A procedure which would be natural in a citizen of an Aegean island community in the seventh century BC would cease to be natural to the poet or acceptable to his audience long before the age of Augustus. It would cease to be natural, in fact, before the age of Perikles. This reflection must make us wonder whether Aristotle was right in thinking that in frr. 22D and 74D Archilochos was employing a literary device for the expression of *his own* views. It is also of some importance for our assessment of Kritias's famous judgement on Archilochos.[67] Kritias said (fr. 44DK) that we should not have known so much to the discredit of Archilochos if the poet had not told us himself, for example, that he was a lecherous adulterer and that he had thrown away his shield. How far was Kritias right? And how far are we today right when we assume, unless we have positive evidence to the contrary, that whenever a fragment of an early Greek poet contains a first person singular it comes from a genuinely autobiographical poem? Are we sure – to take a crucial example – that Archilochos himself threw away his shield in combat against the Saioi? I put this question because consideration of pre-literate song has left me no longer sure. But, in case anyone still feels that data derived from cultures greatly inferior in material development, organization and rationality to archaic Greece are irrelevant, it is not impossible to base a similar plea on Greek data alone. I cited earlier a fragment of Alkaios and one of Anakreon. These came into the question solely because they exhibit feminine participles and adjectives in agreement with a first person singular and thus indicate beyond doubt that the poet is assuming a personality other than his own. But, if and when the poet assumed a personality which was male but still not his own, should we expect that the poem – let alone a line or two cited from it by metricians or anthologists – would reveal to us that it was not autobiographical? Even if the poet declared his hand as Horace does, the bare citations which constitute most of our knowledge of early Greek lyric would not tell us whether or not he declared it. A similar consideration is raised by two more fragments of Anakreon (*PMG* 376, 378), both cited by Hephaistion as specimens of verse-forms, which say respectively (376) 'Now I have launched myself from the White Cliff and dive into the grey sea, drunk with passion' and (378) 'I fly towards Olympos on light wings'. In both cases the nature of what is said proves that the poet is envisaging an imaginary situation; but if and when he envisaged a situation which, although equally imaginary to him at the time of composition, is physically possible or even commonplace – e.g. elaboration of the themes 'I am angry', 'I am lonely' or 'I am in love' – how could the ancients know, and how could we know from the type of citation on which we have to depend, whether the situation was actual or not?

The approach to the fragments of Archilochos which I am by now implicitly advocating is open to two objections, both of which are, in my submission, insufficient.

---

[67] Cf. Treu, *Archilochos* 156ff, on the Greeks' attitude to Archilochos and their predilection for moral judgements on poets.

First, it may be said: surely a poet would not risk ill fame by composing in the first person singular songs which did not actually refer to his own experience but might be interpreted as doing so. The answer to this objection is that everything depends on the conventions of the society in which he lives. If the first person in a song is generally taken to refer to the poet, then obviously he will not risk damage to his own reputation. If, on the other hand, it has been accepted for generations – as it is accepted in so many preliterate cultures – that a poet in making a song may assume any personality he likes, the possibility that all his songs will be taken to refer to him will not occur to him. The community in which he composes a song knows its context; other communities in which it is sung will not know or care who composed it, nor will they necessarily know or care what its original point and meaning were.[68] The spread of literacy is likely to change this attitude.[69] As a poet becomes accustomed to the idea that his songs will be known in many different communities, now and in the future, not simply as good songs but as *his* songs, and that when collected and transmitted they will represent *him* to posterity and will compete powerfully with the oral tradition of his valour in battle and other virtues, a new concept of the relation between his own personality and the whole body of his work will form itself in his mind.[70] Of course this concept was already present and active in Greek society in the time of Archilochos. My argument is that it coexisted and competed with a different concept, that a song, once composed and sung to people who knew its composer and the circumstances of its composition, drifted loose, as it were, from its composer. In Greek society the problem is complicated by the existence of a third concept, that of the poet as moral teacher. The balance between these different concepts was not the same for any two genres of poetry, nor was it the same for any two periods or regions. My concern is to rescue from neglect a primitive concept which seems to me of fundamental importance for the interpretation of songs composed in a period of transition from preliteracy to literacy.

The second objection is that my approach to the fragments is more than cautious; it is agnostic to the point of nihilism, and if it is valid it implies that we no longer know about Archilochos many things which, in common with the Greeks themselves from the Classical period onwards, we have always believed that we knew. Part of the answer to this objection is Plato's: we must go where the wind of reason blows, however barren the shore upon which it casts us. For my part, I would be content if I were able to demolish some portion of what has lately been built upon such foundations as the fragments of Archilochus provide. I can, however, offer a less uncompromising answer. I do not suggest, or believe, that the fragments in which Glaukos or Perikles is addressed express emotions other than those of the poet himself. I do suggest

[68] Cf. p. 108 n. 49.
[69] Cf. Burn 160f.
[70] Cf. Theognis 19ff.

that the poet's own standpoint is only one among the standpoints which he adopted in the composition of poetry. The fragments may tell us less of Archilochos's own life than we thought they did; but they tell us no less than before what standpoints he preferred to adopt, what emotions he preferred to express, and what topics he preferred to develop; and these are the elements which compose his personality as an artist.

DISCUSSION

Wistrand. May I take up a question which relates also to the lecture and discussions of yesterday and the day before? Archilochos's language is, on the whole, the traditional epic language, as Mr Page emphasized yesterday. There is, however, a certain amount of independence, in that the non-Ionic elements of epic language are, generally, avoided. Mr Scherer made a point of that in his lecture. Now this seems to me to be a remarkable fact, for surely Archilochos mastered the whole of the epic language and could have used any part of it if he had wanted to. I had thought that for an archaic poet there was one great linguistic distinction, that between his own vernacular which he learnt in his everyday life, and the poetic language which he learnt in the school of the epic poets. But now it seems that for Archilochos the line of demarcation is between non-Ionic epic language on the one hand and on the other hand the Ionic dialect both as it appeared in the epics and as it was used in daily speech. This union of epic and contemporary Ionic would be much easier to understand if we accept Mr Dover's view that the gap between epic language and contemporary Ionic was considerably less than it is generally supposed to be, because many of the words and forms which the chance of transmission make us regard as exclusively Homeric may in fact have lived on in archaic time; they may have existed in the folksongs which Mr Dover has dealt with today. I should very much like to believe that Archilochos, when he spoke about himself and addressed his fellow-citizens, employed a language which he felt to be his own language, and not *die epische Kunstsprache*.

Dover. My view of the 'gap' between epic language and the language of Archilochus is largely determined by the fact that although there are so few archaic Ionic inscriptions they so often present us with words which in literature are known only from epic or early Ionic poetry. These inscriptions show us, moreover, many words which do not occur in extant literature at all, but which, if we found them in a papyrus and not in an inscription, we should call 'poetic'. Therefore I always assume that a word found in early poetry belongs to the spoken language of the time, unless we have positive evidence – as we sometimes have – to the contrary.

I do not want to draw upon ethnological material to excess, but I must mention the fact that in many primitive cultures there exist songs composed entirely in archaic dialect, and when new songs are composed they draw upon this dialect in varying degrees – and indeed upon neighbouring languages, feeling, that this kind of 'seasoning' is appropriate to poetry.

As for folksongs: some of these transmitted to us in Greek may be very old, but I am not sure which ones. For that reason I thought it best not to cite any; I do not want to complicate the issue by introducing songs which may be influenced by literature.

Page. On the first part of his paper, I should like to ask Professor Dover for further enlightenment on two points. First, does he exclude the possibility that elegiac poetry may have developed independently in Ionia and in the Peloponnese, going different ways, though perhaps originally from some common source? Secondly, on the fragment οὐ φιλέω μέγαν στρατηγόν, is not this very much in the spirit of Homer? The descriptions of Tydeus and Iros are essentially the same; and it is to be noticed that when Homer wishes to describe a particular individual, such as Thersites, he does just what Archilochos is doing – he uses a detailed and highly specialized vocabulary, including numerous ἅπαξ εἰρημένα.

On poems of the type of Charon the Carpenter: I suggest that the comparable examples in Alkaiow and Anakreon were in fact recited by women and written for that purpose. The entertainment of his friends by the poet at a symposium may well include not only an αὐλητρίς but also a female colleague who recites a poem specially composed for the occasion.

The examples from Archilochos are of a different type. In the case of Charon, Professor Dover allowed that there may have been an explicit statement or indication of the speaker's identity; but he seemed to suggest that there may have been no such indication in the piece quoted by Aristotle. I find this rather hard to accept, and in fact I wonder if the lines following those quoted by Aristotle may not give the name of the father, Ἀρχηνακτίδης, and a reference to the daughter, πάις, together perhaps with an indication of the cause of the trouble, γάμος.

Professor Dover's final observations are of the highest importance. No doubt Kritias thought he could quote Archilochos himself to prove that the poet was the son of a slave-mother: but we must reckon with the possibility that this and other statements are founded on poems which had nothing to do with Archilochus himself.

Dover. 1 I have certainly considered the possibility that elegy developed independently in two different regions, but the morphology and phonology of Tyrtaios, especially when contrasted with what happens in verse inscriptions, seem to me to rule it out. Of course, if Tyrtaios was not a Spartan, the whole problem assumes a different complexion; but I think he was.

2 I agree that there is much that is Homeric in οὐ φιλέω μέγαν στρατηγόν. In summarizing two opposing hypotheses I mentioned the fragments which have in fact formed the basis of arguments.

3 In χρημάτων ἄελπτον it is possible that Aristotle's interpretation was based simply on the occurrence, somewhere in the poem, of the words 'my daughter'. Perhaps he believed that Archilochos had no daughter; perhaps he

was right. Of course Charon must have been named somehow in οὔ μοι τὰ
Γυγέω. I am very interested indeed in the suggestion that ἔμε δείλαν and ἐκ
ποταμοῦ may actually have been sung by women; but in this connection I
should like to mention the possibility that there was a much greater mimetic
element in the singing of poems than we know about. Miming in character is
extremely common in the performance of primitive song, and the words
naturally do not betray this.

4   In the interpretation of any fragment whatsoever of Greek poetry we
must ask: do we know who is speaking, and in what connection? Usually the
answer is 'no'. Sometimes we may learn something from the Greek quoter
who had the entire poem before him and could see obvious things in it which
we cannot; but a situation in which a Greek is drawing on biographical anecdotes for his own interpretation of the fragment is something of which we
must beware.

Pouilloux. Le scepticisme dont M. Dover témoigne à propos des renseignements que nous apporte Archiloque sur sa vie et les événements de son temps
me paraît particulièrement précieux. Les historiens m'ont en effet reproché
parfois de ne pas assez demander aux fragments d'Archiloque pour recon-
struire l'histoire primitive de la colonisation thasienne. Je dois avouer qu'en
présence de certaines reconstructions extrêmement ingénieuses (mais com-
bien fragiles!), j'ai toujours eu une certaine timidité. Aujourd'hui, après avoir
entendu M. Dover, j'ai peur non plus de n'en avoir pas assez dit, mais d'en
avoir trop dit. Je partage entièrement sa manière de voir pour aborder l'utili-
sation historique des fragments. Puisque, d'autre part, M. Dover a abordé la
question des inscriptions métriques archaïques, je voudrais simplement lui
poser une question, ainsi qu'aux philologues et métriciens qui sont ici:
lorsque j'ai publié l'inscription du *mnèma* de Glaucos, je n'ai pas cru pouvoir
la ranger parmi les inscriptions métriques. Or W. Peek la tient pour telle
puisqu'il l'a publiée dans l'addendum à ses *Grab-Versinschriften I*. Pensez-vous
que l'on puisse, sans altérer le texte, donner une forme métrique satisfaisante
à cette inscription?

Sur un autre point, l'exposé de M. Dover, comme d'ailleurs celui de
M. Page hier, me paraît soulever une question. Sans doute M. Kontoleon
nous a-t-il montré qu'en raison des rapports très étroits entre Paros et Milet,
Archiloque appartenait encore au monde ionien et 'homérique'. Les exposés
d'hier et d'aujourd'hui, en attirant l'attention sur la communauté du langage,
insistent encore davantage sur cette appartenance. Et pourtant, entre l'art
géométrique du VIIIᵉ siècle en son début, et l'art ionien qui paraît sur la
céramique des années 650 à Thasos, la différence est considérable, comme s'il
y avait eu tout à coup, non pas une conquête technique – la technique des
potiers de l'époque géométrique atteignait une véritable perfection de formes
et de combinaisons linéaires – mais une révolution dans l'esprit même de
cette décoration. Il y a une quinzaine d'années, M. P. de La Coste-Messelière,
dans une communication à l'Académie des Inscriptions, s'était attaché à
montrer que les décorateurs des vases géométriques avaient été enfermés dans

un véritable carcan de conventions et d'interdictions; en 650, cette barrière de défenses et de craintes est assurément levée. Or tout se passe comme si, en littérature, cette différence n'existait pas. Est-il possible d'en discerner les raisons?

Reste enfin la question, toujours reprise depuis le début du siècle, de la créance que l'on peut donner aux comparaisons tirées de l'étude des civilisations dites primitives et de leurs créations. Ne s'agit-il pas toujours, dans ces créations, de poèmes relativement courts et d'un formulaire assez limité? Même si on estime qu'Archiloque suit à sa manière un courant de chanson populaire, les conditions n'étaient-elles pas radicalement différentes par le seul fait qu'il avait derrière lui Homère et Hésiode. Même s'il n'a été à l'origine qu'un créateur parmi d'autres, et dont les œuvres ont survécu seulement parce qu'elles étaient meilleures, la seule présence de la poésie homérique, lui fournissant comme la matière première de son expression et de sa technique, ne modifie-t-elle pas absolument les données? Même si la méthode comparative peut apporter des indications sur les formes de littérature liées à un mode de société donnée, ne croyez-vous pas qu'il serait dangereux de vouloir pousser trop avant cette comparaison, de vouloir y trouver des raisons déterminantes pour expliquer la poésie grecque du VIIᵉ siècle?

Dover. I certainly cannot scan the Glaukos inscription. There are inscriptions which contain a single metrical phrase, and one may be in doubt about the composer's intention; but the Glaukos inscription seems to me undoubtedly prose.

I would rather not express any opinion on the relation between developments in poetry and developments in the visual arts. It is possible, after all, for different arts to develop independently and even in different directions.

I do realize that the Parians were not savages, and certainly the cultures to which I have referred compose songs on a smaller scale than Archilochos. Certainly, too, Archilochus had Homer and Hesiod behind him; I want to emphasize that he *also* had a tradition of popular song behind him.

Treu. Mit sehr viel besseren Argumenten als je zuvor wurde gezeigt, dass Tyrtaios von Homer abhängig ist, nicht umgekehrt. Auch dass nun vom Ethos des Dichters gesprochen wurde, freut mich besonders. Ich stimme der Datierung des Kallinos und Archilochos in die gleiche Zeit gern zu; Strabons Satz darf nicht dahin gedeutet werden, dass Kallinos einer anderen Generation angehöre. Stilunterschiede und thematische Unterschiede zwischen Elegien und Iamben habe auch ich bei Archilochos noch nicht finden können, möchte aber doch fragen, ob nicht manche Themen einem Genos vorbehalten bleiben, die Tierfabeln z.B. den Epoden (fast nur ihnen). Bei aller Gleichzeitigkeit von Iamben und Elegien in Inschriften glaubte Friedländer lokale Unterschiede annehmen zu können, näml. Fehlen iambischer Inschriften in einigen Gebieten (war es Korinth?). Bei Paus. x 7.4 ist das Epigramm und die historische Tatsache authentisch; wenn er die Aulodie düster nennt, so ist dem wie allen Motivierungen gegenüber Skepsis am Platz.

Bezeugt ist threnodische Elegie für die Peloponnes nicht. Die Frage der Herkunft der Tierfabeln wurde nicht berührt und ist ja auch kaum zu beantworten; kommt die Fabel, wie ich anzunehmen geneigt bin, aus dem Osten, so rückt – nach Prof. Kontoleons Ausführungen – Milet in den Vordergrund. Dass Prof. Dover Material aus Volksliedern anderer Völker heranzog, freute mich ganz besonders. Das lettische Volkslied war in meiner Heimat noch durchaus lebendig; manches ist mir von dort vertraut. Wenn bezweifelt wurde, ob das Charon-Gedicht (22D) einen paradoxen Schluss gehabt haben könne, ob Archilochos Ironie kenne, so hätte hier durch einen Vergleich mit Volkstümlichem der Zweifel gemindert werden können, – auch wenn man von H. Fränkels Rekonstruktionsversuch absieht (Tr. 198f). Es gibt in vielen Sprachen das sog. epilogische Witzwort; eine schöne Sentenz wie 'Immer feste druff!', durch das Folgende – 'sprach der Hahn und stieg von der Henne' – hinterher zum komischen Paradoxon umgekehrt. Dass sog. mimetische Lieder entsprechender Kostümierung bedürfen oder als Aussagen von Mädchen vorgetragen zu denken sind, bestreite ich. Bei einer solchen Annahme würde übrigens – wenn wir uns nicht den Dichter selbst als χοροδιδάσκαλος vorstellen – am Rande die Frage der Schriftlichkeit erneut auftauchen.

Mit 'the song became artistically respectable' wurde das Hauptproblem berührt. Es konnte scheinen, als bestünde nun eine besondere Schwierigkeit, zu unterscheiden zwischen imagined and actual situation, zwischen mimetischem Pseudo-Ich und echter, persönlicher Selbstaussage. Dass es in nicht wenigen Fällen gar keinen Zweifel für mich gibt, dafür sei τὸ πρὶν ἑταῖρος ἐών [79aD] nur ein Beispiel. Musen sind übrigens durch anthropologisches Vergleichsmaterial sonst nicht zu belegen; sie sind nicht aus dem volkstümlichen Lied entlehnt.

Dover. The animal fables of Archilochos seem to have been composed only in epodic metres; my remarks on the essential community of ethos between his elegies and other genres were based on the fact that all the elements of the former are to be found in the latter, not *vice-versa.*

In saying what I did about Echembrotos and Sakadas I assumed that enough was known about their work to afford a basis for the motivation which Pausanias suggests.

I avoided reference to European or Near Eastern folksong because of the possibilities, however remote, that it might have been influenced by the diffusion of Greek motifs and art-forms.

I am very grateful for the information that a paradoxical ending is common in popular proverbs. In what I said about οὔ μοι τὰ Γύγεω, I mean simply that it is very difficult to give it the point which Horace's *Epode 2* has.

By 'making songs artistically respectable' I meant that the fact that Archilochos did not express his poetic genius by composing epic must be taken fully into account by anyone who wishes to deny any development of ideas during the seventh century.

Most certainly κύμασι πλαζόμενος . . . τὸ πρὶν ἑταῖρος ἐών expresses the emotions of the poet himself.

The community in which and for which Archilochos composed was not the whole of Paros, or of Thasos, but simply the people he knew.

Bühler. Eben war davon die Rede, dass Fabeln bei Archilochos nur in den Epoden vorkämen. Eine Gegeninstanz in Fr. 48D (in den Jamben). Ein Wort noch zur Bedeutung von ἴαμβος im Fr. 20D. Herr Dover hat davor gewarnt, dass wir den späteren Gebrauch im metrischen Sinn ohne weiteres auf die Frühzeit rückprojizieren. Er hat auch Zeugnisse dafür angeführt, dass das Wort auf trochaïsche Tetrameter und Hinkiamben angewendet wurde. Dieser Gebrauch scheint mir nicht so ungewöhnlich, da das trochaïsche und das iambische Versmass tatsächlich etwas Gemeinsames haben. Ich kann aber immer noch nicht recht glauben, dass das Wort ἴαμβος je in Bezug auf Distichen gebraucht wurde.

Dover. The interpretation of οὔτ᾽ ἰάμβων οὔτε τερπωλέων is so full of ambiguity that we must leave open the possibility that for Archilochos the term ἴαμβοι includes elegiac poems.

Treu. Horaz nennt seine Epoden *iambi*, Theokritos (*Epigr.* 21) unterscheidet bei Archilochos Iamben und Elegien (ἔπεα).

Page. I should like to raise the question whether anybody can explain to me why this kind of personal poetry had so short a life in Greece. It begins with Archilochos and ends with Anakreon. It never existed again; in Athens it never existed at all. Personal loves and hates and experiences are never again expressed in lyrical or iambic metre, except on a very small scale in the Hellenistic period. So far as this kind of personal poetry ever does recur, it is conveyed by a different channel, the Epigram.

Treu. Ein einzigartiges, ja erschütterndes Phänomen ist das Ende der persönlichen Lyrik bei den Griechen (oder sollte man lieber sagen, ihr Zurückkehren in den Schoss des Volkes?). Aber was von ihrem Ende gesagt wurde, gilt auch von ihrem Anfang.

Snell. Es ist vielleicht zu bedenken, dass die archaische Lyrik nicht ganz so 'persönlich' ist, wie wir zunächst annehmen, da das, was wir 'persönlich' nennen, noch stark als Einwirken der Gottheit gefasst wurde (Archilochos: Ares und Musen, Sappho: Aphrodite usw.). Die Sublimierung der Götter machte die Götter zu erhaben, als dass man in ernster Poesie solch ein Eingreifen darstellte. Auch die Skulptur zeigt, dass 'grosse' Kunst von dieser Art des 'Persönlichen' absieht. Hier liegt ein Grundproblem der 'Klassik'.

Treu. Sehen können wir, – um zunächst beim Feststellbaren zu bleiben, – wie ein Zweig der Lyrik, die Chorlyrik, bei Alkman in hohem Masse fähig, auch persönliches Sentiment auszudrücken, den Weg zum Dithyrambischen einschlägt. Sie lebt in der Tragödie weiter. Sehen können wir, wie im Hellenismus das pointierte Epigramm ein Ersatz für die Lyrik geworden ist – und wie Theokrit aus der Lyrik den Refrain aufnimmt in hexametrische Dichtung.

Dover. Would it be possible to call Empedokles a 'personal' poet? The most trivial circumstances may cause a change of fashion; we cannot always expect to know the reasons.

There is a splendid example of a love song in the *Ecclesiazusae* (δεῦρο δὴ δεῦρο δή) through which we may glimpse non-literary 'personal' poetry in the classical period.

Treu. Das Volkslied stirbt am Schlager: alles, was stirbt, stirbt an etwas. Aufs Ganze gesehen, erliegt die Tragödie der Philosophie. Lange zuvor war die persönliche Lyrik der Tragödie erlegen (mag auch scheinbar eine zeitliche Lücke bleiben). Den sozialen und politischen Verhältnissen ist diese geistige Entwicklung vorausgeeilt; die Tragödie ist der attischen Demokratie voraus.

Wistrand. In der lateinischen Literatur erwacht die persönliche Liebes-poesie bekanntlich zu einem neuen Leben. Dabei ist es doch eine Frage, wie ernst diese Dichtung als persönliches Bekenntnis zu nehmen ist. Mit Sicher-heit möchte ich das eigentlich nur für Catull zu behaupten wagen. Bei ihm hat man sogar das Gefühl, dass ein Gedicht wie 76 *Si qua recordanti* malgré lui entstanden ist, weil die Gefühle zum Ausdruck drängten, während sein eigentlicher Kunstwille eher in den grossen Gedichten zu sehen ist.

Page. Sincerity in love-poetry is surely to be found in Propertius almost if not quite as much as in Catullus.

Bühler. Auch bei den Epigrammen ist es oft schwer, den Anteil des Persön-lichem von dem des Künstlerische und Sprachlichen zu unterscheiden.

Dover. Even if Latin love elegy were not 'serious', it would still be an import-ant art-form.

ADDITIONAL NOTES

P. 98, 'three separate jokes'. ἐν δορὶ κεκλιμένος, not in comfort on a κλίνη; bad local wine, not the wonderful wine associated with the region in myth (*Od.* ix 196 ff.); and – this is purely speculative – sarcastic use of a notion 'ready-made (*sc.* by others)' in μᾶζα μεμαγμένη.

P. 98, n. 6, on κορώνη. *KOPONE* appears as the name of a girl in an erotic scene on a red-figure vase, *ARV*² 113 no. 7.

P. 106, on 'the chronological order Homer–Hesiod–Archilochos'. I would not now take it for granted that Hesiod was later than Homer.

P. 107, 'immeasurably more civilized'. I repent of this arrogant statement, and of 'in-ferior in . . . rationality' on p. 113.

P. 112, n. 66. The best example is A. *Se.* 6, and cf. (cited by Hutchinson *ad loc.*) *X* 107, S. *OT* 6, 397, 1366.

11

Review of Lasserre and Bonnard's *Archiloque*

Archiloque: Les Fragments, texte établi par François Lasserre, traduit et commenté par André Bonnard (Les Belles Lettres, Paris 1958) cxiii + 105 pp.

During the last few years papyri and inscriptions have greatly enriched our knowledge of Archilochus. In the Budé edition the whole of the new material has been incorporated; so have many glosses and citations of suspected Archilochean origin, and some late verses which may be imitations of Archilochus. Although testimonia are separately assembled (pp. ciiiff), some of them are included also among the fragments, and others are found in both categories; no less than six, not one of them a fragment in the accepted sense of the word, are extracted from Critias B44; and occasionally they are versified, e.g. 'fr. 19' ⟨Χάρων ὁ τέκτων . . . Θάσιος⟩. It is a pity that a door so hospitably open should be shut in the face of the Strasbourg Epodes (frr. [79a]–[80]D).

Many scholars have devised contexts for fragments of Archilochus and have reconstructed the themes of poems. It might be thought that the most serious responsibility of the editor of a fragmentary text is to put asunder what the literary historian has joined, and that in printing ἔχουσα θαλλὸν κτλ. and ἡ δέ οἱ κόμη κτλ. as a single fragment Diehl lapsed from his usual standards. LB hold the opposite view. As one might expect from Lasserre's book *Les Épodes d'Archiloque* (Paris 1950; see *CR* ns ii 18f), the epodes have been subjected to the most thoroughgoing reconstruction. Under 'epodes' LB print 136 fragments. Of these, eight are explicitly assigned to the epodes by ancient sources, no one of them to any particular epode. A further seventeen (or twenty-three, if all LB's emendations are right) are unambiguously epodic or asynartete in metre. LB, however, allocate all but one of their 136 fragments to one or other of fourteen poems. The justification which they offer is only partial; for the full story the reader must turn to Lasserre's book. This situation is unsatisfactory in principle, and particularly so since the extent of the edition's dependence on the book is left uncertain (p. 49 n.), some of the arguments of *Les Épodes* have been invalidated by new papyri and second thoughts, and others are demonstrably unsound. To take 'Epode 1' as an example:

(i) 'Fr. 164' Λυκαμβὶς ἀρχή· ὁ Κρατῖνος ἐν Νόμοις (fr. 130K), τὸν πολέμαρχον δηλῶν, πρὸς ὃν ἀπεγράφοντο τὰς τοῦ ἀπροστασίου καὶ ἐπικλήρου δίκας. Λυκαμβίδα δὲ εἶπε τὴν ἀρχὴν ἐπεὶ ἐπολέμησεν Ἀρχίλοχος τῷ Λυκάμβῃ. So Hesychius (omitting καὶ ἐπικλήρου and ἐπεὶ κτλ.) and Photius. Lasserre (*Les Épodes* 35) says, 'Lycambès avait donc assimilé Archiloque à un hors la loi et l'avait accusé de vouloir détourner l'héritage de sa fille.' But the gloss is a combination of a frigid explanation, πολέμαρχοι ~ ἐπολέμησεν, with irrelevant information on the functions of the polemarch. It is not hard to improve on the explanation. Lycambes was the traditional victim of invective (cf. Luc. *Pseud.* 2); hence Λυκαμβὶς ἀρχή is either an office which people vilify or an office one holder of which, in the circumstances which Cratinus had in mind, was vilified. There seems then no justification for printing Critias B44 Ἐνιποῦς υἱὸς ἦν τῆς δούλης as 'fr. 165' in 'Epode 1'.

(ii) Fr. 167 (*EM* 26.23) ὡς δ' ἂν σε θωῖῃ λάβοι = Kallim. fr. 195.22. Philoxenus is very probably the source of the citation in *EM*; but in view of the evidence assembled by Pfeiffer on Kallim. fr. 23.15 Lasserre is wrong in arguing (*Les Épodes* 37) that Ἀρχιλόχῳ cannot be a mistake for Καλλιμάχῳ in *EM* (as it sometimes is) because Philoxenus did not quote poets as late as Callimachus. Having once vindicated the fragment to Archilochus, LB make it fit 'Epode 1' by translating: 'pourtant ⟨tu avais déclaré⟩ que tu étais prêt à subir un châtiment ⟨si tu violais ton serment⟩.'

(iii) Frr. 159 and 166 are addressed inimically *to* Lycambes; but fr. 176 is *about* an enemy (ἐκεῖνος), the person of the verb in fr. 160 (reconstructed from later adaptations) is wholly uncertain, and it is frivolous to expand fr. 161 τίς ἄρα δαίμων κτλ. by translating: 'quel dieu, *dis-moi*, fâché *contre toi* et à quel propos ⟨t'a poussé à agir ainsi⟩?' (my italics).

(iv) Lasserre, having rashly said (*Les Épodes* 45) that Archilochus attacked Lycambes only in 'Epode 1', found a place in it for Δωτάδης, glossed by Hesychius: Δώτου υἱὸς ὁ Λυκάμβας. The generalization is now imperilled by the iambic fr. 42 (*P. Oxy.* 2312 fr. 4a), and the gloss is now referred to fr. 43.7 (*P. Oxy.* 2312 fr. 5a.7) ἀμφ[ὶ Δω]τάδεω πατρ[. It should be observed that the contexts of frr. 40–2D and 92bD are now shown by the papyri (*P. Oxy.* 2312 fr. 14.2f, 2310 fr. 1 col. i 41, 2316.11) to be different from what was devised for them in *Les Épodes*.

I chose 'Epode 1' as my example because it is by far the strongest of LB's reconstructions. Seven of its nineteen fragments (counting 171.1–4 and 5–7 as two) are metrically epodic, of the form *ia trim* + *ia dim*, and eight more could be. Fr. 159 πάτερ Λυκάμβα κτλ. has a good claim to be the opening line of the first epode, since it is the ancient metricians' stock example of *ia trim* + *ia dim*. The fragments relating to the fable of the fox and the eagle are made intelligible by Aesop's version, and the applicability of the fable to Archilochus' relations with Lycambes is apparent from a portion of the biographical tradition which may rest wholly on the poems. The other reconstructions of epodes cannot claim comparable support, and LB's note on fr. 179 provides a neat comment on them: 'fragmentum Archilocho tribuit Bergk huicque epodo Lasserre quod alii cuiquam minus convenire videtur'.

The grouping of elegiac, iambic, and trochaic fragments is less ambitious. It is chiefly designed to determine the addressees of various poems, and relies heavily on the evidence of the reconstructed epodes.

The following details require comment: Fr. 7 ἐν δορὶ κτλ.; see now Bowra, *AFC* vi 37ff. Fr. 8.1 εἰμὶ δ' ἐγώ, 'et je suis . . .'; an emphatic anti-thesis is required. Fr. 10 Αἰσιμίδη κτλ.; there are no adequate grounds for supposing 'un échec . . . lors d'une campagne electorale'. Fr. 13.3 ψυχὴν δ' ἐξεσάωσα; the archaic reflexive αὐτὸν (cf. Schwyzer, *Gr. Gr.* ii 196), which rightly interested the commentators on Plato, is surely original, ψυχήν being an accommodation to Attic usage. Fr. 20.11 = fr. 36D is a long shot, since -]μεν[◡ is all that Lasserre and Lobel agree on in *P. Oxy.* 2312 fr. 19.5 + 2319 fr. 2.12; 2311 fr. 1(b).7 has a stronger claim to be fr. 36D. Fr. 46.2 κύβδα δ' ἦν πονευμένη; why '*puis* se laissait . . .'? Fr. 51 ⟨χολὴ τῆς ὕδρης⟩ does not scan; if a fragment is to be created here, why not ⟨ὕδρης χολήν⟩? Fr. 54 σὺν θεοῖ[σ' ἀντήσεται; but ἄντεσθαι has no future, and see Page, *CR*, ns vii 192. Fr. 62.5 ὑπερκ]ύδαντ' ἴδη⟨ι⟩; K]υδαντίδη? (cf. Lobel, *ad loc.*). Fr. 77.4 ζηλωτὰς[does not scan; presumably ζηλωτὰ σ[. Fr. 85.1 ἔλπομαι; why 'j'en fais le vœu'? Fr. 94.2f οὔτε τίμον εἰσένεικας ⟨− ◡ Μυκονίων δίκην⟩ / οὐδὲ μὲν κληθεὶς ⟨ἐσ⟩ῆλθες; I doubt whether anything can be devised for − ◡ which will make grammatical sense. Fr. 197.3 τὴν νηδὺν τὴν ἀθλίαν does not scan. Fr. 198 δὲ μεδέων (*ia*) is metrically unlikely. Fr. 239 ἀλλ' ἀπερρώγασι is also unlikely in an asynartete of the type 4 *da* + *ith*. Fr. 271 πολλὸς δ' ἀφρὸς κτλ. is more likely to refer to a boar (cf. Ar. *Lys.* 1255ff) than to a river-god in the guise of a bull.

Lasserre has collated the papyri, and offers many readings substantially different from Lobel's, e.g. *P. Oxy.* 2310 fr. 1 col. i 21 γεν[ειδ]ε[π]ι (*που* s.l.), 48 διαψεγοι, col. ii 33–6 ('valde dubitans') πολύ[. . . νιπτ[. . . φαμενγα[ρ . . . χερσονδε[.

By contrast with the reconstructions of the poems, the introductory chap-ters on the life of Archilochus, his language, and the history of his text are often cautious and sceptical, especially on Archilochus's alleged travels (pp. xixf) and mercenary service (pp. xxif). On the eclipse, LB perhaps go too far in suggesting that the speaker of χρημάτων ἄελπτον κτλ. is the poet's own father recalling an event long past to justify his generalization. I just cannot make the lines sound like that; and the article in τὸν πατέρα . . . τῆς θυγατρός may well be 'reciprocal'; cf. Gortyn Code iv 23 τὸν πατέρα τῶν τέκνων . . . κάρτερον ἦμεν.

Part of LB's assessment of the importance of Archilochus in the history of literature is marred, as I believe, by a fundamental error. From the fact that he was the first Greek to compose personal poetry which was transmitted to posterity in writing they seem to infer that he actually invented this kind of poetry; and upon this inference they build elaborate sociological and historical hypotheses (pp. xxv ff), for which they strangely claim the support of [Long.] *Subl.* 13.2–4. Do they really believe that Greeks of the tenth or fifteenth or twentieth century BC sang nothing but hexameters about the deeds of gods and heroes?

12

Review of Tarditi's *Archilochus* and Prato's *Tyrtaeus*

1 *Archilochus*, fragmenta edidit, veterum testimonia collegit Iohannes Tarditi, Collana di testi critici 2, Lyricorum Graecorum quae exstant 2 (Ateneo, Rome 1968) viii + 35 + 298 pp.

2 *Tyrtaeus*, fragmenta edidit, veterum testimonia collegit Carolus Prato, Collana di testi critici 3, Lyricorum Graecorum quae exstant 3 (Ateneo, Rome 1968) ix + 102* + 153 pp.

These two volumes are similar in format to each other and to Gentili's *Anacreon* (Rome 1958). Both include a long introduction, a very full bibliography, testimonia, text, apparatus criticus, phraseological parallels (these, by contrast with Diehl[3], are kept separate from the apparatus), an index verborum, an index auctorum and a concordance of numeration (both introduce a new numeration, which could hardly have been avoided in the case of Archilochos but might perhaps have been avoided for Tyrtaios). In addition, Tyrtaios is given a detailed commentary but no translation, Archilochos a translation and no commentary but a conspectus of classified linguistic and metrical data and an index to the testimonia. Both books are generously constructed; big margins are indeed desirable in editions of fragments, but the space given to the translation of one-word citations from Archilochos seems extravagant. The standard of printing is high, but there is some accentual and phonological confusion (notable ε/η and ο/ω) in Tarditi.

1 *Archilochus*. Tarditi's introduction is historically less rigid than Bonnard's in the Budé edition, but still tends (e.g. p. 4*) to treat the time at which short poems began to be transmitted in writing as if we knew it to be the time at which poems of Archilochean type were first composed and disseminated. Similarly, he treats fr. 174 (= 94D) ὦ Ζεῦ πάτεϱ Ζεῦ κτλ. and fr. 187 (= 84D) Ζεύς ... μάντις κτλ. as a 'superamento della teologia omerica', without regard for the possible contexts in which these sentiments — and I say 'sentiments' deliberately, not 'thoughts' — were uttered. Again, he takes fr. 166 (= 88D) 3f νῦν δὲ δὴ πολὺς / ἀστοῖσι φαίνεαι γέλως as evidence that people

really did laugh at Lykambes – as if 'you are a laughing-stock', in the mouth of an enemy, were a statement of objective fact.

More cross-references among fragments and testimonia would be helpful, notably fr. 109.1 ~ 171.3, 119.4 ~ 123.1f, T9 ~ E₁ col. ii 50, T10 col. i 1 ~ T60, T17 ~ T56 and T64, T43 ~ T169. Fr. 284 (= 146B) could well be included among the testimonia, and T102 (Luc. *Am.* 3 τὴν φωνὴν δ᾿ ἴσην τῇ Λυκάμβου θυγατρὶ λεπτὸν ἀφηδύνων) may be thought to deserve inclusion among the fragments, even without the reconstruction offered (fr. 208LB) by Lasserre. Leutsch's emendation of Ἀρχίλοχον πατεῖς (T17) to Ἀρχιλόχου πατρίς needs a warning reference to Ar. *Av.* 471 and Pl. *Phdr.* 273a, and the same warning is required on Eustathios's interpretation of Ἀρχίλοχον πεπάτηκας (T64).

The poems are classified by metre, but a few adjustments to the classification are desirable. 'Iamboi' and 'tetrametra' are not mutually exclusive terms, as Arist. *Rhet.* 1418b28 demonstrates, and 'trimetra' would have been preferable to 'iamboi'. The distribution of very short fragments between trimeters and epodes, or between epodes and asynarteta (e.g. fr. 212 = 118D) is more often in doubt than Tarditi allows, and there is no point in calling frr. 208–12 (= 111, 113, 116–18D) 'incertae sedis asynarteti'; in particular, if Bergk's βακχίησιν is adopted in fr. 208, the fragment belongs to the same category as frr. 162ff (= 107ffD). Fr. 191 (= 152B) Καρπάθιος τὴν μάρτυρα could as well be elegiac as epodic. Fr. 198 (= 34D) is printed as ἀλλ᾿ ἀπερρώγασι / μύκεω τένοντες, with the note 'metrum restituit Lasserre', but Lasserre's belief in ithyphallics of the form — ∪ — × — — (followed by Tarditi, p. 210) needs better justification than has yet been offered.

P. 6*: it is sad to see χειρὶ παχείη in φ 6, where the epithet describes the firm flesh of a woman on whom the wrinkles of age have not yet appeared, still being treated as a 'formula con il suo significato puramente metrico'. P. 8*: I hope 'estatica ammirazione', describing fr. 25 (= 25D) is a misprint for 'estetica ammirazione'. P. 16* n. 249 (and again on fr. 207 = 120D): Tarditi errs in treating the subscription to the scholia on Aristophanes' *Birds* (cf. the subscription of *Clouds*) as if it were a scholion on the last three lines of the play. Fr. 4.8: 'at nescio quid Thessalis cum Pariis fuerit'; but since nothing about Paros is legible in this unintelligible papyrus, the question does not arise. Fr. 42 (= 47D): 'fortasse . . . agitur de Nesso centauro cum Deianira colloquente'; but a dialogue involving ferrymen (cf. Arist. *Meteor.* 356b12ff) is at least as likely. Fr. 45 (= 113B): τά is unwelcome with the name of a festival, and the metre is rescued by its deletion. Frr. 162, 163 (= 107fD): it is worth pointing out (cf. p. 208) that Hephaistion 27.15ff failed to observe that there is synizesis in ἐρέω and φιλέειν. Fr. 167 (= 88AD): is not ἐδράξω slightly more probable than εἴληφας? Fr. 197 (= 112D) 3: since A. R. iv 1524 is quoted as a parallel for v. 2, it would be worth quoting Theokr. 13.48 ἀπαλὰς φρένας for v. 3. Fr. 203 (= 104D): Ar. *Ec.* 956f is hardly a parallel for δύστηνος ἔγκειμαι πόθῳ, given the very different sense of the verb. Fr. 204 (= 117B): if Hdn. i 189 yields a fragment, it is πόλις, not Πάρος. Fr. 233 (= 135B): I do not know why

Tarditi insists on ἆι, when the sources (and the rest of Greek) say ἆ. Fr. 281: 'parum verisimile puto Archilochum egisse de Homeri Margite'; but there is nothing against it in principle, given Alkman fr. 145 (*PMG*) and Κάλαινος (*sic*) *ap.* Paus. ix 9.5.

2   *Tyrtaeus.*

Prato's text takes account of the information given by L. Koenen, *RhM* xcvi (1953) 187ff, on fr. 10 (= 1D), but was sent to press just too soon to take account of M. L. West, *Ztschr. f. Pap. u. Epigr.* i (1967) 173ff. It is good to see *GVI* 749 included in the very full collection of *testimonia*, although the reference is given only to its original place of publication; elsewhere in the commentary epitaphs are cited from *GVI*, but no indication is given of their origins and dates. The linguistic, prosodic and metrical data assembled in the introduction (pp. 48*ff) might have been augmented by a fuller discussion of digamma, details of vocalic contraction and its avoidance, and the main contrasts between early elegy and the exiguous but instructive remains of later elegy from Xenophanes to Kritias.

Two problems necessarily dominate the interpretation of Tyrtaios: one is the relation between his verses, the rhetra given by Plutarch, and the Delphic oracle; the other is the relation between Tyrtaios's portrayal of fighting and the weapons and tactics of his time. Despite a full discussion which rests on judicious use of an ample bibliography, there remain aspects of these problems with which Prato has not entirely got to grips.

L. H. Jeffery, *Historia* x (1961) 145ff, perceived the analogical importance of *SEG* ix 3 (Cyrene) for the interpretation of the rhetra; note especially her judgement (147 n. 29) that 'in effect, the blueprint' (i.e. the text of the rhetra, in Lakonian prose) 'would be sent to the Pythia for her endorsement'. We may compare also *SEG* ix 72, the religious prescriptions in Cyrenaean prose which are introduced by the words Ἀπόλλων ἔχρησε. There is no good reason why Tyrtaios should not have described the rhetra as an oracle and paraphrased it in verse. The syntactical difficulty of frr. 1b (= 3bD) 3f, 14 (= 3aD) 3f, is in no way solved by referring to passages in which ἐπιστάμενος functions as a predicative adjective; the relevant parallels are such passages as *IG* i² 6.57ff ἄρχειν δὲ τὸν χρόνον τῶν σπονδῶν τοῦ Μεταγειτνιῶνος μηνὸς ἀπὸ διχομηνίας καὶ (*sc.* continue) τὸν Βοηδρομιῶνα καὶ τοῦ Πυανοψιῶνος μέχρι δεκάτης ἱσταμένου.

As for the references to fighting: Prato takes ἀσπίδας εὐκύκλους in fr. 10.72 (= 1.58D) as 'allusione evidente ai cerchi concentrici' of the type of pre-hoplite shield discussed and illustrated by A. M. Snodgrass, *Early Greek Weapons and Armour* (Edinburgh 1964) 52ff; but εὔκυκλος seems a very natural epithet (so Snodgrass 181) of the circular hoplite shield (incidentally, on p. 110 Prato reverses the meanings of ἀντιλαβή and πόρπαξ). In fr. 8.23f μηρούς τε κνήμας τε κάτω καὶ στέρνα καὶ ὤμους / ἀσπίδος εὐρείης γαστρὶ καλυψάμενος the problem of κνήμας τε κάτω is not tackled; it may be that a very large hoplite shield could be 'felt' to protect the shins (cf. Snodgrass 181, on the Olympia shield with a diameter of 1.2m.), but hoplites did after all depend on greaves for protection of the shins. I would prefer to regard κνήμας τε κάτω as a slightly clumsy parenthesis, comparing O 344 τάφρῳ καὶ σκολόπεσσιν ἐνιπλήξαντες ὀρυκτῇ, S. *Ichn.* 109 ἀλλ᾽ αὐτὰ μὴν ἴχνη τε χὠ στίβος τάδε κείνων ἐναργῆ.

P. 6 n. 31: the plural ἐλεγεῖα is not 'molto spesso usato, già alla fine del V secolo, per indicare una serie di distici'; the two examples which Prato quotes are the only two before Aristotle. Fr. 6.7f: Hes. *Op.* 399f should be added to the parallels. Fr. 7.31 εὖ διαβάς: cf. Archil. fr. 60 (D). 4; and for μενέτω E 527 is perhaps the most important parallel. Fr. 8.1f: four dashes in these two lines do not seem quite the right punctuation. Fr. 8.17: Ahrens's emendation ἀρπαλέον is not really disposed of by reference to the Spartan military doctrine of Plu. *Lyc.* 22.9; the point of ἀρπαλέον would be, 'an enemy will be only too glad to stab you in the back if you run away'. Fr. 8.24: Ar. *Ach.* 1123 τῆς ἐμῆς sc. ἀσπίδος (= γαστρός) is relevant to ἀσπίδος εὐρείης γαστρί. Fr. 8.37: ἐς αὐτούς might mean 'at the enemy themselves' (*sc.* 'and do not throw wildly in their general direction'), but, if it means simply 'at the enemy', the reference of the pronoun being understood from the context, cf. Ar. *Nu.* 1079. Fr. 9.2: the genitives need a word of explanation. Fr. 9.40ff: Theognis 935ff, mentioned in the commentary, could well be cited among the parallels.

These are mainly minor criticisms. There is plenty of interesting material and sensible discussion in the introduction and commentary.

13

Pindar, *Olympian Odes* 6.82–6

δόξαν ἔχω τιν᾽ ἐπι †γλώσσᾳ· ἀκόνας λιγυρᾶς†
ἅ μ᾽ ἐθέλοντα προσέρπει καλλιρόαισι πνοαῖς,
ματρομάτωρ ἐμὰ Στυμφαλίς, εὐανθὴς Μετώπα,
πλάξιππον ἃ Θήβαν ἔτικτεν, τᾶς ἐρατεινὸν ὕδωρ
πίομαι κτλ.

82 *punctum post* γλώσσᾳ hab . ABH *P. Oxy.* 1614; om. cett.   λιγυρᾶς ἀκόνας Bergk
83 προσέλκει Ε^{γρ} (-οι) G^{γρ} Η^{γρ}; cf. Σ^A   -ρόαισι *P. Oxy.* : -ρόοισι codd.

Professor A. J. Beattie has recently reminded us[1] that δόξαν ἔχειν ἐπί *c. dat.* means 'I have a reputation for . . .'. His point is valid even without the limitation '*ἐπί c. dat.*'. δόξα is a common word in Pindar, and with the exception of *N.* 11.24 ἐμὰν δόξαν ('judgement') and possibly *O.* 10.63 ἐν δόξᾳ θέμενος εὖχος 'expectation', he uses it in the sense 'reputation', 'fame', 'glory'. δόξαν ἔχειν 'have a reputation' is normal from the sixth century onwards, e.g. Alc. D14.12, Solon 1.4, *IG* xiv 652.3, Pind. *P.* 8.24, E. *Md.* 540, fr. 659.10 (= Critias fr. 15), Th. iv 126.5; cf. the many examples of δ. λαβεῖν, δ. εὑρεῖν, δ. φέρειν, etc. On the other hand, the sense 'entertain a belief' is unexampled before the fourth century. In any case, 'I have a belief' (or 'illusion', or 'sensation') 'of a whetstone upon my tongue' is not a Greek form of metaphor and does not mean 'There is, as it were, a whetstone upon my tongue.' It follows that unless we fail to make sense of *O.* 6.82ff by translating δόξαν as 'reputation' we need not consider the many interpretations[2] which translate it otherwise.

Professor Beattie, reading ἐπὶ γλώσσας ἀκόνᾳ λιγυρᾶς (which retains the word-order of the manuscripts) and ἀλλ᾽ for ἅ μ᾽, interprets thus: 'I have a certain reputation for the sharpening power of my tongue; but' (i.e. despite the effectiveness of my native talent, as shown by its power over other men) 'I am glad that Metopa approaches me and inspires me.' My interpretation differs from his in that (i) the coyness 'I have a certain reputation' seems to me

[1] *CR*, ns vi 1f.
[2] Including those of the scholia, which uniformly explain δόξα as δόκησις. This in turn is paraphrased by Σ^{ΒΕ} as ὃ δοκῶ περὶ τῶν ἀνδρῶν.

to conflict with the tone of Pindar's other references to himself (E. *El.* 939 is perhaps the earliest example of τις with the overtone 'good' or 'big'), and (ii) I think that good sense can be made of ἅ μ'.

τιν' I take to be purely informative, as in *P.* 4.247 καί τινα οἶμον ἴσαμι βραχύν, *N.* 9.6 ἔστι δέ τις λόγος ἀνθρώπων; thus δόξαν ἔχω τιν'. . . ἅ. . . = 'Among the good things said of me, there is one which . . .', or 'I have one (claim to) fame, (among others), which . . .'.

Since, on any interpretation, 83 says something about poetic inspiration, the most natural sense for the rest of 82 is: '(which acts as) a whetstone to my tongue,[3] (making it) clear-sounding', a phrase in apposition to δόξαν.[4] This sense would be given by ἐπὶ γλώσσας ἀκόναν λιγυρᾶς. My only doubt is whether the relation between a whetstone and that which it sharpens is properly described by ἐπί c. gen. If not, then (i) if Pindar wrote προσέρπει in 83, ἐπί c. gen. could express arrival, as commonly, the form of the expression being determined by the movement implicit in 83: '(which, acting as) a whetstone, (comes) to my tongue (and makes it) clear-sounding'; or (ii) if Pindar wrote προσέλκει – as I think he did – we may, with Bergk, transpose the last two words of 82, keeping the terminations as in the manuscripts, ἐπὶ γλώσσᾳ λιγυρᾶς ἀκόνας, in which case λιγυρᾶς is a transferred epithet and the genitive is appositional (cf. E. *Su.* 715 ὅπλισμα τοὐπιδαύριον. . . δεινῆς κορύνης): '(consisting of) a whetstone upon my tongue (which makes my tongue) clear-sounding'.

Manuscripts and papyrus agree on προσέρπει, but προσέλκει is recorded as a v.l. in manuscripts of one branch[5] if the Vatican family and is also clearly implied by the explanation προσάγει in Σᴬ. Let us defer decision for a moment, treating the first half of 83 as 'which ——s me', and consider the second half.

καλλίρ(ρ)οος is applied exclusively to rivers and springs; cf. the wide distribution of Καλλιρ(ρ)όη as a name of springs and water-nymphs. The words καλλιρόαισι πνοαῖς therefore tell us at once something about the nature of the δόξα; it has a connection with a river or spring; and 84 is specific: 'my mother's mother, a Stymphalian (nymph), flowery Metopa, who bore Theba, whose sweet water I drink'. So far, then: 'Among the good things said of me, there is one . . . which ——s me πνοαῖς of a lovely stream, (namely) . . . Metopa.' To take the person Metopa in apposition to a relative pronoun which refers to the reputation grounded upon that person seems to me no harder than calling a person a glory, reproach, or grief; cf. *Il.* xvi 498–9 σοὶ γὰρ ἐγὼ καὶ ἔπειτα κατηφείη καὶ ὄνειδος ἔσσομαι, xxii 435 καί σφι μάλα μέγα κῦδος ἔησθα ζωὸς ἐών.[6] Anyone who does find it objectionable may

---

[3] For Pindar's metaphorical treatment of γλῶσσα see Beattie, *loc. cit.*, Woodbury, *TAPA* 1955, 31, and Pearson, *CR* xlv 210. Of many examples, *N.* 7.70–2 is perhaps the most striking.

[4] So Σᴮᴱ: ὃ δοκῶ περὶ τῶν ἀνδρῶν, τοῦτό μοι ἀκόνη ἐστίν, and ὀξὺς ὢν ὀξύτερος γίνομαι παρ' ἀκόνης τῆς δοκήσεως θηγόμενος.

[5] In both, according to Turyn's stemma; but I am following Irigoin here.

[6] Appositional phenomena discussed in Kühner–Gerth, *Gr. Gr.* i 282.1A1, 284.6, Schwyzer, *Gr. Gr.* ii 615 Zus. 1, may also have some relevance here.

punctuate strongly after 83 and take ματρομάτωρ as the beginning of a fresh statement, understanding ἐστίν.

Returning now to 83: our choice is between (i) 'which approaches me – and I welcome it – *with* the πνοαί of a lovely stream', and (ii) 'which draws me – and I do not resist it – *to* the πνοαί, etc.' (cf. *I.* 6.69 ἄστει κόσμον ἑῷ προσάγων). Since the gods may 'breathe into' a man strength, the power of song (Hes. *Th.* 31), or an impulse to action (*Od.* xix. 138–9), the boy Alcimedon by his victory at Olympia πατρὶ δὲ πατρὸς ἐνέπνευσεν μένος (Pind. *O.* 8.70), and the Bacchants on Cithaeron were θεοῦ πνοαῖσιν ἐμμανεῖς (E. *Ba.* 1094), καλλιρόαισι πνοαῖς might perhaps describe the inspiration which Pindar derives from the thought of Metopa. However, while pain, emotions, desires, and hope come to a man (e.g. προσέρπει, προσέρχεται τόδ' ἐγγύς S. *Ph.* 787–8, χαρά μ' ὑφέρπει A. *Ag.* 270, ἵμερος . . . μοι ἐπῆλθε Hdt. i 30.2), and a 'cloud of forgetfulness' comes over the mind (ἐπὶ . . . βαίνει, Pind. *O.* 7.45), subjects of song do not come to Pindar; he goes to them (e.g. *O.* 6.22ff, *I.* 4.3) or shoots them from afar. This consideration tells decisively in favour of προσέλκει; so does ἐθέλοντα, which has more point if Pindar is being moved than if something is approaching him. Recalling ἡδὺ πνεῖν = 'smell good', I suggest that καλλιρόαισι πνοαῖς are the fresh smell of a lovely stream of water, such as may literally 'draw' or 'attact' a man, cf. *Hymn Pan* 9 ῥείθροισιν ἐφελκόμενος (passive) μαλακοῖσιν.

As elsewhere, Pindar blends the literal and the metaphorical inseparably. He means, 'Reflection upon the fact that I am called a Theban stimulates my utterance and induces me to speak of Metopa the mother of Theba.' But he says, 'Among the good things said of me, there is one – it acts as a whetstone to my tongue, making it clear-sounding – which draws me – and I do not resist it – to the smell of a lovely stream, (for it is) my mother's mother, a Stymphalian (nymph), flowery Metopa, who bore Theba. . . .' Compare the similar blending in the same poem, 22ff: 'Yoke me the mules, that . . . I may come to a genealogy; they know the way; throw open the gates of song for them; I must arrive today at Pitana on the Eurotas, (Pitana) who bore Evadne. . . .'

ADDITIONAL NOTE

P. 131, on the overtones of τις. E. *Hcld.* 973 is of course earlier than *El.* 939 (and *Ion* 596) but has a rather special point: 'No one will . . .' – '*I* will; and I am someone.' However, I was at fault in overlooking Kratinos (*PCG*) 59 τούς . . . βουλομένους τινὰς εἶναι.

14

Pindar, *Isthmian Odes* 6.4

In *I.* 6.3–5 the primary manuscripts (BD) have: ἐν Νεμέᾳ μὲν πρῶτον, ὦ Ζεῦ, τὶν ἄωτον δεξάμενοι στεφάνων, νῦν αὖτ᾽ ἐν Ἰσθμοῦ δεσπότᾳ (δέσποτα D) Νηρεΐδεσσί τε πεντήκοντα. Despite the paraphrase of Σᴮᴰ *ad loc.*, which might be thought to point (though rather shakily) to a reading ἐν Ἰσθμῷ, Pindar's use of δεσπότας and δέσποινα (*P.* 4.11, *N.* 1.13, frr. 29 Tur., 130 Tur. 11, 14) compels us to take Ἰσθμοῦ δεσπότᾳ together. The editor's problem is to get rid of ἐν; hence αὖτις Byz., αὖτεν Usener (an invention on the analogy of ἔπειτεν), αὖτε Hermann (for hiatus before Ἰσθμός cf. *I.* 1.9, 32), αὖ τίν Bergk (with δέσποτα).

It happens that these lines are quoted by Σᴮᴰ in the hypothesis of *I.* 5 (Drachmann iii 240.22): there, while Σᴮ has αὖτ᾽ ἐν, as in the text of *I.* 6, Ζᴰ has αὖτε. Bury took this seriously, as evidence that the author of Σᴮᴰ had αὖτε in his text; Schroeder and Mommsen may have thought this, but their critical notes on *I.* 6 do not make it clear. Other editors, whether they adopt αὖτε (e.g. Bowra, Turyn) or merely mention it, attribute it to Hermann and say nothing of Σᴰ.

There is, I believe, some additional evidence that Bury was right. According to Σ's metrical analysis of *I.* 6, the words νῦν ... δεσπότᾳ constitute the seventh colon of the strophe. This colon is analysed thus: (Dr. iii 250.6) τὸ ζ′ δίμετρον ἰαμβικὸν ἀκατάληκτον μετὰ τοῦ ε′ εὕρηται. The words μετὰ τοῦ ε′ εὕρηται are puzzling ('sensu cassa', Dr.). ε′, according to the usage of the Pindar Σ, should refer to the fifth colon. εὕρηται cannot then have its usual sense 'is found, *sc.* in other passages' (cf. Σ *recc.*, Abel i 62.12, Eust. on Hom. *Il.* i 8, etc.). It could mean 'is found, *sc.* in some texts' (cf. εὕρομεν, Σᴬ Hom., Dindorf i 54.2, etc.), but 'the seventh colon is found in some texts with the fifth' is a strange textual comment to find in a metrical analysis. 'The analysis of the seventh colon is found in some texts with that of the fifth' (so Boeckh, Abel) makes sense, but it is hard to see why Σ should find so obvious a mistake worth mentioning. Nor is the easy emendation εἴρηται (cf. Dr. iii 1.13) helpful.

The metrical analyses in the Pindar Σ, ostensibly applicable to the whole poem, sometimes refer without warning to the first triad only. So in the

analysis of the first colon of the epode of *I*. 6: τὸ α΄ ἐκ Σαπφικοῦ τοῦ ἐνδεκα-
συλλάβου Πινδαρικόν. ἤ τοι (Pauw; ἤτοι *codd.*) κοινή ἐστι; in which the last
words can only refer to line 17, the first colon of the *first* epode, ὔμμε τ᾽ ὦ
χρυσάρματοι Αἰακίδαι. Again, in *I*. 8, ἤ νον μακρά (Dr. iii 269.143) refers to
πόνον in line 8 of the first strophe. On this analogy, we may suspect that μετὰ
τοῦ ε΄ εὕρηται conceals a reference to line 4: read μετὰ τοῦ ε· εὕρηται ⟨ ... ⟩,
meaning '(the seventh colon is an iambic dimeter acatalectic) *with the* ε', i.e.
'the ε of αὖτε being unelided'. It is not easy to supplement the lacuna. We
expect a metrical, not a textual, comment; but the natural comment, that
hiatus occurs elsewhere before Ἰσθμός, would be startling in a Greek Σ and
can hardly be entertained (I owe this warning to Dr R. Pfeiffer). Probably
something more banal must be supplemented, e.g. εὕρηται ⟨δὲ πολλὰ ἐκ
πλήρους γεγραμμένα⟩. Be that as it may, μετὰ τοῦ ε makes sense. I suppose
therefore that the author of the metrical analysis of *I*. 6 had αὖτε in his text
and thought it worth while to warn the reader against elision. Similarly, the
author of the hypothesis of *I*. 5 read αὖτε, which Σ^D preserved there, while Σ^B
altered it to αὖτ᾽ ἐν to conform with his already corrupted text of *I*. 6. (On
Σ^B's treatment of quotations, see Turyn, *Philologus* 1935, 117.)

ADDITIONAL NOTE

On εὕρηται ⟨δὲ πολλά ...⟩. Cf. Σ Ar. *Eq.* 941a ἐστὶ δὲ πολλὰ κτλ., Σ *Ra.* 1263
ὥσπερ καὶ ἄλλα πολλάκις.

15

Some Neglected Aspects of Agamemnon's Dilemma

Interpretation of the *Agamemnon* in general and of its first choral sequence in particular has tended to proceed on two assumptions: first, that Aeschylus could have given an answer (not necessarily a simple answer) to the question, 'Was Agamemnon free to choose whether or not to sacrifice his daughter?'; and, secondly, that he composed the play in such a way that if we try hard enough we can discover his answer. I submit in this paper an interpretation which replaces both these assumptions with an alternative trio of hypotheses for which, I think, a case can be made: first, that Aeschylus was well aware that in real life we cannot know the extent to which an agent was able to choose whether or not to commit a particular act; secondly, that in *Ag.* 104–257 he has portrayed realistically the manner in which people respond to the commission of an extraordinary and disagreeable act by a respected agent; and, thirdly, that the aspect of Agamemnon's predicament which made the most powerful impression on Aeschylus and his audience is an aspect to which modern interpreters of the play have seldom alluded even by implication. I would not be so rash as to assert that Aeschylus never concerned himself with the question of responsibility, nor that his concepts of justice and retribution are of small interest, but I am not satisfied that 'with all the powers of his mind', as Professor Lesky puts it,[1] 'he wrestled with the problem arising from the conflict between human existence and divine rule', nor do I take the view that a dramatist passionately involved in metaphysics and theology is a wiser and greater man than one who devotes the powers of his mind to concrete problems of poetic and theatrical technique. The scale of values adopted by interpreters of early Greek tragedy has certainly been affected, and has perhaps been somewhat distorted, by the dominant position of philosophy in European culture and education.

It is normal and salutary practice in discussing Aeschylean morality and theology to issue a warning against the anachronistic importation of Christian ideas into the fifth century BC. This warning could profitably be extended, strengthened and made more specific, and in the category 'Christian' we

---

[1] *JHS* lxxxvi (1966) 85.

should include not only peculiarly Christian ideas but also some modern ideas which have been widely adopted by Christians, others which may be reflexes of Christianity,[2] and traditional ingredients of Christianity which have roots in the Hellenistic or even in the Classical period.

In the first place, people who believe both that God is just, with an inclination to mercy, and also that many of us are destined to eternal pain have a strong motive for insisting, irrespective of such empirical evidence as might be thought relevant, that somehow or other each of us is truly responsible for his own moral choices and deserving of punishment for wrong choice. In Aeschylus's time, however, the notion of judgement and differential treatment after death was no more than one among several λόγοι on the subject of the afterlife (*Su.* 230f),[3] so that there was no eschatological compulsion to take up a firm position on the question of free will, either on the popular or on the philosophical level. Even in the late fourth century, funeral speeches, where Christian analogy might have led us to expect a fervent expression of faith, treat the notion of a sentient afterlife as no more than plausible and generally acceptable (Dem. lx 33f, Hyper. vi 43). Abundant epitaphs (notably of the third century BC) which allude to 'the place of the pious' coexist with many which seem to preclude differentiation between the good and the bad or explicitly treat the survival of a sentient soul as a mere hypothesis; cf. the death-bed agnosticism of the pious Cyrus in Xen. *Cyr.* viii 7.19–22.

Secondly, Christian treatment of faith as a virtue has generally encouraged people to declare themselves 'sure' or 'convinced' on many moral questions, both general and particular, which do not in fact offer grounds for being sure. The Greek seems on the whole[4] to have had a better grasp of the relation between belief and evidence and to have been less reluctant to keep alternatives open, except (see below) when personally involved in immediate conflict with an adversary and thus under the necessity of *using* one alternative to the exclusion of others.

Thirdly, and most important, the Christian distinction between God and Caesar and Christian insistence on the magnitude of the moral claims of each of us upon his fellows provide a foundation for a concern that no individual should be unjustly punished, written off as irredeemable or sacrificed as a means to an end. While the influence of explicitly Christian ethics has declined in the present century, that concern has been intensified, in those Western societies

---

[2] It is difficult to imagine, for instance, that the cry 'We are all to blame!' (*sc.* for everything), popularized by Ugo Betti, could have been echoed so widely and so often in any culture which had not inherited an oppressive sense of human worthlessness and guilt, even though many of those who have recourse to it most readily have no intention of contrasting man with a transcendent deity.

[3] In tragedy generally, as in oratory throughout the fourth century, death is regarded as the end of suffering even (e.g. Lys. vi 20) for an impious man whose suffering is inflicted by angry gods. Perhaps Plato's Cephalus does not speak for everyone in saying (*R.* 330DE) that when a man is old and near to death he is tormented by the fear that the stories he laughed at when he was young may be true after all.

[4] S. *El.* 400 (Chrysothemis) πατὴρ δὲ τούτων, οἶδα, συγγνώμην ἔχει is unusual; contrast ibid. 355f (Electra).

which have escaped totalitarianism, by liberal assertion of the individual's rights against the state, neo-liberal compassion (sometimes 'justice' to its proponents and 'sentimentality' to its opponents, neither very accurately), and a spectacular growth in scientific knowledge of the determinants of behaviour. One consequence of this is an anxiety that a man who commits a wrongful act while in a psychotic or neurotic condition should not be treated as if he had committed it in furtherance of a sane and rational intention. The Classical Greek offers a strong contrast with Christian and modern attitudes alike. He tended to 'nationalize' his gods to such an extent that (at least in public utterance) the application of 'pious'/'impious' converged upon that of 'patriotic'/ 'unpatriotic'. Furthermore, to him the question raised by wrongdoing was not so much, 'How can this *person* be dealt with fairly?' as 'What reaction to this *situation* will safeguard the interests of the community?' Many of his moral judgements imply that he regarded the state not as a roof over the head of a big family of individuals expressing and fulfilling themselves each in his own way, but as an organization – like a regiment or a firm – in which the individual has a function to perform; and in organizations, now as then, negligence may be held as culpable as treachery and promotion or honour depends more on results than on good disposition. Attic law on involuntary homicide made no provision for what English law calls 'diminished responsibility', and there is no sign in the Classical period that anyone thought it should. When the chorus in *Ag.* 1407ff contemplate the possibility that Clytaemnestra has been rendered insane by something that she has eaten or drunk, they still assume that she will be outlawed and cursed. A Greek orator often calls his opponent 'demented', 'crazy', and the like, but not in extenuation, for his purpose is rather to suggest the mercy could only have undesirable consequences. The same view could be taken of ineradicable defects of character: cf. Dem. xxv 33 'Who would not, as far as he possibly could, avoid (*sc. τὸν ἀπονενοημένον*) and put out of the way (*ἐκποδών*) the man afflicted by this vice (*sc. ἀπόνοια*), so as not to encounter it even by accident?' and Dem. xx 140 *παντάπασι φύσεως κακίας σημεῖόν ἐστιν ὁ φθόνος, καὶ οὐκ ἔχει πρόφασιν δι' ἣν ἂν τύχοι συγγνώμης ὁ τοῦτο πεπονθώς*. It was perfectly possible to argue, with a hypothetical reference, that action proceeding from ignorance (e.g. Dem. xix 98–101) or from an ungovernable temperament (e.g. Dem. xxi 186) should receive lenient treatment, but 'bad or mad?' and 'wicked or sick?' are disjunctions which the Greek would not have found it easy to discuss at all without first formulating the issue in many more words than we require to make it intelligible in English.[5] If the orators are not felt to be satisfactory evidence for the attitudes of the mid-fifth century,[6] we may

---

[5] Note especially Dem. xix 267 'Those responsible for this felt no shame . . . *οὕτως ἔκφρονας . . . καὶ παραπλῆγας τὸ δωροδοκεῖν ποιεῖ*, where insanity (i.e. an abnormal shamelessness and recklessness) is treated as a *consequence* of wrongdoing.

[6] No comprehensive affirmation or denial of its relevance is rational. It will be found on reflection that circumstances can arise in which the application of fourth-century evidence to a fifth-century problem is argument *a fortiori*.

recall how readily the dramatists use νόσος and νοσεῖν to denote not only sickness and madness but intransigence, error, vice, misfortune, failure and poverty. When an actual conflict arose between fairness to an individual and what were conceived to be the best interests of the community, the latter prevailed, and punishment intended as an exemplary deterrent was deliberately inflicted on men 'forced' into misdemeanour by their circumstances (Aeschines i 87f, Dem. xxiv 123). In Lys. xiii 52, where the issue is one of duress or rational error, it is argued that in the case of an act which has really serious consequences for the community no attention should be paid to the agent's plea that he acted ἄκων; the truth or falsity of the plea is to be treated as immaterial, presumably so that anyone contemplating such an act in future may know in advance that if he is caught there is no possible way out for him.

When we theorize about criminal responsibility or about free will and determinism, it is quite easy for us to construct a hypothetical case of such a kind that we can judge the agent guilty or guiltless. We can do this by being careful not to go on feeding ingredients into the construction beyond a point at which definite judgement is still possible. Equally, we can take a real case of which we have personal knowledge and pass judgement on the agent's responsibility after we have withdrawn our attention from all those elements in the case which make a clear decision difficult. In the one case we facilitate decision by refraining from addition, in the other we facilitate it by subtraction. If, however, we honestly attempt to take into account every consideration which is relevant to a case involving a person whom we know well, we can never find it easy, and usually find it impossible, to decide whether he could or could not have acted otherwise. If we happen to be people empowered to give judicial or disciplinary decisions, or when we serve as jurors, we are always put into the position of basing our verdicts on a fraction of the relevant evidence; the rules of the courts, combined with the need to finish one case and pass on to the next, see to that. The law, in fact, must pretend that firm and correct answers to a question of responsibility can be given, and it is hard to see how any system of law could operate on any other basis. Equally, an organization cannot afford, in most cases, to take into account the problematic aspects of responsibility. When it is not our job to punish, reward or return a verdict, we are free to stop pretending and admit that we do not really know the answer.

The considerations listed above suggest that Aeschylus and his contemporaries were even less constrained to pretend, since the hypotheses, beliefs, attitudes and traditions which can make a decision on responsibility so painful for many of us did not exist in sufficient strength to make difficulties for them. It is moreover questionable whether Aeschylus had ever heard, read or even imagined any argument or problem of a kind which philosophers, ancient or modern, would regard as proper to moral philosophy. If by chance he had, it is unlikely that it had anything to do with free will and determinism, in view of the failure even of the powerful philosophical minds of the following century to comprehend the true nature and dimensions of that problem. Yet

Aeschylus will have observed that some actions seem to be more easily explicable and predictable than others; he will also have observed that the view we express about the responsibility for a given act depends above all on whether we are attacking or defending. The classic example of a disagreement on responsibility is to be found in Euripides' *Troades*, where Helen (945–50) exculpates her flight and adultery by the trite (cf. Ar. *Nu.* 1079–82) claim that she was a victim of the irresistible Aphrodite, while Hecuba (987–93) angrily rejects this excuse, putting the blame on Helen's own lust and greed. To adopt Aristotelian terminology (*Eth. Nic.* 1113b31), Helen locates the ἀρχή of her adultery outside herself, and Hecuba insists on relocating it within her. Pasiphae in Euripides' *Cretes* refuses absolutely to accept responsibility for her love of a bull (fr. 82 [Austin] 9f νῦν δ᾽, ἐκ θεοῦ γὰρ προσβολῆς ἐμηνάμην, / ἀλγῶ μέν, ἐστὶ δ᾽ οὐχ ἑκούσιον κακόν, 29f κἀγὼ μὲν ἡ τεκοῦσα κοὐδὲν αἰτία / ἔκρυψα πληγὴν δαίμονος θεήλατον), but Minos in his anger behaves (44ff) as if he had not even heard her argument. In *Ag.* 1475ff, 1497ff, Clytaemnestra, exploiting the chorus's apostrophe (1468ff) to the 'δαίμων of the Tantalidai', attributes the murder of Agamemnon to that supernatural power of which she was only the tool; whereupon the chorus are at once provoked into repudiation of her claim (1505f), and then as promptly go into reverse with the admission (1507f) πατρόθεν δὲ συλλήπτωρ γένοιτ᾽ ἂν ἀλάστωρ. Confronted by Orestes in *Ch.* 910, Clytaemnestra pleads that a μοῖρα was παραιτία of Agamemnon's death, to which Orestes retorts that her death too is apportioned by a μοῖρα. They are not arguing about philosophical or legal theory. Aeschylus represents Clytaemnestra as clutching in turn, like anyone else (real or fictional) in a desperate predicament, at every imaginable means of putting off her own death, while Orestes brushes aside anything which might frustrate the act to which he is impelled – as he has told us (*Ch.* 298–305) – by a powerful combination of fear, hatred and shame.

Between declared adversaries, the issue is simple: what I did right is to my credit, and what I did wrong was not my fault; what you did wrong was your fault, and what you did right was no doing of yours (cf. Agamemnon to Achilles, *Il.* i 117f). Complexity is introduced by pre-existing loyalties and obligations. Kallistratos, the speaker of Dem. xlviii, attacks Olympiodoros in terms familiar to us in fourth-century oratory (52 ἀδικεῖ ... διέφθαρται ... παραφρονεῖ, 56 οὐ μόνον ἄδικος, ἀλλὰ καὶ μελαγχολᾶν δοκῶν), but feels obliged to temper his onslaught with embarrassment (52) and charity (58, cf. 3) because Olympiodoros is his brother-in-law (1f). Where the speaker is not a contestant but only indirectly involved, reluctance to over-simplify the issue and take sides on the allocation of responsibility is the product not only of conflict between emotional reaction and the claims of partisanship, but also of maturity, experience and intelligent reflection. Since the chorus of *Ag.* are old men, loyal to their king but no more disposed than most Greeks to servility or to the suppression of normal human reactions, and reflection on antecedent events is a common formal function of a Greek chorus, we might expect to find their treatment of the sacrifice of Iphigenia characterized by caution, doubt and ambivalence in everything that concerns the responsibility for it as an *act*, contrasting with unambiguous revulsion against it as an *event*. It seems to me that this expectation is entirely fulfilled.

One of the most striking aspects of the chorus's narrative is its indirectness. The chorus do not at any point commit themselves to the assertions that Artemis was offended, that Artemis caused the bad weather which prevented the fleet from sailing, that Artemis demanded the sacrifice of Iphigenia, or that Artemis caused the bad weather to cease when the sacrifice had been performed. Instead, they say:

131–57   Calchas interpreted the omen of the eagles and the hare as signify-
          ing that Artemis might be hostile to the expedition and might
          prevent it from sailing. (His actual utterance is reported, 126–55.)
184–98   Bad weather prevented the fleet from sailing.
198–204   Calchas declared that Artemis should be propitiated by sacrificing
          Iphigenia: μῆχαρ . . . μάντις ἔκλαγξεν προφέρων Ἄρτεμιν (199–
          202).
205–27   Agamemnon was in a quandary (again, his actual utterance is
          reported, 206–17); but eventually ἔτλα δ᾿ οὖν θυτὴρ γενέσθαι
          θυγατρός (224f).
228–47   Iphigenia was sacrificed.

Three omissions from this narrative are noteworthy. We are not told why Artemis was angry; there is no hint at any form of the alternative legend (known to Hesiod, frr. 23a.21ff, 23b Merkelbach–West) that Artemis miracu-lously rescued Iphigenia; and we are not told that when the sacrifice had been performed the weather cleared. It may reasonably be felt that the third of these items hardly constitutes an important omission, because the Greeks did, after all, proceed to besiege Troy. I suggest, however, that it acquires some sig-nificance in the light of what the chorus do say (see below) at the point where they might have said, 'And so the wind abated . . .'. If the chorus had spoken directly of a clearing of the weather after the sacrifice, they would have taken a step towards giving us the impression that they are satisfied of the necessity of the sacrifice. Such an impression would have been greatly strengthened if they had committed themselves to an explanation of Artemis's anger or reported any singular circumstances which would hint at the substitution of an εἴδωλον for the girl whose throat was apparently cut. But such commitment is precisely what they avoid; for in their narrative, as in real life, the figure of the seer stands all the time between laymen and the mysterious intentions of the gods, and they cannot know whether his interpretation of events was correct or not.

It does not seem to me very likely, despite the temperamental instability and arbitrariness of deities in legend, that we are meant to believe that because a certain event in the animal world was distasteful to Artemis she therefore vented her anger on the humans whose enterprise, through no fault of theirs, was symbolized by that event. Those who do believe this speak from a position of strength, because they have the text on their side and do not have to reconstruct any ὑπόνοια. Yet we must remember that some measure of protest against the theological implications of much inherited legend had already been voiced by the time of the *Oresteia*, and I doubt whether Aeschylus's audience would have had any difficulty in seeing a mantic reasoning underlying Calchas's interpretation: 'This is an event which has an ominous character relevant to our enterprise. It is *also* an event which is distasteful to Artemis. I infer from *that* aspect of the event that *if* any deity is going to thwart our enterprise (131 οἷον μή τις κτλ.), it will be Artemis.' Speculation on *why* Artemis should want to thwart their purpose is irrelevant to that line of reasoning, and in any case unprofitable, since divine motives are commonly not ascertainable.[7] When the bad weather came, Agamemnon did not oppose (as he might have done) any judgement of his own to that of his seers (186 μάντιν οὔτινα ψέγων). The 'remedy' prescribed by Calchas was effected. The words uttered by the chorus at the conclusion of the narrative, τέχναι δὲ Κάλχαντος οὐκ ἄκραντοι (149), have four distinguishable implications: (i) Calchas said that Iphigenia must be killed, and killed she was; (ii) Calchas said that the bad weather would then stop, and stop it did; (iii) Calchas said that Troy would fall, and we may therefore still hope for its fall; (iv) Calchas uttered obscure but undoubtedly menacing words (151–5) about consequences of the sacrifice, and we cannot but fear that they will be fulfilled.[8]

By passing immediately from affirmation of the skill of Calchas to 'learning by suffering' (249f δίκα δὲ τοῖς μὲν παθοῦσιν μαθεῖν ἐπιρρέπει), thence to the reflection that to guess at the future is not only useless but an anticipation of grief (250–2 τὸ μέλλον δ' ἐπεὶ γένοιτ' ἂν κλύοις· πρὸ χαιρέτω· ἴσον δὲ τῷ προστένειν), and eventually to an expression of hope that all may be well (255 πέλοιτο δ' οὖν τἀπὶ τούτοισιν εὖ πρᾶξις), the chorus sound again a sequence of notes which we first heard in 121 αἴλινον αἴλινον εἰπέ, τὸ δ' εὖ νικάτω, after their description of the eagles' devouring of the hare: the event has a menacing aspect, which makes them fear future evil, but they hope and wish for future good (as one does), and they are acutely aware that they cannot know in

---

[7] In saying this I do not mean to deny that Aeschylus and his audience may well have had in mind a good reason why Artemis should have acted as an enemy to Agamemnon: Hugh Lloyd-Jones, *CQ* ns xii (1962) 190, points out that in Homer Artemis, like Apollo and their mother Leto, is an ally of Troy (*Il.* xx 39f, 67–72, xxi 470–513); cf. B. Daube, *Zu dem Rechtsproblem in Aischylos' Agamemnon* (Zürich and Leipzig 1939) 149f – who, however, will not accept partisan deities in Aeschylus. The objection of R. D. Dawe (*Eranos* lxiv [1966] 14), that this role of Artemis is insufficiently conspicuous in Homer, is far from cogent, since different people recall different details. One would not have thought, for example, that Menelaus would have been remembered as μαλθακὸς αἰχμητής, a sneer rhetorically applied to him on one occasion (*Il.* xvii 588) by Apollo for the purpose of rousing Hector; but Pl. *Smp.* 174c – a passage criticized by Ath. 178a–e – indicates that he was so remembered, and that is a datum relevant to *Ag.* 122f.

[8] On the menacing character of seers' utterances and the predominantly pessimistic reactions to them cf. (with reference to *Ag.*) H. Klees, *Die Eigenart des griechischen Glaubens an Orakel und Seher* (Stuttgart n.d.) 88f.

prospect whether good or evil will prevail. The refrain αἴλινον κτλ. is repeated (139) after Calchas has proclaimed his fear of Artemis's hostility, and again (159) after his enigmatic reference to an enduring μῆνις. Agamemnon too hopes (217 εὖ γὰρ εἴη),[9] but does not know, that the consequences of obeying Calchas will be good. The chorus's famous affirmation of the power of Zeus (160–83) arises out of the conflict between hope and fear voiced in the refrain of 159.[10] The 'burden of care' is only to be 'cast from the mind' (165f) by recognition that it is not we who decide the outcome of events, but Zeus; I take the mood of these words to be essentially one of resignation, as in 250–2, and, if the chorus feel a 'relief' in contemplating the power of Zeus, it is the feeling of liberation which comes from mature acknowledgement of the limitation of one's own powers, not the euphoria induced by trust in an infinitely good deity. Naturally, we want Zeus to be inflexibly just and stern when it is we who are injured and aggrieved, but in other circumstances, particularly when we are on the same side as the person on whom the execution of justice may fall, we should feel easier in mind if Zeus were not so just.[11] καὶ παρ' ἄκοντας ἦλθε σωφρονεῖν (180f) is a statement of fact, not of faith, and can be uttered by a person of any religion or of none; χάρις βίαιος (182) is a grim oxymoron emphasizing the difference between χάρις from man to man and the corresponding transaction from god to man. Of course the 'learning by suffering' which Zeus has decreed (177f) has its positive side, especially if the sufferer survives (cf. Croesus to Cyrus in Hdt. i 207.1 τὰ δέ μοι παθήματα ἐόντα ἀχάριτα μαθήματα γέγονε), and in any case we can learn from the suffering of others. But its negative side, stemming from Hom. Il. xvii 32, xx 198 ῥεχθὲν δέ τε νήπιος ἔγνω, Hes. Op. 218 παθὼν δέ τε νήπιος ἔγνω, is much more relevant to the story of divination, hidden gods and human dilemmas; Zeus has so constructed the universe (denying man prescience as he once denied him fire) that we *cannot* understand whether we are taking the right course of action *until* we have experienced the consequences of that course.

I am not for a moment suggesting that Aeschylus was a rationalist who wished to discredit seers, or that he intended us to imagine the Argive elders as having progressed to the sceptical view expressed by the messenger in E. *Hel.* 744–57 (applauded by the chorus, 758–60), let alone the cynicism of E. *IA* 518–21. I suggest simply that Aeschylus was an observant, well-informed

---

[9] These words have been called 'cynical', 'sceptical' and 'despairing'; they are in fact a cliché (cf. Fraenkel *ad. loc.*) naturally uttered by a Greek embarking on unwelcome means to a desired end.

[10] Fraenkel (113) speaks of a 'sharp break' between 159 and 160, and in justifying this break (114) he treats the chorus as having reached 'a point of utter ἀμηχανία'. Dawe (2f) is right to question the appropriateness of this hyperbole, but goes to the other extreme in saying, 'There is *nothing* in the preceding verses which can be made to yield *any* point of attachment to the Hymn to Zeus' (my italics). 159, prompted by the menacing obscurity of Calchas's concluding utterance, is a very good point of attachment to a pair of stanzas which say in effect, 'Zeus will decide, anyway, and it is pointless to speculate in advance.'

[11] Rightly emphasized by A. J. Beattie, *CQ* NS v (1955) 15. In E. *Phoen.* 154f the Paidagogos says of Polyneikes' army σὺν δίκῃ δ' ἥκουσι γῆν· / ὃ καὶ δέδοικα μὴ σκοπῶσ' ὀρθῶς θεοί.

and reflective Greek who realized the magnitude of the predicament in which commanders of armies sometimes found themselves. An unusual event occurs, probably ominous but not immediately intelligible; or natural forces – wind, an eclipse, an earthquake – suggest that a supernatural being is communicating some uncertain intention. The commander may be no better equipped to decide on the action appropriate to these intimations than he is to set a fracture or paint a shield. He must go to his experts, the seers, and when he has listened to their interpretations he must decide whether to trust them and act on their advice, risking disaster if they turn out to be mistaken, or to defy and overrule them, trusting in his own judgement and risking punishment from gods and men if the seers prove to have understood the divine intention correctly. Hector in E. *Rh.* 63–9, describing wryly and with a touch of sarcasm how he yielded to his seers against his own sound military judgement, is modelled equally on the Hector of *Il.* xii 195–250, who scorns Poulydamas's scruples over a strange omen, and on scores of commanders in the Classical period. The issue could be of great moment, as the Athenians learned to their cost in August 413, when the seers' interpretation of the eclipse of the moon imposed a fatal delay on the departure from Syracuse; in criticizing Nicias for acceding to the superstitious fears of his men Thucydides (vii 50.4) may imply that Demosthenes, left to himself, would have stood up for a more practical view. A seer, after all, did not normally (there are exceptions) claim to operate solely or primarily by divine inspiration; he exercised a τέχνη. A certain Polemainetos, a seer of the generation after Aeschylus, bequeathed his books on divination to his friend Thrasyllos, who was thereby enabled to earn a good living as a seer himself (Isoc. xix 5–7, cf. 45). Xenophon, who was no sceptic, represents Cambyses as teaching his son Cyrus (*Cyr.* i 6.2) the essentials of divination so that he may interpret signs when no professional is available and may not be at the mercy of seers (ἐπὶ μάντεσι) should they wish to mislead him. Wherever arts and skills are exercised, error and fraud are possible, and to suppose error or fraud is a natural reaction to a distasteful divination. Oedipus, infuriated by Tiresias, accuses the old man of venality and deliberate falsehood (S. *OT* 378–89). The chorus, with less reason to be angry but much reason to be worried, take refuge in the reflection that one cannot know whether a seer is right: 499–503 ἀνδρῶν δ᾽ ὅτι μάντις πλέον ἢ 'γὼ φέρεται, / κρίσις οὐκ ἔστιν ἀληθής· / σοφίᾳ δ᾽ ἂν σοφίαν / παραμείψειεν ἀνήρ. To a Greek there was no impiety in recognizing the lessons of experience and the limitations of certainty. After all, when Odysseus in *Il.* ii 284ff urges the Greeks to stay at Troy and reminds them of the omen of the snake and the sparrows, although he ends his recital with the robust declaration, 'all that will be fulfilled' (330), he begins it with 'stay for a while, that we may learn *whether or not Calchas's prophecy is true*' (299f). In thee circumstances, are we to believe that Aeschylus means the chorus to take it for granted, without question, either that Calchas's interpretation of the will of Artemis was correct or that it was incorrect, and is it mere chance that for some reason he composed the lyrics in terms (186, 201, 248–50) which point to the opposite intention?[12]

Agamemnon, as reported by the chorus, regarded the army's demand for the sacrifice of his daughter as θέμις (214–17; it is misleading to say 'the chorus call the sacrifice θέμις', let alone, 'Aeschylus calls the sacrifice θέμις').[13] Agamemnon was quite right; it was undoubtedly θέμις for an army embarked on an enterprise which it felt to be just to demand the life of someone else's daughter in obedience to the prescription of an eminent seer. That the enterprise itself was righteous the chorus do assert: the abduction of Helen was a gross offence against Zeus Xenios (61, cf. 362ff, 748), so that the Greek expedition had the goodwill of Zeus. This does not mean that the chorus are inhibited from observing that the effort to punish Troy has already inflicted on the Greeks loss and suffering out of all proportion to the recovery of one man's wife (62, 225, cf. 448); enforcement of law, human or divine, not uncommonly produces a situation more heavily fraught with suffering than anything that can be confidently attributed to the original infringement of law. Again, reference to Zeus Xenios in no way implies that Zeus must necessarily have approved every act performed in furtherance of the expedition. The expedition was the instrument which he used for the chastisement of Troy; it also proves to have afforded an opportunity to create circumstances setting in motion a train of events which give effect to the curse uttered by Thyestes. Similarly in Isaiah 10.5ff the Assyrians are treated as an instrument employed by God for the chastisement of Israel, but not as themselves enjoying God's favour, for they are destined to eventual punishment and destruction when they have served their purpose. Gods, like men, often use the tools most readily available.

[12] N. G. L. Hammond (*JHS* lxxxv [1965] 47) makes the important point that Agamemnon's dilemma 'is very familiar to those who are engaged in a war and exercise command', but, whereas he formulates the crucial question as, 'Is one to stop or is one to take an action which will involve the death of innocent persons?', I would put more emphasis on (i) the relation between commander and seer, to which, perhaps, a partial modern parallel might be afforded by uncertainties over the interpretation of meteorological and intelligence reports, and (ii) the notorious fact that when we are responsible for the safety of others we commit cruelties which we would not commit purely in our own interests. Dawe's criticism (19) of Hammond seems, if I have understood it aright, to suggest that we should try to forget that fighting in battles was one of the experiences which formed the author of *Oresteia* and that personal acquaintance with commanders who had taken difficult decisions is likely to have been another. Why we should even permit ourselves to forget such a thing, I am not clear.

[13] Even if περιόργῳ ⟨σφ'⟩ is a mistaken emendation of περιόργως in 216, the connection of thought between 212f and 214ff and the order of phrases point to the army, not to Agamemnon, as the subject of ἐπιθυμεῖν; cf. the discussion by Dawe 16–18. I cannot agree with Lesky (82) that Agamemnon himself comes to feel a 'passionate desire' for the sacrifice; I dare say he passionately desires the end to which the sacrifice appears to be a means, but that is a very different matter. The analogies between *Ag.* 205–27 and *Se.* 653–719, to which Lesky (84) draws attention, are indeed interesting; but so are the great differences between the situation of Eteocles, who has good reasons for hating Polynices and a real need to kill him, and that of Agamemnon, who has had no occasion to feel anything but affection for his daughter.

The stanza 218–27, ἐπεὶ δ' ἀνάγκας ἔδυ λέπαδνον, so far from making a statement about Agamemnon's responsibility, precludes even the raising of a genuine question about it. δῦναι can be used both of deliberate and voluntary movement (e.g. A. fr. 461M, S. *Ant.* 1217, of entering a cave) and of totally involuntary movement (e.g. *Ag.* 1011f οὐκ ἔδυ πρόπας δόμος, where the preceding nautical imagery suggests the translation 'sink'). The 'yoke-strap of ἀνάγκη' is a variant of the common image 'yoke of ἀνάγκη', suggested by the fact that oxen and horses go under the yoke not because they want to but because man forces them to (cf. Pind. *P.* iv 234f βοέους δήσαις ἀνάγκᾳ / ἔντεσιν αὐχένας). ἀνάγκη is applicable to any physical, legal or moral force to which resistance is shameful, painful, perilous or for any other reason difficult. If the force is exercised by a deity upon a mortal, difficulty amounts to impossibility; this impossibility may be recognized by anyone who has decided that the force is divine, but the decision must precede the judgement that resistance is actually impossible.[14] Many ἀνάγκαι are resistible in principle: shame and fear (Pl. *Ep.* 7.337a), which we can sometimes overcome; lust (Pl. *R.* 485d), against which shame can sometimes be deployed effectively; the power of alcohol (Ba. fr. 20B.6f γλυκεῖ' ἀνάγκα . . . κυλίκων), to which few of us surrender our will in its entirety; or the moral and social obligation to maintain our parents (Is. vii 32, with the implication that it 'necessarily follows' as a matter of logic), which ungrateful children evade. The Spartan envoys at the Persian king's court successfully resisted, by refusing to prostrate themselves, the ἀνάγκη brought to bear on them by his bodyguard (Hdt. vii 136.1). [Xen.] *Cyn.* x 14 prescribes the 'only way out' (ἀπαλλαγή . . . μία μόνη) for a hunter caught in a nasty ἀνάγκη ('predicament'), on the ground with an angry boar over him. Agamemnon's predicament was that only five courses of action (nine, if we include as an option with four of them the despatch of Iphigenia to a safe refuge) were open to him, all disagreeable or perilous: suicide; flight; disbanding the expedition; waiting obstinately to see if Calchas would be proved wrong by the return of good weather; and obedience to Calchas. In E. *Phoen.* 896–985 Creon, faced by Tiresias with a demand for the sacrifice of his son Menoikeus, is torn by the fury, grief and despair which we can imagine also in Agamemnon, and he puts his son's preservation first; his plans are frustrated by the boy's own patriotism and courage, and we may in any case feel that the ground has been cut from under his feet by one powerful retort of Tiresias (922), ἀπόλωλεν ἀλήθει' ἐπεὶ σὺ δυστυχεῖς; Agamemnon took the course which most people with Greek values and presuppositions would have felt bound to regard as dictated by honour, justice, piety and the overriding obligation to subordinate one's own life and

---

[14] I do not understand how Denniston and Page (xxiv n. 4) find it possible to say, 'the word means "necessity", "compulsion", *always*' (my italics) 'with a connotation of *inevitability*' (their italics). Apart from the instances quoted above, cf. *Pe.* 587, quoted below (p. 148).

the lives of one's dependants to the common good.[15] We must remember not only Euripides' treatment of the sacrifice of Chthonia by Erechtheus (especially fr. 50 [Austin] 14–21, 37–9) but the use which Lycurgus (*Leocr.* 98–101) makes of the story in addressing a jury. It is not very important whether we refer Agamemnon's 'yoke-strap of compulsion' to the forces which determined the particular course on which he eventually embarked or to the predicament which so limited the range of possible courses.[16] It is, in my submission, important that neither he nor anyone else could be certain – as certain as one would wish to be before killing one's own child – that his seer had interpreted the will of the gods correctly, and this dimension of his dilemma seems to me emphasized by the terms in which the chorus tells the story.

The chorus use very harsh words (219–23) in describing how Agamemnon accepted the sacrifice as the right alternative. They react in this way because the cutting of a girl's throat as if she were a sheep constitutes a pitiable and repulsive event; whether it is necessary or unnecessary, commanded by a god or the product of human malice or perversity, makes no difference to the emotional reaction of the chorus (or of any other reasonable person) to such a sight or story.[17]

They describe by implication Agamemnon's state of mind as αἰσχρόμητις τάλαινα παρακοπά (222f) because anything against which one feels a revulsion, aesthetic, moral or empathetic, is αἰσχρός, and because Greek emotive language (cf. p. 137 above) was normally indifferent to any distinction between a cruel, wicked or reckless act committed by a manifestly insane person and a comparable act committed by those whose behaviour did not otherwise afford comprehensive evidence of insanity. They also call Agamemnon's state of mind 'impious, impure, unholy' (219f δυσσεβῆ ... ἄναγνον ἀνίερον) because Greek emotive language exploited to the full the assumption that what is offensive to the speaker, or to man in general, is also offensive to the gods; this is evident from (*inter alia*) the widespread use of θεοῖς ἐχθρός as a general term of abuse and disapproval (cf. Philoctetes' addressing of Odysseus as ὦ θεοῖς ἔχθιστε in S. *Ph.* 1031), the readiness of the

---

[15] H. D. F. Kitto, *Form and Meaning in Drama* (London 1959) 5, calls the sacrifice 'assuredly . . . a price which a man of courage and sense would refuse to pay'. It is perfectly possible to pass an adverse moral judgement on Agamemnon by some modern standard, but I feel pretty sure that many an Athenian in Agamemnon's place would have thought that courage and sense demanded the sacrifice; in Clytaemnestra's place, he would have thought the opposite; and in the chorus's, he would have *felt* as they do and would have changed his *opinion* frequently about the claims of courage and sense.

[16] The phrasing of the sentence strongly suggests the former, and editors have normally taken it so.

[17] Lesky (82) remarks, 'I must object to the attempt to disparage these words of the chorus as a personal opinion or even a misunderstanding on its part'. For my part, I must object to the implications of the word 'disparage', to the suggestion that a value-judgement is something other than a 'personal opinion' and to the treatment of 'misunderstanding' as a meaningful word in the discussion of this particular passage.

orators to apply ἀσεβής, δυσσεβής or ἀνόσιος indiscriminately to conduct of which they disapprove (cf. Lycurg. *Leocr.* 93, where εὐσεβεῖς is the antonym of κακοῦργοι), and the comic use of (e.g.) ἱερόσυλος as a term of abuse in cases which have nothing to do with the literal meaning of the word.[18] This consideration may be helpful in respect of another Aeschylean passage which does not seem to have received a satisfactory interpretation in terms of religion and law,[19] *Su.* 9f γάμον Αἰγύπτου παίδων ἀσεβῆ τ' ὀνοταζόμεναι ⟨διάνοιαν suppl. Weil⟩. Whether Aeschyulus or any of his contemporaries could have demonstrated to the satisfaction of a level-headed ἐξηγητής that it was *impious* of a commander to sacrifice his daughter when told by his seer that Artemis demanded it, I greatly doubt.[20] Did the contemporaries of Euripides think that it was impious of Erechtheus to sacrifice Chthonia? It is a singular fact – especially singular if we have Aristophanes' *Frogs* fresh in our minds – that Euripides transfers the sacrifice and self-sacrifice of princes and princesses to the plane of rhetoric, whereas Aeschylus brings us down to earth and makes us feel what such a thing is really like. Since his chorus are not giving a considered judgement as theologians, philosophers or legal consultants, but discharging their emotions in words, the question, 'But was it really *impious?*' is perhaps inappropriate.

My emphasis on the representational and strictly dramatic aspects of *Ag.* 104–257, at the expense of its speculative and theological aspects, impinges on the difficult question of positive characterization in choruses. That the Eumenides and the panic-stricken women of *Se.* 78–180 coexist in the same dramatic corpus as choral stanzas which could be uttered by people of either sex and any age, status or nationality suffices to show that distinctiveness of choral characterization is a matter of degree, and that questions about this aspect of the chorus in any given play are not answerable by recourse to interpretative dogma.[21] There is no lack of parallels for a choral utterance which

---

[18] Cf. Alexis fr. 15, where one character remarks successively οὐδὲν ἀσεβεὶς οὐδέπω and ἁγνεύεις ἔτι while another checks through the items of a shopping-account. The important boundary in the usage of words which carry, or can be made to carry, an emotive charge does not lie between the serious and the humorous but between the technical, informative or objective (philosophy, science, exegesis, jurisprudence) and the artistic, manipulative or subjective (poetry, *expressive* drama, oratory, conversation).

[19] Cf. A. F. Garvie, *Aeschylus 'Supplices': Play and Trilogy* (Cambridge 1969) 215ff.

[20] Cf. F. Schwenn, *Die Menschenopfer bei den Griechen und Römern* (Giessen 1915) 121–40, on the part played in Attic and other Greek myths by human sacrifice, especially the sacrifice of a princess, on the command of an oracle. D. Kaufman-Bühler, *Begriff und Funktion der Dike in den Tragödien des Aischylos* (Bonn 1955) 63, 72f, 78f, maintains that the sacrifice of Iphigenia is an offence against divine Dike, and that Artemis cannot have required it; this amounts to saying that Calchas was wrong, but Kaufman-Bühler does not follow up the dramatic implications of that. The same criticism may be made of Wilamowitz, *Aischylos: Interpretationen* (Berlin 1914) 166, upon whose conviction that Aeschylus is rejecting legends about deities demanding human sacrifice Kaufman-Bühler's fuller exposition is based.

[21] Fraenkel (248), criticizing interpretations of 475–87 (see p. 149 below), will not allow a chorus to 'function as an ordinary character'. Ctr. R. P. Winnington-Ingram, *CQ* NS iv (1954) 25f, on elements of consistency in the characterization of the chorus of *Ag.*

reveals and expresses an irrational frame of mind. In *Ag.* 1132f the chorus's rhetorical question, 'What message of good comes to men from oracles?' carries the implication that oracles and inspired utterance *always* foretell evil; the implication is false, but emotion notoriously prefers 'always' and 'never' to a judicious 'sometimes'. In *Ag.* 757f δίχα δ' ἄλλων μονόφρων εἰμί carries the suggestion that the belief that only impiety, not innocent prosperity and good fortune, provokes divine punishment is novel, or at least rare; this suggestion is not borne out by the available evidence, but contrasting a view explicitly with another and asserting its originality is one mode of emphasis. The chorus of Persian elders in *Pe.* 584–90 τοὶ δ' ἀνὰ γᾶν Ἀσίαν δὴν / οὐκέτι περσονομοῦνται, / οὐκέτι δασμοφοροῦσιν / δεσποσύνοισιν ἀνάγκαις offers a related phenomenon. Conceivably the retreat of Xerxes was followed by widespread revolt in the Persian empire; or possibly Aeschylus at the time of writing believed, for one reason or another, that the empire was or had lately been in revolt; but since the epitome of Ctesias has nothing to say about this, and there is no Oriental documentary or archaeological evidence to suggest it, I would suppose that Aeschylus made his chorus utter a gloomy generalization about revolt simply because that is what they would be likely to say in their situation.[22]

If, however, we are seeking a really substantial parallel for interpretation of *Ag.* 104–257 in representational terms, we must consider *Ag.* 355–488, where – as seems obvious to me, and quite out of the question to many others – a sequence of reactions of an irrational but entirely familiar type is portrayed realistically.

355–402	Troy has fallen, and her fall is just punishment for the sin of Paris.
403–28	Helen's flight inflicted great sorrow on Menelaus.
429–58	And the war has inflicted great suffering on the Greeks, so that there is resentment against the Atridae.
459–74	And victory may incur divine hostility.
475–87	Perhaps it is not true – who knows? – that Troy has fallen.

If we speak of a 'sequence of thought' here, we must make it plain that we do not mean a *logical* process of inference from premises to conclusion.[23] It would be nonsensical to argue: '(a) Troy has fallen. (b) I am apprehensive about what will follow its fall. (c) *Therefore* perhaps it has not fallen.' But the narrative statement, 'They believed that Troy has fallen; then they reflected on some possible consequences of its fall; *therefore* they doubted whether it

---

[22] The use of Ἀσία, Ἀσίς and cognate words in the *Persae* makes it very unlikely that 584ff refer to the Aegean coast of Asia Minor.

[23] Wilamowitz, *Griechische Verskunst* (Berlin 1921), 185f, reconstructs what could be called a rational process, in so far as it ostensibly leads to a conclusion that the gods *cannot* have allowed Agamemnon to capture Troy ('iustitiam divinam eis ipsis, qui poenas demeruerunt, triumphum concessisse quis potest credere?'), but an infusion of irrationality is needed (cf. Fraenkel, 247) to justify 'qui poenas demeruerunt'.

had fallen', would describe a particular case of a common *causal* process,[24] and it is this case which Aeschylus has put before us in dramatic terms. Fraenkel (246–9), admitting that anyone in the situation of the Argive elders 'will naturally be the prey of contradictory emotions', regarded Aeschylus as bringing one element of that emotional complex into exceptional – and, he seems to imply, unrealistic – prominence in order to create a dramatic contrast between the return of doubts and the arrival of the herald who confirms the news of the fall of Troy. Denniston and Page treat this contrast as the least unsatisfactory explanation so far proposed, but are even less inclined than Fraenkel to compromise with what he called Hermann's 'expedient of a subtle psychological speculation' (247; cf. ibid. 'flimsy psychological speculation', which seems to refer to Wilamowitz and Kranz as well as to Hermann).[25] The rhetoric of 'expedient' and 'flimsy' is too crude to do much harm, but that 'subtle' and 'speculation' should be used rhetorically as derogatory terms is more to be regretted, for the interpretation of Greek poetry cannot easily dispense either with subtlety or with speculation. The derogatory use of 'psychological' is more serious, and it would be a pity if we allowed ourselves as a matter of course to be provoked by the mere mention of psychology into adverse reactions which would have surprised the Victorians.[26] The situation is curiously confused by the willingness of those who profess mistrust of psychology to propose interpretations which do not seem to differ in kind from what they criticize in others, e.g. Fraenkel (145) on what he regards as a contradiction between *Ag.* 249–54 and 255–7: 'The behaviour of the Chorus here is just as full of contradictions and just as natural as under certain conditions the behaviour of men at their prayers often is . . .'.

Most people would probably agree without more ado that no interpretation of a Greek text is likely to be right, except by a fluke, if it depends on the assumption that the author consciously adhered to a psychological theory which, so far as our evidence goes, contradicts such psychological theories as were held in antiquity, especially if it is a theory dependent on modern experimentation which for technical reasons was not within the capacity of the ancients. Everyone, on the other hand, would agree that some intellectual and emotional processes seem to be universally distributed throughout known

---

[24] It may often be observed that when a participant in a discussion begins with 'I say that, because . . .', he proceeds sometimes to give the grounds on which his conclusion is based, but at other times to make a purely autobiographical statement. Denniston and Page describe 475ff as an 'unmotived rejection of the theme on which the whole of [the chorus's] song was founded'. This is fair so long as 'unmotived' is taken in the limited sense 'logically unfounded', but the *cause* of the chorus's rejection of the news has in fact been fully presented to us in the course of the song.

[25] Hermann in his note on 454, of which Fraenkel quotes only the first half, suggested that the chorus's deep mistrust of Clytaemnestra conflicts with, and eventually prevails over, their joy in victory. W. Kranz, *Stasimon* (Berlin 1923) 159f, offers an interpretation which has certain affinities with Hermann's, Wilamowitz's (see n. 23 above) and that which I have suggested, but also stresses the dramatic contrast with the arrival of the herald. Fraenkel eventually (248f) comes very near to admitting what he began by rejecting.

[26] Cf. (e.g.) George Eliot's letters to John Blackwood, 29 February 1860 and 9 July 1860.

human cultures. Different cultures have adopted different theories about such processes, and they have differed in the assurance with which they regard their own theories as simple common sense dictated by nature and shared by all good and sensible people; our own traditional culture has failed as much as any to recognize the extent to which what it calls common sense is a set of beliefs, assumptions and denials founded on a highly selective treatment of experience, and we have always to reckon with the possibility that the Greeks took for granted as self-evident some psychodynamic principles which occasion surprise when they surface after being submerged for a couple of millennia. No one, however, can fairly be called a psychologist unless he thinks both rationally and systematically on the subject of thought and feeling; Plato and Aristotle were psychologists in so far as they theorized explicitly on that subject, while Aeschylus, so far as our evidence goes, was not. But that is not to say that Aeschylus did not observe accurately, or that the theory implicit in the dramatic representation which he founded on observation was inferior to anybody's explicit theory. The article to which H. J. Rose gave the unfortunate title 'Aeschylus the Psychologist' (*SO* xxxii [1956] 1ff) would more properly have been entitled, 'Realism' (or 'Realistic Characterization', or 'Realistic Representation') 'in Aeschylus'.

This leads us into a second reason which sometimes makes an interpreter of Aeschylus shy of saying anything which others may dismiss as an excursion into psychology: the fear that he may be assumed to have committed himself to an unfashionable extent to the view that Aeschylus intended to create characters which would be at the very least self-consistent and even on occasion unique but totally convincing individuals, and the further fear that he may compound his offence by noticing occasions on which choruses behave like recognizable individuals. I do not think that anyone should be in a hurry to take up a dogmatic position on these questions; there is nothing like enough agreement on which elements in a given play amount to a significant degree of consistency in characterization and which do not.[27] When, if ever, there is a greater measure of agreement, we shall be in a better position to consider how far, and in what circumstances, characterization is sacrificed to other dramatic purposes.[28] In the meantime, it may be useful to see how many passages in Greek drama are explicable without residue as realistic portrayal of irrational processes, familiar to us from introspection and observation, working upon matter furnished by Greek beliefs and values and expressing themselves in Greek terms.

---

[27] For example, the description of Agamemnon as μάντιν οὔτινα ψέγων (186) and his reply to Clytaemnestra in 934, εἴπερ τις εἰδώς γ' εὖ τόδ' ἐξεῖπεν τέλος, create a consistency in the character of Agamemnon. About the fact of consistency, there can be no argument; it is simply there, under our eyes; the argument can only be on whether the consistency is due to mere coincidence or to the poet's design. Of course, if R. Merkelbach (in *Studien zur Textgeschichte und Textkritik* [Cologne 1959] 168ff) is right in his rearrangement of lines between 932 and 945, *cadit quaestio.*

[28] I find myself in essential agreement with the argument of Mrs P. E. Easterling (in a paper read to the Classical Association in April 1972) that dramatic effect is diminished to the extent to which the characters whose interaction constitutes the effect are deficient in credibility and intelligibility.

16

The Red Fabric in the *Agamemnon*

Did Aeschylus mean to present us in *Ag.* 810–974 with a great commander who is tired but patient, shrewd but courteous? Or with an arrogant and suspicious tyrant, whose pride surfaces at the slightest pretext? He answers the welcoming speech of his wife with words not of consolation or affection but of reproof, with a sarcastic joke about the length of her speech, criticism of its obsequious fulsomeness, and a refusal to tread on the red fabric which the women slaves have spread out on the ground before his feet. Eventually he allows himself to be persuaded to perform that action, because he is vanquished by an argument to which we are all inclined to yield: 'Please, I beg you! What I am asking is so important to me, but it costs you so little. In this moment of victory show your compassion and your generosity by freely granting me what I ask.' This appeal, which I have paraphrased and amplified, naturally makes Agamemnon see himself in the role of the king at the banquet, who listens to any request from his guests, or the king in judgement, who displays his power as much by indulgence to the weak as by humiliation of the strong. I take it for granted that most of us would yield to such a temptation. But before he comes to that point, his resistance is weakened by a couple of arguments which are rational in form and do not depend on the personal relationship between the conqueror and his suppliant wife.

The first argument is (933): 'Would you, through fear, have vowed to the gods to do this (ἔϱδειν τάδε)?', i.e. 'Can you not imagine a situation in which you would have said to a god, "Save me from this danger, and I vow that when I have returned home I will tread on costly fabrics"?' Agamemnon says yes, admitting that he would have done that if 'someone who knew well' – that is to say, a skilled seer – had so advised him.[1]

Now the second argument. Clytemestra goes on (935): 'What would Priam

---

[1] The resumption of the essential point in 963 leaves no doubt that τάδε refers to treading on the fabric, not to the refusal (cf. Fraenkel's commentary, ii 421f). It follows that one must opt for ἐξεῖπεν, Auratus's emendation, in place of ἐξεῖπον (FTr). If Merkelbach (*Festschrift Jachmann* [Cologne 1959] 168–71) is right in his rearrangement of the passage, giving the question to Agamemnon and the answer to Clytemestra, the argument of this paper is not invalidated.

have done in your opinion, if he had accomplished this?' (εἰ τάδ᾽ ἤνυσεν, i.e. 'if he had won what you have won'). Agamemnon replies, 'I am sure he would have walked on patterned (*sc.* fabrics)'. From this the following exchange develops (937ff):

> *Cl.* Do not, then, show respect for human blame.
> *Ag.* But the voice of the people has great power.
> *Cl.* He who provokes no jealousy earns no admiration.

Agamemnon makes no direct reply to that, but remarks on his wife's wish – unwomanly, in his view – for conflict; then comes the queen's final appeal to her husband.

Each of the two arguments raises a problem. First: in what circumstances and with what motives would a seer have said to a commander, 'You can escape this danger by vowing to a god to tread on costly fabrics when you reach home safely'? Secondly: what exactly is the purpose of trying to make Agamemnon behave as Priam would have behaved? Agamemnon's reluctance to tread on the fabric was produced in part by his conviction that such honours belong to the gods alone (922 θεούς τοι τοῖσδε τιμαλφεῖν χρεών); any mortal who accepts such an honour incurs danger (923f ἐν ποικίλοις δὲ θνητὸν ὄντα κάλλεσιν βαίνειν ἐμοὶ μὲν οὐδαμῶς ἄνευ φόβου).

If Agamemnon means that the gods will be angry at his action, how can he imagine that a seer could have told him to promise the gods something which they would regard as insulting to themselves?

Let us begin by asking how far his fear of walking on the fabric really is fear of the gods. It is true that what he says in 921–30 entirely agrees with the hypothesis that he is afraid of the resentment of the people of Argos against a mortal king who enriches his own return by ingredients worthy of a god. That is confirmed explicitly by his reference to the people in 938 φήμη ... δημόθρους. Nevertheless, when we take 946f into account, it is obvious that religious fear cannot be excluded:

> καὶ τοῖσδέ μ᾽ ἐμβαίνονθ᾽ ἁλουργέσιν θεῶν
> μή τις πρόσωθεν ὄμματος βάλοι φθόνος.

Although in all probability the word θεῶν here goes with ἁλουργέσιν ('on these coloured fabrics which belong to the gods') rather than with τις ... φθόνος ('some divine resentment'), the addition of πρόσωθεν ('may no look of resentment strike me from afar') leaves no doubt that Agamemnon is alluding here to divine resentment, because that word πρόσωθεν occurs five lines later with reference to the supervision which the gods exercise over human actions, and we find it elsewhere in tragedy with the same connotation.

We have to conclude, therefore, that one and the same act, walking on the fabric, has two quite different aspects, one offensive to the gods and the other in certain circumstances acceptable.

The fabric is called πετάσματα (908) because Clytemestra orders it to be spread out; it is πετάσματα in so far as it πετάννυται.[2] Thereafter it is called εἵματα (921, 960, 963); it is woven (ὑφαί 949, cf. 960), dyed (βαφαί 960; cf. ἀλουργῆ 946) and patterned (ποικίλα 910, 923, 936). The fabric is not a carpet,[3] and treading on it will spoil it. We have to think – and I am speaking not of the theatre, but of the area in front of the palace evoked by the theatrical portrayal – of a fabric of exquisite workmanship put on to a ground covered with sharp stones and defiled by the excrement of dogs, pigs and children, by urine, sputum and dirt of all kinds. By taking off his sandals Agamemnon reduces the risk of breaking the threads, but nothing can prevent the underside of the fabric from being soiled. He speaks in fact (948f) of 'wasting the wealth of the house',[4] and Clytemestra replies to that (958–62) that the house is rich enough to afford the loss. She adds something (963–5) which throws light on the earlier question she addressed to her husband: 'I would have vowed to tread on many fabrics if I had been told by an oracle that it was necessary in order to bring you back safe' (ψυχῆς κόμιστρα τῆσδε).

The notion that an oracle could declare to a wife 'Promise that if your husband comes back safe you will tread on and spoil costly fabrics' is a variant on the common notion that it is possible to secure the goodwill of a god by vowing to dedicate a costly object in his temple or to sacrifice to him many fine animals, and it reminds us that the practice of sacrifice involves at least two different religious principles. In any given sacrifice either of these principles may predominate, or both may be blended.

On the one hand, we can present a god with something pleasing to him by reason of its beauty or its exceptional value. If the gift is inanimate, we can most easily transfer ownership of it to a god by dedicating it to him in his temple, just as one gives a valuable or beautiful present to a friend, who will keep it thereafter in his house. The performance of songs, dances and plays at a festival can be regarded as a gift of human energy to the gods, both for their pleasure and for ours. If the gift is alive, we can offer it to the gods by abandoning it – rather as we may leave milk outside the door for the fairies, even though we know that it is the hedgehogs which drink it – or we can treat its destruction as a means of transferring it from the human to the super-human world; after all, we have no other mechanism of transference at our disposal.

On the other hand, man abases himself in sacrifice. Men are the subjects of the gods, and a ruler feels himself threatened by the power, wealth and achievements of his subjects (cf. the myth, of popular type,[5] related by

---

[2] On the semantic analysis of substantives ending in -μα I have learned much from the (unpublished) St Andrews doctoral dissertation (1977) of Dr A. Kapsomenos, 'Aspects of the Vocabulary of Aeschylus' 370ff.

[3] Fraenkel (on 909) speaks of 'carpet-like fabrics'.

[4] φθείροντα πλοῦτον necessitates Schütz's emendation δωματοφθορεῖν (σωματοφθορεῖν FTr).

[5] Cf. *JHS* lxxxvi (1966) 41ff.

Aristophanes in Plato's *Symposium*, in which the boldness of the human race threatens the gods and provokes drastic counter-measures from them). Just as in some animal species a subordinate individual can ensure the tolerance of stronger members of the group by pretending to be an infant or a female or an adversary already overcome, so man can conciliate the gods – and escape the fate of the tallest trees, which are struck by lightning (Hdt. vii 10ε) – by reducing his own wealth or power. In their note on *Ag*. 933f Denniston and Page rightly point to the story of Polykrates, who followed the advice of Amasis (Hdt. iii 40–3) and tried to avert more serious calamities by voluntary infliction of a misfortune on himself. He threw into the sea a ring of exceptional beauty and value, and so tried to become an object of compassion rather than jealousy. Aeschylus makes use of this idea also in *Ag*. 1005–14, where the image of the ship which is lightened and saved by casting a portion of its cargo into the sea alludes to the need for abstention from excessive acquisition.[6] A more positive development of this aspect of sacrifice is the acceptance of loss and suffering as an annihilation of one's own will and a total submission to the ruling god. When Abraham brings himself to sacrifice Isaac, he is not presenting God with a Ganymede, but showing that he is ready to carry out any command whatsoever, no matter how painful.

The interaction between these two aspects of sacrifice is exemplified by the two different traditions which concern the killing of Iphigeneia. In the *Agamemnon* her immolation is the terrible price which the king has to pay to Artemis for abeyance of the wind. In Hesiod fr. 23a.15–26 the sacrifice is accompanied by a transference of the girl from the human to the superhuman world; Iphigeneia becomes immortal. According to E. *IT* 18–24 Agamemnon once promised Artemis to sacrifice to her the most beautiful creature born in his kingdom that year (ὅτι ... ἐνιαυτὸς τέκοι κάλλιστον). He was thinking, of course, of the sacrifice of an animal whose beauty would gladden both the goddess and the mortals who would take part in the sacrifice and enjoy eating the animal; but fifteen years later, when the fleet was immobilized at Aulis, the seer reminded him that he had not paid the debt, because the most beautiful creature born that year was in fact his daughter, and now it fell to him to mourn her loss.

According to Clytemestra's reasoning, treading on the fabric is a perfect example of the second aspect of sacrifice; the destruction of one's own property serves the purpose of self-abasement and so wins the favour of the gods. I cannot find in Greek literature any parallel which is absolutely conclusive; yet the idea must have existed in Athenian society in Aeschylus's time, or the words 'Would you have promised . . .?' and 'I would have vowed . . .' are unintelligible. The sacral aspect of the situation does not enter Agamemnon's head until he has revolted against what seems to him luxurious and arrogant. Clytemestra persuades him that one can look at the

---

[6] The relation between the two passages is noted by Blass, *Mélanges Henri Weil* (Paris 1898) 11–13.

situation from an entirely different point of view and justify what at first sight seemed unjustifiable. In this way we sometimes persuade a friend to do something to which he was at first opposed; and sometimes we are right. But it should be noted that Clytemestra has changed her tack. Her first reference to the fabric, when she asked Agamemnon not to put on the ground 'the foot which trampled Troy' (906f), was entirely adulatory. Agamemnon's refusal compels her to use her reserve arguments.

Now let us look at the second argument put forward by Clytemestra: 'What, do you think, would Priam have done?' In the fifth century there was always a tendency to regard the Trojan War as a model of the conflict between Asia and Europe which culminated in the Persian Wars. Sophocles takes this assimilation much further than Aeschylus,[7] but the representation of Trojans in Phrygian costume goes back to vase-painters of the early fifth century. In the *Agamemnon* the assimilation finds expression (1050ff) in the un-Homeric assumption of Clytemestra that Cassandra may not understand Greek.[8] Since Agamemnon reproves Clytemestra's welcome as barbaric adulation (918–20), the proposal that he should imitate the Asiatic king whom he has conquered seems strangely maladroit; yet he accepts it.[9] Why? In Clytemestra's question and Agamemnon's answer there is a psychological realism. When I speak of 'psychology', I do not mean modern theories designed to trace psycho-dynamic mechanisms, but ways of speaking and acting which, when we have observed them in ourselves, we can find everywhere in Greek tragedy, conspicuous even on the surface, not hidden in the darkness of the unconscious. Once I am in conflict with an adversary, I become vulnerable to the temptation to act as I think he would have acted. A variety of fears creates this temptation: the fear of appearing less virile and aggressive, or of putting myself at a disadvantage by excessive scruples. Moreover, I am convinced that I am in the right and my opponent in the wrong, so that an act committed in furtherance of my own intentions seems to me different from the same act committed by him in furtherance of his. That way, many cruelties are perpetrated; and, if in saying so I stir a few memories of forty years ago, that is not unintentional. It must be added that neither the conflict nor the temptations which accompany it are extinguished by victory. Even when the feared and hated enemy or boss or parent has long been dead, we can continue, in our attitudes and behaviour, a shadow-fight against him. Clytemestra does not want to risk a hardening of Agamemnon's refusal by recalling Priam as Asiatic king; she gets the reply she wants by means of the phantasm of Priam as victor (εἰ τάδ' ἤνυσεν). Agamemnon yields to the temptation of refusing on any account to be inferior to his dead enemy.

[7] Cf. Helen Bacon, *Barbarians in Greek Tragedy* (New Haven, Conn. 1961) 101ff.

[8] There is a splendid irony in this passage, since Cassandra understands more than anyone; cf. H. Diller, *Entretiens de la Fondation Hardt* viii (1961) 48f (= *Kleine Schriften* [Munich 1971] 425f).

[9] Verrall comments, 'Priam is no argument, it is the king's very ground of objection.' Verrall saw the paradox; yet it is precisely the argument which 'is no argument' which helps to overcome Agamemnon's objection, and Verrall was not interested enough in why that should be so.

Clytemestra's following words, 'Do not, then, show respect for human blame', resume both of the two arguments which I have described above. Since Agamemnon admits that he might have vowed to the gods to tread on the fabric, he has no divine resentment to fear; and, since she has awakened his pride by her reference to Priam, she feels sure now of her ability to make him treat human jealousy with contempt. He says that what he fears is the hostility of his subjects, and Clytemestra has the last word by suggesting, as Pindar suggested to Hiero (*P.* 1.85f) that jealousy is not easily separated from prosperity.

Although I think that good psychological observation is one aspect of Clytemestra's second argument, there is one further consideration which in my view helps to explain why Aeschylus introduced the motif of red fabric into the play; and, if I am on the right lines, it explains also why the encouragement to follow Priam's (hypothetical) example has to be made explicit.

To the modern student of Greek drama, whose interest is normally focused on the central, classical period of Greek literature and, within that period, on those few authors whose work has survived, it should not be difficult to recall a series of remarkable events which happened less than twenty years before the production of the *Oresteia* and which must have made a deep impression on the Greek world: a series of events which in its structure presents an obvious resemblance to Agamemnon's sudden passage from power and glory to the shame of a squalid death. They are, however, events which, for reasons which I will try to explain, even the most discursive commentators on Aeschylus have refrained from mentioning; I refer to the career of Pausanias, regent of Sparta, a career of which Herodotus describes the zenith and Thucydides the nadir.

At the battle of Plataea Pausanias commanded a vast and heterogeneous panhellenic army. By defeating the Asiatic army commanded by Mardonius he won a victory which Herodotus (ix 64) called 'the best there has ever been'. His dedicatory inscription at Delphi described him as Ἑλλήνων ἀρχηγός. A few years later he died of hunger in a Spartan sanctuary, under the eyes of the ephors who had decided to get rid of him. This transition from panhellenic command to a lonely and unheroic death is the essential point of resemblance between Pausanias and Agamemnon. Aeschylus has chosen to insert one further element which brings out even more clearly how much the structure of the fate of each of them has in common with that of the other.

It was hard for Pausanias to exact obedience from one of his Spartan commanders, and he treated his Athenian allies with exemplary sensitivity; but in 478, as head of a panhellenic fleet at Byzantium, he alienated the allies by his arrogant and tyrannical behaviour. Immediately after the battle of Plataea, according to the tradition reproduced by Herodotus (ix 82), he had drawn a lively contrast between Greek frugality and Asiatic luxury; but when he had been deprived of his naval command and returned to Byzantium with a ship of his own he adopted Persian clothing and lifestyle and travelled with a non-Greek bodyguard (Th. i 130). Thus the Greek victor yielded to the temptation to adopt the manners which Asiatics regarded as appropriate to a person of his status.

Now we can recall not only Agamemnon's initial refusal to tread on the red fabric but also the importance acquired in overcoming his resistance by the argument 'Do what Priam would have done.' There is no doubt of the utility of subjecting Greek tragedy to structural criticism which discovers identical schemes in different parts of the same play,[10] but it must also be recognized that there are structures and schemata common to certain historical events and the dramatic themes of a poet influenced by those events. The fact that no commentator on the *Agamemnon* has mentioned Pausanias may be due to a decision on the part of commentators that the differences between the fate of Pausanias and the fate of Agamemnon are more important than the resemblances. It may, on the other hand, simply be due to the fact that Greek literature and Greek history are commonly studied in separate compartments, and a fortunate combination of circumstances has enabled me to study and teach both at the same time, so that I very readily treat as historical events both the political vicissitudes of a Spartan regent and the creative process which went on in the mind of an Athenian poet of genius. A third reason is to be sought in an understandable reaction against various attempts to 'decipher' a drama as if it were an allegorical or enigmatic presentation of contemporary political issues – a reaction which has discouraged us from asking what relations can link a drama to the experience of the person who wrote it and the experience of those who saw it. I am not in sympathy with the allegorical interpretation of tragedy, because such interpretations seem to me to underrate to a very great extent the force with which the tragic myths can operate directly on our emotions without any help from political passions. I observe, nevertheless, that in certain plays there is a deliberate insistence on links between the heroic world and contemporary politics (e.g. the treatment in *Eumenides* of the Argive alliance and the functions of the Areopagus). It appears that in certain other plays some elements of the heroic world have been distorted to make them fit a contemporary situation; for example, the 'democratization' of the Argive monarchy in Aeschylus's *Suppliants* and of the Athenian monarchy in the *Suppliants* of Euripides. In most tragedies I do not find evidence of this 'updating' of myths.

In pointing to the analogy between Agamemnon and Pausanias I do not mean that Aeschylus sought to communicate to his audience any reflection or sentiment about Pausanias, Sparta or the Persian Wars. I am simply proposing an exploration of the poetic process which generated the *Oresteia*, asking myself why Aeschylus wanted to introduce the motif of the red fabric into Agamemnon's return and why he put into Clytemestra's argument the question, 'What would Priam have done?' I am not satisfied with the usual

[10] E.g. Anne Lebeck, *The Oresteia: a Study in Language and Structure* (Washington, D.C. 1971) 80ff; cf. C. W. Macleod, *Maia* NS vi (1975) 201ff (= *Collected Essays* [Oxford 1983] 41ff).

explanations, which emphasize the arrogance and impiety of Agamemnon and exploit in various ways the concept that the gods now look on him with hostility or the concept that the character alienates himself from our sympathy by revealing his true nature and displaying his pride.

Is it suggested that if Agamemnon had categorically refused to tread on the fabric a messenger from Zeus would have stayed Clytemestra's hand at the moment when she was poised to give the fatal blow? And that the fulfilment of the curse of Thyestes would have been deferred – perhaps to the next generation? The revenge long planned by Aegisthus, son of Thyestes and seducer of Clytemestra, and the sequence of events set in train by the sacrifice of Iphigeneia (which gave Clytemestra a strong motive for revenge) converge inexorably on the killing of Agamemnon. Can we believe that the gods were still undecided when he was about to enter the palace? And that they said to one another, when he walked on the fabric, 'Now he no longer deserves our protection; he has shown himself impious, and so it is right that he should die'?

As for the mortal spectators of the play, they can easily see that Agamemnon is induced by arguments of slight weight to abandon his original position; but that is very different from saying that from now on they will enjoy participating in the murder of the conqueror of Troy by his adulterous wife and her cowardly lover. Even if the act of treading on the fabric was universally regarded as a serious offence against the gods, that would not necessarily imply *moral* shock or revulsion on the part of the audience. The act is more like that of a man smoking a cigarette while filling a tank with petrol in hot weather than that of a man planting an explosive device in his rival's car. Our reaction to stupidity is different from our reaction to evil. We are all victims of the severity of the gods, and can sympathize with one another. Undoubtedly we share the horror expressed by the chorus in their description of the sacrifice of Iphigeneia, but we can also understand – and Aeschylus has made sure of that – the intractability of the dilemma in which Agamemnon found himself because of the seer's verdict. If we were members of an ancient culture in which it was possible to say that killing enemies is an inexpressible joy (Xen. *Hi*. 2.15) or that the most agreeable and admirable way of living consists in taking by force the property of non-Greek peoples (Xen. *HG* v 1.16f), we would not shudder at hearing Agamemnon boast of his panhellenic victory and the destruction of Troy. We know that Clytemestra will kill him treacherously and that her death at the hands of her son will be approved by Apollo. In Euripides' time Agamemnon and Orestes were judged more harshly, and no doubt among the spectators of the *Oresteia* there were some who were disposed to judge those two characters harshly. However, Aeschylus did not intend to facilitate too sharp a judgement, but imparted to his characters a lifelike complexity. If he had wished us to be repelled by Agamemnon's treading on the fabric, he would have composed the episode in black and white instead of using subtle shades.

How the spectators of Greek tragedy related the extraordinary events taking place on stage to the circumstances of their own experience, and how far Aeschylus intended to emphasize that relation, are problems to which critics have given diverse answers. I suggested a few years ago[11] that Aeschylus could not have described Agamemnon's difficult situation at Aulis – given the expert religious interpretation which Agamemnon was in no position to refute – without thinking of the difficulties encountered by contemporary commanders whenever their judgement conflicted with the recommendations of their seers. There is no lack of reference to such conflicts in other plays, and I take it for granted that the audience of the *Oresteia* regarded them as a phenomenon common to the past and the present. This presupposition finds some confirmation in certain passages of the *Agamemnon* in which Aeschylus has chosen words in such a way as to bring out an essential identity between present and past and make the heroic age up-to-date. For example, he uses Athenian technical terminology when he speaks of Paris's offence against Menelaus: 41 ἀντίδικος, 534 ὀφλών . . . ἁρπαγῆς τε καὶ κλοπῆς δίκην;[12] and he uses the nautical term σέλμα in a figurative sense to distinguish between degrees of power (183, 1617f). The continuous loss of life among the combatants in the Trojan War is presented in terms of the arrival of urns filled with human ashes (434ff), an experience very familiar to the Athenians of the fifth century. Of particular significance is the tormented question which Agamemnon poses in his dilemma (213f): πῶς λιπόναυς γένωμαι συμμαχίας ἁμαρτών. He sees himself simultaneously exposed to two reproaches: that as an individual he has failed in his highest duty (an offence which in Attic law was called λιποναύτιον or λιποστράτιον, according to whether a fleet or a hoplite force was concerned), and that as representative of a city he has defaulted on that kind of collective obligation which had already provoked not only deep discord within the Athenian empire (cf. λιποστράτιον Th. i 99.1 and λιποστρατία vi 76.3) but also an inflexible decision on the part of the Athenians. The form of this Aeschylean passage is meant to emphasize the identity of the problems common to commanders of the heroic age and those of contemporary Greece.

Plato, considering the function of tragedy in his ideal state, was concerned above all with the effect which the behaviour of tragic characters could have on the moral character of the audience. Plato belonged to the classic tradition of literary criticism which is manifested in a crude form in Old Comedy and reappears, with much greater psychological refinement, in Aristotle. I would like to encourage critics to adopt a radically different standpoint in order to observe the interdependence of characters and spectators and to study the genesis of theatrical portrayal in the communal experiences in which the playwright himself participated.

---

[11] See pp. 135–50 above.
[12] Cf. Fraenkel on 41.

ADDITIONAL NOTES

P. 153, on sacrifice. *Entretiens de la Fondation Hardt* xxvii (1980) is devoted entirely to *Le Sacrifice dans l'antiquité*. I find myself in particular sympathy with the contribution of H. S. Versnel (135–94), who declares (184) 'My interest starts where the "original" functions of these rituals got lost to sight, whereas the rituals themselves did not disappear. . . .' Students of the Classical world should not shirk the attempt to understand the attitudes and presuppositions which caused the Greeks to take sacrifice for granted as a necessary ingredient of the relations between mortals and gods.

P. 156, on Pausanias's conduct and fate. P. J. Rhodes, *Historia* xix (1970) 387ff argues cogently that Thucydides uncritically followed a tradition hostile to Pausanias. I should also add that between Aeschylus's time and Thucydides' the portrayal of conquerors on the tragic stage (including precisely the scene which I have been discussing) may well have made its own contribution to the picture of Pausanias entertained by Athenians. My argument therefore requires an important qualification: Aeschylus's portrayal of Agamemnon's behaviour was influenced by the fate of Pausanias *if* the Thucydidean version, or something very like it, was widely entertained at Athens by 458.

17

The Political Aspect of Aeschylus's *Eumenides*

The ransacking of tragedy for indications of the political views of tragic poets is seldom profitable and may be disastrous.[1] But *Eumenides*, like much that Aeschylus wrote, is unusual, and one of its unusual aspects is the clarity and persistence with which the hearer's attention is engaged in the political present as well as in the heroic past; one might almost say, directed away from the past and towards the present. The nature of this redirection, and its implications, if any, for Aeschylus's own standpoint, are no new problem. My reason for discussing it once more is that not enough attention has been paid to the immediate dramatic context of the passages by which this redirection is effected or to the relation between these passages and the language of Greek politics in general.

I. THE CENTRAL STASIMON 490–565

(i) 490–3

> νῦν καταστροφαὶ νέων
> θεσμίων, εἰ κρατή-
> σει δίκα<τε>καὶ βλάβα
> τοῦδε μητροκτόνου.

Editors of Aeschylus have assumed[2] that these words cannot mean what they appear to mean: 'Now new ordinances are overthrown, if the cause pleaded, and the injury done, by this matricide are going to prevail.' The old laws, not the new, it is said, are in danger of overthrow, and it can only be the old laws

---

[1] See G. Zuntz, *The Political Plays of Euripides* (Manchester 1955), pp. 55ff for destructive and effective criticism of some common assumptions about historical allusions in tragedy.

[2] Strictly speaking I should except Stanley's expansion 'Nunc eversio novarum legum, *sc.* Apollinis et Minervae, juniorum deorum, si accusatio et punitio huius parricidae obtinebit' and Potter's translation (1759, repeated later in some minor English translations) 'Confusion on these upstart laws!' The latter does not commend itself as a piece of translation, and the former requires us to understand 'for otherwise . . .' with πάντας ἤδη κτλ.

which the Chorus defend and lament. Attempts to escape the *prima facie* meaning have taken the following forms:

(a) Emendation to give the sense 'overthrow of old ordinances' (ἕνων κ. θ., Cornford), 'overthrow of ordained laws' (κ. νόμων θ., Ahrens), 'overthrow of my ordinances' (ἐμῶν κ. θ., Weil), or 'change to new ordinances' (μεταστροφαὶ ν. θ., Meineke).

(b) Interpretation of νέων θεσμίων as subjective genitive, giving the sense 'overthrow (*sc.* of old ordinances) by new ordinances' (Scholefield, Schütz, Wecklein).

(c) Acceptance of νέων θεσμίων as objective genitive, with the sense 'overthrow of ordinances, making them new' (Paley, cf. *PV* 309 μεθάρμοσαι τρόπους νέους, where, however, μεθ- makes all the difference, or 'end in new ordinances' (Wilamowitz, cf. *Su.* 442).

We shall not get an answer to this problem by considering the words in isolation. Elsewhere in Greek καταστροφή with a genitive means 'overthrow of' or 'end of', not 'overthrow by' or 'end in'. Again, we often find in Aeschylus a *nomen actionis* with a genitive which is shown by the context obviously and immediately to be subjective, e.g. *PV* 546 τίς ἐφαμερίων ἄρηξις; or objective, e.g. *Ag*. 224–6, ἔτλα δ᾿ οὖν θυτὴρ γενέσθαι θυγατρός, γυναικοποίνων πολέμων ἀρωγάν; we sometimes find a genitive the analysis of which is obscure but immaterial for the argument or picture, e.g. *Eu*. 546–8 καὶ ξενοτίμους ἐπιστροφὰς δωμάτων αἰδόμενός τις ἔστω, *Pe*. 396–7 κώπης ῥοθιάδος ξυνεμβολῇ ἔπαισαν ἅλμην; we shall not readily find examples in which the decision between the two types of genitive is both vital and obscure. These considerations militate against interpretations (b) and (c) above, and appear to pose two plain alternatives: either the *prima facie* meaning must be accepted, and the stasimon interpreted accordingly, or we must emend. Yet we are already begging the question. If the *prima facie* meaning is really as absurd as editors assume, the genitive does not fall into the category 'both vital and obscure', and the singularity of καταστροφὴ νέων θεσμίων = καταστροφὴ ἐς νέα θέσμια is no more objectionable than any other singularity of expression in tragedy.

I believe that the initial assumption is itself mistaken, the product of misapplied logic and of a failure to see and hear the development of the play stage by stage as it were with the ears and eyes of the original audience. We do not and cannot know what political preoccupations were uppermost in the minds of the audience which entered the theatre one day early in 458 to witness the *Oresteia*. We may base some reasonable inferences on what we know of the history of the time, inferences which may be false in so far as there may have been immediate preoccupations which were trivial *sub specie aeternitatis* and are unknown to us. Of one thing, however, we may be sure. When *Eumenides* begins, no spectator, unless he is a very frivolous spectator, is thinking about politics. His attention is engaged by the terrible predicament of Orestes, pursued by one supernatural entity for his obedience to another. The first hint of the link which is to be made between past and present is given by Apollo's command and assurance in 79–84, the assurance being repeated in 224. Orestes invokes Athena's help, Apollo knows what the future holds, but it is the Chorus, not Orestes or Apollo, who ask Athena to decide the case (433–5). In so doing they are seeking a characteristically Greek solution to an otherwise unresolvable dispute, οὔτοι προδώσω against οὔ τι μὴ λίπω ποτέ. Athena with hesitation accepts the charge, but for its execution proclaims her intention of instituting a court which will not only judge the case of Orestes but will endure for ever . . . θεσμόν, τὸν εἰς ἅπαντ᾽ ἐγὼ θήσω χρόνον (484).

We should not be well advised here to use our knowledge of the conflict which is to develop after the verdict, the conflict between the young gods on one side and the old gods on the other, still less our knowledge of the expressions used by Aeschylus to describe supernatural conflicts in other plays, e.g. *PV* 149–51. We must allow Athena's decision its full dramatic weight. For the purposes of the story at this point, the Chorus must be regarded as entrusting the decision to Athena in the confidence (not uncommon in litigants) that an impartial judge is bound to decide in their favour. The new institution which Athena proclaims is thus from their point of view an ally, an executive instrument for the enforcement of their law. For the audience, Athena's words θεσμόν . . . θήσω are the decisive link between the heroic saga and the circumstances of their own time. It is therefore natural that the opening of the stasimon should be about the new institution. νῦν indicates approaching crisis or decision or conflict, as in *Pe*. 405 νῦν ὑπὲρ πάντων ἀγών, Hdt. i 11.2 νῦν τοι δυῶν ὁδῶν παρεουσέων, Γύγη, δίδωμι αἵρεσιν, etc. The words which follow νῦν say 'new institutions will be overthrown if Orestes is acquitted', and mean 'the fate of this new court hangs upon this case; if Orestes is acquitted, it will be overthrown, and if he is condemned, its authority will be assured'.

This interpretation seems to me preferable to the assumption that despite their ἐπιτροπή to Athena and the audience's interest in her θεσμός the Chorus are lamenting the imminent overthrow of old laws by new. So far I have based this preference on what has led up to the stasimon; it can also be supported by reference to the sequence of thought within the stasimon itself.

(ii) 494–516   πάντας ἤδη τόδ᾽ ἔργον εὐχερεί-
                            -ᾳ συναρμόσει βροτούς κτλ.

τόδ᾽ ἔργον most naturally refers to the possible victory of Orestes' plea; for its use as a mere demonstrative, cf. *Pe*. 765–6 Μῆδος γὰρ ἦν ὁ πρῶτος ἡγεμὼν στρατοῦ · ἄλλος δ᾽ ἐκείνου παῖς τόδ᾽ ἔργον ἤνυσεν. 'If Orestes is acquitted, no parents will be safe from their children; we shall not punish sin; in vain will men seek relief.' As the picture takes shape, they pass from prediction in the future tense to description in the present: 'Let no one call upon us; the house of Justice is falling.' Why will they not punish sin? On the usual interpretation, this will be a petulant revenge on humanity for the crime of an Athenian court. This may indeed be do, but their threat is more easily intelligible if they are to be conceived as having already surrendered their jurisdiction to the new court, while retaining the power of punishing the criminals detected and convicted by that court. The point will then be: 'If the court, the instrument in the creation of which we have acquiesced, fails to exercise the function for which it is created, we shall not carry out our side of the arrangement.'[3]

(iii) 517–65. At this point begins one of the most singular passages in tragedy. Up to the words πίτνει δόμος δίκας (516) all is blood and thunder; with the judicious ἔσθ' ὅπου τὸ δεινόν εὖ there is an immediate and striking drop in the temperature, and it is only in 553ff, where the ship of the sinner is dashed to pieces and the god laughs at him, that warmth and colour come flooding back into the words. The sequence of thought is this:[4]

517 Fear has its place.
522 Without fear, there is no justice.
526 But there should be neither too much fear nor too little.
534 From justice comes prosperity.
538 Therefore respect justice,
542 for injustice is punished.
545 Therefore respect your parents.
550 From justice comes prosperity,
553 but injustice is punished by loss of prosperity.

If at the beginning of the stasimon the Chorus are lamenting the overthrow of old laws by new, 517ff must be taken as meaning 'We, the Erinyes, have our place.' In that case, when we come to 526ff μήτ' ἀνάρχετον βίον μήτε δεσποτούμενον αἰνέσῃς, words which have overwhelmingly political, not religious, associations, we must suppose either that the sequence of thought makes an unheralded transition from supernatural authority to political authority, or else that the words are used of supernatural authority and mean 'do not approve either of an (imaginary) world in which the gods exercise no authority or of a world in which men', in Solon's words, ἤθη δεσποτῶν τρομούμενοι, 'are the slaves of the gods'. Neither interpretation is utterly impossible, but neither is attractive. If the words are political, the transition is exceedingly abrupt. If they are religious, the novel conception of a life which is

---

[3] If the MSS οὔτε γάρ in 499 is rejected and Elmsley's οὐδὲ γάρ adopted, I translate 'we shall not punish *either*'. But I am not certain that οὔτε is impossible. The antithesis between 'we, the βροτοσκόποι, shall not punish' and 'one man will ask another' does not seem essentially different from the antitheses expressed by οὔτε/δέ in the examples in Denniston, *Greek Particles* 511. If there is a difference, it lies in the size and complexity of the οὔτε member.

[4] Cf. J. Seewald, *Untersuchungen zu Stil und Komposition der Aischyleischen Tragödie* (D.-Greifswald 1936) 25ff.

not ruled by the gods needs a more explicit introduction, and it is pointless for the Chorus to decry a life in which the gods exercise the power of masters and to recommend in its place a 'mean'. The acceptance of the stasimon as concerned from the outset with the Areopagus removes these difficulties. τὸ δεινόν will then be taken by the audience as referring to political authority, and the transition to μήτ᾽ ἀνάρχετον κτλ is smooth and natural.

Kranz called this central portion of the stasimon a 'tragic parabasis'.[5] This judgement contains a measure of truth in so far as the relation between Chorus and audience seems closer here than elsewhere in tragedy, not least in the imperatives αἰνέσῃς (529) and αἴδεσαι (539), the latter introduced by σοι λέγω[6] – the second person of the potential optative with ἄν has a less personal flavour, cf. S. OC 1218 οὐκ ἂν ἴδοις ~ Tr. 113–15 τις… ἂν… ἴδοι – and the quasi-imperative αἰδόμενός τις ἔστω (549), with which we may compare Alcaeus A6.12 νῦν τις ἄνηρ δόκιμος γε[νέσθω, Callinus 1.9 ἀλλά τις ἰθὺς ἴτω ~ Tyrt. 8.3–4, and in prose literature many similar orders and exhortations to troops. Yet, although the total effect may be compared with a parabasis, the literary affinities of this stasimon are to be sought rather in paraenetic elegy. It is there that we shall find the casting of political and moral maxims into the form of an address to an individual, the rhythm, vocabulary, and sentiments of 530–1 παντὶ μέσῳ τὸ κράτος θεὸς ὤπασεν, ἀλλ᾽ ἄλλα δ᾽ ἐφορεύει and 534 δυσσεβίας γὰρ ὕβρις τέκος ὡς ἐτύμως, the 'ring-form' of the argument as a whole (cf. Callinus fr. 1), and the illogical drift of mood and picture, e.g. 499 οὐδὲ γὰρ βροτοσκόπων κτλ ~ 542 ποινὰ γὰρ ἔπεσται (cf. Solon fr. 1).[7]

II. ATHENA'S SPEECH 681–710

When Apollo and the Chorus have argued their cases, Athena, before the voting of the court, addresses to Ἀττικός λεώς (681) exhortation which in part repeats the content of the stasimon. Her speech may be divided into three sections.

683–95. 'This court will endure for ever … and reverence for it will restrain crime for ever, provided

> αὐτῶν πολιτῶν μὴ †πικαινόντων νόμους.
> κακαῖς ἐπιρροαῖσι βορβόρῳ θ᾽ ὕδωρ
> λαμπρόν μιαίνων οὔποθ᾽ εὑρήσεις ποτόν.'

The point of αὐτῶν is: 'my court will play its part, if the citizens *for their part* do not …' or 'unless the citizens, *on their own initiative* (i.e. contrary to what I

---

[5] W. Kranz, *Stasimon* (Berlin 1933) 172.

[6] In treating this phenomenon as unusual I am thinking of tragic choral lyric; outside tragedy, we may find ἢ οὐχ ὁρῇς; and διαφάδαν τί τοι λέγω; in Alcman fr. 1. 50, 56, and second person imperatives in Pindar.

[7] Cf. Kranz 303.

now ordain) . . .' πικαινόντων is a *vox nihili*, and I would accept either Thomson's τι κινούντων (the usual word for altering institutions)[8] or Wieseler's τι καινούντων (cf. Th. i 71.3, iii 82.3; denominal verbs in οὖν are abundant in Aeschylus). I keep the θ' of the manuscripts and punctuate with the MS. F after νόμους on the grounds that Aeschylus more often than not allots one or more complete lines to a *gnome* at the end of a speech or definable portion of a speech (twenty-four examples out of some thirty in the *Oresteia*), and frequently introduces such a *gnome* in asyndeton, e.g. *Ag*. 1359, *Ch*. 780.[9] We may compare the asyndeton characteristics of lines which are metaphorical or otherwise colourful, e.g. *Eu*. 253, *Ag*. 322. Within the *gnome*, ἐπιρροαί is the flowing or pouring of new liquid into, and on top of, the liquid which is there already; its point for the context is that it represents bad new laws added to the existing body of law. So in 853–4 οὑπιρρέων γὰρ τιμιώτερος χρόνος ἔσται πολίταις τοῖσδε there is an image of time accumulating, new time flowing, as it were, on to old time; and in Hdt. ix 38.2 ἐπιρρεόντων δὲ τῶν Ἑλλήνων καὶ γινομένων πλεύνων . . . συνεβούλευσε Μαρδονίῳ τὰς ἐκβολὰς τοῦ Κιθαιρῶνος φυλάξαι, λέγων ὡς ἐπιρρέουσι οἱ Ἕλληνες αἰεὶ ἀνὰ πᾶσαν ἡμέρην καὶ ὡς ἀπολάμψοιτο συχνούς the point is clearly that fresh troops were coming in to swell the numbers of those already there.[10] Thus this part of Athena's speech means: 'Do not change, by bad new laws, the court which I have instituted.'

The second part, 696–9, is again introduced in asyndeton, which gives it a flavour of Hesiodic ὑποθῆκαι, cf. *Op*, 342–67. The words

τὸ μήτ' ἄναρχον μήτε δεσποτούμενον
ἀστοῖς περιστέλλουσι βουλεύω σέβειν,
καὶ μὴ τὸ δεινὸν πᾶν πόλεως ἔξω βαλεῖν.
τίς γὰρ δεδοικὼς μηδὲν ἔνδικος βροτῶν;

follow closely the argument of the Chorus in 517–31.

The third part, 700–6, is extravagant praise of the Areopagus, ending with the words εὑδόντων ὕπερ ἐγρηγορὸς φρούρημα γῆς καθίσταμαι.

III. THE POLITICAL CONTENT OF 490–565 AND 681–710

The verbal coincidences between the stasimon and Athena's speech, together with the unique character of each of them and the uniqueness of their relation, entitled us to take them together in enquiring into their political content.

---

[8] Cf. Thomson, *ad loc.*

[9] Cf. Paley and Sidgwick, *ad loc.*, and G. Bromig, 'De Asyndeti Natura et apud Aeschylum Usu' (Diss., Göttingen 1879) 25ff.

[10] Dodds in *CQ* ns iii (1953) 19–20, offers a different interpretation of the Herodotus passage and draws from it a different conclusion on the point of κακαῖς ἐπιρροαῖσι.

(i) *The mean*. Political language, like the language of ethics, is characterized by the use of 'value-words', which convey little to the hearer until he knows the presuppositions and political associations of the speaker. If we hear a man say of a labour dispute, 'This demands a *just* solution', we do not know, until we know more about the man himself, what kind of solution he would call just. In Greek, as in English, 'just' is a value-word, but the Greeks differed from us in three important respects: in their approval of the repetition, in poem after poem and play after play, of passages which, however elaborate and colourful their language, constitute not a philosophical argument but a simple act of religious formality, the acknowledgement that justice is good and injustice bad; in the respect which men of differing political views paid to law, custom, tradition, and antiquity; and in the extent to which they agreed in treating right behaviour as a mean between extremes.

In consequence we find that the words of Pericles in Th. ii 37.3, τὰ δημόσια διὰ δέος μάλιστα οὐ παρανομοῦμεν, τῶν τε αἰεὶ ἐν ἀρχῇ ὄντων ἀκροάσει καὶ τῶν νόμων, and of Lysias ii 19, describing prehistoric Attica as ὑπὸ νόμου βασιλευομένους, remind us of a similar description of a dissimilar constitution by Demaratus in Hdt. vii 104.4, ἔπεστι γάρ σφι δεσπότης νόμος. Plato, speaking as a critic of democracy, alleges that in a democracy the citizen exults in disobeying the magistrates (*R*. 562d), but, unless the orators gravely mislead us, such exultation would have been ill received by a fourth-century jury. Ἀναρχία[11] is the oligarch's description of democracy (e.g. Pl. *R*. 558c), δουλεία, with which I take δεσποτούμενος βίος to be synonymous, the democrat's description of oligarchy (e.g. Lys. ii 56, Th. vi 40.2); but democrats do not boast of their ἀναρχία, nor do oligarchs claim to impose δουλεία. Μέσος, with the related but etymologically different concept μέτρον, μέτριος, is among the oldest 'value-words' in Greek ethics,[12] and what a democrat would call an extreme an oligarch would represent as a mean; thus Megabyxus, arguing for oligarchy in Herodotus's famous Persian debate, treats the ὕβρις of a monarch and the ὕβρις of a people as the frying-pan and the fire (iii 81), and Plato, *Lg*. 693d, 756e, speaks of the authoritarian state which he is constituting as a mean between Persian monarchy and Athenian democracy. When someone says, as both the Chorus and Athena do, 'Avoid the extremes of anarchy and despotism; the mean between the two is right', he is not necessarily speaking as a 'moderate democrat' or as a member of a 'centre party'. He is using words which, if we view them from the standpoint of archaic Greek morality in general, merely recommend a reflective rather than a violent attitude to politics. Neither democrats nor conservatives could cavil at these words; neither could claim that Aeschylus was speaking for them

---

[11] I grant that to Aeschylus ἀνάρχετος (ἄναρχος) βίος is primarily a life in which one has no ruler (cf. Fraenkel's note on *Ag*. 883), whereas to Plato the words describe primarily the behaviour or attitude of a man who behaves as if he had no ruler, but I do not think the distinction is material for my argument.

[12] Cf. Theognis 335, Solon fr. 16, and in general H. Kählreuter, 'Die Μεσότης bei und vor Aristoteles' (Diss., Tübingen 1911).

and against their opponents. This is not to say that a value-word could not be appropriated by a political party and used so frequently by them that it came to be associated with them and was avoided by their opponents; this eventually happened to οἱ βελτίους, and I suspect that it happened to μέσος also. For the present I am interpreting Aeschylus's μέσος in the light of archaic poetry, not late fifth-century politics; the justification of this choice will be considered below.

(ii) *New and old laws*. In 693–5 Athena appears to be not only prohibiting interference with the court which she has established but also generalizing this prohibition and giving a warning against adding bad laws to good. It is precisely the general character of the *gnome* which makes it hard to accept without demur the common interpretation that Aeschylus here intends to accept the reform of the Areopagus which had already taken place but to issue a warning against going any farther. When we remember that the period was one in which the laws had been, and were still being, changed and augmented,[13] the whole passage has a very reactionary ring; and I should find this conclusion inescapable but for one curious circumstance. Aristotle, *Ath*. 25.2, describes Ephialtes' reduction of the powers of the Areopagus thus: ἅπαντα περιείλετο τὰ ἐπίθετα δι᾽ ὧν ἦν ἡ τῆς πολιτείας φυλακή. The word ἐπίθετος, 'attached' or 'superimposed', seems to be first attested in Antiphon the Sophist fr. 44, col. i 25, where the demands of law are described as ἐπίθετα vis-à-vis nature. We do not know whether this view of the reform represents an historian's construction or the claim actually made at the time by the democrats,[14] but I can see no good reason for rejecting the second possibility. Such a claim needed to survive orally for only fifty years at the most; it would then have received a new lease of life in the political arguments provoked by the reactionary movements of the late fifth century, and its perpetuation thereafter would be ensured by historical and political literature. Its truth or falsity is, of course, quite a different question.

Anyone, of any political complexion, may say 'do not add bad laws to good'. Any Greek was predisposed to defend a law which could be given the authority of age; a democrat, as well as a conservative, may invoke tradition when it serves his purpose, as when Cleon and Alcibiades in Th iii 37.3 and vi 18.7, both in different circumstances and for different reasons, exploit the principle νόμοις ἀκινήτοις χρῆσθαι. A democrat may indeed invoke tradition even in the midst of a programme of reform, provided that he can represent his reforms as the restitution of original right and – by a process familiar in our own time – represent the most obvious innovations (jury-pay, for example) as consequential administrative measures involving no great issues of principle. Euripidean tragedy freely attributed contemporary democratic principles to the Athens of the heroic age, and this anachronism is expressed

---

[13] Cf. Jacoby, *Fr. Gr. Hist*. IIIb Supplement, i 338–9, ii 244–5.
[14] Cf. Jacoby, ii. *loc. cit*.

in its extreme form in the *Epitaphios* of Lysias. Lest we should suppose it a sophistic phenomenon, we must remember that in Aeschylus's *Supplices* the Argive king handles the primitive democracy of Argos as cautiously, though with less constitutional necessity, as the Euripidean Theseus does primitive Athens. Thus Athena's words, so far from being a reproach against reform of the Areopagus or a warning against further reform, may well be an adaptation of arguments used by the reformers themselves.

(iii) *Homicide*. So far, it seems that neither the Chorus nor Athena have uttered anything that is unambiguously partisan. Yet in the last part of her speech Athena invests the Areopagus with a dignity and power which are to our way of thinking inappropriate to a homicide court and seem to transform it into the most exalted instrument of the state's authority. Have we here, for the first time, something incompatible with acceptance of the democratic reforms?

We think of murder as a 'private' crime and of revolution as action on the political plane. Although the distinction was made by Greek legal procedure, it was alien to Greek political theory. The Greek community conceived politics (not always rightly) and practised them (not always fruitfully) as a system of rivalry between individuals, a kind of competitive ladder. This is abundantly demonstrated by many political careers in the fifth and fourth centuries, and it is pertinent to recall one imaginary career, that of the defendant in the first Tetralogy of Antiphon. This man has incurred suspicion because as an enemy (ἐχθρός) of the murdered man he has been worsted by him in a long battle of γραφαί (α 5). One of the roads which had to be travelled by an aspirant to political power lay through the courts, and the foundation for the defeat of an opponent in the assembly was laid by defeating him before a jury. Consequently, the Greeks did not put murder and stasis into separate compartments; they clearly perceived that an authority which restrains and punishes homicide is the first step in progress from the life of beasts to the life of a human community, and upon the preservation of that authority the continued existence of the community ultimately depends. They often speak of jealousy, murder, and stasis in the same breath; to Thrasymachus (fr. 1) ὁμόνοια is the antithesis alike of private quarrels and public sedition; cf. Democritus fr. 245, φόνος γὰρ στάσιος ἀρχὴν ἀπεργάζε-ται. To Demosthenes (xx 157) homicide is the most serious concern of legislation, μάλιστ᾿ ἐν ἅπασι διεσπούδασται τοῖς νόμοις. In the same passage Demosthenes speaks of the Areopagus as a special court for a special crime; Isocrates (iv 39) represents the reference of homicide cases to Athens as the first step out of ἀναρχία taken by the primitive Greek world; and their words enable us to understand the prestige and political authority with which Athena in the third part of her speech invests what was to the Athenians, democrats and conservatives alike, not only the oldest homicide court in Athens but the oldest in the Greek world.

In arguing that the political language of *Eumenides* is neutral, and for that very reason reconcilable with unreserved acceptance of the democratic revolution, I have assumed that by 458 BC:

(a) μέσος had not yet been appropriated, if it ever was, by the language of conservatism.
(b) The theory, which we find expressed in the fourth century, that the restraint of homicide is the fundamental principle of society, was already accepted.
(c) The anachronistic belief in prehistoric democracy was already current.

Disproof of the first assumption would invalidate my interpretation, and disproof of either of the other two would throw some doubt upon it. There is, however, a further political aspect consideration of which will make my three assumptions necessary.

IV. THE ARGIVE ALLIANCE

When Orestes first approaches the statue of Athena, he salutes her with a brief prayer for her goodwill, a conventional prayer of arrival (235ff). When the Chorus have caught him up and again besiege him, he invokes Athena more elaborately and more urgently, prefacing the direct invocation with a promise that in return for her help Argos will be her faithful ally for ever; that is to say, the ally of Athens, for throughout the play Athena is identified with Athens to a degree unparalleled in the case of any other tutelary deity and comparable only with Pindar's treatment of eponymous nymphs. The promise of an Argive alliance is twice renewed: once at the end of Apollo's testimony (667ff) and again, most fully, in Orestes' expression of gratitude after his acquittal (762ff).

Is it possible to interpret these references as politically neutral? It is true, and natural, that the note of the play as a whole is one of assurance. Athens is fighting the right wars, with the right allies, and has the right institutions; given internal harmony, glory awaits her. The differences between the end of *Eumenides* and the prayer for Argos in *Su.* 625ff are instructive. In *Supplices* the order and relative importance of the prayers are dictated by the dramatic context; hence the aversion of war, μάχλος ᾿Αρης, takes first place (633–9; cf. 663–6), while the aversion of stasis receives the briefest mention (661–2). In *Eumenides* the words of both Athena and the Chorus are determined not by the dramatic context but by the political circumstances of 458 BC; hence war is welcomed (θυραῖος ἔστω πόλεμος, 864–5), Ares is linked with Zeus as honouring φρούριον θεῶν, the champion of the Greek gods against the barbarian (918–20), but stasis and faction are the danger most to be feared (858–66 and especially 976–87). This is well adapted to a situation in which, on the one hand, Aegina was being besieged, the Long Walls were being built, an expeditionary force was in Egypt, there had lately been hard fighting in the

Megarid, and more trouble was imminent in Central Greece, while, on the other hand, Ephialtes had been murdered and (Th. i 107.4) there was a section of the community willing to enlist Spartan help for the overthrow of the democracy. As society depends on the restraint of violence, so survival of the perils of war depends on ὁμόνοια.[15]

In so far as a political situation was made the subject of tragedy at all, propriety demanded that it should be treated with optimism and confidence; it was presumably the conspicuous lack of this tone in *The Fall of Miletus* which got Phrynichus into trouble. Aeschylus neither made nor wanted to make Phrynichus's mistake; to this extent *Eumenides* could be conceived as containing a conventional message of assurance. But the threefold reference to the Argive alliance invites contrast with political aetiology elsewhere in Tragedy, e.g. the prophecy of Eurystheus in E. *Hcld*. 1026ff, Athena's dictation of an Argive alliance in E. *Su*. 1183ff, the foundation of the Attic tribes in E. *Ion* 1575ff, etc. These have their place in the concluding scenes of plays, as do references to the foundation of places (e.g. E. *El*. 1275ff) and cults (e.g. E. *IT* 1449ff). *Eumenides* differs from all of them in introducing the Argive alliance at so early a stage in the play and in referring to it three times. Secondly, the alliance was an achievement – or perhaps it would be more accurate to call it a gesture – of the democrats, inseparable from their renunciation of the Spartan alliance to which the conservative elements in Athens gave their loyalty. The Spartan alliance was the product of common effort and common suffering in the Persian War; the Argive alliance had a distinctly ideological flavour and could be supported by tradition only in so far as Argos and Athens alike had suffered at the hands of Cleomenes. A man who resented the perils which Athens had incurred in consequence of Sparta's enmity and one who resented the process of democratic reform were blaming the same group for both policies.

Aeschylus broke with tradition in laying the scene of the trilogy in Argos instead of Mycenae; he almost certainly broke with tradition in associating the foundation of the Areopagus with the story of Orestes.[16] If he was positively conservative in sentiment, it is difficult to believe that he would have written the *Oresteia* in anything like the form which it actually has. If he was in principle democratic, but mistrustful of the continuation of democratic reform, he has concealed his mistrust impenetrably.

V. PERICLES AND DELPHI

Clara Smertenko, in *JHS* lii (1932) 233, pointed out certain analogies between the fortunes of Orestes and those of the Alcmaeonidae. Her

---

[15] Cf. Democritus frr. 250, 255; C. O. Müller, *Dissertations on the Eumenides of Aeschylus* (Cambridge 1835) 121–2; H. Kramer, 'Quid valeat ὁμόνοια in litteris graecis' (Diss., Göttingen 1905).

[16] Cf. Jacoby i 22ff.

suggestion that *Eumenides* could not fail to remind the audience of Pericles' family has not commended itself; but where a play is so heavily charged with political implications one cannot dismiss without enquiry the suggestion of one further implication. The analogy amounts to this: Orestes by his crime incurred the enmity of the Eumenides. Apollo purified him at Delphi and declared him innocent. The Eumenides refused to accept either the purification or the declaration, but it was Apollo who was in the end vindicated. The Alcmaeonidae were originally expelled because Megacles incurred the emnity of the Eumenides, by slaughtering suppliants at their altar. Despite this, they were highly favoured by Delphi,[17] which must mean one of three things: either Delphi did not believe the story about Megacles, or it did not regard the curse as a relevant obstacle to the favour of Apollo, or it purified the Alcmaeonidae and made an end of the matter. Of these three alternatives, the difficulties inherent in the first two are obvious, and the third is supported by other occasions on which Apollo of Delphi prescribed the means by which men might be absolved from offences against other gods, e.g. Hdt. i 19.2, Paus. ix 8.2. None the less, the validity of the Delphic absolution was implicitly denied when the curse was used by Cleomenes as a pretext for his expulsion of the Alcmaeonidae and by the Spartans in 431 to discredit Pericles.

Now, before it can be said that this has any bearing upon the play, we need to know whether or not the curse was used as a stick with which to beat Pericles at this early stage of his political career. Direct evidence is entirely lacking, but the indirect evidence is cogent. First, as we saw, the curse was invoked both fifty years earlier and thirty years later. Secondly, it is clear that a belief in the vengeance of the dead and the power of a curse could be publicly assumed in the late fifth century; cf. Antiphon iv. β 8, etc., Andoc. i 130–1. Thirdly, although Aeschylus and others found it necessary to believe in the reconciliation of traditional conflicts within the supernatural, I doubt whether the average man had any difficulty in believing that the Eumenides could persecute a family which Apollo had accepted. Fourthly, it was common form in politics to damage a man's reputation by recalling the misdeeds of his ancestors; cf. Antiphon fr. 1, Ar. *Eq.* 445–9, Isoc. xvi *passim*. I do not believe that political loyalty itself determined Aeschylus's attitude to Delphi, still less that he had Pericles' descent in mind[18] when he put into the mouth of Apollo (657ff) a view of genetics held by some of the early philosophers; but I do not think that it is possible to avoid the conclusion that the audience perceived after reflection that on this issue as on others the implications of the play were in Pericles' favour.

---

[17] Cf. G. W. Williams, 'The Curse of the Alcmaeonidae', *Hermathena* lxxviii–ix (1951–2), esp. lxxviii 45 n. 27, 49.

[18] Smertenko 234.

VI. ALLEGORY

I have considered the play throughout as representing a strange event in the heroic past, involving mortal and immortal persons, and have made no reference to Justice, Sin, Law, Order, or any of the other abstractions which are sometimes supposed to be the 'real' subjects of Aeschylean tragedy. I confess that I have little sympathy with scholars who speak as if a theological theory is a proper and adequate subject for tragedy while the murders of a husband and a mother are not. No story is so barren that it has no religious or moral implications; the same may be said of many actual events. Since the Greek poets translated abstractions into the concrete terms of personal relations, I prefer to think of tragedy as being concerned with persons; and I would explain, for example, Athena's somewhat illogical reason for voting in favour of Orestes (736ff) by saying that Aeschylus gives her these words because that is what he thinks Athena would have said.

Similar considerations militate against the suggestion of Sir Richard Livingstone, in *JHS* xlv (1925) 120, that the play contains political allegory, the reconciliation of the Chorus in the last scene representing, and thus promoting, the reconcilation of the conservatives to the democratic reforms. The scene lacks one essential characteristic of allegory. The participants are not, to a Greek, fictions or abstractions, but real gods, and the issue of the conflict between them is itself a matter of so high an importance that there is no room for allegory. It is a conflict which mattered on more than a purely intellectual plane to any contemporary of Aeschylus who thought at all seriously about religious tradition and practice. Past conflict within the realm of the supernatural was guaranteed by tradition.[19] Present conflict between deities worshipped in the same community and prayed to for the same blessings was to many, if not intellectually unthinkable, at least emotionally insupportable. This problem could be met in several ways. A man could accept tradition and plead his own incompetence to pass judgement, he could choose between alternative traditions, he could reject tradition as a whole, or he could supplement it, as Aeschylus did, by the supposition of points in time at which the traditional supernatural conflicts were resolved.

VII. EPIMETRUM: EGYPT AND PALLENE

Orestes calls upon Athena in the familiar εἴτε/εἴτε form of prayer, 292–7:

$$\text{ἀλλ᾿ εἴτε χώρας ἐν τόποις Λιβυστικῆς,}$$
$$\text{Τρίτωνος ἀμφὶ χεῦμα γενεθλίου πόρου,}$$

---

[19] On the role of tradition in Aeschylus's theology, cf. F. Solmsen, *Hesiod and Aeschylus* (Ithaca, N.Y. 1949) 197.

τίθησιν ὀρθὸν ἢ κατηρεφῆ πόδα,
φίλοις ἀρήγουσ᾽, εἴτε Φλεγραίαν πλάκα
θρασὺς ταγοῦχος ὡς ἀνὴρ ἐπισκοπεῖ,
ἔλθοι.

It is not surprising if many editors have seen in these lines reference to the foreign wars of Athens. The expedition to Egypt was undertaken originally in support of Inaros, 'king of the Libyans adjoining Egypt' (Th. i 104.1). The Phlegraean plain was presumably located by Aeschylus, as it was by Herodotus (vii 123.1) in the peninsula of Pallene, i.e. near Potidea. Potidea was a colony of Corinth, and, her mother city being at this time at war with Athens, may have been giving trouble.[20] All this looks persuasive at first glance, but I am not sure that it survives enquiry.

1 The Athenian force in Egypt fought in the Delta, not in Libya. Aeschylus certainly drew a distinction between the two in *Su*. 279ff. Λιβυστικαῖς γὰρ μᾶλλον ἐμφερέστεραι γυναιξίν ἐστε ... καὶ Νεῖλος ἂν θρέψειε τοιοῦτον φυτόν, Κύπριος χαρακτήρ τε κτλ. Herodotus (ii 15–17) shows not that some Greeks included the Delta in Libya, but that they made it begin with the west bank of the Nile and ignored the Delta.

2 In 293, before we come to the suggestive words φίλοις ἀρήγουσα,[21] the river Triton is specified. Herodotus (iv 180) located this in the far west of Libya. We do not know whether the alternative location of Lake Tritonis at Euesperides was known to Aeschylus,[22] and in view of (1) it would help us a little if we did. The Athena of legend was closely associated with Lake Tritonis, as γενεθλίου reminds us, and cf. Hdt. *loc. cit.*

3 The political flavour of φίλοις ἀρήγουσα is weakened when we recall that Orestes has called upon Athena ἐμοὶ μολεῖν ἀρωγόν (288–9).

4 We have no independent evidence of trouble at Potidea at this time, and the Phlegraean plain, as being the scene of the victory of the gods over the giants (Pind. *N*. i 67), in which Athena took a prominent part (E. *Ion* 988ff), is naturally associated with her.

In the present state of our knowledge it would be incautious to interpret these lines as anything but an invocation of the type which names localities favoured by the god, cf. Theocr. i 123. The problem is not dissimilar to Athena's words on her arrival (397ff): 'I have come from the Scamander, where territory has been given to Athens in perpetuity.' Seven years after the *Oresteia* Sigeum earned the commendation of Athens for its conduct in circumstances of which we know nothing (*SEG* x 13). Seven years, at a

---

[20] Cf. *Athenian Tribute Lists*, iii 321.

[21] Kranz 107 ignores the intervention of 293.

[22] It does not seem to me necessary to accept the inference of A. Herrmann in *Rh. Mus.* lxxxvi (1937) 69–70 from Ap. Rhod. iv 1490 that this alternative location is pre-Herodotean and implied by Pindar's Fourth Pythian.

distance of over two thousand, does not sound a long time, but it is. No doubt the Troad was a scene of actual or potential conflict with Persian forces at this time, but that is true of other areas of the Aegean. Conflict with Mytilene over the Troad was a phenomenon of the sixth century, not the fifth.

ADDITIONAL NOTES

P. 166, on ἐπιρρεῖν. The late W. L. Lorimer drew my attention to Pl. *Lg*. 793d οὐ χρὴ θαυμάζειν ἐὰν ἡμῖν πολλὰ ἅμα καὶ σμικρὰ δοκοῦντα εἶναι νόμιμα ἢ καὶ ἐθίσματα ἐπιρρέοντα μακροτέρους ποιῇ τοὺς νόμους.

P. 168, on the invocation of tradition. Henry VIII's Act in Restraint of Appeals (1533) made use of the idea that he was simply reasserting the ancient rights of the kings of England *via-à-vis* the Papacy. Similarly, the 'destalinization' of the Soviet Union after 1956 was often presented as a return to Leninism.

18

The Speakable and the Unspeakable

The late Robert Lowell's *Oresteia*[1] is a set of three plays in English bearing an intermittent resemblance to three plays which Aeschylus wrote in Greek. It is presented in the preface and on the dust-jacket as a 'translation' or 'version' of the *Oresteia* of Aeschylus. Lowell said that his purpose was 'to trim, cut, and be direct enough to satisfy my own mind and at a first hearing the simple ears of a theater audience'. The trimming and cutting has certainly been brutal: more than a third of all that is uttered in Aeschylus's *Eumenides* goes unrepresented in Lowell's *Furies*. Lowell's *Orestes* (~ Aeschylus's *Choephori*) drops the curtain at Orestes' cry 'You don't see them, but I do', and in *Agamemnon* the passage of two hundred lines (1372–576) in which the chorus confronts Clytaemestra is reduced to half-size in Lowell. An abridged translation, or a translation of an abridged play, is fair enough, so long as the publisher's advertisement is candid; but Lowell's 'translation', which not only cuts but also, always without warning, imports material quite alien to the original, misrepresents both the intentions of the author as dramatist and the character of the culture to which he belonged. Innocent readers of Lowell are led to believe, for example, that Pylades had a speaking part in the opening scene of *Choephori*, that Orestes put on his father's tomb not two locks of his own hair (*Ch*. 6f) but eagle's feathers dipped in blood and tied with hair (Lowell 53, 59), and that at *Ch*. 1015f Orestes trips himself up in Agamemnon's fatal robe and says, 'Not yet, not yet, I am entangled in my kingship'. Similarly, 'huge' is a disastrous addition in '[Thyestes] kicked the huge table over' (*Ag*. 1601), for Greek tables were tiny; the notion that Clytaemestra's slaves welcomed the victorious Agamemnon with '*wailing*' (Lowell's stage-direction, 28) and '*howling like wolves*' (*Ag*. 919f) does violence to the Greek sense of occasion; and the allegation of Lowell's chorus in *Ch*. 24–31 and 423–8 that Clytaemestra personally inflicted on them the bruises and scratches of ritual mourning is an absurdity of which the origin is not easy to determine.

    Now, a scholar–reviewer criticizing a poet–translator cannot easily win,

---

[1] Robert Lowell, *The Oresteia of Aeschylus* (Faber and Faber, London 1978).

though he can have a good try. The popular belief that the scholar's effort to understand a text actually causes his imagination to atrophy is complementary to the belief that a professional poet, no matter how many errors of detail he may make in translating another poet, must necessarily achieve 'fidelity to the spirit of the original'. This notion is not to be discarded outright as cant, for there are occasions, notably in the translation of topical allusions in comedy, when the systematic replacement of one set of persons or institutions by another is justified. There are also occasions on which it is helpful to make explicit what is implicit in the Greek: for instance, replacing 'the god' by a proper name in certain contexts is an unobtrusive way of integrating explanatory comment into the text and saving the reader from puzzlement or misapprehension. When, however, Lowell turns *Ag*. 167–73 and *Eu*. 641 into a bleak statement that Zeus 'castrated his own father', he not only picks on the wrong god (for it was Zeus's father Cronus who castrated *his* father Uranus) but makes Aeschylus accept and perpetuate precisely the kind of myth which, for his purposes in the *Oresteia*, he would have rejected.

What goes wrong in this genre of pseudo-translation is not just ignorance of the literature and culture to which the original work belongs, but narrowness of vision and indifference to character, plot and the intelligence and imagination of the original author. A translator can go badly astray through giving his emotional response to a passage in isolation precedence over cool scrutiny of the relationship between that passage and one of the major themes of the play. For instance, when the chorus tells us what Agamemnon said when the seer told him that only by sacrificing his daughter could he assuage the wind that prevented the fleet from sailing, the Greek text (206–8) has, literally,

> heavy on-the-one-hand fate not to obey,
> heavy on-the-other-hand fate if I shall slaughter child.

Here Vellacott's Penguin translation has

> Disaster follows if I disobey;
> surely yet worse disaster if I yield
> and slaughter my own child.

In some circumstances it might be pedantic to cavil at the mistranslation of a positive as a comparative and even at the importation of 'surely' and 'my own'; but to imply that Agamemnon immediately recognized his dilemma as no true dilemma is simply to spoil Aeschylus's presentation of the moral issue itself, other people's thoughts and feelings about it (including the chorus's) and its function in the fulfilment of Thyestes' curse.

More culpably, when Lowell omits Clytaemestra's contemptuous reference to the death of Iphigenia as 'a spell to charm the winds of Thrace' (*Ag*. 1418) he sacrifices (presumably for 'the simple ears of a theater audience') one of the most illuminating moments in the play; in condensing *Ch*. 113–16, where the chorus forces recollection of Orestes into Electra's consciousness, he trivializes Electra; and in transforming *Eu*. 644, 'detestable monsters, hated by the gods', into 'monsters fed on anarchy and boredom' he forgets, or does not care, that 'anarchy' is the very last thing with which an intelligent adversary would associate the Furies, especially after 490–565.

Something could be forgiven if Lowell had written good English poetic variations on an Aeschylean theme, but one of the conspicuous features of his poetry is incongruous images which, so far from stimulating new perceptions of reality, provoke incredulous laughter by their amateurish insensitivity. Here are some examples: 'crouching like a dog on one elbow' (*Ag*. 3), 'like a forged coin rung and rejected on the touchstone' (*Ag*. 390f), 'they fed it their daughter's milk' (*Ag*. 724), 'they threw their votes in the urn of blood' (*Ag*. 815f), 'it's noon, the sun loiters in mid-sky, but night's dark chariot is rushing on' (*Ch*. 661f, which says nothing whatever about noon or anything except the lateness of the hour), 'listen, the sword slides gently from the scabbard' (somewhere in the neighbourhood of *Ch*. 790–837).

Fidelity to the spirit of the original in translating poetry is achieved not by intuition but by finding out what the spirit of the original was; and that is hard work. Not every occupant of the Regius Chair of Greek at Oxford in the course of its long history has accomplished notable work of that kind; but the present Regius Professor, Hugh Lloyd-Jones, understands as well as anyone in the world what Aeschylus said, why he said it, and what the *Oresteia* conveyed to the Athenians in the middle of the fifth century BC. One distinctive feature of his translations[2] is the running commentary occupying the lower part of each page. This includes an occasional warning (of a kind generally eschewed by translators, as if they feared a charge of pedantry) when the Greek text is corrupt or its interpretation controversial, essential information about the thought and behaviour of the Greeks in Aeschylus's time, and indication, spare and lucid, of moments in the trilogy which make all the difference to our understanding of its personalities and themes. A translation designed for the general reader two millennia distant from the author needs some such commentary, and a handful of notes at the back of the book is no real substitute. Unless readers are helped to distinguish between what is Aeschylus and what is simply Greek, there is a high risk not only that their evaluation of Aeschylus as an original dramatist will be distorted but that even the most thoughtful translation of what he said will convey a misleading impression of what he had in mind. Lloyd-Jones's notes on *Ch*. 438 (literally, 'then may I, having slain, perish!'), *Eu*. 667–73 (Apollo's shameless bribe to the Athenian court) and *Eu*. 735–40 (the motivation of Athena's casting vote for acquittal) are excellent examples of what is wanted. Here and there some more would be welcome, particularly on the rhetorical organization of *Ag*. 1372–576, where Clytaemestra, beginning with a kind of warrior's boast,

---

[2] Aeschylus, *Oresteia: Agamemnon, The Choephoroe (The Libation Bearers), Eumenides (The Kindly Ones)*, tr. Hugh Lloyd-Jones (Duckworth, London 1979).

continues through logic, grievance, defiance, demonology and opportunistic excuses, and on the quick succession of alternative means by which she tries to evade her fate in *Ch*. 904–30. Consideration might also have been given to the possibility that Cassandra's words in *Ag*. 1330, literally, 'and I pity these (*sc*. nearer) things much more than those (*sc*. further) things', mean that Cassandra's pity for human misfortunes (1327–9) exceeds her self-pity for her own imminent death (1323–6) – a surprising sentiment, but it would not be the only surprising sentiment in *Agamemnon* (cf. 951f). On *Ag*. 1484 the note, 'the early poets saw no inconsistency between the belief that Zeus determines all things and the freedom of men to make their own decisions' is puzzling unless one realizes that 'all things' refers not to the fall of a sparrow but to the ultimate outcome of a chain of events. Something seems wrong in the stage-direction at *Eu*. 565, where Orestes 'enters' although left on stage at 487.

The translator of a play has two tasks, one compulsory and the other optional. The compulsory task is to say what the author said; the option, to be taken if he wants the play performed, is to say it in a way which actors will relish speaking and an audience relish hearing. Recent experience in translating some passages of Aeschylus for studio production and hearing the actor's views on the relative 'speakability' of alternative phrasings suggests to me that, while Lloyd-Jones has accomplished the first task so well that a reviewer determined to criticize could only scratch around with a degree of desperation, he has not attempted the second; but neither he nor his publisher claims, even by implication, that his translation is designed for performance. The Greeks of Aeschylus's time thought it right that poetry should be strongly differentiated from prose in vocabulary and word-formation and to some extent in syntax and morphology; but the modern English public thinks otherwise. It has little taste for distinctively poetic vocabulary; it is embarrassed by the verbalization of groans as 'Woe!' and 'Alack!', and even by the intrusion of the literary conjunction 'for' into dialogue; and its tolerance of participal and subordinate clauses is low. I cannot easily believe that lines such as Lloyd-Jones's translation of *Ag*. 1366,

> Must we truly, inferring from his cries of pain,
> guess that the man has perished?

or of *Ch*. 169,

> To what man or what deep-girdled maiden can it belong?

would be spoken with conviction in the modern theatre. Some enterprising theatrical company may already have proved me resoundingly wrong; if it has, that is an encouraging sign that audiences can take greater variety of style than might have been supposed.

The Serpent Son of Raphael and McLeish[3] comes on the market under a handicap, for it was the translation used, with minor modifications, in the BBC2 production of the *Oresteia* in March 1979, a production which has done much to put people off Greek drama. However, any viewer benevolent enough to endure the suppression of Aeschylus's well-considered design in the first half-hour of the trilogy in favour of the producer's notion of what we might prefer, and resolute enough to shut his eyes and use his ears when insulted by one silly costume after another, was rewarded by hearing some poetry of distinction. The translators have chopped Aeschylus down into short and simple sentences, with abundant use of loose apposition and exclamation. The Watchman's utterance at *Ag*. 22–4 becomes

> Light! Light! There in the dark night
> The day-gleam, the dawn, the beacon
> To set all Argos dancing. Luck at last!

They are right to do this, for the relation between sentence-structure and emotive charge is not the same in modern English as in ancient Greek. If the English translation is to be acted, it must carry the same charge; and that dictates a radical difference of sentence-structure. In the second place, Raphael and McLeish exploit with great skill the wealth of monosyllabic words available to the English poet and the variety of effect that can be achieved by slipping from the ding-dong of monosyllables into the swirl of longer words or by pairing words unequal in size but equal in impact. For example, *Eu*. 303–6, in which the chorus-leader introduces the 'binding-song' of the Furies, says, literally,

> Do you not speak in reply, but reject my words,
> fattened for me and consecrated?
> You will feast me actually living, not slaughtered
>   at an altar;
> and you will hear this song binding you.

Raphael and McLeish translate this as

> Nothing to say? Your flesh
> Is fat for us,
> Our sacrificial dish.
> Not for you the knife,
> Quick execution –
> I sup on living flesh.
> Hear, now, the spell
> That binds your soul to death.

[3] *The Serpent Son* (Aeschylus, *Oresteia*), tr. Frederic Raphael and Kenneth McLeish (Cambridge University Press, Cambridge 1979).

One can pick holes: 'reject my words' is jettisoned, 'consecrated' and 'altar' are run together in 'sacrificial'; I miss 'altar' and the threat in the future tense, offer a sly welcome to 'quick', but then start at 'execution', which has the wrong associations. The holes having been picked, the temptation to patch is irresistible: what about

> Our consecrated dish.
> Not for you the knife,
> Quick at the altar – ?

Translations, once made, should be tinkered with indefinitely, and if Raphael and McLeish come back in ten years' time with their second thoughts or twentieth thoughts we shall have an even better theatrical version of the *Oresteia* than they have given us already. The short introduction could profitably be revised sooner; 'the winds would not blow' (*sc.* at Aulis) and 'Klytemnestra . . . pinned his arms . . . while Aegisthus cut him down' would be surprising statements even from someone who had read the play just once, and from a translator they are inexplicable.

ADDITIONAL NOTE

P. 177, on the translation of *Ag*. 206–8. Through a disastrous error (which I was able to correct, but not excuse, in the next issue of *Essays in Criticism*) I attributed Vellacott's three lines to Louis MacNeice.

19

Review of Brooks Otis, *Cosmos and Tragedy*

Brooks Otis, Cosmos and Tragedy: An Essay on the Meaning of Aeschylus, ed. with notes and a preface by E. Christian Kopff (University of North Carolina Press, Chapel Hill 1982) xiii + 119 pp.

Few classical scholars can resist the temptation, sooner or later, to write about the *Oresteia*. The late Brooks Otis, best known for his work on Virgil and Ovid, planned a book on 'how pagan and Christian writers and thinkers attempted to . . . move beyond the tragic limitations that seem built into human life', and *Cosmos and Tragedy* is the execution of that part of his plan which concerned Aeschylus in general and the *Oresteia* in particular.

In *Eumenides*, the last play of the trilogy, Aeschylus made some use of the distinction, prominent in Hesiod's *Theogony*, between older and younger generations of gods; so the Furies, 'old' goddesses, lament Orestes' acquittal as an outrage perpetrated against them by Apollo and Athena, and threaten revenge on Athens, but are persuaded by Athena to settle there instead as revered possessors of a sanctuary. Otis (like others before him, in differing degrees) believed that Aeschylus's dominant concern was with theodicy; that is to say, that Aeschylus used the tragic myth of the House of Atreus to exhibit the replacement of an 'old régime', in which vengeance was automatically exacted by the Furies without regard for the commensurability of guilt and punishment (pp. 44, 46, 52), by a 'new order' in which justice was guaranteed by Zeus (pp. 14, 20, 66, 95).

In the course of his argument Otis says much that is true, though little that is original, about each step in the unfolding of the story. His remarks on the different degrees of guilt of Agamemnon, Klytaimestra and Orestes, as judged by human standards, are not without interest (pp. 8f), but I doubt, for reasons given in *JHS* xciii (1973) 66f (repr. above, pp. 135–50), whether Aeschylus meant us to see a 'fierce personal complicity' of Agamemnon (p. 26, cf. p. 145 above) in his army's desire to sacrifice his daughter.

Otis's view of Aeschylus's general intention is not, of course, refuted by the fact that it does not seem ever to have occurred to an ancient Greek, for we have every right to interest ourselves in aspects of Aeschylus which did not interest ancient critics, historians, or philosophers. The real trouble is that *Eumenides*, where we might have expected a comparatively clear revelation of whatever cosmic scheme Aeschylus chose to illustrate by the myth, is hard to reconcile with any such scheme. Otis treats Apollo's 'curious apology for matricide' (p. 87), which 'avoids the ethical question' (p. 93), as 'required by the logic of the trilogy' and 'explicable when we consider its relation to the impartiality of the court'; he dismisses 'the indifference of the Erinyes to Agamemnon's fate' as 'a belated development' (p. 86); and while admitting that 'to oppose father-right to mother-right is to confuse the moral issue altogether' he considers that 'it is not the justification of matricide but the setting up of a system that will prevent it and other crimes that constitutes the *raison d'être* of the Areopagus' (ibid.). When interpreters of Aeschylus say things like that, the probability that they have themselves misconceived the moral issues is quite high. How can the setting up of a court *prevent* crimes more effectively than the certainty of supernatural vengeance? Athena – who, incidentally, is very far from 'preserving that appearance of judicial impartiality' (p. 87; see *Eu*. 737) – in fact promises the Furies (*Eu*. 934) that inherited human sin will continue to provide them with victims.

The intention of a Greek tragic poet is best recovered from the relation between inherited data and innovation in his handling of a myth. Aeschylus's innovations in the *Oresteia* are exceptional in scale and audacity. They have their origin in his exultation in the fortunes of his own city, and one of them is identification of the demons – curses, 'Furies', 'Erinyes' – who pursued Orestes with the 'August Goddesses' worshipped at Athens. Considerations of this kind are passed over by Otis; perhaps he felt, as many do, that it is intolerable if the cosmos of a great poet turns out to be a parish.

20

Aeschylus, *Fragment 248M*

Athenaeus 51c: μόρα δὲ τὰ συκάμινα καὶ παρ᾽ Αἰσχύλῳ ἐν Φρυξὶν ἐπὶ τοῦ Ἕκτορος·

ἀνὴρ δ᾽ ἐκεῖνος ἦν πεπαίτερος μόρων.

(= Aeschylus, fr. 248 Mette = 264 Nauck[2] = 147 Weir Smyth).

The play had the alternative title Ἕκτορος λύτρα, and Priam's ransoming of Hector's body was represented in it (Aristophanes fr. 678). The line quoted by Athenaeus is a grisly joke (spoken, therefore, by a Greek and not by Priam or any other Trojan) spun out of the mockery of the dead Hector by the Greeks in *Il.* xxii 373f:

ὦ πόποι, ἦ μάλα δὴ μαλακώτερος ἀμφαφάασθαι
Ἕκτωρ ἢ ὅτε νῆας ἐνέπρησεν πυρὶ κηλέῳ.

ἀνὴρ ἐκεῖνος points the same contrast; and for πέπων = μαλακός = 'unwarlike', 'cowardly', cf. *Il.* ii 235. When Hector had been repeatedly stabbed on the battlefield (*Il.* xxii 371, xxiv 420f) and dragged back to the Greek camp at the tail of Achilles' chariot (*Il.* xxii 395ff) his body would have had a horrible resemblance to overripe mulberries; cf. Demetrius Ixion's etymology μόρα ~ αἱμόρροα (Ath. 51f).[1]

The closest parallel to Aeschylus' expression is Theopompus Comicus fr. 72 μαλθακωτέρα σικυοῦ πέπονός μοι γέγονε. Other obvious parallels come from poetry which lacks serious pathos (not all, of course, involve two senses of the same word as different as the two senses of πέπων exploited by Aeschylus): Epicharmus fr. 154K and Sophron fr. 34K, ὑγιώτερος (*sic*) κολοκύντας; Theocr. 7.120 ἀπίοιο πεπαίτερος; ibid. 11.20ff λευκοτέρα

---

[1] We must ask (without any assurance of an answer) *why* Athenaeus thought he knew *which* fruit was denoted by μόρα in Aeschylus' line; all fruits become πέπων, but not all are the same colour. In this connection Dr D. C. C. Young has drawn my attention to 1 Macc. 6.33: καὶ τοῖς ἐλέφασιν ἔδειξαν αἷμα σταφυλῆς καὶ μόρων τοῦ παραστῆσαι αὐτοὺς εἰς τὸν πόλεμον.

πακτᾶς κτλ. (adapted and exaggerated by Ovid, *Met*. xiii 795ff); Catullus 25.1ff 'mollior cuniculi capillo . . . idemque turbida rapacior procella'.

I can credit Aeschylus with a harsh joke on an enemy's lips; I could not so easily credit him with these words if they were spoken, as is commonly believed, by the mourning Priam in praise of his son's gentle manners (cf. *Il*. xxiv 767ff)[2] – any more than I could believe that he would seriously describe a man's intelligence as πυκνότερος βάτων.

---

² So most recently W. Schadewaldt, *Hermes* lxxi (1936) 65 (= *Hellas und Hesperien* [Zürich and Stuttgart 1960] 207), to whom the metaphor seems eminently Aeschylean. G. Hermann, *Opuscula* v (Leipzig 1834) 158, did indeed refer the line to Hector's body, but to the body after its miraculous cleansing; Eustathius on *Il*. ii 235 explains πεπαίτερος as ὡριμώτερος, and Hermann went too far in equating ὥριμος and ὡραῖος.

21

ΗΛΙΟΣ ΚΗΡΥΞ

Sophocles, *Trachiniae* 97–102:

"Άλιον "Άλιον αἰτῶ
τοῦτο καρῦξαι τὸν Ἀλκμήνας πόθι μοι πόθι [μοι] παῖς
ναίει ποτ᾽, ὦ λαμπρᾷ οτεροπᾷ φλεγέθων,
ἢ ποντίας αὐλῶνας ἢ δισσαῖσιν ἀπείροις κλιθείς.
εἴπ᾽, ὦ κρατιστεύων κατ᾽ ὄμμα.

98 alt. *μοι* del. Triclinius

When we mortals do not know where in the world someone is, the Sun knows, for he traverses the whole earth and sees everyone and everything. The scholiast on this passage of Sophocles adduces a conflated citation of *Il*. iii 277 Ἥλιός θ᾽ ὃς πάντ᾽ ἐφορᾷς and *Od*. xi 109 Ἡελίου, ὃς πάντ᾽ ἐφορᾷ, and the Homeric concept persists in tragedy (e.g. A. *PV* 91, S. *OC* 869).[1] Having seen, the Sun can tell; Ares and Aphrodite thought that they could deceive Hephaestus, ἄφαρ δέ οἱ ἄγγελος ἦλθεν Ἥλιος (*Od*. viii 270f). In a passage of *h. Hom. Cer*. (69ff) which comes very close to Sophocles in spirit,[2] Demeter visits the Sun and implores him, 'You who look down on all earth and sea . . . tell me truly of my dear child, if you have seen her anywhere, who has gone off with her. . . .' The women of Trachis do not have a goddess's freedom of the cosmos, but they understandably express their feeling, 'If only the Sun could and would tell me . . .!', in an extravagantly direct prayer to the Sun. In the light of the passages cited, it is a reasonable presumption that Sophocles is using καρῦξαι as practically synonymous with μηνῦσαι or with ἀπαγγεῖλαι, and εἰπέ in 102 seems to confirm this.

Since it is the function of a herald to communicate something to a community or army as a whole, κηρύττειν may be used figuratively in poetry to contrast clear, loud, open or widespread disclosure with suppression or secrecy. The contrast is explicit in E. *Cretes* fr. 82 (Austin) 29–34 κἀγὼ μέν . . .

---

[1] See further Roscher, *Myth. Lex*. i 2019f.
[2] Cited by Erfurdt Soph. *ad loc*.

ἔκρυψα ... σὺ δ᾽ ... πᾶσι κηρύσσεις τάδε and *Cressae* fr. 460 (Nauck) 2f περιστεῖλαι καλῶς κρύπτοντα καὶ μὴ πᾶσι κηρύσσειν τάδε; cf. A. *Ch.* 1026 κηρύσσω ('declare', 'proclaim') φίλοις κτανεῖν τε φημί, S. *Ant.* 87 πολλὸν ἐχθίων ἔσει σιγῶσ᾽ ἐὰν μὴ πᾶσι κηρύξῃς τάδε (Antigone's retort to Ismene's anxious προμηνύσῃς... τοῦτο μηδενί), *El.* 606 κήρυσσέ μ᾽ εἰς ἅπαντας, εἴτε χρῇς κακὴν κτλ., E. *Andr.* 436 κήρυσσ᾽ἅπασι ('you can tell the world, for all I care' is the implication), *Hcld.* 864 βροτοῖς ἅπασι λαμπρὰ κηρύσσει μαθεῖν κτλ. In certain other passages κηρύσσειν is used of communication between mortals and immortals (as between states or armies): A. *Ch.* 4f κηρύσσω πατρὶ κλύειν ἀκοῦσαι (Orestes to his father's soul), 124ff κηρύξας ἐμοὶ τούς γῆς ἔνερθε δαίμονας κλύειν ἐμὰς εὐχάς (addressed to Hermes and exploiting Hermes' role as divine herald), E. *Hec.* 147 κήρυσσε θεούς (where loud and public invocation is also appropriate), *Ion* 991 εἰς οὓς αὐδὰν καρύξω (Creusa apostrophizes Apollo, cf. 907 ὠή, τὸν Λατοῦς αὐδῶ κτλ.). Finally, distinction between κηρύσσειν and ἀγγέλλειν seems doubtful in E. *Hel.* 1491–4 καρύξατ᾽ἀγγελίαν... Μενέλεως ὅτι... ἥξει and S. *El.* 1105 εἰ τὸν ἀγχιστόν γε κηρύσσειν χρεών (with reference to the announcement of a visitor's arrival).

Nevertheless, there is evidence to suggest that the audience of the *Trachiniae* is more likely to have taken τοῦτο καρῦξαι κτλ. in the sense, 'make a proclamation, *asking* where ...' than in the sense '*tell me* where ...'. Some κηρύγματα convey information; but others ask for it, the question often (but not always) implying an invitation to action.[3] The most straightforward example is afforded by the Megarian in Ar. *Ach.* 748f, who says ἐγὼν δὲ καρυξῶ Δικαιόπολιν ὅπα. Δικαιόπολι, ἢ λῆς πρίασθαι χοιρία; Since he wants to sell, there is a superficial resemblance to the κηρύγματα of the market (cf. the fishmongers of Antiphanes fr. 125.1f), but there is a much more important difference; whereas merchandise, not the customer, normally κηρύττεται, i.e. 'is offered publicly for sale', 'is advertised for sale' (e.g. Antiphanes fr. 168.3f), the Megarian means 'I will call out to discover where Dikaiopolis is'. An interrogative κήρυγμα is required to get information about a crime or a criminal: Andoc. i 112 ὁ κῆρυξ ἐκήρυττε τίς τὴν ἱκετηρίαν καταθείη, Dem. xxv 56 'He broke out of the prison and escaped ... and she hid him in safety for the first few days, ἃς ἐζήτουν καὶ ἐκήρυττον οἱ ἔνδεκα', Antiphon ii γ 2 τὸ κακούργημα (a man and his slave murdered in the street at night) ἂν ἐκηρύσσετο ~ δ 6 εἰ δὲ ἐκηρύσσοντο ἢ μή ἄλλοι τινὲς κακοῦργοι, τίς οἶδεν; κηρύττειν a runaway slave is to describe him ὑπὸ κήρυκος and to ask 'Who has seen him? Who knows where he is?' Allusion is made to this formula in Luc. *Fug.* 27 τὸ νῦν δὲ ἅμα κηρύττωμεν · εἴ τις ⟨εἶδεν⟩ ἀνδράποδον Παφλαγονικόν... μηνύειν ἐπὶ ῥητῷ. Meleager 37 (Gow-Page; *Anth. Pal.* v

---

[3] By 'invitation' I mean (e.g.) Hdt. ii 134.4 κηρυσσόντων Δελφῶν ... ὃς βούλοιτο κτλ. (on interrogative ὅς in Hdt. cf. Kühner–Gerth, *Gr. Gr.* ii 459), Dem. xliii 5 τοῦ κήρυκος κηρύττοντος εἴ τις... βούλεται κτλ. Eur. *Phoen.* 47f τἀμὰ κηρύσσει λέχη ὅστις... μάθοι is a step further away from 'Who wants...?' in the direction of 'If anyone... there is a reward....' J. Oehler in *RE* xi 355–7 (*s.v.* κῆρυξ) does not give enough weight to invitations and requests for information in his summary of the functions of heralds.

177) is a conceit founded on it: κηρύσσω τὸν Ἔρωτα ... ἔστι δ' ὁ παῖς γλύκυδακρυς κτλ.[4] In Moschus 1 (= Anth. Pal. ix 440) it is Aphrodite herself who issues the proclamation about Eros, ὅστις ἐνὶ τριόδοισι πλανώμενον εἶδεν Ἔρωτα, δραπετίδας ἐμός ἐστιν · ὁ μανύσας γέρας ἕξεῖ (2f), but here he is not her slave (despite δραπετίδας) but her son, as the first line of the poem declares: ἁ Κύπρις τὸν Ἔρωτα τὸν υἱέα μακρὸν ἐβώστρει.

What did a Greek family do when a small boy failed to come home? The obvious mechanism was a κήρυγμα describing him and asking who had seen him, the ancient equivalent of the police message on the radio. This much we can infer without actual examples, but I suspect that an example underlies the anecdote derived by Plutarch (Alc. 3.1) from Antiphon (fr. 66 Thalheim): 'As a boy he ran away from home to one of his lovers, Democrates. Ariphron wanted to ἀποκηρύττειν him, but Pericles would have none of this. If he is dead, said Pericles, we shall know it only one day sooner διὰ τὸ κήρυγμα, but if he is safe (σῶς) the rest of his life will be ruined (ἄσωστος)' – sc. because his absence from home will have been revealed, and gossip will do the rest. ἀποκηρύττειν elsewhere refers to disposal by sale (which is not relevant here), prohibition (Xen. HG v 2.27) or the formal disowning of a son by his father,[5] e.g. Aeschines Socraticus Alc. (P. Oxy. 1608.39), Pl. Lg. 928e (coupled with ἀπειπεῖν, cf. E. Alc. 773 ἀπειπεῖν ... κηρύκων ὕπο). Ariphron might indeed have proposed ἀποκήρυξις if he know where Alcibiades had gone; but Pericles' answer makes sense only if the boy's whereabouts were not known and the proposal was for a κήρυγμα declaring him lost and asking for information. Thalheim (RE i 2836, s.v. ἀποκήρυξις) accepted the prima facie interpretation of the word here, exceptionally, as 'ausrufen ... ein verloren gegangenes Kind'. Is it not more likely that Plutarch or a source intermediate between him and Antiphon conflated two anecdotes, one involving a proposal of ἀποκήρυξις and the other involving an interrogative κήρυγμα?

If the Trachinian women are asking the Sun not simply to tell them where Herakles is but to ask the human race, 'Where is Herakles?', the closest parallel[6] to their request is not, after all, Demeter's in the Homeric Hymn but Ajax's in S. Aj. 845ff, 'Sun ..., when you see my native land, draw rein and tell (ἄγγειλον) my aged father ... of my fate'.

Three elements reinforce, in varying degrees, the interpretation of Tr. 97ff for which I argue. First, the agonized repetition of πόθι; but this is perhaps too

---

[4] A good example of an advertisement (second century BC) describing some runaway slaves, asking for information on them and promising a reward, is to be found in P. M. Meyer, Juristische Papyri (Berlin 1920) no. 50 (165).

[5] In Dem. xxxix 39 the issue seems to be not the disowning of a son by his father but the father's revocation of the name which he had given his son; Demosthenes may, however, be referring to the fact that ἀποκήρυξις deprives the son of his patronymic and demotic and thus alters his total official name.

[6] Two passages of A. Ag. have just a nuance of the concept that the Sun seeks and transmits information: 632f, 'No one knows, so as to bring clear report (ἀπαγγεῖλαι τορῶς), except the Sun ...', and 676, 'If some ray of the Sun discovers (ἱστορεῖ) him alive ...', i.e. 'if he is alive somewhere on earth'.

common a Sophoclean phenomenon to bear much weight. Secondly, the syntactical isolation of παῖς, which superimposes a suggestion of 'Where is the child?' upon 'Where is the son of Alcmena?' Thirdly, the expression of 'Herakles' in the form τὸν Ἀλκμήνας: again, this is so common that by itself, considered separately from the other elements in the passage, it tells us nothing, but we must remember that in any small community such as an Attic deme a young child is more likely to be identified as his mother's than as his father's. That, I think, is why Pindar *O*. 1.46f says of the disappearance of the young Pelops οὐδὲ ματρὶ πολλὰ μαιόμενοι φῶτες ἄγαγον, and I would not rule out the possibility that the common designation of Herakles as 'son of Alcmena' was the germ from which the conceit developed by Sophocles in *Tr*. 97ff grew.

The most obvious objection to this interpretation is εἰπέ in 102. If καρῦξαι is 'make an interrogative proclamation', then it seems that εἰπέ must mean either 'utter (*sc*. the question which I have asked you to utter)' or 'tell me (*sc*. when the question which I have asked you to utter has been answered)'. No one could feel comfortable with either of these alternatives, given the frequency of εἰπέ or εἰπέ μοι in comic dialogue (e.g. Ar. *Ach*. 157, *Eq*. 1361, *Nu*. 200) following and reinforcing a clause or word-group which contains an interrogative word. I think, however, that 100f make the second alternative unobjectionable. Professor Lloyd-Jones has shown (*CQ* NS iv [1954] 91–3) that those lines do not mean 'on land or sea' but refer specifically to the entrance to the Black Sea and the Pillars of Hercules. Thus the chorus, having asked the Sun to put a question to the world, go on to speculate themselves, saying in effect, 'Is he . . .?', which is a fresh stage in their thought and dissociates εἰπέ from τοῦτο καρῦξαι. Finally, there is the objection that κηρύττειν is a repetitive process; does not the aorist καρῦξαι militate against my interpretation? Other things being equal, yes; but I do not think that other things are equal. There is quite a difference between hiring a herald to plod from one agora to another and asking the Sun to proclaim in a divine voice, once and for all, a question which will reach to the ends of the earth.

ADDITIONAL NOTE

The argument of this paper is criticized in detail by the late T. C. W. Stinton, *CQ* NS xxxvi (1986) 337ff. Anything that Tom Stinton said about a problem in tragedy deserves respect, and I was glad to find that he agreed at least to characterize my interpretation as 'not impossible', although it 'founders on one vital point', '*tell* me . . .'. The reason I have not consigned my paper to oblivion is that I would still like to know what image formed in the mind of the Athenian hearer as the words τοῦτο καρῦξαι πόθι μοι unfolded – especially if the last word of the verse was παῖς, but even if it was not. And I am not persuaded that Stinton was right in taking Ar. *Ach*. 748 ἐγὼν δὲ καρυξῶ Δικαιόπολιν ὅπα to mean 'I will summon Dikaiopolis to where (the sale is).'

22

Greek Comedy

A. METHOD

1 The Twentieth Century

Papyri and inscriptions pose new problems and spring many surprises, but they may also answer questions already asked. The physical unearthing of new material is not in all circumstances more exciting than that kind of discovery which is ultimately the product of reflection; and a spark is often kindled by the mere juxtaposition of facts long familiar in isolation. For these reasons I propose to discuss in this section, A, progress in interpretation which may have been stimulated by the discovery of new material but was not dependent on this material for its success. In B I shall describe the three principal categories of discovery, and in C I shall try to summarize the present

In referring the reader to books and articles I have tried to preserve a balance between two different and often conflicting criteria: importance in the history of the study of Greek comedy, and accessibility to the British reader in the 1950s. I have often omitted works which in their time represented significant progress in favour of accessible modern works which summarize the results of half a century's study.

In the citation of comic fragments:

K refers to Kock's *Comicorum Atticorum Fragmenta*
D refers to Demianczuk's *Supplementum Comicum*
S refers to Schröder's *Novae Comoediae Fragmenta*
P refers to Page's *Greek Literary Papyri*

In addition to the abbreviations current in *L'Année Philologique* I have used the following special abbreviations:

DFA	Sir Arthur Pickard-Cambridge, *The Dramatic Festivals of Athens* (Oxford 1953)
DTC	A. W. Pickard-Cambridge, *Dithyramb, Tragedy, and Comedy* (Oxford 1927)
NCh	M. Platnauer, *Comedy*, in *New Chapters in the History of Greek Literature, Third Series* (Oxford 1933)
SLGC	T. B. L. Webster, *Studies in Later Greek Comedy* (Manchester 1953)
Wil., *Ar*.	U. von Wilamowitz-Möllendorff, *Aristophanes Lysistrate* (Berlin 1927)
Wil., *Men*.	Id., *Menander: Das Schiedsgericht* (Berlin 1925)

state of what seem to me the five most significant problems with which we are confronted by the old and the new material in combination.

A scholar who tries to explain a difficult passage of a Greek text may be conceived as exploring a complex of concentric circles; the innermost circle encloses the immediate context of the passage, the outermost the whole of human experience. The right path to pursue is long and spiral; the average interpreter of Greek comedy in the nineteenth century tended to follow a path that was short and straight. Atomizing his text, he considered each sentence in its relation to the lexical, grammatical, and metrical norms continuously extracted by learning and devotion from his vast inheritance.[1]

Twentieth-century work on comedy shows two characteristics which stand in particular contrast to the purely linguistic approach. One is the development of what I would call 'generic studies', the extension to literary form of the methods of collection and classification previously applied to linguistic data; these methods have been particularly fruitful when applied to recurrent dramatic situations.[2] The second characteristic is the realization, as yet imperfect and erratic, of the full implications of the simple truism that comedy is *drama*; these implications will be discussed in section 2 below.

In contrasting one century with another one necessarily commits a double injustice: an injustice to the past, in that the most stimulating and fruitful of modern enquiries may turn out to be no more than the following-up of hints long unheeded but plainly given by individual scholars a century ago; and an injustice to the present, in that anyone who still sees comedy through the eyes of a Kock or a Blaydes may share the credit which rightly belongs to those who do not. Nevertheless, if the nineteenth-century scholars who were influential in their own day are viewed in contrast with the twentieth-century scholars who have been influential in ours, I believe that the distinction made above is valid.

If the historian of the future is ever asked whether there was any one man in this century whose influence on the study of comedy was outstanding, he may well say: Wilamowitz. Superficially, this may seem a surprising choice, for the bulk of Wilamowitz's work on comedy is not large, and there are others – Alfred Körte most obviously – who might reasonably claim prior mention.[3] But Wilamowitz was no waster of words, and methodologically he has had no equal; much of his work should be read not as a systematic exposition of data but as intellectual protreptic illuminated by provocative examples. He owed his understanding of comedy to his sustained determination to take the

---

[1] Cf. S. G. Owen's obituary of Blaydes in *JAW* xxxii (1909) 37–9.

[2] F. Leo, 'Der Monolog im Drama', *AGG* NF x.5 (1908), esp. 113–19, on the investigation of poetic forms in general; W. Kock, *Der Personarum Comicarum Introductione* (Breslau 1914); K. Kunst, *Studien zur griechisch-römischen Komödie* (Vienna/Leipzig 1919); A. Perkmann, 'Streitszenen in der griechisch-römischen Komödie', *WS* xlv (1926–7), xlvi (1927–8).

[3] We must also be aware of the presence of a ghost: Georg Kaibel, who died in 1901 in the prime of life. It is not easy to set a limit to the services which his prodigious scholarship would have rendered to the study of Greek comedy had he been given another thirty years of life.

Greeks as he found them and to his refusal to believe that metre and politics, palaeography and religion, cannot be studied by the same man at the same time.

2 *Action and Language*[4]

Van Leeuwen was long perplexed by the dramaturgy of *Acharnians*, but in his edition of 1901 he solved the problem to his own satisfaction: 'Dicaeopolidem . . . in ipsa urbe celebrare parva Liberalia, quorum tempus legitimum dudum praeteriit, fingentem se rure versari . . . Lamachum autem et Euripidem vicinos [*sic*] Dicaeopolidi fingendo comicus fines arti suae concessos non est egressus.' Now van Leeuwen was an intelligent editor who had gone far to free himself from purely verbal preoccupations,[5] but he had not freed himself from the characteristic attitude of the nineteenth century towards dramaturgy: the acceptance of the 'three unities' as fundamental and the grudging admission of occasional departures from these unities by virtue of 'comic licence'. The fact is that in Old Comedy the moment and the episode were everything, and all consistency of place, time, character, personality, and logic could be sacrificed to them.[6] It might be said that Aristophanes made great demands on the imagination of his audience – provided we understand that the poet did not regard himself as asking for a concession and his audience was not conscious of granting one. This concentration on the comic moment is characteristic of several types of popular comedy in our own day. Perhaps the man who is brought up on Molière and Shaw, who listens in to *Studies in Interpretation* but never to *Take It From Here*, is not altogether to be trusted with Aristophanes.

The reader who makes a serious effort to put himself in the place of the ancient audience will find Aristophanic dramaturgy at once more acceptable. Progress in the archaeology of the Greek theatre[7] has facilitated this imaginative effort, but in interpreting a text it is also necessary that we should always see in the mind's eye the movements and gestures of the speakers and

---

[4] No complete exegetical editions of Aristophanes have appeared since those of J. van Leeuwen (Leyden 1893–1906) and B. B. Rogers (London 1901–6). Rogers' scholarly equipment was defective, and though the force and ingenuity of his translation endeared him to the amateur he has not been taken seriously by the professional; but he sometimes hit the nail on the head (cf. Ed. Fraenkel, *Eranos* xlviii (1950) 84 n. 1, on *Av*. 267). Of the editions of separate plays the most significant are: W. J. M. Starkie's *Wasps*, *Acharnians* and *Clouds* (London 1897, 1909 and 1911 respectively), R. A. Neil's *Knights* (Cambridge 1901), Wil., *Ar.*, L. Radermacher's *Frogs* (*SAWW* cxcviii.4 [1921]), and K. Holzinger's commentary on *Plutus* (*SAWW* ccxxviii.3 [1940]). Of contributions in periodicals: Wilamowitz, 'Uber die *Wespen* des Aristophanes', *SPAW* 1911; V. Coulon's articles in *REG* xxxv (1922) – xliv (1931); K. Holzinger, 'Erklärungen umstrittener Stellungen des Aristophanes', *SAWW* ccviii.5 (1928) and ccxv.1 (1933).

[5] Wil., *Ar*. 7 is grossly unfair.

[6] F. Krause, *Quaestiones Aristophaneae Scaenicae* (Rostock 1903); Wilamowitz, *SPAW* 1911, 481–5, and *Hermes* lxiv (1929) 470–6; W. Kranz, *Hermes* lii (1917) 585 n. 1; O. J. Todd, 'Quomodo Aristophanes Rem Temporalem in Fabulis suis Tractaverit', *HSPh* xxvi (1915).

[7] A. W. Pickard-Cambridge, *The Theatre of Dionysus at Athens* (Oxford 1946).

hear in the mind's ear the sound of their voices.[8] It is an encouraging sign that in the Teubner third edition of Menander the *actio* appears above the apparatus; but we are still unskilled in visualizing gesture. Editors of *Frogs* do not seem to remember that line 1434, ὁ μὲν σοφῶς γὰρ εἶπεν, ὁ δ'ἕτερος σαφῶς, was spoken by a live man with mobile hands, so that data on μέν and δέ are of limited relevance.

In many nineteenth-century scholars the mind's ear was as undeveloped an organ as the mind's eye. In fr. 1K of Antiphanes a speaker is declaiming in tragic style; someone else at last exclaims τί λέγεις; and he replies τραγῳδίαν περαίνω Σοφοκλέους. And here is Kock's comment: 'non video cur non maluerit scribere περαίνω Σοφοκλέους τραγῳδίαν, versu haud paullo modulatiore'. With a sudden shock we realize that to Kock Greek was not a real noise that once issued from the mouths of real men, but a set of visual symbols to be manipulated by rules which were excellent up to a point but defective in so far as they were based on only a portion of the relevant facts. It is strange that when so much work has been devoted to the vocabulary of Greek comedy so little thought has been given to its characteristic groupings of words and structure of phrase,[9] and for this deficiency our reluctance to speak the words of the text aloud is to blame.

Study of vocabulary has concentrated on the distribution of words; in Menander to establish his relation to the Koine[10] and in Aristophanes to uncover the different literary and cultural strata which make up his astonishing edifice of poetry. The substratum of Aristophanic language is presumably colloquial, though the boundaries of colloquial Greek are much harder to determine than those of colloquial Latin. It may often be identified by expressions which recur in the popular speech of Byzantium and modern Greece,[11] or by terminations of a type associated with colloquialism in Latin.[12] Overlying this substratum is the language of parody. Parody of serious poetry, especially of tragedy, is comparatively easily detected and isolated,[13] but a more subtle parody, or a kind of allusion which shades into parody, is seldom completely absent from any passage of Aristophanes. In particular, many words and terminations[14] are associated with certain specialized vocabularies, e.g. with medicine or philosophy or formal rhetoric; it has been well remarked that the editor of Aristophanes needs inverted commas.[15]

---

[8] Wil., *Ar.* 7, 38–9, and *Hermes* lxiv (1929) 466–70.

[9] Wil., *Men.*, 156; W. Dittmar, *Sprachliche Untersuchungen zu Aristophanes und Menander* (Weida 1933) is a step in the right direction.

[10] Chr. Bruhn, *Ueber den Wortschatz des Menanders* (Jena 1910); D. B. Durham, *The Vocabulary of Menander* (Princeton, NJ, 1913).

[11] G. P. Anagnostopoulos, 'Γλωσσικὰ Ἀνάλεκτα Γ', Ἀθηνᾶ xxxvi (1924), esp. 42–4.

[12] Ibid., 52–7.

[13] A. C. Schlesinger, 'Indications of Parody in Aristophanes', *TAPhA* lxvii (1936) and *AJPh* lviii (1937).

[14] C. W. Peppler's articles in *AJPh* xxviii (1907), xxxi (1910), xxxvii (1916), xxxix (1918), xlii (1921).

[15] J. D. Denniston, 'Technical Terms in Aristophanes', *CQ* xxi (1927).

The late-nineteenth-century school which regarded linguistic abnormality as aesthetically objectionable or even morally depraved is not a good master in the study of comic language. Just as in metre the divergence of comic practice from tragic has to be recognized,[16] and premature theorizing has merely hindered the essential task of discerning and describing metrical phenomena, so in language the student of comedy must adopt a non-committal and positivistic approach. Even in the field of vocabulary the essential material has not yet been wholly reduced to a serviceable form. We have an Index to Aristophanes,[17] but – while it is ungracious to carp at a work which we use not only with gratitude but also with relief that we did not have to do the job ourselves – it is to be deplored that all such indices for the sake of a few hours' more work and a few shillings more in printing costs omit the plausible variants. No comprehensive index to the comic fragments has been compiled since the mid nineteenth century.[18] Furthermore, most of the existing studies of comic vocabulary would be of shorter length but greater weight if their authors, before labelling a word 'colloquial', 'technical', 'poetic', etc., on the purely positive evidence had asked and answered the vital question: 'How else could the poet have said it?'

3   Comedy and Society

Not all the humour of comedy is verbal, and not all the verbal humour is readily appreciated without effort. The analysis of humour is never popular, thanks to the superstition that a joke explained is no joke. Fortunately, useful classificatory work has been done on some obvious types of humour in comedy,[19] but there is much in the Greek sense of humour and sense of fantasy which is elusive. The enjoyment of tremendous indecency in close conjunction with refined literary criticism no longer presents a serious problem, for the unparalleled restraint imposed on the written word by the convention of the nineteenth century has died the death of all excesses; contemplation of the cold and arrogant savageries which our own world perpetrates makes us turn with something like relief to Aristophanic lechery. For the understanding of those aspects of comedy which are really alien to our own culture we cannot do better than look to the modern Greeks. Anyone who has seen dancing in a Greek village will not discount the final clause in *V.* 1524–30 τὸ Φρυνίχειον ἐκλακτισάτω τις ὅπως ἰδόντες ἄνω σκέλος ᾤζωσιν οἱ

---

[16] J. W. White, *The Verse of Greek Comedy* (London 1912), gives valuable data on metres κατὰ στίχον, but his analysis of lyric metres is too theoretical; on problems of responsion, Wilamowitz, *Griechische Verskunst* (Berlin 1921) 470–86, and M. Platnauer, 'Antistrophic Variations in Aristophanes', in *Greek Poetry and Life* (Oxford 1936) 241–56.

[17] O. J. Todd, *Index Aristophaneus* (Cambridge, Mass., 1932).

[18] Demianczuk's *Supplementum Comicum* and Jensen's and Körte's editions of Menander contain *indices verborum*. K. Klaus, *Die Adjektiva bei Menander* (Leipzig 1936), is an excellent analysis of part of Menander's vocabulary.

[19] H. Steiger, 'Die Groteske und die Burleske bei Aristophanes', *Phil.* lxxxix (1934); H. W. Miller, 'Comic Iteration in Aristophanes', *AJPh* lxvi (1945), cf. lxv (1944).

θεαταί. On a more sophisticated level, there is hardly an incident, hardly even a phrase, in Nikos Kazantsakis' novel *Zorba the Greek* which has not an alien ring to ears which know only English, but no one who has read Aristophanes will raise his eyebrows at a remark such as 'Many are the joys of this world – women, fruit, ideas', which the *New Yorker* picked out for sarcastic comment.

Though the attention paid to the audience's sense of humour has been scanty, much has been paid to its intellectual attainments, and it is commonly represented as sceptical in religion and intimately conversant with great poetry. The case for its scepticism rests primarily on its tolerance of the discomfiture of Poseidon in *Birds* and the discreditable antics of Dionysus in *Frogs*. Yet the conclusion that Athenian society in the late fifth century was in general sceptical of traditional religion[20] is not easily reconciled with the evidence from other sources, and rests on a failure of the imagination. To understand pre-Christian religious attitudes requires a great imaginative effort, and those who make it are commonly regarded as imposters by those who cannot. The intimate association of the gods with the fabric of ordinary Greek life is something which might be better understood by a Papuan than by a bishop, and perhaps best of all by the medieval Christian, whose humour was full of casual blasphemy[21] and prompt to interweave the comic and the tremendous.[22] The fact is that the Greek gods had human pleasures and understood laughter; at the right time and place they could take a joke.[23]

The case for the literary discrimination of the Athenian audience rests on the fondness of comedy for literary topics[24] and above all for parody. But it has been remarked that criticism of poetry in comedy tended to be criticism of the poet's person (real or conventionalized) rather than of his art;[25] and the humour of para-tragedy lies not in the choice of the particular tragic passage but in the use of tragic language as such in a comic context. The audience could detect that tragedy was being parodied without identifying lines from *Telephus* or *Medea*, and the stance and voice of the actor would show them that it was there to be detected.[26] Even if they recognized the original and remembered its source, it may be that the majority of the allusions in comedy

---

[20] G. Keller, *Die Komödien des Aristophanes und die athenische Volksreligion seiner Zeit* (Tübingen 1931), esp. 16; M. P. Nilsson, *Greek Piety* (Oxford 1948) 77.

[21] P. Lehmann, *Die Parodie im Mittelalter* (Munich 1922) 39–40, 55–6, 208.

[22] E.g. the persistent intrusion of comic elements in the Alsfeld Passion Play (ed. R. Froning, *Das Drama des Mittelalters* vols ii–iii [Stuttgart n.d.]: cf. P. Scherer, *Geschichte der deutschen Litteratur* [Berlin 1883] 247–8) or the comic treatment of Noah and his family in *The Chester Pageant of the Deluge* (ed. E. Rhys in *Everyman and Other Interludes* [London 1909]); cf. G. Murray, *Aristophanes* (Oxford 1933) 2.

[23] Wilamowitz, *Der Glaube der Hellenen* (Berlin 1931) i 43 and ii 96–8; H. Kleinknecht, *Die Gebetsparodie in der Antike* (Stuttgart–Berlin 1937) 116–22.

[24] G. W. Baker, 'De Comicis Graecis Litterarum Iudicibus', *HSPh*. xv (1904).

[25] A. E. Roggwiller, *Dichter und Dichtung in der attischen Komödie* (Zürich 1926) 18–28.

[26] A. Römer, 'Ueber den litterarisch-ästhetischen Bildungsstand des attischen Theater-publikums', *ABAW* xxii (1905), esp. 68.

are allusions to lines which the poet knew from experience were widely disseminated;[27] and to remember ἡ γλῶσσ' ὀμώμοχ' ἡ δὲ φρὴν ἀνώμοτος is not the same thing as forming a critical judgement on *Hippolytus*. Again, the poet may often have amused himself by recondite allusions which he did not expect his audience to appreciate;[28] experience of the modern 'little' revenue suggests that the uninformed majority will readily join in the laughter of the few and feel more flattered than insulted by an appeal to their discrimination.

Attempts to use comedy as evidence for Athenian society and economy are valuable and productive,[29] but the material needs very cautious handling. It is not only that the closest attention must be paid to the context, for that is a necessary principle of all interpretation. The sociologist using comedy must deal with two special difficulties, the autonomous comic myth and the nature of comic statement. The fidelity of comedy to ordinary life can be overrated; as well as the farmer of real life, there is the conventional farmer of comedy, and the two may differ. Comic conventions tend to lag behind the times; in the comic papers of our own day sergeant-majors wear waxed moustaches, countrymen chew straws, and dons spend their whole adult life in serene senility. In comic statement there is no room for judicious accuracy; it must be forceful and slick and capture the audience's interest. Antiphanes (fr. 191K) says that everyone was familiar with the stories of tragedy, Aristotle (*Poet*., 1451b) that few were. Even making allowance (which way, incidentally?) for their difference in date, they cannot both be right, and no one who reads the Antiphanes fragment with attention can hesitate long on which to believe. Thus the sociologist who takes comic convention and comic statement at face value will go very wide of the mark; but he can make very good use of comedy if he is prepared to ask what makes a joke a joke, and what presuppositions must be shared by author and public if comedy is to be intelligible.[30]

Much of what has been said above applies also to the political historian's use of comedy. The history of the discussion of such passages as *Eq*. 173–4 ('Cast your right eye on Caria and your left on Carthage') or the embassies to and from Persia in *Ach*. 61–124[31] emphasizes the complexity of the issues involved and the difficulty of deciding between the claims of pure fantasy, faithful parody of actual events, and exploitation of ideas that were in the political air. The whole methodological problem was attacked in 1873 by Müller-Strübing's *Aristophanes und die historische Kritik* with a determination and acumen only slightly vitiated by an undertone of mad laughter and a

---

[27] Ibid. 76–8.

[28] Schlesinger 313–14; Roggwiller 7.

[29] V. Ehrenberg, *The People of Aristophanes* (Oxford 1943, 2nd edn 1951).

[30] I have argued this at greater length in a review of Ehrenberg's book in *Cambridge Journal* v (1952) (= pp. 279–82 below).

[31] H. Weber, *Aristophanische Studien* (Leipzig 1908) 30–43; Ed. Meyer, *Geschichte des Altertums* (Stuttgart–Berlin 1901) iv 366–7; A. Ruppel, *Konzeption und Ausarbeitung der Aristophanischen Komödie* (Darmstadt 1913) 6.

number of unlikely solutions of particular difficulties; it is perhaps due for an equally thorough re-examination.

It is always hard to interpret a political allusion until one knows what axes the writer is grinding, and at first sight Old Comedy appears to have ground one large axe busily and continuously. Aristophanes is still popularly regarded as a conservative who used comedy as a medium for glorifying the Athens of Aeschylus and attacking all that was new in politics, literature and philosophy. Now, no reasonable man will deny the presence of a serious element in comedy, quite apart from the personal feud between Aristophanes and Cleon. The fact that the privilege of Comic ridicule was suspended by law from 440/39 and 437/6 shows that it was not always regarded as a light-hearted family game; nor can we read Aristophanes without becoming aware of passages which strike home in a way that fun does not. Such subjective feelings are a poor basis for argument, but they are facts and we must take cognizance of them.

The common view of Aristophanes as a preacher has to contend with the coincidence that to judge from the fragments the other poets of Old Comedy all belonged to the same crusted minority. Croiset[32] attempted to meet this difficulty by suggesting that comedy was traditionally the favoured art-form of the conservative, suspicious Attic farmers, and that its character and development were determined by the sympathies of this appreciative audience.

But the presentation of Aristophanes, to say nothing of other poets, as spokesman or instrument of a party or class is easier to sustain on a first reading than on a second. Any consistent picture of his views which we can be constructed from snippets of chorus or dialogue, chosen without regard for speaker or context, can be confronted by different pictures constructed on the same principle. Aristophanes was a dramatist of genius; he had a keen eye for the absurdities inherent in all conflicts of temperaments and ideas, and he was concerned, *qua* dramatist, to exploit them.[33] Thus in *Clouds* his purpose was not to persuade his audience of the immorality of Socrates but to bring together Strepsiades, Pheidippides and Socrates, each in his own way an ass, and work out, with dramatist's logic, what happens.

Moreover, comedy by its very nature makes certain demands on its practitioners. In Aristophanes, as in popular comedy of all ages, people are presented as they appear to the Common Man, who is tough but comfort-loving, shrewd but uneducated, caustic but unpolished, irreverent and intolerant of the unfamiliar. With the Common Man as foil, 'Euripides' and 'Socrates' are composite characters exhibiting the features popularly attri-buted to the intellectual, and their individuality is to some extent suppressed in order to secure their conformity to accepted comic types.[34]

[32] M. Croiset, *Aristophane et les Partis à Athènes* (Paris 1906), English tr. by J. Loeb (London 1909).

[33] A. W. Gomme, 'Aristophanes and Politics', *CR* lii (1933).

[34] W. Süss, *De Personarum Antiquae Comoediae Atticae Usu atque Origine* (Bonn 1905) 10–22; A. Weiher, *Philosophen und Philosophenspott in der attischen Komödie* (Munich 1913) 16.

It may also be true that the good comic writer is almost inevitably committed to rebellion – or reaction; it does not matter which we call it – against the established order and the fashions and movements of his day.[35] The same facet of his mind that makes him fertile in comic invention makes him sceptical and independent. Wit and cant do not live comfortably together, and for all its fierce virtues Athenian public life was not lacking in cant.

B. DISCOVERY

1   *The Text of Aristophanes*

The pursuit of manuscripts in the libraries of Europe, or the re-examination of manuscripts last collated by Bekker or Dindorf, is no less an act of discovery than the extraction of a papyrus fragment from the sands of Egypt, and I make no further apology for dealing at this point with the establishment of the text of Aristophanes.

Comparatively speaking, we are now well informed on the manuscripts of Aristophanes,[36] but little of the essential data was available before the end of the nineteenth century. Important collations were then made by von Velsen, Zacher and Zuretti, and later by White, Cary[37] and Coulon. The Oxford Text of Hall and Geldart[38] was defective even for its time; for the sake of brevity it suppressed much of value in the apparatus, though room was found for many mediocre conjectures. Coulon's Budé edition[39] is the first which gives an accurate and discriminating apparatus. Much remains to be done,[40] especially on what were in Byzantine eyes the major plays, *Plutus*, *Clouds* and *Frogs*, and until it is done final judgement on the stemmata so far proposed[41] should be reserved. The upper reaches of the stemma are unlikely to be seriously refashioned, but for the lower reaches we have to take our editors' work on trust; it is a pity that Coulon did not publish a systematic *eliminatio*.

The contribution of the papyri has been interesting but not exciting.[42] A Berlin papyrus[43] gives us some help with the dialect of the Megarian in *Acharnians*, and warns us of the complexity of the tradition by agreeing in

---

[35] Cf. 'Beachcomber' and 'Timothy Shy'.

[36] Listed by J. W. White, 'The Manuscripts of Aristophanes', *CPh* i (1906).

[37] E. Cary, 'The Manuscript Tradition of the *Acharnians*', *HSt* xviii (1907); J. W. White and E. Cary, 'Collations of the Manuscripts of Aristophanes' *Aves*', *HSt* xxix (1918), and 'Collations of the Manuscripts of Aristophanes' *Vespae*', *HSPh*. xxx (1919); cf. O. Bachmann's preface (vi–xxx) in K. Zacher's edition of *Peace* (Leipzig 1909).

[38] F. W. Hall and W. M. Geldart (eds), *Aristophanis Comoediae* (Oxford 1900, 2nd edn 1906).

[39] V. Coulon (ed.), *Aristophane* (Paris 1923–30), 5 vols, with French translation by H. van Daele.

[40] See now D. Mervyn Jones, 'The Manuscripts of Aristophanes' *Knights* (I)', *CQ* NS ii (1952).

[41] Van Leeuwen, *Prolegomena in Aristophanem* (Leyden 1908) 270–9; Coulon i xii–xviii; G. Pasquali, *Storia della Tradizione e Critica del Testo*, 2nd edn (Florence 1952) 194–201; cf. Mervyn Jones 172 n. 1, 175–6.

[42] Pasquali 196–8 somewhat exaggerates their importance.

[43] *BKT* v.2 (1907) 100–5.

error with the Codex Ravennas at *Ach*. 791. It is satisfactory, but not surprising, that a papyrus of *Thesmophoriazusae*[44] refers to the old man in the play as κηδ᾽, i.e. κηδεστὴς Εὐριπίδου, not as 'Mnesilochus',[45] and preserves a stage-direction ολολυ[at 277;[46] the same papyrus tantalizingly gives us only the first few letters of the difficult line 809, which van Leeuwen pusillanimously deleted.

The editor of Aristophanes can profit more than the editor of any other Greek author from the citations of the text in other authors, and from the scholia. Coulon's edition is the first which presents the material from these sources satisfactorily in the apparatus. The citations have now been catalogued,[47] and apart from the right readings which they sometimes afford they throw some light on the interrelation of the extant manuscripts; this is particularly true of the numerous citations from Aristophanes in Suidas.[48]

A definitive edition of the scholia is in preparation, the only complete edition to date being Dübner's of 1842, which is not adequate. The scholia on *Birds* have been edited separately by White.[49] Rutherford's *Scholia Aristophanica*[50] unfortunately comprised only the scholia of the Codex Ravennas. The Ravennas is a handsome and venerable manuscript, but its scholia are for the most part an abbreviated and garbled version of what appears in a fuller and more intelligible form in the Codex Venetus. To publish them by themselves, with only passing references to the Venetus, was absurd; and, though the absurdity was quickly and decisively exposed,[51] it imposes on undergraduates to this day.

Before proper use can be made of scholia something must be known of their origin, and here the papyri have provided many helpful clues. The bare format of early dramatic texts brings home to us the magnitude of the ancient commentators' responsibilities; fragments of learned commentaries and of texts with a greater or smaller degree of marginal annotation reveal not only the nature of the commentaries themselves but also the possible relationships between separate commentary and marginal note. The outlines of the history of the ancient study of Aristophanes are now tolerably clear.[52] White believed

[44] *PSI* 1194.

[45] Cf. van Leeuwen on the *dramatis personae* of *Thesmophoriazusae*.

[46] Cf. the Ravenna Scholiast: ὀλολύζουσι· τὸ ἱερὸν ὠθεῖται.

[47] W. Kraus, 'Testimonia Aristophanea', *Wien. Akad. Denkschr.* lxx. 2 (1931).

[48] Coulon, *Quaestiones Criticae in Aristophanis Fabulas* (Strasburg 1907).

[49] *The Scholia on the 'Aves' of Aristophanes* (Boston 1914).

[50] 3 vols (London 1896).

[51] A. Römer, *Studien zu Aristophanes und den alten Erklärern Desselben* (Leipzig 1902); note especially (2) the amusing example *V*. 1326.

[52] Wilamowitz, *Einleitung in die griechische Tragödie* (= *Euripides Herakles* vol. i, chs 1–4) (Berlin 1907) 179–84; P. Boudreaux, 'Le Texte d'Aristophane et ses Commentateurs', *Bibl. Ec. Fr. Ath.* cxiv (1919); J. Steinhausen, Κωμῳδούμενοι (Bonn 1910); White, *The Verse of Greek Comedy* 384–421; A. Gudeman, 'Scholien (Aristophanes)', *RE* ii. 2 cols 672–80. The mention in a recently published letter of the second century AD of 'books vi and vii of Hypsicrates' Κωμῳδούμενοι' is an interesting glimpse beyond the great ancient scholars whose names we already knew (*P.Oxy.* 2192).

that a late commentary on Aristophanes was transferred wholesale to the margins of an Aristophanes codex in the fourth or fifth century AD, and that this codex was sole ancestor of the minuscule archetype of our extant manuscripts.[53] What we know of codices, Christian and secular, from the fourth to the ninth century AD, does not support this hypothesis,[54] and the fact that the extant scholia on a given passage often repeat the same explanation several times, introducing each repetition by ἄλλως, suggests that the archetype in fact accumulated its scholia from the relatively sparser marginalia of not one but many earlier manuscripts.[55] Thus, although the Aristophanes scholia are ultimately the product of the ancient study of Aristophanes, the genealogy of any given scholion may be very different from that of its immediate neighbour.

2   The Text of Menander[56]

Until the end of the nineteenth century the Greek text of Menander was known only by the very numerous citations in later authors and anthologies; and these, being mainly gnomic in character, gave little idea of the sight and sound and movement of a Menandrean play. In 1897 a papyrus fragment containing eighty lines of *Georgus* was discovered; a few years earlier a parchment fragment at St Petersburg had been identified as belonging to *Phasma*. A fragment of *Colax* was published in 1903 (a second was to come in 1914), and then in 1905 came the discovery of the mutilated Cairo codex, comprising very substantial parts of *Epitrepontes*, *Perikeiromene* and *Samia*, with some smaller items, including the hypothesis and opening scene of *Heros*.

Of these plays *Epitrepontes* has attracted the most attention – for which its quality as well as its comparatively extensive preservation is responsible – and a summary of its history since 1905 may serve as a specimen of the work devoted in this century to the constitution of the text of Menander.[57]

The Cairo codex was originally made up of quaterniones, and each quaternio consisted of four sheets folded and placed one inside another to make sixteen pages. When the codex was found, the quaterniones had been separated from each other, and many lost; those that had not been lost were largely disrupted, and what remained was pieces of half-sheets. It was found that the best preserved half-sheets could be placed in an approximate order

[53] *The Scholia on the 'Aves'* lxvii–lxxii.
[54] G. Zuntz, 'Die Aristophanes-Scholien der Papyri', *Byzantion* xiii (1938) and xiv (1939).
[55] Zuntz 601–4; cf. Boudreaux 171–88.
[56] The most recent critical text is A. Körte's third Teubner edition (1938: K³); C. Jensen's (Berlin 1929: J), is extremely useful and more easily obtainable in Britain than Körte's. F. G. Allinson's Loeb edition (Cambridge, Mass., 1921: A) is the only text really accessible in Britain, but it is out of date in some important respects. K³ and J include only the plays known from papyrus and parchment fragments; the citations have now (1954) appeared in the Teubner series.
[57] Pp. 9–13 A, ix–xi, xix–xxi J, viii–x K³.

either by their physical configuration or on the grounds of their content. From this it emerged that within each quaternio the four sheets had originally been so placed that a side with vertical fibres uppermost alternated with a side with horizontal uppermost; thus when the quarternio was completely made up pages 1 and 16 would have had horizontal fibres, pages 2 and 15 vertical fibres, 3 and 14 vertical, 4 and 13 horizontal, 5 and 12 horizontal, and so on. This naturally reduced the number of alternative positions possible for the fragments which were not easy to place by content. Körte's second Teubner edition of 1912 was able to print ten of the original pages (i.e. the greater part of three folded sheets) in their correct order in the first half of the play, and four (i.e. one folded sheet) in the second; mutilated pieces of another four half-sheets were given an approximate location, and the position and extent of the completely missing portions were accurately estimated.

The Cairo half-sheet known as Z, which had been excluded from *Epitrepontes* by Körte and placed by others in the early part of the play, was then given its correct place by the observation that it bore the marginal number ς'. This was not a page-number, for the half-sheet of *Heros* bore the page-numbers $\kappa\theta'$ and λ' while Z's number was on one side only. But considered as the first sheet of the sixth quaternio, or by its content – Pamphile is being urged by her father to divorce her husband – it fits well into the gap between Smicrines' realization of his son-in-law's bad behaviour and Habrotonon's recognition of Pamphile.

An Oxyrhynchus papyrus (*P. Oxy.* 1236) published in 1914 gave us a mutilated portion of the text of *Epitrepontes* which overlaps the text of one of the best-preserved Cairo half-sheets and one of the minor Cairo fragments. This at once introduced order into a part of the play which in Körte's 1912 edition had been extremely uncertain.

The parchment fragment in Russia which contained a piece of *Phasma* exhibited also forty-odd lines of a play which van Leeuwen and Capps recognized as *Epitrepontes*. Körte in 1912 did not admit these lines, and those who referred them to *Epitrepontes* were not agreed on the position in the play which they should occupy. It is now accepted that they give us the end of the original first act and the beginning of the second, and thus precede the parts extant in the Cairo codex.

Mention must also be made of a papyrus first published by Weil in 1879 and for long attributed (as it was by its ancient copyist) to Euripides. It is not itself a fragment of a dramatic text, but a speech transcribed from a play; a daughter is addressing her father who has evidently urged her to divorce her husband. The ascription to Euripides was palpably wrong, and Professor Robertson[58] suggested that the speech is not merely the work of Menander but is actually Pamphile's reply to her father in *Epitrepontes*. The argument is persuasive, and if two lines had been irrecoverably mutilated it might well

[58] D. S. Robertson, 'An Unrecognized Fragment from Menander's *Epitrepontes*?', *CR* xxxvi (1922); *NCh* 168; fr. 34P; p. 132 J, 143 K³.

have won general acceptance; those lines, however (19–20) ἀλλ᾽ ἔστ᾽ ἐμοὶ μὲν χρηστός, ἠπόρηκε δέ· σὺ δ᾽ ἀνδρί μ᾽, ὡς φής, ἐκδίδως νῦν πλουσίῳ are not quite the point which Pamphile would have made in her actual situation. Körte, while accepting Menander's authorship on linguistic grounds,[59] has excluded the speech from *Epitrepontes* in his third edition. Interest in the particular problem of whether we are concerned here with Pamphile's reply to Smicrines seems to have allayed the more general suspicion which should have been aroused by the fact that so long and serious a speech in a style so near tragedy is without parallel in New Comedy.[60]

Apart from the plays already mentioned, fragments of *Citharista*,[61] *Coneiazomenae*,[62] *Perinthia*,[63] *Misumenus*,[64] and *Theophorumene*[65] have been identified by content on grounds of varying cogency; in the *Theophorumene* fragment the coarsely abusive ἱππόπορνε strikes a discordant note for Menander. The Cairo codex also gives us some sixty lines of a play not yet identified, and the so-called *Comoedia Florentia*,[66] stylistically the essence of Menander, does not very readily suggest any of the known titles.

3 Didascaliae and Similar Records

Fragments of inscriptions which recorded victories at dramatic festivals or names of poets and actors were known well before the end of the last century, but it was not until 1906 that Wilhelm was able to determine the precise nature of the original inscriptions and assign the fragments their relative positions.[67] Wilhelm's conclusions have since been corrected or augmented in minor details,[68] and a few additional fragments have been recovered.[69] We are concerned with four types of document, three from Athens and one from Rome. The Athenian documents are:

(i) The so-called 'Fasti', in which were recorded the names of the victorious διδάσκαλος and χορηγός in tragedy and comedy at the Dionysia each year.[70]

---

[59] 'Euripides oder Menander?', *Hermes* lxi (1926).

[60] Page *ad loc.*

[61] P. 370 A, 96 J, 104 K³.

[62] P. 398 A, 110 J, 120 K³.

[63] P. 420 A, 120 J, 130 K³.

[64] P. 408 A plus fr. 52P; P. 112 J, 122 K³; *NCh* 169; add now W. Schubart, *BSAW* xcvii.5 (1950) no. 22; *SLGC* 184.

[65] P. 101 K³; fr. 55P.

[66] *PSI* 126; P. 128 J, 138 K; fr. 54P; Schubart, *loc. cit.*; E. Ulbricht, *Kritische und exegetische Studien zu Menander* (Leipzig 1933) 4–26.

[67] A. Wilhelm, 'Urkunden dramatischer Aufführungen in Athen', *Sond. öst. arch. Inst.* vi (1906); reviews by E. Capps, *AJPh* xxviii (1907), and Wilamowitz, *GGA* 1906.

[68] A. Dittmer, *The Fragments of Athenian Comic Didascaliae [sic] Found in Rome* (Leyden 1923); *IG* ii² (1931) 2318–25; the material is now published and discussed in *DFA* 103–26.

[69] *Hesperia* vii (1938) 116–18, and xii (1943) 1–11.

[70] The victorious tribes in the men's and boy's choruses were also recorded, and after *c.* 450 the victorious tragic protagonist; the comic διδάσκαλος was normally, but not necessarily, the poet.

(ii) The Didascaliae, which recorded under each archon-year all the plays performed at the festival concerned, in the order of the prizes obtained, together with the names of the poets and the protagonists.
(iii) The victor-lists; these included a list of all the comic poets who had ever won the first prize at the Dionysia, arranged in order of first victories, and a similar list for the Lenaea. In both lists the total number of his victories at the festival concerned was entered against each poet's name.

The fragments from Rome appear to come from a document which listed all the comic poets with the titles of their plays, each poet's plays being dated and arranged in order according to the prizes obtained.

The extant fragments of the Fasti give us the names and dates of seven victorious comic διδάσκαλοι from Magnes in 473/2 to Alexis in 348/7; they also record the fact that an old play was revived in 340/39 and that this was the first occasion of such an occurrence. The Didascaliae give us no certain information on comedy before 313/12; 289/8 is well preserved; after which, excepting a few undatable fragments, we pass to the early second century. Although in that century comedy was presented at the Dionysia in only one year in three, and on each occasion an old play was revived, we can also see that five new plays were performed on each occasion; the record appears to have ended in the last quarter of the century. The victor-lists of comic poets are well preserved for both Dionysia and Lenaea in the fifth century, and for the Lenaea in the fourth. Thanks to the literary evidence and the few but valuable pieces of the Fasti, some fixed points in the chronology of the victor-lists can be established, and it can be stated with certainty that comic poets first competed for prizes at the Dionysia between 490 and 480 (probably 486) and at the Lenaea about 440. The problem of the two Apollodori is also settled by the occurrence of the name Apollodorus with a first Lenaean victory c. 320 and a first Dionysian victory at least forty years later.

The extant portions of the inscription from Rome provide valuable information on the chronology of the plays of Callias in the fifth century and Anaxandrides in the fourth, and somewhat scrappier information on Teleclides, Lysippus and Aristomenes.

C. HISTORY OF COMEDY

1 Genre and Individual

The epigraphic records combined with the literary evidence have made it possible to construct an outline chronology of Greek comedy,[71] and unless

[71] P. Geissler, *Chronologie der altattischen Komödie* (Berlin 1925); H. Oellacher, 'Zur Chronologie der altattischen Komödie', *WSt* xxxviii (1916); Webster, 'Chronological Notes on Middle Comedy', *CQ* NS ii (1952); R. J. T. Wagner, *Symbolarum ad Comicorum Graecorum Historiam Criticam Capita Quattuor* (Leipzig 1905).

new material is discovered it is unlikely that any substantial additions will be made to what is now generally accepted. But to arrange titles in chronological order is not the same thing as interpreting the extant fragments and discovering what the plays themselves were about. Wherever we have a title and handful of fragments, in almost every case we have inherited from Meineke, Bergk and Kock a more or less tentative and partial reconstruction of the play. These reconstructions are sometimes brilliant and persuasive, but it is to be regretted that many of them have now crystallized into dogma; unthinkingly we tend to accept even the numerical order of the fragments of a play in Kock as giving their original relative position. All the comic fragments need now to be re-examined from top to bottom and the traditional reconstructions treated – for their own good – with the utmost scepticism. In particular, the manifold contextual possibilities of each fragment should be taken into account, and we should resist the temptation to draw too facile a conclusion, chronological or otherwise, from the allusion in a fragment to a known person or historical event.[72]

One of many reasons for undertaking such an examination is the desirability of knowing where to draw the boundaries between Aristophanes and Aristophanic comedy and between Menander and Menandrean comedy. Until recently the bulk of our evidence for New Comedy was the Roman adaptations, and, although it was known who had written the originals of many of the adaptations, it was hard to draw essential distinctions between these original authors and impossible to avoid speaking of New Comedy in generic terms. It would be quite untrue to say that the papyri represented a merely quantitative accession of material.[73] They allow us at least to form a positive conception of Menander[74] independently of the Roman adaptations, and it is interesting that the best-preserved of the Cairo plays happens also to show us a character, Habrotonon in *Epitrepontes*, entirely remote from the 'stock-types' commonly regarded as characteristic of New Comedy.[75]

Nevertheless, to characterize Menander in contrast with the Romans is not equivalent to characterizing him in contrast with his contemporaries. The attribution of individual characteristics to Philemon, Diphilus, or Apollodorus of Carystus still rests primarily on interpretation of the Roman plays,[76] and sometimes requires an assumption of uniformity of structure and treatment within the work of a given author which may be a right assumption

---

[72] I have attempted a specimen re-examination in 'Plato Comicus: *Presbeis* and *Hellas*' (ch. 23 below).

[73] The thorough characterization of New Comedy by Ph.-E. Legrand, *Daos* (Lyon–Paris 1910) 64–324, serves to show the relation between the highest common factor of the Roman plays and the highest common factor of Roman plays plus Greek.

[74] A. W. Gomme, *Essays in Greek History and Literature* (Oxford 1937) 249–95; Webster, *Studies in Menander* (Manchester 1950).

[75] H. Hauschild, *Der Gestalt der Hetäre in der griechischen Komödie* (Leipzig 1933) 40–9 (cf. 31–40 on Thais in *Eunuchus*).

[76] *SLGC* 4, 125–83, 205–32.

but cannot as yet be conclusively justified.[77] The papyri stimulated interest in the separation of Greek from Roman elements in the Roman plays, but this work has been most fruitful when its purpose has been to construct a positive picture of the Roman element;[78] attempts to give an equally positive picture of the Greek element[79] tend to be vitiated by an oppressively subjective assumption that the Greeks were dramaturgically impeccable.

The generic nature of the study of New Comedy is well shown by a simple pragmatic test: we now possess about thirty papyrus fragments, some of them of considerable extent, which can clearly be assigned to New Comedy, but we cannot assign them to particular authors. Moreover, in a genre which flourished for so long we cannot clearly distinguish even the main stages of development. For example, an anonymous prologue[80] shows us a light kind of literary criticism familiar in Roman prologues, but we do not know whether it belongs to the time of Menander or to a century and a half later. It would be pleasant to think that another prologue[81] which expounds the situation in lines beginning successively with α, β, γ, etc., belonged to a very late and degenerate stage of the genre, but the papyrus itself, written at the end of the third century BC, imposes a terminus.

Turning now to Old Comedy, I suppose that if we had ever been able to choose what papyri should be discovered we might have recalled Horace's triad (*Sat.* 8.4.1) 'Eupolis atque Cratinus Aristophanesque poetae'. Fortune has been kind; we now have a substantial fragment of Cratinus's *Pluti*,[82] half the hypothesis of his *Dionysalexander*,[83] several good portions of Eupolis's *Demi*,[84] and a fragment[85] which has been assigned solely on the strength of the words (lines 5–6) καὶ φράζεθ' οἶα τἀνθάδ' ἐστ [∪ − ∪−] Προσπαλτίοισιν to Eupolis's *Prospaltii*. In all significant respects this new material confirms the conclusion already drawn from the citations: that Old Comedy combined a relative uniformity of structure with great variety of theme.

The earlier plays of Aristophanes exhibit a strong community of structure which in one element, the parabasis, can be pursued into detail. Although no two plays present the same constituents in exactly the same order, it is possible to construct an ideal schema from which each play deviates in one

---

[77] P. W. Harsh, review of Webster's *Studies in Menander*, *Gn* xxv (1953).

[78] Leo, *Plautinische Forschungen*, 2nd edn (Berlin 1912) ch. 3; Fraenkel, *Plautinisches im Platus* (Berlin 1922); cf. H. W. Prescott, 'Criteria of Originality in Plautus', *TAPhA* lxiii (1932).

[79] G. Jachmann, *Plautinisches und attisches* (Berlin 1931), W. E. J. Kuiper, *Grieksche Origineelen en Latijnsche Navolgingen* (Amsterdam 1936); cf. Gomme 251 n. 2; G. E. Duckworth, *The Nature of Roman Comedy* (Princeton, NJ, 1952).

[80] *Adesp.* fr. 14D; fr. 7S; fr. 60P; *NCh* 178.

[81] *Adesp.* fr. 22.2D; p. 63S; fr. 72(2)P; *NCh* 172–3.

[82] *PSI* 1212; fr. 38P; W. Schmid, *Geschichte der griechischen Literatur* i.4 (Munich 1946) 81–2.

[83] Pp. 31–2D; *NCh* 159–61; Schmid 86–8.

[84] Eupolis frr. 7–12D plus *Adesp.* fr. 40D plus *P.Oxy.* 1240; fr. 40DP; *NCh* 161–3; Schmid 124–32.

[85] *PSI* 1213; fr. 41P; Schmid 114–15 speaks as if not only were the identification certain but the interpretation of the fragment simple and obvious – which is not the case.

respect or another;[86] the later plays deviate increasingly, and *Frogs*, *Ecclesiazusae* and *Plutus* cannot be accommodated under the same schema without impairing its usefulness. Among the new fragments, Aristides' treatment of the Sycophant in *Demi* 61–100 not only recalls the episode *Ach*. 909–28 but by its apparent position in the development of the 'plot' conforms to the structure of *Acharnians*, *Peace* and *Birds*, in which the crisis of the action is followed by a series of episodes illustrating the state of affairs brought about by the crisis. The hypothesis of *Dionysalexander* tells us that in the parabasis the chorus addressed the audience περὶ τῶν ποιητῶν, which recalls *Knights*, *Clouds*, *Wasps* and *Peace*. Only *Pluti* strikes an unfamiliar note by the chorus' address to the audience in the *parodos*. In general the shorter citations often permit us, by coincidence of metre, form, and subject, to assign them to one place rather than another in their original plays.[87]

In theme, however, the position is quite different. We know that mythological burlesque and political allegory, combined in *Dionysalexander*, were common in Old Comedy, but they are absent from the extant work of Aristophanes; the pre-Aristophanic Ὀδυσσῆς of Cratinus possessed some features which induced Hellenistic scholars to associate it with 'Middle Comedy',[88] and Aristophanes' late plays *Aeolosicon* and *Cocalus* appear to have resembled their contemporary *Plutus* no more closely than the plays of the Archidamian War.[89] In full recognition of this variety and inventiveness we should be at least as cautious of generalization about Old Comedy as about, let us say, Aeschylean tragedy.

2   *The Origins of Comedy*

If we possessed a dozen complete plays by different poets of Old Comedy from the period 460–430 BC it might be possible to discover by extrapolation how the genre began. As it is, we cannot extrapolate from Aristophanes. Although comedy changed in his hands, the change was not necessarily in the same direction as the developments before his time; it is therefore unsafe to argue from his early plays that the sequence prologue–agon–parabasis was his inheritance from the early days of comedy.[90] The chorus' address to the audience in the *parodos* of Cratinus's *Pluti* does not imply that the role of the chorus was larger before Aristophanes, but only that the relation between chorus and audience which exists in the Aristophanic parabasis may originally have existed in other parts of the play. The known variety of themes in Old Comedy also discourages extrapolation.

---

[86] Th. Zielinski, *Die Gliederung der altattischen Komödie* (Leipzig 1885); P. Mazon, *Essai sur la composition des comédies d'Aristophane* (Paris 1904); *DTC* 292–328.

[87] M. Whittaker, 'The Comic Fragments and their Relation to the Structure of Old Attic Comedy', *CQ* xxix (1935).

[88] Platonius, Περὶ Διαφορᾶς Κωμῳδιῶν 7; Schmid 80.

[89] Schmid 221.

[90] *DTC* 240–4, 292–311 argues by extrapolation.

Mention should here be made of Cornford's argument[91] that comedy originated as a ritual representing the triumph of the new year over the old and that sequences in this ritual were ultimately responsible for features inherited and preserved by Aristophanes. Cornford's book owed a great deal to the influence of Jane Harrison[92] and to the essentially wise realization of the late nineteenth century that anthropological evidence has a bearing on Greek studies. But the value of anthropology lies in its capacity to suggest possibilities, and Cornford's bland dishonesties and sheer unreasonableness in the use of evidence were not a very good advertisement for it. Throughout the book we are unhappily aware of the great gulf between him and Aristophanes;[93] if only he had sat down to write a comedy before writing about the Origin of Comedy!

The starting point for the study of comic origins is the fact that Aristophanic comedy shows us a regular combination of extremely dissimilar elements, which entitles us to assume that the origin of the genre is complex. The search may be conducted separately through literary evidence and through iconography. Aristotle (*Poet*. 1449a) saw the origin of comedy in οἱ ἐξάρχοντες τὰ φαλλικά, and says (1448a, cf. 1449b) that the Dorians claimed its invention, a claim partly supported by the early date of Epicharmus. Our evidence on the performances of ἰθύφαλλοι and φαλλοφόροι reveals no dramatic element, though there were φαλλοφόροι who 'made fun of the bystanders',[94] and this, combined with the association of Dionysus with phallic ritual,[95] may point at least to a possible origin of the parabasis. In the dramatic element in comedy the two recurrent features which engage our attention are the agon, involving two actors or one actor and the chorus, and the episodes. The attempt to discover a specific origin for the agon[96] is probably mistaken, for contest is hard to separate from drama, and the Greek love of contest is manifest throughout their literature.[97] For the episodes it is natural to look to Epicharmus and the Dorians. Epicharmus,[98] whose fragments show no sign of literary immaturity or undeveloped technique,[99] wrote at least one piece which required three characters,[100] but there is no good evidence that he wrote also for a chorus.[101] He was the first man known

[91] F. M. Cornford, *The Origin of Attic Comedy* (London 1914); cf. *DTC* 329–49.

[92] Murray, 'Francis Macdonald Cornford, 1874–1943', *Proc. Brit. Acad.* xxix 1–6.

[93] E.g. pp. 17, 34, which are vital to his argument.

[94] Semus of Delos *ap*. Athen. 622d; *DTC* 233–7.

[95] Nilsson, *Geschichte der griechischen Religion* vol. i (Munich 1941) 557–61.

[96] H. E. Sieckmann, *De Comoediae Atticae Primordiis* (Göttingen 1906), referred it to Epicharmus.

[97] Radermacher, *Frösche* 21–34; Wil., *Ar.* 14.

[98] For the text of Epicharmus see Kaibel, *Comicorum Graecorum Fragmenta* vol. 1 (Berlin 1899), and A. Olivieri, *Frammenti della Commedia Greca e del Mimo nella Sicilia e nella Magna Grecia* vol. i (Naples n.d.) (expansive where Kaibel is austere, but adds little of real importance); on the poet in general, Kaibel, 'Epicharmos', *RE* vi cols 34–41; *DTC* 353–415; E. Wüst, 'Epicharmos und die alte attische Komödie', *RhM* xciii (1950).

[99] Kaibel cols 37–9.

[100] Fr. 6 (Kai) = 3 (Ol.); *DTC* 389–90.

[101] *DTC* 405–6; Wüst 342.

in later times to have put comedies into written form, but it is doubtful whether he created the genre from nothing,[102] and the existence of rudimentary comic drama in Dorian communities is indicated by the evidence relating to Sparta[103] and Megara.[104]

So far, so good. The literary evidence points to a combination of an indigenous chorus (presumably called a κῶμος and associated with Dionysus, probably also associated with him as part of a phallic ritual) with an episodic drama introduced from the Dorian world. We should beware of extending this dependence on Dorian comedy from form to matter. Indigenous fairy-tales certainly made their contribution, and comic narrative had an Ionian ancestry; the citations from Archilochus and the new papyri of Hipponax[105] reveal a colourful ferocity of language and a startling obscenity which are strongly reminiscent of Old Comedy.

The archaeological enquiry into origins begins from the costumes of actors and chorus.[106] The extant plays, together with many titles of lost plays, imply that the chorus most frequently represented animals, women, foreigners or abstractions. Choruses of men disguised as animals, dancing in unison to a flute-player, appear on Attic black-figure vases much earlier than comedy as we know it;[107] the vases tell us nothing of the god or festival with whom such choruses were associated, and in particular there is no known point of contact between them and phallic ritual.

No representation of the comic actor exists which can be referred with certainty to the fifth century, but two red-figure vases of the very early fourth century[108] show that he wore (a) a grotesque mask, (b) tights, with a padded stomach and buttocks, (c) a large artificial phallus. The internal evidence of Aristophanes points also to the phallus as a common, if not universal, feature of the actor's costume.[109] These elements appear singly or in combination on Corinthian vases of the early sixth century. Most important are two figures which appear in a representation of the return of Hephaestus with Dionysus;[110] they have grotesque faces, with wild hair and beards, prodigious

---

[102] Kaibel col. 39.

[103] *DTC* 228–30.

[104] *DTC* 274–84.   [105] Archil. fr. 28, Hippon. fr. 14A. 1–9; cf. Schmid 70 nn. 14, 16.

[106] Körte, 'Archäologische Studien zur alten Komödie', *JDAI* (1893); A. Greifenhagen, *Eine attische schwarzfigurische Vasengattung und die Darstellung des Komos im VI Jahrhundert* (Königsberg 1929); Humfry Payne, *Necrocorinthia* (Oxford 1931) 118–24; E. Buschor, 'Satyrtänze und frühes Drama', *SBAW* 1943.5.

[107] J. Poppelreuter, *De Comoediae Atticae Primordiis* (Berlin 1893); M. Bieber, *History of the Greek and Roman Theater* (Princeton, N.J. 1939) figs 76, 77, 79; *DTC* 245–6, figs 16–18. The vase which shows men riding on real dolphins and ostriches (Bieber fig. 78) is of very doubtful relevance for drama; E. Bielefeld, 'Delphinreiter Chor', *AA* 1946/7, answers the ill-conceived suggestions of F. Brommer, 'Delphinreiter', *AA* 1942.

[108] Bieber fig. 121; (*DTC* fig 32 is expurgated) and S. P. Karouzou, *AJA* 1 (1946) 132–8 and fig. 10.

[109] *DFA* 234 n. 2; more cautiously, *DTC* 237 n. 1, Körte 65–9, Wüst *PhW* 1942, col. 460. See now W. Beare, *CQ* NS iv (1954) 64ff.

[110] Bieber fig. 83; Payne 121–2 and fig. 44G; Buschor 20–1 and fig. 10; Greifenhagen 60.

phalli, and short chitons which throw stomach and buttocks into prominence. In isolation this vase would justify the suggestion that the actor's costume in Old Comedy originated in the portrayal of a kind of satyr, but there is other evidence which complicates the issue. On another Corinthian vase[111] we find (a) a flute-player with a dancer who wears a mask and a short padded chiton, (b) two creatures called Εὔνους and Ὀφέλανδρος, naked and of normal shape except for Ophelandrus's unduly large phallus, carrying a wine-jar, (c) a naked figure called Ὀμρικός, with a very large phallus, (d) two naked men in the stocks, with a woman standing by, and a wine-store. The names point to Dionysiac demons,[112] and the natural interpretation of the vase is that it portrays a story about them. As often in vase-painting, the kind of association intended between demons and dancer is open to very different interpretations, but at the least we can say that masked padded dancers existed in sixth-century Corinth and were considered by a painter an appropriate subject for association with a story about Dionysiac demons, and at the most it can be argued that the scene on the vase portrays a comic performance[113] – which does not explain comedy but only raises its date and associates it with Corinth. Unmasked padded dancers, without the phallus, are common on Corinthian vases and appear on Attic vases, under Corinthian influence, in the mid-sixth century;[114] they are occasionally associated with Dionysus,[115] and once with a figure who wears the phallus as well as padding.[116] The discovery of early sixth-century comic masks at Sparta,[117] which accord well with the literary evidence for rudimentary drama there, has no archaeological point of contact with the Corinthian iconographic tradition.

The abundant evidence adduced in the last fifty years has not solved the problem but at least it has clarified the questions which need answering. It seems probable that the actor's costume was in origin a portrayal of a kind of satyr, and that this portrayal was practised in the Peloponnese in the sixth century; it seems certain that comic episodes, in which the actors used masks, were also practised then in the Peloponnese; but when and why were the two combined, so that a man dressed in imitation of a satyr when he was portraying the doings of beings other than satyrs? Secondly, when and why were characteristics of the animal-chorus and the φαλλοφόροι combined in one chorus – or has Aristotle's ἐξάρχοντες τὰ φαλλικά put us on a wrong scent?[118] Thirdly, when and why were the two elements, actors and chorus, each perhaps of a double origin, combined in the same performance?

[111] Körte 90–2; Bieber fig. 85; *DTC* 273–4; Greifenhagen 57–9, 66 n. 128; Payne 122.

[112] Cf. Anecd. Bekk. i 224 οἱ δὲ Ὀμβρικός ὑπὸ Ἁλικαρνάσσεων Βάκχος.

[113] Payne seems to have thought this, *loc. cit.*

[114] Greifenhagen 65–6; CVA Pays-Bas, Musée Scheurleer, xxvi 4–5, shows some men dressed as women among padded dancers.

[115] Payne 121–2.

[116] Payne pl. 34 n. 2.

[117] *DTC* 254–6.

[118] Nilsson pl. 35 nos 2–3 shows a red-figure vase on which there are two representations of the ritual phallus being drawn along on wheels by a crowd of men; in one scene, a giant silenus stands

3   *The Structure of New Comedy*

The Cairo codex gives us fifty well-preserved lines of the prologue of *Perikeiromene*, spoken by the personified Agnoia. In this prologue the situation from which the plot develops is expounded in detail, and in lines 7–8 we read: ... τῆς παιδός, ἣν νῦν εἴδετε ὑμεῖς ... In other words, a scene preceded the appearance of Agnoia. So in *Heros* the play opens with a scene between Getas and Daos; after fifty lines, the text is mutilated, but in the *dramatis personae* Ἥρως θεός is listed third, after Getas and Daos. Similarly, in the prologue of the '*Comoedia Florentina*' Tyche says (3–4) οὗ δ᾿ εἰσελήλυθ᾿ ὁ θεράπων ἐν γειτόνων ἀδελφὸς οἰκεῖ. ... It thus appears to have been Menander's practice to open the play with a dramatic scene and arouse the interest of the audience before entrusting the clarification of the situation to the speaker of the prologue.[119] Roman comedy exhibits this feature only in *Cistellaria*, whose original, as we now know, was Menander's *Synaristosae*.[120] The treatment of the prologue in the other poets of New Comedy is discernible only by inference from the Roman evidence.

In the St Petersburg fragment of *Epitrepontes* (32–5) Simmias says to Chaerestratus, 'Let's go in here to see Charisius', and Chaerestratus replies, 'Yes, let's go. There's a gang of young men coming this way, half-drunk, and I think it's not a good time to get in their way.' This is followed in the text by the word *XOPOY*; after which Onesimus enters and begins a monologue in which (apparently) no reference is made to the 'gang of young men half-drunk'. Similarly in *Perik.* 71–6 (141–6A) Daos calls out to the slaves indoors, 'A whole lot of drunken young men are coming ... I must go and look for my master. ...' and off he goes to find Moschion. Then comes *XOPOY* in the text, immediately followed by a well-preserved dialogue between Daos and Moschion in which nothing is said of drunken young men. At *Epitr.* 242 (201AJ), *Sam.* 270 (413A), *Comoedia Florentina* 45, and in an anonymous fragment,[121] the entry *XOPOY* occurs without any reference in either the preceding or the following words to the presence or nature of the chorus; at *Heros* 54 (p. 300A) and in a second anonymous fragment[122] the lines preceding and following *XOPOY* are unreadable; and at *Epitr.* 584 (764A) the presence of *XOPOY* in the original is an inference from the spacing of the preserved right margin.

These facts appear to warrant three generalizations. First, that the chorus continued to be used in New Comedy, but as an entr'acte and not as a

---

over the phallus, in the other a naked giant man with rounded stomach. H. Herter, *Vom Dionysischen Tanz zum komischen Spiel* (Iserlohn 1947) 17, sees in this figure the link between phallic ritual and the dancers with padded stomachs.

[119] Wil., *Men*. 142–9.
[120] Fraenkel, 'Das Original der *Cistellaria* des Plautus', *Phil* lxxxvii (1932).
[121] *Adesp*. fr. 17D; fr. 3 col. iiiS; fr. 66(e)P.
[122] *Adesp*. fr. 23D; fr. 4 col. vS; cf. fr. 65 (*ad fin.*) P.

participant in the action; secondly, that at least in Menander it was represented as a κῶμος; and, thirdly, that its presence and nature might be referred to on its first appearance but not on its subsequent appearances. The limited basis of these generalizations is obvious; their strength is the fact that the instances of *XOPOY* are preserved by the purest chance and not to illustrate a thesis. Körte tries to implicate the chorus more closely in the action[123] by suggesting that, for example, at *Perik*. 76 (146A) they were the friends of Polemon mentioned at 55–6. But the attempt to identify the composition of the possible choruses in Menander (especially *Epitrepontes*) and the Roman adaptations made it necessary to suppose that the same group of dancers appeared in different guises in the same play and that on occasions a group was present on the stage during part of the action, in readiness for an entr'acte, but not referred to in the dialogue.[124] Körte later retracted his argument.[125] None the less, it was pointed out[126] that a passage of Terence, *Heaut*. 170ff, suggests at least one occasion in Menander[127] in which the chorus was something more than a passing κῶμος. Chremes there says, 'I must go and remind Phanias to come and have dinner with me.' He goes off; the stage is empty; he returns, saying, 'They tell me he's come to me already. . . . Well, I'm keeping my guests waiting. . . .' His departure from the stage is not dramatically necessary in Terence's play; in Menander's, it could have been the cue for the entry of his guests as a κῶμος and their performance of a song and dance, after which they would have entered his house.

When the presence of the chorus was recognized as a characteristic of New Comedy, the question of its relevance to the traditional five acts was naturally raised. The five-act division as we know it in Terence is very old,[128] and Donatus *Praef. Ad*. 1.4 'quinque actus . . . choris divisos a Graecis poetis' suggests that if we had a play of Menander absolutely intact we should find *XOPOY* four times, dividing the play into five blocks of approximately equal dramatic weight. Roman comedy for the most part, though not without some awkwardness at times, admits of this partition.[129] Of the originals, we can only say that it suits *Epitrepontes* very well and is reconcilable with what we know of the other plays. Considerations other than the extant texts certainly support it. Once the role of the chorus had become stereotyped, we should expect a large measure of agreement on the amount of work that could fairly be demanded of it. The 'laws' of Greek drama, such as the 'law' of three actors in tragedy, had their origin not in legislation or in ritual but in economic fair play. What could be expected of the choregus and the state helped to determine what was expected of the poet.

[123] Körte, 'Χοροῦ', *Hermes* xxxix (1904).
[124] E. Bethe, 'Der Chor bei Menander', *BSG* lx (1908).
[125] 'Kömodie', *RE* xi col. 1268.
[126] R. C. Flickinger, 'Χοροῦ in Terence's *Heauton*', *CPh* viii (1912) 24; K. J. Maidment, 'The Later Comic Chorus', *CQ* xxix (1935) 20–1.
[127] Cf. the didascalia to *Heaut*.: 'Graeca est Menandru'.
[128] Legrand 464–7; Wil., *Men*. 120–1.
[129] Legrand 467–90.

4   *Middle Comedy*

XOPOY is a phenomenon not confined to the new Menander. It has always been there in the text of the two latest extant plays of Aristophanes, *Ecclesiazusae* and *Plutus*; which shows that the virtual elimination of the chorus from the action in New Comedy was the end of a process begun in Aristophanes' own day. The intermediate process may be inferred from one fragment of Alexis and another which *may* be Alexis. In the former (fr. 107K) we recognize the formula which we saw in Menander: 'I see a κῶμος approaching . . .'.[130] The latter is a papyrus fragment[131] attributed to Alexis on the admittedly slender grounds that it has (22–3) εὖ γε καὶ [παλ]αιστρικῶς and Phrynichus *Ecl*. 218 says παλαιστρικός· "Αλεξίν φασιν εἰρηκέναι, ὁ δὲ ἀρχαῖος παλαιστικὸν λέγει. It presents a scene in which a group of people is addressed as ἄνδρες (18, 26) and replies as ἡμεῖς οἱ παρόντες (24); *XOPOY* occurs also in a mutilated context. It does not follow that the ἄνδρες, of whom all but one could be mute characters, were also the performers of the choral entr'acte (cf. the *advocati* of Plautus *Poen*. 504–816), but the fragment constitutes *some* evidence that Alexis may represent the turning-point in the history of the comic chorus.

The attempt to trace through the fragments of the fourth-century comic poets the development of elements common to Old and New Comedy and the origins of elements characteristic of New Comedy constitutes the true study of Middle Comedy. As a positive category, 'Middle Comedy' is unsatisfactory[132] – for us, though not for the ancients. It was ignored by Kock, who thought it a label devised by the Hadrianic age. In this he was historically wrong,[133] but methodologically justified. The poverty of our positive conception of Middle Comedy is well illustrated by the readiness with which an anonymous papyrus fragment is assigned to Old or New Comedy but not to Middle. Our knowledge of Middle Comedy rests on the citations, on a papyrus fragment,[134] and on the *Persa* of Plautus, the original of which should probably be dated earlier than Alexander – not because of its historical allusion, which is not as specific as it looks,[135] but on negative grounds, the difficulty of dividing it into five acts[136] and the difference of its theme and treatment from what we regard as characteristic of New Comedy.

Hellenistic theory regarded as typical of Middle Comedy the absence of political criticism and the popularity of the mythological burlesque.[137] This

---

[130]   Leo, 'Χοροῦ', *Hermes* xxxix (1904).

[131]   Fr. 48P; *NCh* 166.

[132]   Leo, 'Der Monolog im Drama' 38–46.

[133]   Körte, *Komödie* cols 1257–8.

[134]   N. 131 above, and fr. 47P, probably from the Διὸς γοναί of Philiscus: memorable for the line ἔχρησε γὰρ Κρόνῳ ποθ' Ἀπόλλων δραχμήν; *NCh* 164–6.

[135]   H. W. Prescott, 'The Interpretation of Roman Comedy', *CPh* xi (1916) 135 n. 2; Fraenkel, *Plautinisches* 89 n. 2; but cf. Maidment 15 n. 8.

[136]   Wil., *Men*. 121 n. 1.   [137]   Platonius 11.

generalization is acceptable provided that it is not interpreted too rigidly. Mythological burlesque was much older than the fourth century, and the Ὀδυσσῆς of Cratinus was described as 'Middle' just as Aristophanes' *Cocalus* looked forward to the plots of New Comedy. We should therefore think of Middle Comedy not as generating several wholly new types of plot but as establishing a preference for some old types of plot over others.

Extant titles suggest that plays no less political in theme than *Acharnians* and *Knights* continued to be written for the first two decades of the fourth century,[138] and the citations show many acrimonious political allusions down to the last quarter of the century.[139] That ancient theory concealed the gradualness of the decline in political content may be due to the rapid reduction of the role of the chorus and the consequent elimination of the type of parabasis in which the chorus, irrespective of the content of the rest of the play, spoke directly to the audience of matters of contemporary political interest.[140] The reason for the change suggested in antiquity, the temporary suppression of free speech in 404/3, is unacceptable.[141] We know there were political plays in the twenty years after 404; and, if we did not know it, we should naturally have supposed that the democratic restoration of 403 brought with it a redoubled enthusiasm for outspoken criticism. If a political reason must be sought, it is legitimate to recall that the unique position of Pericles created an abnormal political situation in the quarter-century after his death. Men prominent in political life were ambitious to achieve a comparable προστασία. In such a society politics tend to be conceived in terms of personal prestige. The political orgasm of 404/3 made a break with the past and inaugurated a fresh tradition; the audience of *Plutus* did not think politically in the same terms as the audience of *Knights*.

Alternatively, the reason might be literary. Since the aging but infinitely adaptable Aristophanes was in the vanguard of the change, it is worth entertaining the idea that he consciously envisaged a dissemination of Attic comedy in the Greek-speaking world comparable to the dissemination of tragedy; and if, comedy was to achieve this, it could do so only in a form such that a knowledge of Athenian political personalities was not necessary for its appreciation.

Turning from generalizations to details, the student is constantly struck by the essential continuity of comedy. The *Miles Gloriosus* recalls Lamachus in *Acharnians*.[142] An incident in an anonymous fragment (conceivably Philemon),[143] where one speaker seems to be deliberately mystifying another by conveying information a syllable at a time, reminds us of the verbal game

[138] *SLGC*, pp. 26–8.
[139] *SLGC*, pp. 37–49.
[140] Cf. Platonius 8.
[141] Platonius 4, but cf. Maidment 3–7.
[142] F. Wehrli, *Motivstudien zur griechischen Komödie* (Zürich–Leipzig 1936) 101.
[143] *Adesp*. fr. 16(h)D; fr. 2(e)S; fr. 64(4)P; *NCh*, p. 176.

of the slaves in *Eq*. 21–6. In a fragment of Timocles[144] a ghastly pun compels one speaker to break the dramatic illusion and cry to the audience 'Stop, for heaven's sake! No whistling!' The two houses of *Ecclesiazusae* foreshadow the New Comedy stage, though the spirit of Old Comedy is lively enough to allow them to be a different pair in different parts of the play.[145] The essential continuity of the comic tradition in manner as well as substance strikes the ear at once if Eupolis fr. 159K and Terence *Eunuchus* 247ff are read side by side;[146] in the one, a chorus of κόλακες describe their way of life, and in the other the parasite Gnatho describes his.

Let me pursue in greater detail one final example of comic continuity. At one end of the scale, the Aristophanic parabasis frequently tends away from specific personalities and towards generalized social and political criticism; at the other, the *sententiae* of New Comedy include reflections on contemporary morality. These two extremities are linked by an example from the latest stage of Old Comedy, Pl. Com. fr. 22K, 'Our laws are like cobwebs . . .', and one from Middle Comedy, Xenarchus fr. 4K, 'Our young men are intolerable! . . .'[147] To these we may now add the telling words from an anonymous fragment:[148] κἄπειτα τῆς ἐκκλησίας κατηγορεῖ ἕκαστος ἡμῶν, ἧς ἕκαστος αὐτὸς ἦν.

The apparent continuity of a literary tradition may, however, reflect only persistent elements in the society which provided the material for Old and New Comedy alike. In *V*. 1351–9 Philocleon says to the flute-player, 'Be nice to me, and one day I'll buy you as my concubine. . . . I can't do it yet, because I've no property of my own. . . . My son keeps an eye on me, and he's a hard, mean man. . . . I'm the only father he's got!' We recognize here a comic reversal of a situation familiar in New Comedy: the dissolute son, the courtesan, the strict father. Yet I should be reluctant to infer that this situation was already familiar in Comedy by the time of *Wasps*.[149] The reference is rather to a situation which occurred in real life, or was commonly believed to occur; compare Thurber's drawing of a man saying to a girl in a crowded hotel lounge, 'You wait here, and I'll bring my etchings down.'

The change from Old to New Comedy was not in all respects leisurely and logical. The fourth century hastened the pace by two distinct innovations; one was the rapid rise in the hetaera as a comic character,[150] and the other was the revolutionary change in comic costume. Between Old Comedy and New the comic actor abandoned the short chiton and padding and phallus for ordinary dress.[151] The date and circumstances of the change are not known,

---

[144] Timocles fr. 2D; fr. 22S; fr. 51(b)P.

[145] Wil., *Ar*. 206; Fraenkel, 'Dramaturgical Problems in the *Ecclesiazusae*', in *Greek Poetry and Life* (Oxford 1936) 257–76.

[146] Fraenkel, *De Media et Nova Comoedia Quaestiones Selectae* (Göttingen 1912) 74.

[147] Ibid., 88.

[148] *Adesp*. fr. 12bD; fr. 45(a)P.

[149] This inference is drawn by Wehrli (24).

[150] Hauschild (see n. 75 above).

but evidence has been adduced from the so-called phlyakes vases from South Italy.[152]

Φλύακες were South Italian performers of burlesque.[153] As a literary form, these burlesques are associated particularly with the third-century writer Rhinthon; but the vases concerned are anything up to a century earlier. They show scenes of mythological burlesque or of everyday life; the male characters wear sometimes a short chiton, sometimes tights, nearly always a prodigious phallus. As the scenes are often being enacted on a low stage reached by steps, it seems likely that the grotesque features of the characters are meant to be masks, though they differ from real masks in wearing the expression appropriate to the moment. In one scene the three participants are uttering words which can be put together to make one and a half iambic trimeters.[154] A vase which stylistically is dated late in the series portrays an old man without the phallus.[155] If this single example were supported by others, so that it became possible to say for certain that the phallus disappeared from the phlyakes vases about such-and-such a date, the argument for their connection with Middle Comedy would be immeasurably strengthened, and an approximate date could be given for the essential change in comic costume at Athens. As matters stand, the connection is doubtful. The stage portrayed on the vases is not the Attic theatrical stage, but similar to one which appears on an Attic vase portraying a non-dramatic solo dancer;[156] at the most, therefore, the phlyakes vases would show us the adaptation of Attic comedy to a South Italian stage. But, while it is often possible to describe a phlyakes-vase scene as representing a known Middle Comedy, it is never necessary; and, when we recall Epicharmus in the early period and Rhinthon later, it is difficult to see in the phlyakes vases anything but a drama wholly Western Greek in inspiration.[157] So far as the physical appearance of the characters is concerned, iconographic burlesque independent of dramatic burlesque may have exercised some influence; the Kabeirion vases from Thebes prove that such an iconographic tradition existed in the fourth century.[158]

Pollux iv 143–54, describing the masks of comedy, presents us with a set of highly-developed conventions which may well go back to the late fourth-century practice at Athens. Representations of masks in the middle or early fourth century[159] are too few to enable us to trace the growth of the Pollucian conventions. A few experiments in designing comic masks will soon show that

[151] *DFA* 234–5.

[152] Webster, 'South Italian Vases and Attic Drama', *CQ* xlii (1948).

[153] E. Wüst, 'Φλύακες', *RE* xx cols 292–306; L. Radermacher, 'Zur Geschichte der griechischen Komödie', *SAWW* cii.1 (1925).

[154] Bieber fig. 381; Webster 25.

[155] Bieber fig. 394; Webster 20; cf. also Bieber figs 357, 392, 402?

[156] *JHS* lxv (1945) pl. v; but I am not sure that *DFA* 237 is right to associate this with dancers on tables (*JHS* lix [1939] 25) or small table-like objects (ibid. 10).

[157] Pickard-Cambridge, 'South Italian Vases and Attic Drama', *CQ* xliii (1949); *DFA* 236–8.

[158] Bieber figs 90–1.

[159] Bieber figs 122–35.

there are not an infinite number of distinguishable grotesqueries, and to point out the affinities of specimens from different places and dates is not necessarily to reveal a historical connection between them.[160]

5 Comedy and Tragedy

The tragic affinities of New Comedy were recognized in antiquity, and Satyrus's *Life of Euripides*[161] summarizes them thus: 'quarrels between husband and wife, father and son, servant and master, or situations involving sudden change of fortune, substitution of children, violation of girls, and recognition by rings and necklaces; for all this is really the mainstay of New Comedy, and it was Euripides who perfected it'. The taste of the fourth century, as is independently demonstrated by Aristotle's *Poetics*, differed from ours in admiring one element in tragedy above others: the dramatic recognition. From tragedy this theme passed into comedy, with the difference that, whereas in tragedy the outcome of the plot was predetermined by myth and the poet's choice of means necessarily limited, in Comedy only the *kind* of outcome could be known and the changes which could be rung on the means were almost unlimited.[162]

It must not be supposed that at any particular moment in the fourth century the development of Comedy was interrupted by a swift and decisive turning away from the comic tradition towards the tragic. As already remarked, Aristophanes himself used a recognition-plot, and the characteristic plots of New Comedy emerged by a process of selection, not revolution, from the infinite variety of Old and Middle Comedy. Furthermore, many tragic features in New Comedy which at first appear independent are probably to be interpreted as necessary consequences of the new type of plot. This is certainly true of the expository prologue, demanded by the complexity of the plot; the purely comic element in the ancestry of the prologue is not important.[163] Again, a complex narrative plot cannot be reconciled with the discontinuities of time and place allowed by the inventive fantasy of Old Comedy. A character in New Comedy must be something more than a series of reactions to episodes designed to be enjoyed individually; it is therefore not surprising that Menander's technique of characterization reminds one of Euripides.[164]

Despite Philemon's remark (it comes from an anthology, and the original

---

[160] Webster, 'The Masks of Greek Comedy', *BRL* xxxii.1 (1949), arguing from widely distributed fourth-century terracotta statuettes, extends the Pollucian conventions as far as possible into Middle and Old Comedy.

[161] Von Arnim, *Supplementum Euripideum* (Bonn 1913) 5.

[162] Cf. Antiphanes fr. 191K.

[163] Legrand 495–8 makes the most of it; cf. Aristophanes fr. 335K (Schol. *Th.* 298), Philyllius fr. 8.

[164] Pasquali, 'Menandro ed Euripide', *A&R* xxi (1915), argues for a more direct derivation of characterization from Euripides.

context is unknown)[165] Εὐριπίδης . . . ὅς μόνος δύναται λέγειν, New Comedy does not present any obvious linguistic or stylistic affinities with Euripidean tragedy. The comic confections of the Aristophanic vocabulary have gone, and what remains is effortless and elegant, less colourful, but essentially colloquial; and verbal reminiscences of Euripides which have been detected in Menander are not impressive either in numbers or in fidelity.[166]

New Comedy is best regarded as the product of a long-standing convergence of Comedy and Tragedy. Just as we found it possible to trace the development of certain recurrent features throughout Old, Middle and New Comedy, so it is possible to trace many of them beyond Old Comedy to tragedy. For example, the severance of choral lyrics from the development of the action, which for us first appears in *Ecclesiazusae*, cannot be considered in isolation from the irrelevant ode in E. *Hel*. 1301–68 and Aristotle's attribution to Agathon of the introduction of ἐμβόλιμα into tragedy (*Poet*. 1456a).[167] This important structural development can be supported by a number of minor details. It is amusing (but perhaps no more) to recognize in E. *Phoen*. 196 what might be regarded as the tragic prototype[168] of the formula 'Here comes a crowd – let's get out of the way.' The *narratio convivialis*, which may be discerned as the context of many citations from comedy, has a splendid ancestor in *V*. 1299–1323, but in reading that passage of *Wasps* we are at once reminded of E. *Alc*. 747–72.[169] The same point is illustrated by consideration of the parallel development of the monologue[170] and the narrative speech[171] in tragedy and comedy.

Similarities of detail between tragedy and comedy should not be taken as necessarily implying a consistent one-way influence. They do, however, remind us that tragic and comic poets were familiar with each other's work and wrote for performance before the same audience in the same theatre. The demands made by this coexistence in identical theatrical conditions were the same demands, and often found the same solutions.

'The curse of specialization' is nowadays a *locus rhetoricus*, and for that reason may before long command no more respect than *loci* of more impressive pedigree. It suffers from the disadvantage that, whereas farmers really are happier than tyrants and a philosophical turn of mind really does confer more lasting pleasure than a discriminating palate, it is not altogether obvious that Classical studies will prosper if everyone renounces the standards which he knows to be attainable only by specialization. But, if any lesson is to

---

[165] Philemon fr. 3D; fr. 23S; fr. 50(b)P.

[166] Collected by E. Sehrt, *De Menandro Euripidis Imitatore* (Giessen 1912); but many of his examples are inappropriate or exaggerated; *Georg*. 79ff ~ E. *Hp*. 403–4 is not very happy, and Men. fr. 348K is a paratragic commonplace (cf. Ar. frr. 1, 155K).

[167] Flickinger, *CPh* vii (1912) 31–4.

[168] Körte, *Komödie* col. 1268.

[169] Fraenkel 13–32.

[170] Leo *op. cit*. (n. 132 above), esp. 36.

[171] Fraenkel 6–12.

be drawn from this brief survey of Greek comedy, we might do worse than to recollect the end of Plato's *Symposium*. Aristophanes may have agreed with Socrates' argument, in so far as it applied to poets, only for the sake of peace and quiet; but, had the argument been applied to scholars, he might well have opened both eyes to agree τοῦ αὐτοῦ ἀνδρὸς εἶναι κωμῳδίαν καὶ τραγῳδίαν ἐπίστασθαι ἐξηγεῖσθαι.

APPENDIX (1967)

The study of Greek comedy during the last few years has been dominated by the discovery of more Menander. We now have *Dyskolos* virtually complete (first published as *Papyrus Bodmer IV* in 1958; edited as an Oxford Classical Text by Hugh Lloyd-Jones in 1960; edited with an extensive introduction and commentary by E. W. Handley [London 1965]), substantial portions of *Sikyonios* (edited by R. Kassel in the 'Kleine Texte' series, 1965) and new fragments of *Misoumenos* (edited by E. G. Turner, *BICS* Suppl. XVII). *Dyskolos*, produced in 316 BC, is not a great play, but as an item in the history of comedy it is full of interest, not only in its formal aspects (it is divided into five parts by four irruptions of a chorus [cf. p. 211], and its final scene is composed mainly in iambic tetrameters) but also in its characterization and in some of the sentiments and attitudes which it expresses.

New discoveries in the field of Old Comedy have been confined to the medieval manuscripts. A Paris manuscript (suppl. gr. 463) has corrections and scholia which are in the hand of Demetrius Triclinius himself (W. J. W. Koster, *Autour d'un manuscrit d'Aristophane écrit par Démétrius Triclinius* [Groningen, 1957] – but the suggestion that the main text is also written by Triclinius has not been generally accepted). A hitherto unnoticed manuscript, Holkhamensis 88, proves to be a good copy of the Triclinian edition of eight plays of Aristophanes (N. G. Wilson, *CQ* NS xii [1962] 32ff). The publication of the scholia on Aristophanes, under the general editorship of Koster, has so far given us only Johannes Tzetzes' scholia on *Plutus*, *Clouds*, *Frogs* and *Birds* (Groningen and Amsterdam 1960–4), but the preparatory work has brought to light from fourteenth-century manuscripts undeniably ancient scholia which are missing or curtailed in the Ravennas and Venetus, and a coherent picture of Byzantine editions of Aristophanes is beginning to emerge (see the articles by Koster and Holwerda in *Mnemosyne* from 1952 onwards).

Frogs has been edited, with a commentary, by W. B. Stanford (2nd edn, London 1963), and *Peace* by M. Platnauer (Oxford 1964). The late J. M. Edmonds' edition of *The Fragments of Attic Comedy*, published in four volumes (Leyden 1957–61), is not at all what was wanted; it abounds in mistakes, confusions, superficial judgements and irresponsible emendations, and the editor's belief that he could read a marginal and interlinear paraphrase (vol. iiib, appendix) in the Cairo codex was a delusion.

The evidence for the origins of comedy is now presented in T. B. L. Webster's substantially revised edition (Oxford 1962) of Pickard-Cambridge's *Dithyramb, Tragedy and Comedy*. Problems of production are discussed in Webster's *Greek Theatre Production* (London 1956) and P. D. Arnott's *Greek Scenic Conventions in the Fifth Century BC* (Oxford 1962). Webster's book contains a short list of works of art which, in one sense or another, 'illustrate' comedy, and he has published complete lists in *BICS* Suppl. IX and XI. A. M. Dale in *JHS* lxxvii (1957) 205ff has argued that only one door into the σκηνή was available to Aristophanes, and that this holds good even for those scenes (notably in *Acharnians*, *Clouds* and *Ecclesiazusae*) where the words of the text imply more than one door; there are (in the present writer's opinion; cf. *Proc. Camb. Phil. Soc.* 1966, 2ff) weighty arguments against this hypothesis, but its opponents must admit that it has forced upon us a salutary reappraisal of Aristophanic theatrical production.

Among the numerous books written during the last ten years on various aspects of the art of Aristophanes three are noteworthy: C. F. Russo, *Aristofane autore di teatro* (Florence 1962), which, although marred by errors of detail, investigates practical theatrical problems of the kind which editors of texts often ignore; H.-J. Newiger, *Metaphor und Allegorie* (Munich 1957), which deals with types and degrees of personification in Aristophanes; and J. Taillardat, *Les Images d'Aristophane* (2nd edn, Paris 1965), an exceedingly thorough account of Aristophanes' vocabulary, with many illuminating comments on individual passages.

ADDITIONAL NOTE

Since 1967 a great deal has happened in the study of Greek Comedy, and many more fragments of ancient texts (of New Comedy in particular) have been published.

Having now edited one play of Aristophanes and investigated the textual transmission of two others, I could not now describe Coulon's apparatus criticus as 'accurate and discriminating' (p. 198). I also regard my statements (p. 197) about the social and political aspects of Aristophanic Comedy as crudely simplistic.

23

Plato Comicus: *Presbeis* and *Hellas*

I. Two beliefs are commonly held about the *Presbeis*: that it was in some sense 'about' the embassy of Epicrates to Persia (Bergk, *Comm. de rel. comm. Att.* 389; Meineke, *FCG* i 182; Kock, *CAF* i 632; Wilamowitz, *Sb. Berlin* 1921, 736), and that it involved an attack upon Epicrates comparable in scale to the attacks on Cleophon, Peisander, and Hyperbolus in the comedies which Plato named after them (Meineke, *loc. cit.*; Schmid–Stählin, *Gesch. d. gr. Litt.* i.4 148). Yet the former belief is demonstrably false; and the latter, though conceivable, is not supported by any positive evidence. Let us look at the relevant fragments. Athenaeus 229e–f:

μέχρι γὰρ τῶν Μακεδονικῶν χρόνων κεραμέοις σκεύεσιν οἱ δειπνοῦντες διηκονοῦντο . . . Ἀριστοφάνης δὲ ὁ κωμῳδιοποιός, ὅν φησιν Ἡλιόδω-
ρος . . . Ναυκρατίτην εἶναι γένος, ἐν τῷ Πλούτῳ τῷ δράματι κατὰ τὴν τοῦ ὁμωνύμου θεοῦ ἐπιφάνειαν τοὺς ἰχθυηροὺς φησι πίνακας ἀργυροῦς ἀναφανῆναι . . . Πλάτων δ' ἐν Πρέσβεσι· (fr. 119K)

κᾆτ' ἔλαβον Ἐπικράτης τε καὶ Φορμίσ⟨ι⟩ος
παρὰ τοῦ βασιλέως πλεῖστα δωροδοκήματα,
ὀξύβαφα χρυσᾶ καὶ πινακίσκους ἀργυροῦς.

κατέλαβον codd., corr. Meineke

Meineke's correction is certain; καταλαβεῖν is the wrong word for taking bribes, and κᾆτ' > κατ- is common. τοῦ βασιλέως must refer to the King of Persia, for (i) the point of the passage in Athenaeus is that golden vessels were oriental (cf. Ar. *Ach*. 73–4), (ii) Plu. *Pelop*. 30, Athen. 251a–b describe (ultimately, I think, from Theopompus *Philippica* x; cf. *Fr. Gr. Hist.* 115 F 92) how Epicrates, on returning from an embassy to Persia, was alleged to have taken bribes, but turned it off with a joke which the Ecclesia received kindly. This story makes it unlikely that Plato is referring to the visit of Timocrates to Greece in 395 (Xen. *HG* iii 5.1; cf. the absence of any mention of Phormisius in *Hell. Ox.* 2.2). The Persian king commonly gave exotic presents to ambassadors (cf. Ar. *Ach*. 63 ~ Antiphon *ap*. Athen. 397c ~ Pl. *Chrm*. 158a). Presumably Epicrates as ambassador was presented with golden vessels, which his enemies called bribes; he was able to laugh this off in an assembly not normally well disposed to its representatives who were bribed.

If the practice of the orators is any guide, τοῦ βασιλέως used of the *Persian* king should not be the first mention of him in the context (cf. Isoc. iv 145, 179, v 88, viii 98, xii 106, 162; Dem. xiv 6, xxiii 200; in Dem. xiv 2 the manuscripts differ over the article; in id. xv 9 they all have it, wrongly, in a quotation from a decree). Thus these lines of Plato form part of a longer context – as κᾆτα suggests in any case – on dealings with Persia.

The embassy must be either referred to as outside the action of the play or actually portrayed – caricatured – within it. The apparent evidence for the latter dissolves on scrutiny.

1 Athen. 424a:

κύαθον δ᾽ ἐπὶ τοῦ ἀντλητῆρος Πλάτων εἴρηκεν ... ἐν Πρέσβεσι· (fr. 120K)

κυάθους ὅσους ἐκλέπτεθ᾽ ἑκάστοτε.

Bergk (392) conjectured ἐκλεπτέτην, to make an iambic trimeter, positing Epicrates and Phormisius as subject. But (i) there are other metrical possibilities; Telesillean, ⟨× —⟩ κυάθους ὅσους / ἐκλέπτεθ᾽ ἑκάστοτε (for the short open vowel-ending cf. Ar. *Pax* 1351); more doubtfully, iambic, ⟨× ∪ ∪⟩ κυάθους κτλ. or ... ἑκάστοτ᾽ ⟨∪ ∪ ∪×⟩ (but cf. White, *The Verse of Greek Comedy* 48). (ii) The sense forbids us to take κυάθους ἐκλέπτετε as referring to ἔλαβον δωροδοκήματα.

2 Σ Ar. *Ec*. 71:

Ἐπικράτους] οὗτος μέγαν πώγωνα ἔχων ἐπεκαλεῖτο σακεσφόρος· καὶ Πλάτων ὁ κωμικός φησιν· ἄναξ ὑπήνης Ἐπικράτες σακεσφόρε. (fr. 122K)

Not quoted as from the *Presbeis*; Meineke (183) put it there. But it is not addressed to a character on the stage; it is an invocation, treating Epicrates as a god; cf. ἄναξ Πόσειδον (Ar. *V*. 143 et al.) and especially ὦ Σουνιέρακε χαῖρ᾽ ἄναξ Πελαργικέ (Ar. *Av*. 870).

3 Anon. in Arist. *Eth. Nic*. iv 7.15 (*Comm. in Arist. gr*. xx 200):

τῶν Λακώνων ἐσθὴς εὐτελὴς ἄγαν ἱστορεῖται Ξενοφῶντι· διὰ ταῦτα καὶ σκώπτουσιν αὐτοὺς οἱ κωμῳδοποιοί, ὡς Πλάτων ἐν Πρέσβεσι· (fr. 124K)

χαίρεις, οἶμαι, μεταπεττεύσας αὐτόν διακλιμακίσας τε τόν † ὑπηνόβιον σπαρτιοχαίτην ῥυποκόνδυλον ἑλκετρίβωνα.

διακλιμακεύεσθαι codd., corr. Porson cl. Hesych.
διακλιμακίσας· διαπαλαίσας. ὑπηνοβότον Naber

Bergk thought of Epicrates' beard and took αὐτόν as referring to him, thus making him an Athenian laconizer. But (i) Anon. in Arist. says nothing of laconizers; ἡ τῶν Λακ ώ ν ω ν ἐσθής ... σκώπτονσιν αὐτούς. (ii) the whole character and political record of Epicrates (Dem. xix 277, *Hell. Ox.* 2.2) exclude the possibility that he was a laconizer. There is no need to explain his conduct in 392/1 (Philochorus *ap.* Did. in [Dem.] x col. vii ~ (Andoc. iii *passim*) as sentimental laconizing.

There is thus no reason to suppose that the *Presbeis* was 'about' the embassy of Epicrates. Such an interpretation is as if we possessed *The Tempest* only in fragments and inferred from

> You three
> From Milan did supplant good Prospero;
> Exposed unto the sea, which hath requit it,
> Him and his innocent child

that the title of the play referred to a storm which fell upon Prospero.

Fr. 119 comes from a narrative speech (the stages linked by εἶτα, κᾷτα, κἀντεῦθεν) complaining about Athenian policy; cf. Praxagora Ar. *Ec.* 170–240 (similar in substance, very different in style), Hermes Ar. *Pax* 603–48 (a different metre), and above all Dicaeopolis Ar. *Ach.* 496–556. *Ach.* 535–7 are peculiarly similar in style to fr. 119; the first two lines might almost be from a historian, the third is purely comic.

Fr. 124 shows that one of the characters in the play was a Spartan. I suggest that the plot concerned a 'private', i.e. comic, embassy (cf. Trygaeus, and the private peace of Dicaeopolis) perhaps to Persia, perhaps to Sparta.

II. The most important fragment of the *Hellas* comes from two versions of a grammatical note on *Il.* i 135–7, in Eustathius and in Σ *Il.* Cod. Paris. Reg. 2766 (v. Greg. Cor. ed. Schäfer 48):

Πλάτων ἐν Ἑλλάδι· (fr. 24K) εἰ μὲν σὺ τὴν θάλατταν ἀποδώσεις ἑκών· εἰ δὲ μή, ταῦτα πάντα συντριαινῶν ἀπολέσω.

ἐν Ἑλλάδι om. Eust.; σύ] σοι Eust.; ταύτην post ἀποδώσεις hab. Σ; συντριαινῶ ἀπώλεσα Σ

The text is metrically ambiguous, and I have attempted no restoration. Poseidon is speaking (Bergk 384, rightly; cf. esp. Ar. *Nu.* 566–7). ταῦτα πάντα ... ἀπολέσω is a deliberate, conscious threat (contrast Ar. *Eq.* 99, Cratinus fr. 187K); hence ταῦτα πάντα must somehow be the property of σύ. Whom is Poseidon threatening? Athens, on behalf of Sparta, said Bergk and Meineke (i 169), no doubt thinking of the cult of Poseidon at Taenarum. Sparta, on behalf of Athens after Aegospotami, said Kock (i 606) and Geissler (*Chronologie der altattischen Komödie* [Berlin 1925] 66), so Murray (*Aristophanes* [Oxford 1933] 67) calls the play 'imperialist'. No one seems to have considered the possibility that Poseidon may be speaking to Conon and his Persians after Cnidus; a preferable alternative, for these reasons:

(i) To call a theme too serious for Old Comedy is rash, always; but if there were such themes, would not Athens' struggle for survival 410–404, especially with a god taking sides, be among them?

(ii) Conon's victory was not only *not* a move in a struggle for survival; it did not even give unmixed pleasure to the Athenians; cf. above all Lys. ii. 59 (less important, but interesting, the irony of Pl. *Mnx*. 245c–246a).

(iii) The *Hellas* was called also *Νῆσοι* (Suid. *s.v.* Πλάτων iv 1708 Adler), suggesting that the issue it raised was command of the *sea*; but the issue between Sparta and Athens 410–404 was more than that.

(iv) Phot. Berol. 88.14: ἀμαυρός· θηλυκῶς· Πλάτων Ἑλλάδι· (Pl. Com. fr. 1 Dem.) αὐτὴ δ' ἀμαυρὸς ἀσθενὴς τ' ἐγιγνόμην. (ἐγενόμην cod., corr. Reitzenstein).

For ἀμαυρός, dignified and even tragic when applied to persons, cf. Eur. *Andr.* 204. Körte, *Bu. Jb.* 1911, i 251, suggested that this line is spoken by Hellas, rescued and reproaching her rescuers for past neglect; for the rescue theme cf. Ar. *Pax* and Ar. fr. 26 Dem. (Körte 270).

If this interpretation is right, it follows from ταῦτα πάντα that part of the scene is set either in Persian territory or in the presence of Conon's fleet. But it does not follow either that the play was 'anti-Conon' or that it was 'pro-Conon'. Gods in Comedy can change their minds (cf. Ar. *Pax* 400–27), and Poseidon may have changed his after speaking fr. 24.

Addendum. Pl. Com. fr. 183K (*ap*. Plu. *Them.* 32.3) was assigned by Sintenis (ed. Plu. *Them*. 1832, *ad loc*.) to the Ἑλλάς. Perhaps he was right, even if for wrong reasons. The words ὁ σὸς δὲ τύμβος κτλ. must be addressed either to Themistocles or to his ghost; clearly, to his ghost, or we should be dealing with an historical comedy, a monstrosity. Are they a prophecy or a promise? A prophecy to a ghost needs a νέκυια or a κατάβασις; a promise needs neither, and there could be no more suitable time for prayers, and corresponding promises, to the ghost of Themistocles than after Cnidus (cf. Lys. ii. 42). What view of the whereabouts of Themistocles' remains (disputed at this time, cf. Plu. *Them*. 32.2) is presupposed by these lines I do not know.

24

The Style of Aristophanes

The stylistic analysis of Aristophanes has to contend with one peculiar difficulty. Generally one can define the style of an author by comparing him with other authors of the same genre; for example, we can characterize the style of Euripides by contrasting it with that of Sophocles. But no complete work of any poet of Old Comedy except Aristophanes has survived; and the existing fragments and citations are not a sufficient basis for a comparison between Aristophanes and Eupolis or Cratinus. Therefore we cannot define the style of Aristophanes as an individual, but must content ourselves with a generic description.

In accordance with a traditional procedure, five stylistic categories, five kinds of language, need to be distinguished in the analysis of comic style, and an area of literature corresponds to each of the five.

1 Normal language, to which a seasoning, so to speak, of the other languages is added.
2 The spoken language, which rarely enters into serious poetry. The phenomena of spoken language are found, apart from comedy, in those passages of Platonic dialogue which have a dramatic or discursive rather than a philosophical character;[1] in some utterances reported by Xenophon; and sometimes also in the rustic or domestic conversations of Herodas and Theocritus. A special category, which must necessarily be assigned to the spoken language, comprises anatomical and physiological words which occur also in the iambographers but are never used even by medical writers.
3 Technical language – or, rather, technical languages.
4 The language of serious poetry: epic, lyric, tragedy. Within this category we must distinguish parody, which raises some problems of method requiring discussion later.
5 Peculiarly comic language; above all, words which are intrinsically funny.

---

[1] Cf. D. Tarrant *CQ* xl (1946) 109ff.

From the stylistic point of view the monologue of Dikaiopolis at the beginning of *Acharnians* serves excellently as a model. From among the linguistic phenomena present in the monologue I will choose a score which will raise the question of the sufficiency of the categories listed above. Are five categories enough? And do the boundaries between them do justice to the complexity of the phenomena? These questions make a rigid classification impracticable, and for that reason I will take the phenomena simply in the order in which they occur in the text.

To begin with 2:

> ἤσθην δὲ βαιά, πάνυ δὲ βαιά, τέτταρα.

The word βαιός occurs often enough in archaic poetry, and in Aristophanes we meet it just twice, here and in *Nu.* 1013, where γλῶτταν βαιάν is contrasted with γλῶτταν μεγάλην. So far, the distribution of βαιός resembles that of κέαρ, which does not occur anywhere in Aristophanes except *Ach.* 5

> ἐγῷδ᾽ ἐφ᾽ ᾧ γε τὸ κέαρ ηὐφράνθην ἰδών.

But unlike κέαρ, whose frequency diminishes continuously in the fifth century in serious poetry (Euripides uses it only in *Medea* and once in *Hercules Furens*), βαιός is found in a fragment (B119) of Democritus: βαιὰ γὰρ φρονήσει τύχη μάχεται. This at once raises the question: was Ionic prose influenced by poetic vocabulary? Or is our notion of prose vocabulary fundamentally distorted by the fact that we read prose through the eyes of a fourth-century Athenian?[2] Moreover, words which seem to be trespassing on the territory of prose do not all have the same origins. For example, νοστεῖν, which apart from *Ach.* 29,

> εἰς ἐκκλησίαν
> νοστῶν κάθημαι

is used by Aristophanes in *Av.* 1270 and *Pl.* 610 and is frequent in archaic poetry from Homer onwards, and also in Herodotus, but is absent from Aeschylus and found only once in Sophocles (*OC* 1386), while Euripides uses it seven times. The Aristophanic contexts do not suggest any intention of parodying serious poetry, and in any case the flavour of νοστεῖν, which we could call 'archaic–Euripidean–Herodotean', would differ appreciably from that of κέαρ, specifically associated with archaic poetry. We have to take account of the simultaneous operation of diachronic changes and regional differences. From the Ionic inscriptions of the fifth century, scarce though they are, we can pick a good handful of words which we would almost

---

[2] G. Lanata *QUCC* v (1968) 22ff examines the relation between poetic and medical vocabulary in the *De morbo sacro*.

certainly define as poetic if they did not occur also in state documents. I am persuaded that not poetry but documents should be the starting-point for the study of the Greek vocabulary of the fifth century; indeed, these documents reveal an aspect of the Attic vocabulary which has nearly always, wrongly, been overlooked. There is no lack of elements common to Ionic and fifth-century Attic but no longer used in fourth-century Attic. For example, the verb θωᾶν (θω(ι)εῖν, θωάζειν) and the noun θωά (θωϊή) are found in Ionic and also mainland inscriptions (θωϊή, Amorgos, s. v/iv [*IG* xii.7 220.3], Miletus, s. v m. [*DGE* 727.12] and Thasos, s. iv [*IG* xii Suppl. 347.II.5]; θωεῖν, Delphi, s. v/iv [*DGE* 323 D.19] and Oeanthea, s. v [*DGE* 363.9]; θωάζειν, Elis, s. vi [*DGE* 412.1]) and in archaic Ionic poetry (θωή, *Od*. ii 192; θωϊή, Archil. *IEG* 329); but in fourth-century Attic prose we catch a glimpse of them only in the word ἀθῷος (= ἀζήμιος). Yet the verb θωᾶν is found in an Attic document of the first half of the fifth century (*IG* i² 4.7) – later, ζημιοῦν would have been used (e.g. *IG* i² 42.7) – and the noun θωά occurs in a law about the βουλή (*IG* i² 114.42) republished about 410. From such examples there seems to emerge a poetic–Ionic–Attic stock of words which Attic prose in the fourth century eschews in general but may on occasion use capriciously, as is apparent from the word occurring in *Ach*. 7,

$$ταῦθ᾽ ὡς ἐγανώθην κτλ.$$

This verb is recorded only twice before the Hellenistic period; Pl. *R*. 411a γεγανωμένος ὑπὸ τῆς ᾠδῆς is the other example. In a fragment of Anacreon (*PMG* 444) cited by Plutarch it is uncertain whether γεγανωμένος is Anacreon's word or Plutarch's: οὐ πόθῳ στίλβων, ὡς ἔφη τὸν παρθένιον Ἀνακρέων, οὐδὲ μύρων ἀνάπλεως καὶ γεγανωμένος. The noun γάνος is poetic, and so is the verb γάνυσθαι, but note Ar. *V*. 612 τούτοισιν ἐγὼ γάνυμαι and Pl. *Phdr*. 234d γάνυσθαι ὑπὸ τοῦ λόγου. These words are absent from Ionic prose, and it is quite likely that they formed part of the spoken Attic of the fifth century, a little old-fashioned in Aristophanes' time and affectionately revived by Plato. There are also some words in comedy which have archaic or vulgar associations and for that reason do not sit comfortably either in Ionic prose or in Attic. Consider, for example, the curious case of ἀργαλέος. This majestic-sounding word is well known in epic and in poetry down to Empedocles. It never occurs in tragedy; but Aristophanes uses it eight times, notably in *Nu*. 451, where it appears in a list of abusive terms recited by Strepsiades:

κύρβις κρόταλον κίναδος τρύμη
μάσθλης εἴρων γλοιὸς ἀλαζὼν
κέντρων μιαρὸς στροφὶς ἀργαλέος υτλ.

The adjective is unknown to Ionic prose, but not to Attic prose: Xen. *Hi*. 6.4 πῶς οὐκ ἀργαλέον ἐστὶ πρᾶγμα (cf. Ar. *Pl*. 1 ὡς ἀργαλέον πρᾶγμ᾽ ἐστίν) and

Aeschines i 61 ἀργαλέος ὢν τὴν ὄψιν. It would not be hard to find analogies in modern languages; vulgar words can have a flavour of archaism out of tune with the literary tradition.

To return now to *Ach*. 2; Dikaiopolis continues

πάνυ δὲ βαιά, τέτταρα.

The repetition of δέ with the intensifying word seems to be unparalleled. Denniston does not mention this passage, perhaps because he took for granted Elmsley's emendation γε (cf. *Pax* 280 οἴμοι τάλας οἴμοι γε). If δέ is right, it may possibly be a phenomenon of rural speech; it does not occur in Platonic dialogues. Whatever the cultural and social differences between city and country (cf. *Ach*. 32ff, Th. ii 15f), we are very ill-informed about any linguistic differences.[3] I imagine that comic technique did not attach importance to rural idiom, any more than (by contrast with modern comedy at popular level) it exploited the solecisms which must have been abundant in the speech of slaves and uneducated people.[4] Nevertheless, it is possible to suspect, here and there in Aristophanes, a rural touch, in the absence of any direct evidence. This suspicion is awakened in me by the use of the word πλᾶτις in 132,

καὶ τοῖσι παιδίοισι καὶ τῇ πλάτιδι[5]

As for τέτταρα, which follows πάνυ δὲ βαιά in 2, it is hard to identify its stylistic category. Dikaiopolis describes in the following lines the things which have pleased him, and there are two of them, not four. It is not surprising that commentators have recalled the Italian expression *quattro passi* and the like but, as van Leeuwen noted, Greek analogies are not close; indeed, in *Ach*. 598 τρεῖς, not τέτταρες, means 'few'. So the possibility remains open that this sense of τέτταρα may belong to colloquial language or rural language.

In 3,

ἃ δ᾽ ὠδυνήθην, ψαμμακοσιογάργαρα.

we are for once liberated from uncertainty. ψαμμακοσιογάργαρα 'sand-hundreds' or 'sand-hundred heaps' is a perfect example of comic invention.

---

[3] J. Taillardat, *Les Images d'Aristophane* (Paris 1965) 12ff is right in his interpretation of Ar. fr. 706 (*PCG*) as referring to differences which we would think of as cultural rather than linguistic in the strict sense.

[4] Cf. pp. 241–6 below.

[5] Aeschylus fr. 451I.26 (*TGF*), classified among 'Dubia' by Radt, has]. δαπλᾶτιδ.[, which seems to bear out the intuitive judgement of G. Björck, *Das Alpha Impurum und die tragische Kunstsprache* (Uppsala 1950) 343, that πλᾶτις is a poetic word. However, the context is not well preserved enough in the fragment to show whether πλᾶτις there means 'wife' or something quite different.

γάργαρα, confined to comedy (Alcaeus Comicus fr. 19, Aristomenes fr. 1) means 'heap', and ψαμμακόσιοι occurs in Eupolis fr. 286 (from *Golden Age*, which, to judge from fr. 290 was produced in Cleon's lifetime). The compound is modelled on some financial terms, such as διακοσιόδραχμα and τριακοσιόδραχμα 'sums of two hundred / three hundred drachmae' (*SEG* x 210 [Rhamnous, s. v]). The verb γαργαίρειν, found in Ar. fr. 375 (*PCG*) and Cratinus fr. 321 (*PCG*),[6] is not exclusively Attic, because it is used by Sophron fr. 30 ἐγάργαιρεν ἁ οἰκία. Timotheus uses it in a serious context, perhaps to give a shock (*Pers*. 107 πόντος . . . ἐγάργαιρε σώμασιν) or perhaps aiming at some other effect through comic style.[7] It does not matter whether the humorous word ψαμμακόσιοι was invented by Aristophanes or by Eupolis or by neither; what is important is that two different poets used it. There are parallels for that; in *Nu*. 57 τί γάρ μοι τὸν πότην ἧπτες λύχνον, 'why did you light me the lamp that's a heavy drinker?' we find for the first time a joke that recurs in Pl. Com. fr. 190 ὠνήσομαι στιλβήν τιν' ἥτις μὴ πότις. What the spectators like once they may like again.[8]

Let us turn now to 4,

φέρ' ἴδω, τί δ' ἥσθην ἄξιον χαιρηδόνος;

Reckoning in purely statistical terms, we have to count χαιρηδών a comic word, because it does not occur anywhere except in this passage. It has been reasonably inferred from Pl. *Cra*. 419c that Plato is unlikely to have known of the existence of χαιρηδών as a synonym of χαρά.[9] That, however, does not tell us whether χαιρηδών is intended to provoke an outright laugh or a smile.[10] Modelled on two other words, ἀλγηδών (Hdt. v 18.4, S. *OC* 513, Euripides seven times, Plato very frequently) and ἀχθηδών (A. *PV* 26, Th. ii 37.2, iv 40.2, Pl. *Lg*. 734a and – for the etymology – *Cra*. 419c), χαιρηδών reflects comic invention which does not differ essentially from invention practised by the tragic poets or by Plato, or indeed from what we would expect to find in the language of sophisticated people. Comic dialogue cannot be considered as uniform stuff seasoned with oddities in such a way that we can separate the parodic and humorous seasoning from the basic material. The comic poet creates his own language as other poets do; for that reason I would prefer simply to locate χαιρηδών in a central stratum of linguistic sophistication.

---

[6] Σ*ΕΓ* is worded in such a way as to imply that the noun γάργαρα occurs elsewhere in Aristophanes, but that was probably not the intention.

[7] There is no good reason why the vocabulary of Philoxenus or of Timotheus should not have been influenced by comedy.

[8] Cf. Taillardat 15ff, 88.

[9] Ed. Fraenkel, *Beobachtungen zu Aristophanes* (Rome 1962) 15f.

[10] Fraenkel recalls χαίρομαι in *Pax* 291, where a non-Greek is portrayed as committing a solecism; but that is a very different matter from poetic invention in the construction of substantives, in which the tragic poets also played an important part.

The case of the adjective τραγῳδικός is no different. It often occurs in comedy; but before classifying -ικός as a comic suffix (which, incidentally, would imply that Plato, who has a great liking for words in -ικός, aligns himself in this respect with comedy) we have to take account of two facts: first, that in a well-known passage of Aristophanes (*Eq.* 1378ff) -ικός is treated as characteristic of literary criticism, or rather, of judgements pronounced by people who regard themselves as cognoscenti; secondly, that by the late fifth century it had already become characteristic of the languages of technology and administration, as is clear from a glance at the index of *IG* i², where we find (e.g.) ἀγαλματοποιϊκός, δημιουργικός, ἐπιβατικός, ληξιαρχικός, λιθοκομικός, τεκτονικός, etc. In the fourth century it continues to extend its domain, e.g. ἀρτοπωλικός, ἐγκτητικός, ὀργεωνικός, πρυτανικός, τειχοποιϊκός. It was not just the sophists or the poets who created the widespread use of the morphemes by which Greek literature was enriched.[11]

In the first part of Dikaiopolis's monologue 8 still has a problem waiting for us,

$$ἄξιον \ γὰρ \ Ἑλλάδι.$$

Here we encounter not only an unusual application of ἄξιος but direct quotation of a half-line of Euripides' *Telephus* (fr. 720 Nauck = 128 Austin). Every time we encounter a quotation from tragedy in a comedy, we naturally suspect parodic intention. This suspicion is not necessarily justified, and in this particular case I do not think it is. There are two motives for parody: one is the desire to turn the critical attention of the audience directly on the tragic material (as, for example, in that scene of *Ach.* in which Euripides appears in person); the second is the desire to exploit the dissonance resulting from the justaposition of elevated poetry and vulgarity.[12] Neither of these motives is applicable to *Ach.* 8. But tragic quotation can be founded upon something which has nothing in common with parody; that is, when an expression drawn from a poem or a play has passed into general use. This phenomenon happens frequently in modern languages, and I do not see any adequate reason for denying that it happened in Greek. I suggest that ἄξιον γάρ may belong to that category. Perhaps we should say the same of ὦ πόλις πόλις in 27, which echoes either S. *OT* 629 or a passage of a tragedy we do not have. (Note that the expression recurs in Eupolis fr. 205, drawn from *Cities*, datable [cf. fr. 238] to the period of Hyperbolus's prominence). A distinction can be drawn, though; in 27, after the familiar imagery of 18ff and the vivid picture presented by 21–6, an effect of comic dissonance is achieved by the contrast

---

[11] A. N. Ammann, *ΙΚΟΣ bei Platon* (Freiburg 1953) attributes the extension of -ικός to the sophists; in his catalogue of words in -ικός most of those which occur in fifth-century inscriptions are missing. C. W. Peppler, *AJPh* xxxi (1910) 428ff. also treats -ικός as an essentially scientific and philosophical phenomenon. Cf. pp. 39–40 above.

[12] On the parody of tragic language in comedy see P. Rau, *Paratragodia* (Munich 1967).

with the solemn exclamation ὦ πόλις πόλις. Compare also ὦ Κραναὰ πόλις in 75, whose tone is in contrast with the plebeian tone of 71f.

In 12,

$$πῶς τοῦτ' ἔσεισέ μου δοκεῖς τὴν καρδίαν$$

we find an expression which recurs in 24,

$$εἶτα δ' ὠστιοῦνται πῶς δοκεῖς.$$

As it happens, a purely statistical consideration can lead to a correct evaluation of this phenomenon. πῶς δοκεῖς or πῶς οἴει / οἴεσθε is found six times in Ar. (apart from *Ach.*, in *Nu.* 881, 1368, *Ra.* 54 and *Pl.* 742), four times in Euripides and once in Xenophon. In three of the four Euripidean passages (*Hec.* 1160, *Hp.* 446, *IA* 1590) πῶς δοκεῖς is parenthetic; in the fourth, *Peirithoos* 38 (Page), it is made to fit the syntax of the sentence: Εὐρυσθέα γὰρ πῶς δοκεῖς ἂν ἄσμενον λέγειν ἂν κτλ. The same can be said of the Xenophon passage, *M.* iv 2.23: νῦν δὲ πῶς οἴει με ἀθύμως ἔχειν. There is no doubt that we are dealing here with an expression belonging to the spoken language, one of many such expressions adopted by Euripides.[13] Note that in 12 δοκεῖς is separated from πῶς, as if the latter were a postpositive particle, and compare Dem. liv 38, where οἶμαι is equivalent to the particle που: οἱ γὰρ οἶμαι βέλτιστοι κτλ.[14]

It may be objected that ἔσεισε is a technical term of medicine; at any rate, we find it in a physiological context when in *Nu.* 1276 Strepsiades says to the creditor τὸν ἐγκέφαλον ὥσπερ σεσεῖσθαί μοι δοκεῖς. In the Hippocratic corpus it is used with reference to bodily shocks, especially of the brain. But a good deal of circumspection is needed when the question of 'technical terms' is raised.[15] They constitute a category which can be divided into four species:

1 Words which have synonyms in ordinary language; for example, 'pyrexia' is a technical term, because one usually speaks of 'fever'.

2 Words which are used in technical language in a sense different from the sense they bear in ordinary language; e.g. 'knot' or 'bundle' in mathematics.

3 Words which have the same sense in technical and in ordinary language but are used more scrupulously and consistently in the former. For example, doctors do not speak of 'horrible' or 'frightful' pain, but of 'severe' pain. Thucydides, in his description of the Plague, uses the adjective ἰσχυρός repeatedly and accurately in just that sense.[16]

---

[13] See P. T. Stevens, *Colloquial Expressions in Euripides* (= *Hermes* Einzelschriften 38 [1976]).

[14] Cf. J. Wackernagel, *Kleine Schriften* (Göttingen 1953) 784f.

[15] The list of medical terms in H. W. Miller, *TAPA* lxxvi (1945) 74ff does not distinguish adequately between ordinary and technical language. The discussion by N. C. Collinge, *BICS* ix (1962) 43ff is a good deal more subtle.

[16] Cf. D. L. Page, *CQ* NS iii (1953) 102.

4 Words which do not appear in ordinary language at all, e.g. 'metatarsal' and 'metathesis'.

Now, in what sense could ἔσεισέ μου τὴν καρδίαν be 'technical'? Given that in ordinary language there does not seem to be any other way of saying what is expressed by those words, I see no reason to include the expression in the category of technical terms.

The interrogative form of 12 reminds us that we have to turn our eyes away sometimes from individual words and look at types of sentence present in the monologue. Dikaiopolis begins with an exclamation which gradually divests itself of its exclamatory character as the sentence proceeds towards its end. Then he poses a question, prefixing the phrase φέρ᾽ ἴδω, which is very common in comedy; and he answers his own question, ἐγᾦδ᾽ ἐφ᾽ ᾧ γε κτλ. Then again an exclamation, which turns into a narrative: ταῦθ᾽ ὡς ἐγανώθην, καὶ φιλῶ κτλ. After the narrative we find again a rhetorical question in 12 πῶς τοῦτ᾽ ἔσεισε κτλ. It is just this alternation of types of sentence which differentiates the language of comedy from tragic language, even from emotional monologues such as that with which *Medea* begins.

The opening words of 13,

$$\text{ἀλλ᾽ ἕτερον ἥσθην κτλ.}$$

each one of which occurs in every literary genre, draws our attention to the pattern of distribution of the individual phenomena taken together. How should Aristophanes' style be characterized in respect of monotony and variation? The sequence is:

1	(exclamation)	ὅσα δὴ δέδηγμαι . . .
2	(continuation)	ἥσθην δέ . . .
3	(continuation)	ἃ δ᾽ ὠδυνήθην . . .
4	(question)	τί δ᾽ ἥσθην . . .
5	(reply)	ἐγᾦδ᾽ . . .
7	(exclamation)	ὡς ἐγανώθην . . .
9	(assertion)	ἀλλ᾽ ὠδυνήθην . . .
		ὅτε δή . . .
13	(assertion)	ἀλλ᾽ ἕτερον ἥσθην . . .
		ἡνίκ᾽ . . .
15	(assertion)	ἀπέθανον . . .
		ὅτε δή . . .
17	(assertion)	ἀλλ᾽ . . . οὕτως ἐδήχθην . . .

Observe the repetitions of words and the degrees of variation: δέδηγμαι (1) ~ ἐδήχθην (18), ἥσθην (2) ~ ἥσθην (4) ~ ηὐφράνθην (5) ~ ἐγανώθην (7) ~ ἥσθην (13), ὠδυνήθην (3) ~ ὠδυνήθην (9) ~ ἀπέθανον καὶ διεστράφην (15); also, ἀλλ᾽ ὠδυνήθην ἕτερον (9) ~ ἀλλ᾽ ἕτερον ἥσθην (13), ὅτε δὴ 'κεχήνη (10)

~ ὅτε δὴ παρέκυψε (16). This aspect of style has tended to be overlooked altogether, and I cannot at the moment present complete lists and analyses as a basis for comparison between authors; but I suggest that one should always consider the style of Greek writers from the standpoint of (among other things) repetition of elements and the avoidance of repetition by means of lexical and syntactical variation. Some writers do not always seem aware of the tedium engendered by repetition; there are others, notably Gorgias, so fond of repetitive patterns that they seem to be trying to put the audience under a spell. Thucydides, and to a lesser degree Isocrates, try so strenuously for variety that the effort itself becomes a stylistic affectation which we notice as soon as we read them attentively. Aristophanes, in this monologue, seems to me comparable with Herodotus, who imposes just enough uniformity and symmetry on his narrative to give an impression of 'naturalness'; if he pushed that 'naturalness' further, he would give an impression of crudity, and if he did not care about it at all he would be in danger of artificiality.

The words ἀπέθανον καὶ διεστράφην (15), with which Dikaiopolis describes his reaction to Chaeris, have a colloquial character because they exaggerate the emotional condition to which they refer and reduce it to physical terms. Compare the English 'I died' in the senses 'I couldn't help laughing' or 'I was terribly embarrassed'; and with διεστράφην compare the common use of 'agony' and 'torture'.

Similarly, παρέκυψε (16) has a comic character because it replaces some such general terms as 'entered' or 'appeared' and is particular enough to evoke a visual image. ἐκεχήνη in 10 is related both to this phenomenon and to the physical exaggeration of 15. The verb is used to denote laughter, surprise, expectation or imbecility; it is comic *par excellence*, because it denotes not the emotional condition itself but one of its physical consequences. Compare English 'I sweated' in the sense 'I was very afraid' or 'I made a great effort'.

In 20 we meet the extended demonstrative αὐτηΐ,

$$ἔρημος ἡ Πνὺξ αὐτηΐ,$$

which recurs in 40,

$$ἀλλ' οἱ πρυτάνεις γὰρ οὑτοῒ μεσημβρινοί.$$

These demonstratives may be considered together with the adverb ἀτεχνῶς in 37,

$$νῦν οὖν ἀτεχνῶς ἥκω παρεσκευασμένος$$

because both are elements common to Aristophanes and prose; but they do not both have the same distribution. ἀτεχνῶς is virtually limited to Old Comedy and Plato. Aristophanes uses it sixteen times, and we find it also in Chionides (fr. 1), Pherecrates (fr. 102) and Eupolis (fr. 282). It is absent from

THE STYLE OF ARISTOPHANES 233

Menander and fourth-century comedy, except Philemon fr. 160.[17] The distribution of the extended demonstratives is in some way similar, because they too are absent from tragedy and the historians; but, unlike ἀτεχνῶς, they are generally avoided by Plato, while they continue to flourish in fourth-century comedy and in some speeches – very frequently in parts of the Demosthenic corpus, and in Lys. xiii, where there are more instances than in the rest of the Lysian corpus put together. How are these curious distributions to be explained? If both phenomena belong to the spoken language, why do the orators, who in general do not like informal language, in so many cases accept οὑτοσί while avoiding ἀτεχνῶς? A simple classification into 'spoken language', 'educated language', 'poetic language' does not suffice, and many subdivisions of the phenomena common to comedy and prose are required. It is as if there was a market of Attic linguistic goods in which each writer could shop according to his taste, remaining free never, or very rarely, to take some of its products. Inscriptions give us little help here, because their variety of subject-matter is limited.

There follow some interesting sentence-connections. In 23,

οὐδ᾽ οἱ πρυτάνεις ἥκουσιν

a positive member precedes the conjunction οὐδέ. As Denniston 190ff observes, in Attic prose οὐδέ and μηδέ connect one negative member to another, whereas in poetry and in Ionic prose they can connect positive to negative. The exceptions are Th. vii 77.1, Lys. xxiv 22, Pl. *Lach*. 198e and *Lg*. 889c, to which Professor D. M. MacDowell has added Gorgias *Palam*. 17 (τῷ δὲ τοιούτῳ βίῳ περὶ ⟨οὐσία⟩ κινδύνων τῶν μεγίστων, οὐδ᾽ ἔχει ἀσφάλειαν) and Alcidamas *Od*. 8 (δεῖ δέ με καὶ τὰ λοιπὰ διελθεῖν ὡς ἔχει μηδ᾽ ἀδίκως οὕτως ἄνδρα σύμμαχον περὶ θανάτου κρίνειν). There, it seems, is an element common to poetry and Ionic – or sophistic – prose.

The syntax of εἶτα δέ in 24 poses a complicated question:

ἀλλ᾽ ἀωρίαν
ἥκοντες εἶτα δ᾽ ὠστιοῦνται πῶς δοκεῖς.

The use of εἶτα, ἔπειτα, κᾆτα, κἄπειτα as conjunctions is conspicuous in comic narrative; in other literary genres they are apt to have a logical rather than a temporal character.[18] The use of κᾆτα and κἄπειτα between a participle and a finite verb on which the participle depends is almost peculiar to comedy, e.g. *Eq*. 391f ἀλλ᾽ ὅμως οὗτος τοιοῦτος ὢν ἅπαντα τὸν βίον κᾆτ᾽ ἀνὴρ ἔδοξεν εἶναι. It is not unknown in Plato: *Grg*. 457b ἐὰν δέ . . . ῥητορικός

---

[17] Compare the distribution of ἀνύσας with an imperative, which is found twenty-five times in Aristophanes but in later comedy is known so far only from Anaxilas fr. 37 and possibly Men. *Dysk*. 201 ναὶ πρὸς θεῶν ἀ[νύσας γ᾽] (cf. Webster).

[18] Cf. pp. 28–9 above.

γενόμενός τις κᾆτα . . . ἀδικῇ, *Phd.* 67e παρασκευάζονθ᾽ ἑαυτόν . . . κἄπειθ᾽
. . . ἀγανακτεῖν.[19] This usage of κᾆτα can thus fairly be assigned to colloquial
language. Yet εἶτα δέ, with apodotic δέ, is not the same thing; apodotic δέ
after a participle, as Denniston 181f notes, is normally associated with a
demonstrative or personal pronoun. The exceptions, in the Hippocratic
corpus and Attic prose, are few. The only example in tragedy is Eur. *Hypsipyle*
fr. 60.10ff [Bond] ὃν . . . πλὴν οὐ τεκοῦσα τἄλλα δ᾽ ὡς ἐμὸν τέκνον
ἔφερβον. In prose there are two examples, Th. vii 33.2 σχεδὸν γάρ τι ἤδη
πᾶσα ἡ Σικελία πλὴν ᾽Ακραγαντίνων (οὗτοι δ᾽ οὐδὲ μεθ᾽ ἑτέρων ἦσαν) οἱ δ᾽
ἄλλοι . . . ἐβοήθουν and a fifth-century inscription, *IG* i² 39.52 ff. τοὺς δὲ
ξένους . . . ὅσοι . . . μή . . ., τοὺς δ᾽ ἄλλους κτλ.[20]

The characteristic κᾆτα appears in 29,

κᾆτ᾽ ἐπειδὰν ὦ μονος,

and then the speech continues with a series of verbs in asyndeton,

στένω κέχηνα σκορδινῶμαι πέρδομαι
ἀπορῶ γράφω παρατίλλομαι λογίζομαι,

– one of which, πέρδομαι, is coarse and naturally does not occur in serious
literature. Asyndeta occur also in 35,

οὐκ ὄξος, οὐκ ἔλαιον,

and 38,

βοᾶν ὑποκρούειν λοιδορεῖν τοὺς ῥήτορας.

Naturally asyndeta can build up a great weight of rhetorical effect (e.g. the
way in which Thucydides describes the last battle in the harbour at Syracuse
[vii 71.4] or the encomium on Eros which Plato puts into the mouth of
Agathon [*Smp.* 197d]). In 34f

ὃς οὐδεπώποτ᾽ εἶπεν ᾽ἄνθρακας πρίω᾽,
οὐκ ὄξος, οὐκ ἔλαιον, οὐδ᾽ ᾔδει ᾽πρίω᾽

there is an echo of many tragic passages, e.g. Eur. *Hp.* 1341ff ὃς οὔτε πίστιν
οὔτε μαντείαν ὄπα ἔμεινας, οὐκ ἤλεγξας, οὐ χρόνῳ μακρῷ σκέψιν παρέσχες.
In general, though, asyndeton in Aristophanic comedy is used not to impart
force to an argument but to give us a vivid series of physical details. Compare

---

[19] In *Phd.* 98c, cited by Dodds on the *Gorgias* passage, καί could have a connective sense.
[20] Cf. p. 42 above.

especially, in 545ff, Dikaiopolis's description of the tumult which would have arisen at Athens if there had been a Spartan provocation.[21]

Finally, 41:

$$οὐκ ἠγόρευον; τοῦτ' ἐκεῖν' οὑγὼ 'λεγον.$$

Compounds of the verb ἀγορεύειν are used, as is well known, to furnish the imperfective aspect of verbs compounded with the aorist εἰπεῖν. The simple verb has a very restricted distribution. Common in epic, Herodotus and Euripides, it almost always refers in Attic prose to speaking in the assembly or to the prescriptions of the law. In Aristophanes, apart from the formula τίς ἀγορεύειν βούλεται; (Ach. 45, Th. 379, Ec. 130) and in another formula (Th. 306), it is found only six times, three of which are οὐκ ἠγόρευον; (apart from Ach. 41, in Pl. 102 and fr. 311 [PCG]). It is noteworthy that the same expression is used by Sophocles, OC 838 οὐκ ἠγόρευον ταῦτ' ἐγώ; – where Oedipus, like Dikaiopolis, manifests strong indignation.[22] It is possible that οὐκ ἠγόρευον; was a fixed phrase of the spoken language even though ἀγορεύειν in the sense λέγειν did not have unrestricted use. It would not be surprising if a rather old-fashioned word survived in a fixed expression at a time when its free use in a variety of circumstances had been forgotten. Compare English 'behold' in the expressions 'Lo and behold!' and 'a joy to behold'.

The second part of 41, τοῦτ' ἐκεῖν' οὑγὼ 'λεγον, recurs in Lys. 240. The combination of τοῦτο with ἐκεῖνο is found in seven other passages of Aristophanes. In two of them, Av. 354 and Ra. 1342, the verb 'be' is omitted – τοῦτ' ἐκεῖνο – while in Pax 516 (ἤδη 'στι τοῦτ' ἐκεῖνο, 'You've done it!') and Ra. 318 (τοῦτ' ἔστ' ἐκεῖν' ὦ δέσποτα) the sentence is complete; in the other instances ἐκεῖνο is only part of the predicate (Ach. 820, Pax 289, Av. 507). Ra. 1342 is of peculiar interest, because the passage is a parody of Euripidean lyrics, and since the emotional treatment of a domestic occurrence is intended to raise a laugh, it may well be that the juxtaposition of tragic language with a colloquial expression is equally meant to be humorous: ἰὼ πόντιε δαῖμον, τοῦτ' ἐκεῖν'· ἰὼ ξύνοικοι, τάδε τέρα θεάσασθε.[23] The justification for assigning τοῦτ' ἐκεῖνο to the colloquial language is to be found in Plato, who uses it at least six times (Phdr. 241d, 252c, Smp. 210e, 223a, Hi. Ma. 296d, Chrm. 166b), on one of those occasions with an obvious tone of familiarity: τοῦτ' ἐκεῖν' ὦ Φαῖδρε, 'Well, there we are, Phaedrus!' Compare Arist. Poet. 1448b 17: confronted by a good portrait of someone we know we exclaim οὗτος ἐκεῖνος. The expression is absent from Aeschylus, unless it has been correctly

---

[21] It would be rewarding to collect and classify comic asyndeta, to match the prose material given by Denniston, Greek Prose Style (Oxford 1952) 99ff.

[22] Jebb ad loc. notes that a poetic elaboration to give the same sense is preferred in OT 973 οὔκουν ἐγώ σοι ταῦτα προύλεγον πάλαι; On the question of colloquial language in Sophocles see P. T. Stevens, CQ xxxix (1945) 95ff.

[23] Rau, however (134), does not agree that the expression is colloquial.

restored in fr. 180 Nauck = 486 Mette. Sophocles uses it twice (*El.* 115, 1178), and Euripides six times (he uses πῶς δοκεῖς too). The most noteworthy of the Euripidean examples is *Or.* 804 τοῦτ' ἐκεῖνο, 'κτᾶσθ' ἑταίρους, μὴ τὸ συγγενὲς μόνον', i.e. τὸ λεγόμενον ἐκεῖνο ἀληθὲς ὂν φαίνεται κτλ.

I have tried to show, first, that to arrive at a just assessment of the style of Aristophanes it is important not to confine oneself to a purely lexical list; important to take account of distributions of choices upon which the hearer's impression of variety or monotony depends. Secondly, even within the limits of a lexical list it is advisable to adopt a system of classification which attaches some importance to the language of inscriptions as well as to literature. It must be remembered that the Attic dialect changed all the time; that our knowledge of the spoken language of the fifth century is necessarily indirect and restricted; and that the comic poet shared with the tragic poet, the orator, the secretary and the craftsman a readiness to enrich the Greek language by the construction of new words.

ADDITIONAL NOTE

I have revised the original footnotes in order to avoid too much overlap with matters discussed in items 2 and 3 of this collection and have updated, where appropriate, the references to corpora of fragments.

25

Language and Character in Aristophanes

In comic plays and novels we sometimes encounter people whose language is so distinctive that we can recall every one of its characteristics and attribute a passage correctly to this or that person even when the context has been forgotten or gives us no help. Two examples which occur to me – and two are enough – are Mrs Malaprop in Sheridan's *The Rivals* or Mr Jingle in Dickens' *The Pickwick Papers*. I daresay we all commit malapropisms from time to time; and, although I have never met anyone who speaks Jinglese, I can at least say that not everyone is equally remote from it. Characters of this kind are intended by their creators to exhibit in a concentrated and exaggerated form linguistic phenomena which in dilute form are widespread; as a rule, each character is distinguished by one such phenomenon. The language belongs to the character in the sense that it must be coherent with the thought, feelings and acts of that character. In respect of coherence, there can be a certain latitude, but, since we do not expect a fictitious character to be a package of discrete traits arbitrarily selected, it is reasonable to regard his or her language as part of the personality communicated to us, just as in ordinary life, if we do not know the temperament and predilections of a friend well enough, we make good the deficiency by attending to the language which the friend uses.

A passage cited from Aristophanes' first play, *Banqueters*, presents us (fr. 205 [*PCG*]) with a dialogue in which one of the two participants speaks a very distinctive language, on which the other comments 'That's from Lysistratus' or 'You've got that from Alcibiades' and so on. We know that in this play Aristophanes portrayed an old man who had two sons of different inclinations and different values. In another citation (fr. 233 [*PCG*]) it seems that the father puts a question to his 'immoral' son about the meaning of some Homeric words, which the son turns aside by asking if his 'good' brother understands legal terms contained in Solon's laws. Apparently Aristophanes contrasted in the play (as he was to do in *Clouds* a few years later) the traditional education in poetry and music with the new enthusiasm (like that shown by Pheidippides after his attendance at the school of Socrates) for the intellectual application of rhetorical technique. At that time, when a man (especially if he was young) could be criticized for too great an interest in litigation or too intimate a knowledge of the law, while at the same time Prodicus, Antiphon and other sophists were trying to 'rationalize' the complexities of the Greek vocabulary, draw distinctions between apparent synonyms, and construct new compound verbs and abstract nouns, the portrayal of an immoral young man contemptuous of tradition, more familiar with legal than with Homeric language and clever in using subtle terms created the possibility of making a perfect match between language and character and producing a stereotype easily identifiable within the limits of comic convention.

One striking feature of the passages from *Banqueters* is that the author does not allow us to perceive for ourselves the kind of language used by the young man; he forces it upon us, because the humour turns upon the language itself; one can say that the language is the subject-matter of the passages. Compare a well-known passage of *Knights* (1375ff), in which Demos describes 'the young men in the scent-market' talking about a lawsuit in which Phaeax was acquitted; their comments consist of a series of invented words ending in -ικός. We do not find anywhere in Aristophanes a young man who simply appears on stage and talks like that; it seems that the poet prefers to make the distinctive language of a certain cultural or social category his explicit subject, serving as a target for ridicule from which we should not be distracted by any concomitant action. Suppose, for example, that *Clouds* had been lost and we possessed only the passages in which Socrates tells Strepsiades to use the term ἀλεκτρύαινα for the female fowl (665f) and to replace κάρδοπος by καρδόπη (677f). We might assume that throughout the play the language of Socrates was consistently characterised by fascinating innovations as a satire on sophistic experimentation. But that would be mistaken, as we can see from the text we have. We have to reckon with an Aristophanic principle of 'one thing at a time', an alternation between the humour of language and the humour of content.

There was a time between the wars when writers of farces for the London stage felt obliged to make room in their *dramatis personae* for a Cockney maid, a Scottish nurse, a Welsh chamber-maid, an Irish cook, an American cousin, a European guest (from what country exactly, did not matter), and (supplementary humour when there was a change of scene from the normal urban ambience to the country) some simple-minded countryfolk whose dialect gave a vague impression of the south-west of England. Given the existence of stereotypes of deviation from the norm in character, over and above linguistic deviation, by the standards of those members of the middle class who lived within fifty miles of London and made up a large part of the audiences in the theatre, there was a certain correlation between language and character in those farces of the twenties and thirties. If the possibility of exploiting it had been denied to the authors, their incompetence in genuine characterization would have been apparent even more quickly than it was. Aristophanes' treatment of cultural deviations on the part of foreigners who could not speak Greek or Greeks who could not speak Attic provides us with a starting-point for investigation of his treatment of those singularities or deviations which could be reflected in language within the Attic community. Old Comedy made good use of the mistakes committed by foreigners; one thinks of the Persian in *Acharnians*, the Thracian god in *Birds* and the Scythian policeman in *Thesmophoriazusae*. In the category of Greeks who do not speak Attic the conspicuous examples are the Megarian and the Theban in *Acharnians*, Lampito and the Spartans in *Lysistrata*, someone who is evidently a Spartan character in Epilycus fr. 3, and what seems to be a constant comic stereotype, from Crates fr. 46 (*PCG*) to Menander's *Aspis*, the Doric-speaking doctor.

The scenes which contain these characters can be divided into two classes; in the first the language is the point of the joke, and in the second it seems to function only as a naturalistic element. When the King's Eye utters the first of his two lines in *Ach*. 100, it is important that he should not seem to be saying what the Athenian envoy has promised, so that Dikaiopolis, asked whether he understands, can reply 'Me? By Apollo, no!' The second line of the King's Eye is rightly interpreted by Dikaiopolis as an insolent refusal, but the Athenian envoy denies that Dikaiopolis has got it right, and offers, on the strength of one syllable, a forced and unconvincing interpretation. Similarly in *Birds* the verdict (1678f) of the Thracian god on the negotiations, rejected by Poseidon as 'the chattering of swallows' – an imprudent image, from which Pisetaerus, as commander of the birds, newly furnished with wings, gains a decisive advantage – is the climactic point of the scene, giving victory to Pisetaerus. By contrast, the sequence in which the Scythian policeman of *Thesmophoriazusae* is a participant could be performed to good effect even if the policeman spoke Greek as good as that of Euripides and the Old Man. His inability to pronounce the name 'Artemisia' without distorting it and his confusion over 'Gorgon's head', are, so to speak, a humorous bonus; nothing in the scene depends for its comic effect on the failure of the other characters to understand him. I would not go so far as to say that the audience was not amused by the clever combination of good iambic trimeters with entirely barbarized morphology; but the humorous potential of the scene is, from our point of view, under-developed. Aristophanes presumably made the Scythian policeman speak the kind of fractured Greek which in all probability Scythian policemen did speak.

In *Acharnians* there is no problem of communication between Dikaiopolis and his visitors from Megara and Thebes, nor is there any problem of that kind between Athenians and Spartans in *Lysistrata*. None of the characters notices non-Attic usage; all respond to the content of the utterances as if it had been correct Attic. Yet, so far as the evidence goes, the dialects seem to be authentic; 'so far . . .' is a significant reservation, because we know nothing from other sources about the Megarian dialect in the time of Aristophanes (we cannot simply use the evidence of fifth-century inscriptions from Selinus without more ado) and very little about the dialect of Thebes at that time.[1] But

---

[1] Regional and genealogical affinities are constantly interlaced, a fact which we accept without demur in the case of documentary inscriptions; consider, for example, the non-Doric definite

at least in the case of the Spartans Aristophanes uses a certain number of non-Attic words, some of which are attested as Doric in other sources (e.g. μνσίδδην = μυθίζειν 'speak', 'say', in *Lys*. 94, 981, 1076 and also in Theocr. 10.58); Laconian dialect did in fact preserve a vocabulary of its own for a long time. It is noteworthy that the adjective ἄφατος in the sense 'extraordinary', 'marvellous' is used three times by Spartans in the play (198, 1080, 1148), on two of those occasions in the expression ἄφατον (*sc*. ἐστιν) ὡς ..., which could be an authentic laconism of the fifth century; but we have to notice also that every playwright has a tendency to use a rare word or expression two or three times in one play and not elsewhere. Aristophanes provides just such an example in *Birds*, where διαμηρίζειν, an obscene verb derived from μηροί 'thighs', occurs three times (669, 706, 1254) but does not appear anywhere else in Aristophanes, despite the conspicuous importance on Old Comedy of the activity which it denotes.[2] Since we find ἄφατον ὡς φρόνιμος 'he's incredibly intelligent' in *Birds* (427), the last extant comedy before *Lysistrata*, and not elsewhere in Aristophanes, it may be that we need plenty of caution in identifying genuine Spartan elements in *Lysistrata*. However that may be, the humorous potential of dialogue between characters speaking quite different dialects does seem to be underdeveloped. Probably Aristophanes simply made Megarians, Thebans and Spartans speak in ways which the audience recognized as genuine because if he had made them speak Attic that would have struck a wrong note with the audience. The tragic poets evidently felt differently. Orestes in *Choephori* says that when he arrives at the palace, concealing his identity, he will speak like a Phocian; but, at any rate in the text we have, there is no trace of recognizable Phocian dialect to be found in his speech to Clytemestra at the door. That is not surprising, in a dramatic genre where legendary heroes of remote times, coming from many different parts of the Greek world, were brought on stage, together with Persians, Lydians and even gods (did they speak Attic on Olympus?). Not even the Phrygian slave of Euripides' *Orestes*, although the poet comes close to self-parody in the portrayal of his unrestrained emotion, is allowed to use incorrect language in his monody; it was left to Timotheus to employ distortions of dubious taste in his lyric narrative of the battle of Salamis.

We have one curious passage of Old Comedy, Strattis fr. 47, in which someone is making laboured fun of the Theban dialect. It comes from a play called *Phoenissae*, which transposed into a comic key the subject of Euripides' tragedy of that name. Strattis plainly distanced himself from the linguistic conventions of tragedy, because in the passage cited someone is complaining in Attic about the strangeness of Theban phonology and vocabulary; they say, for example, τῦκα for σῦκα 'figs', and κριδδέμεν for γελᾶν 'laugh'. If the

---

article in Crete and the submergence of Doric under Ionic at Halicarnassus. On Megarian cf. pp. 297–300 below.

[2] The words ἀπόδος τὸ διαμήριον, painted on an Attic black-figure vase (Beazley, *ABV* [Oxford 1956] 664), demonstrate the antiquity of the compound δι-μηρ-.

quoted words had obscene or absurd associations in Attic, the passage could have been uttered with striking effect by a good comic actor; otherwise its humour is as puerile as that of a speech put into the mouth of an English visitor to Scotland complaining that the Scots say 'brig' for 'bridge' and call children 'bairns', and so on. It so happens that one of the Theban words, σάκτας in the sense 'doctor', means 'sack' in *Pl.* 681 and is recorded by Photius in an obscene sense; another, ὀπισθοτίλη 'cuttlefish', has a vulgarity (in the element -τιλ-) absent from its Attic equivalent, σηπία. I do not know whether we are justified in thinking that all the items in Strattis's list, without exception, are full of implications which escape us because of our ignorance of vulgar Attic, but it is certain that the comic effect of the speech is increased if a series of two or three 'innocent' words leads up to an obscenity, thus keeping the audience in pleasurable suspense. We do not seem to find in Aristophanes any joke of which the point is (as in Strattis) the use of dialect. Even in *Pax* 929ff, where it looks at first sight as if Ionians are being ridiculed for the exclamation ὀΐ, further scrutiny shows that the Ionic word is introduced simply to make the discussion of the sacrifice of a sheep (ὀΐς) comic.

So far I have been concentrating on one important characteristic of Aristophanes' use of linguistic deviation, the principle of 'one thing at a time', in accordance with which we are invited either to turn our undivided attention to the deviation itself or to accept it as background, to which it contributes an element of authenticity, but not to turn our attention to two different levels of humour operating simultaneously. We have to keep this characteristic in mind when we look at the more important problem of deviations attributable to cultural or social status or to peculiarities of personality.

So far as status is concerned, three contrasts suggest themselves *a priori*: between free people and slaves, between the educated and the uneducated, and between city-dwellers and countryfolk.

Those of us who learned Greek the hard way (and there are no easy ways) are reluctant to believe that the Xanthias or Sosias of an ordinary Athenian household always deserved a pure alpha for mastery of Attic syntax and idiom. But there are a lot of things we do not know about Athenian slaves, including the percentage born in slavery and growing up in houses where they heard nothing but good Attic all day. Obviously a household slave was in a much better position to acquire the authentic dialect of his owners than a Scythian archer living in barracks with other Scythians and speaking his own language most of the time or a Lydian working in a team of miners and needing only enough Greek to understand the overseer's orders. If we want to find out how far, if at all, Aristophanes makes slaves utter malapropisms, solecisms or any other distinctive feature of language, we need to look in the first instance at the conversation 'below stairs' of Xanthias and the slave of Pluto in *Ra.* 738ff. We could also take into consideration the dialogues between Xanthias and his master Dionysus in the expectation that there we might find the maximum contrast between vulgar style and high style.

It is unlikely that in respect of linguistic accomplishment a wholly uneducated citizen doing a very humble job could easily be distinguished from a household slave. We make the acquaintance of precisely such a citizen in *Knights*; the Sausage-seller confesses (188f) 'I've no education (οὐδὲ μουσικὴν ἐπίσταμαι) except the alphabet, and I don't even know that well (καὶ ταῦτα μέντοι κακὰ κακῶς).' The central theme of the play, until we come to the magical transformations of the final scene, is the displacement of Cleon by a man of a fibre even rougher than his, vulgarity in person.

As for country and city, a certain expectation of significant difference in language is created by the fact that Aristophanes is apt to emphasize the special virtues of the farmer, and in *Clouds* by the isolation of the countryman from fashion and innovation. Strepsiades at the school of Socrates excuses his untimely knocking on the door by saying (138), 'Forgive me; I live a long way off in the country'. He has already told us in the first scene (41–55) of a cultural disparity between himself and his wife, who was brought up in the city; and it appears from his quarrel with Pheidippides towards the end of the play that Euripides is little more than a name to him, so that before hearing the horrifying recitation by Pheidippides he has no idea of the central theme of Euripides' *Aeolus* (1369–78). We might therefore expect to find in the passages of dialogue between Strepsiades and Socrates, who is expert in so many things, a contrast like that between Squire Western and Mr Supple the curate in book iv chapter 10 of *Tom Jones*.

Sextus Empiricus cites from Aristophanes (fr. 706 [*PCG*]) a passage in which someone is described as having a διάλεκτος ('style' or 'way of speaking' rather than 'dialect') 'which is the ordinary style of the citizen' (μέση πόλεως 'midway in the community') 'neither too effeminate and elegant' (οὔτ' ἀστείαν ὑποθηλοτέραν) 'nor vulgar and gross' (οὔτ' ἀνελεύθερον ὑπαγροικοτέραν). Sextus deduces from this that in Aristophanes' time the Greek of the city differed from that of the country. Taillardat[3] emphasizes that by the fifth century ἀστεῖος and ἀγροῖκος were both freely used in figurative senses, respectively for 'smart', 'witty', 'elegant' and for 'thick-headed', 'coarse', 'vulgar', without reference to the place of origin of the person so characterized. It may be, given the small size of Attica and the readiness with which people went to and fro between the city and the rural demes, that there was no linguistic difference between one locality and another except the differences of intonation and quality of voice which differentiate the localities of an English or Scottish county. All the same, Theophrastus, a century after Aristophanes, treats ἀγροικία (*Char.* 4) not simply as coarseness but as the specific coarseness of the countryman. Considering the rapid succession of linguistic, literary and cultural innovations which characterized the last decades of the fifth century, it is not easy to believe that men like Strepsiades and Dikaiopolis, who spent so much of their time in their rural demes, kept abreast of that rapid innovation; we would therefore expect that the language of the ἀγροῖκος was marked not only by the absence of words and expressions

---

[3] *Les Images d'Aristophane* (Paris 1965) 12–14.

which had become fashionable in the city but even more by the persistence of archaic words which city usage had discarded. It can be shown that some words, common property of Ionic and Attic in the first part of the fifth century, fell into disuse during the period 450–350 (διαβάλλεσθαι in the sense 'deceive' is a case in point),[4] and that is the category of words we would expect to find Aristophanes putting into the mouth of a countryman.

Looking at the chat between Xanthias and the slave of Pluto, we notice at once that they are speaking very self-consciously as slaves, about their ways of getting their own back on their masters. Yet there seems to be no trace of solecism or malapropism in their language. Even the expression μᾶλλα πλεῖν ἢ μαίνομαι 'I'm absolutely crazy about it' (Ra. 751) echoes Dionysus, who uses exactly the same expression in another passage (103) to describe his enthusiasm for memorable lines of Euripides. Equally, ὡς οὐδὲν οἶδ' ἐγώ (749), literally 'as I know nothing', i.e. 'more than anything else I know', can be compared with οὐδὲν γὰρ οἷον 'there's nothing like it' in Lys. 135. Pluto's slave adopts, to denote the extreme pleasure which he derives for giving away his master's secrets, the vulgar expression ἐκμιαίνομαι (753), which means a spontaneous ejaculation of semen. Compare the extravagant terms in which Dikaiopolis, delivering his soliloquy, converts emotional into physical conditions: 'I died, my limbs were dislocated' (Ach. 15), or V. 1469, where the chorus says 'I was poured out', apparently in the sense 'I was transported with joy'; but ἐκμιαίνομαι differs in being unambiguously obscene. Linguistic obscenity is easily identified in Greek literature, perhaps more easily than in many other literatures, because so many anatomical and physiological terms, whether refined or slang, are entirely confined to comedy and to some types – vituperative or strenuously obscene – of archiac iambic poetry; in all other literary genres, including technical works on medicine, they are replaced by euphemisms, although what they denote is made plain enough. It does not happen that some characters in an Aristophanic play use obscene language while others abstain from it. Pluto's slave in that scene of Frogs is treated by the poet as a vehicle for what I call 'climactic obscenity'[5] – that is, the insertion of an obscenity as the second of a pair of elements or the last of a more extended series, after which the joke to which the passage has led up to is discarded and a new starting-point is taken. An example of this technique is to be found in the conversation between Euripides and his relation in the opening scene of Thesmophoriazusae. The old man has never heard of Agathon, and after he has tried to recall various men of that name Euripides speaks a line insinuating (in gross terms) that Agathon as a boy played the prostitute in the dark. This must have raised a laugh in the theatre, and, when that has subsided, Euripides makes a fresh start, 'But let's go to one side; one of his slaves is coming out.' Up to that point Euripides has been contrasted with the old man as a sophisticated intellectual talking to a slow-witted

---

[4] Cf. pp. 24, 226 above.
[5] E.g. Av. 127–43, and cf. my Aristophanic Comedy (London 1972) 38–43.

philistine, and from that point of view the obscenity is incongruous. Aristophanes simply wants at this moment to use the technique of the climactic obscenity, and for that purpose he makes use of the character who is available, without regard for the relation between the character and his language.

Neither the Sausage-seller nor the Paphlagonian, so far as our knowledge of Greek will take us, seems to be guilty of solecism or malapropism. Nevertheless, some citations from lost plays show that the comic poets were not at all averse to exploiting solecism for humorous purposes. According to a scholion on *Ra*. 681 Plato Comicus, in his *Cleophon*, portrayed Cleophon's mother as 'speaking like a foreigner' (βαρβαρίζουσα). Rather than supposing (on the doubtful principle 'where there's smoke, there's fire') that Plato was telling the simple truth and not defaming the old lady, we have to remember that the inadequacy of documentation at Athens, combined with the ease of bribing witnesses, encouraged those who wanted to insult an adversary to allege that he was not of Attic stock or even of Greek birth, but had been illegally enrolled in deme and phratry. The list of those Athenians against whom the comic stage makes this accusation is quite long. The citizenship law of the 450s, which prescribed that a citizen must have not only an Attic father but also an Attic mother, increased the temptation to arouse suspicion of the affinities of an adversary's mother in cases where it might be impossible to question the status of his father. It is a pity that students of Aristophanic comedy do not pay more attention to the fourth-century orators, because the techniques of slander and ridicule, used, for example, by Demosthenes and Aeschines against one another, illustrate the techniques used for the same purpose by Old Comedy.[6] Aeschines declares that Demosthenes' mother came from 'the nomad Scythians', on the strength of which he calls Demosthenes himself a Scythian. Demosthenes' father, wealthy owner of a workshop, is ridiculed as μαχαιροποιός 'knife-maker', which reminds us of Hyperbolus the 'lamp-seller', Cleon the 'tanner' and Cleophon the 'lyre-maker'. The representation of Cleophon's mother as speaking foreigner's Greek was probably a way of validating the hostile imputation, which could be wholly unfounded, that Cleophon was not the son of an Attic mother. Aristophanes in *Ra*. 679f goes further in calling Cleophon himself 'a Thracian swallow perched on a barbarous twig'. Since it is now known that Cleophon was the son of the Cleippides who was *strategos* in 428, it is reasonable to think that, however outrageous his conduct in the assembly may have seemed to those who did not share his political opinions, he belonged to a prominent Athenian family, and if his speech contained personal characteristics they were not to be attributed to foreign influence or lack of education.

Plato Comicus also wrote a comedy called *Hyperbolus*, in which there was a passage (fr. 168) referring to a speech made by Hyperbolus himself. It makes

---

[6] In *Greek Popular Morality* (Oxford 1975) 22–33 I have gone into more detail about the relations between oratory and comedy.

out that he pronounced ὀλίγος as ὀλίος (olíyos?), γίννος as ἵννος (jinnos?) and διητώμην as a trisyllabic word (δητώμην in the text as cited by the *Etymologicum Magnum*, but djeitɔ:mɛ:n is not to be excluded). The disappearance of intervocalic gamma in ὀλίγος and its compounds is attested in documents not long before the middle of the fourth century, and is not uncommon.[7] The conversion of δι- into a complex consonantal sound is suspected in some passages of classical poetry.[8] If Hyperbolus exhibited in his own speech phonological features which became widely disseminated in the classical world, this can be explained as idiosyncrasy rather than as an indication of cultural level. Once again it is a matter not of a character whose qualities are revealed by his language in the course of the action, but of a descriptive passage focused upon language. By his emphasis on these linguistic features the comic poet chose a concrete way of expressing doubts about Hyperbolus's origins. Numerous citations of single words from the comic poets contain some oddities, e.g. ἄσκη for ἄσκησις (Pl. Com. fr. 234) and ᾆσμός for ᾆσμα (id. fr. 235), and the chances are that these come from passages like the passage about Hyperbolus; on the other hand, it may be that they are drawn from scenes in which foreigners are speaking,[9] or even that they represent a sample of the (many) Attic words otherwise not known to us.

Turning now to the contrast between the coarse countryman and the sophisticated city-dweller, and in particular to the dialogue between Strepsiades and Socrates: are there any obviously 'Strepsiadic' words in it? One plausible candidate is the verb τετραμαίνειν 'fear', which is used twice by Strepsiades (*Nu.* τετραμαίνω καὶ πεφόβημαι, 374 τουθ' ὅ με ποιεῖ τετραμαίνειν) but nowhere else by Aristophanes. It occurs in a fragment of Archilochus (*IEG* 23.9) relating a conversation (μὴ τετραμήνῃς μηδέν) and also in the Hippocratic corpus. For that reason it might be an ingredient of the common Ionic–Attic stock which was progressively reduced during the classical period; but it could be one of those words, like διαμηρίζειν in *Birds*, concentrated in one part only of an author's work. Moreover, it appears once more in Attic in a comic fragment of the fourth century, Xenarchus fr. 4 (τετραμαίνοντα καὶ φοβούμενον) – where, unfortunately, we do not know what kind of character utters it.

The Socratic student in conversation with Strepsiades uses big words which are not always intelligible to the old man, e.g. γεωμετρία and the mathematical term παρατείνειν, which Strepsiades takes in a colloquial sense.

Similarly, Socrates tells Strepsiades that the clouds provide intellectuals (or, as he puts it, 'men who do not work') with διάλεξις, περίλεξις, κρούσις and κατάληψις. But Strepsiades matches him, declaring himself inspired by the

[7] K. Meisterhans, *Grammatik der attischen Inschriften*, 3rd edn (Berlin 1900) 75; E. H. Sturtevant, *The Pronunciation of Greek and Latin*, 2nd edn (Philadelphia 1940) 87; Schwyzer, *Gr. Gr.* i 209.

[8] P. Maas, *Greek Metre* (Oxford 1962) 73; A. M. Dale, *The Lyric Metres of Greek Drama*, 2nd edn (Cambridge 1968) 25f n. 2; cf. H. D. Broadhead's commentary on Aeschylus's *Persians* (Cambridge 1960) 281f.

[9] In that case, though, the words would not have interested Pollux, who cites them.

sound of the clouds' song and ready to λεπτολογεῖν, στενολεσχεῖν and ἀντιλογῆσαι. Again, told by Socrates of the poets who are 'nourished' by the clouds, Strepsiades crowns that by a joke in which the vocabulary, morphology and style of dithyrambic poetry are parodied (335ff).

The same principle seems to apply to parody, the creation of words, and obscenity: the joke is uttered by whoever is available, for its own sake, at the moment of Aristophanes' choice, without taking any account of its consistency with the character's cultural or intellectual level. A good example is Strepsiades' reaction to the student's account of the noise which, according to the Socratics, the mosquito produces by expelling air through its bowels. 'I congratulate you', he says, 'on the διεντέρευμα' (166). This is an unusual type of word; no other word in Aristophanes is compounded with δια- and -μα except διανεύματα (*Th.* 124, in the parody of Agathon's lyrics),[10] and it is a formation rare before the last part of the fourth century. Strepsiades is not playing on words, because there is no verb διεντερεύειν, and the simple verb ἐντερεύειν denotes the gutting of fish, which is no help in this context. Strepsiades' διεντέρευμα in fact means that which happens διὰ τοῦ ἐντέρου; Aristophanes is making a literary verbal joke, and the joke is his rather than Strepsiades'.

This intermittent discrepancy between character and language is nowhere more apparent than in parody. Consider, for example, the big speech of the Sausage-seller in *Knights* when he returns from his triumph over Cleon in the council (624ff). This speech fulfils the same function in the comedy as a messenger-speech in tragedy, but its narrative structure, particularly its use of εἶτα or ἔπειτα, is distinctively comic.[11] Let us look at two verses from its opening section (626f):

> ὁ δ' ἄρ' ἔνδον ἐλασίβροντ' ἀναρρηγνὺς ἔπη
> τερατευόμενος ἤρειδε κατὰ τῶν ἱππέων.

'Then he, in the council-chamber, bursting out into words like thunder, charged against the cavalry in monstrous terms.' Two successive verses which both begin with ∪ ∪ — remind us that this is comedy; but the imagery in ἐλασίβροντ' ἀναρρηγνὺς ἔπη is remote from comic vulgarity. The words are parodic, reminding us of passages of Pindar (frr. 144, 180).[12] Later the Sausage-seller says (646) that 'the faces of the councillors cleared up'; διαγαληνίζειν 'clear up' is a *hapax*, and the image (of good weather) is hardly in accord with the cultural level of the man who said at the start that he had 'no education'.

[10] Bentley conjectured δινεύματα, which may be right; but Luc. *Salt.* 64 is relevant, and cf. Wilamowitz, *Griechische Verskunst* (repr. Darmstadt 1958) 341 n. 1.

[11] Cf. pp. 28–9 above. M. Landfester, *Die 'Ritter' des Aristophanes* (Amsterdam 1967) 45 n. 130 does not take sufficient account of the narrative technique.

[12] P. Rau, *Paratragodia* (Munich 1967) considers only the comic parody of tragedy, not of other genres of serious poetry.

The first scene of *Thesmophoriazusae* is heavily laden with parody (in fact, in Agathon's lyrics and his slave's we encounter one of the most intractable of literary problems, a parody of a completely unknown original). Before the sight of the effeminate Agathon in women's clothes, the old relation of Euripides puts to him questions closely modelled on the interrogation of Dionysus by Lycurgus in Aeschylus's *Edonians* (the opening play of the *Lycurgeia*). He tells us in advance that that is what he is doing: 'I'll put questions to you from the *Lycurgeia* of Aeschylus' (134f); it is as if in a modern comedy a rough countryman began a soliloquy with an explicit reference to *Hamlet* and went on to recite two or three verses of Hamlet's famous soliloquy. Aristophanes parodies serious poetry for more than one reason: sometimes to draw our attention to the poetry itself, asking in effect, 'Isn't it like that? And do you like that pretentious stuff?', sometimes to achieve the humour of incongruity – when elevated language is used in a situation of domestic life or superimposed on a gross obscenity – and sometimes when the content of a few well-known verses exactly suits the situation which has arisen from the comic plot. Whatever its occasion, parody remains the author's, and the character who utters it is his mouthpiece.

At first sight another aspect of the opening scene of *Thesmophoriazusae* appears to contradict that generalization. Agathon, entreated by Euripides and at the same time ridiculed by the old man, expresses himself almost entirely in tragic language and, which gives his lines their most distinctive character, in tragic rhythm, because very few of the trimeters he utters contain more than twelve syllables. One part of what he says can refer to the plays of the real Agathon (of whose work we have only a very few citations), particularly the distich in which he declares sententiously that it is right to endure misfortune without seeking to evade it:

> τὰς συμφορὰς γὰρ οὐχὶ τοῖς τεχνάσμασιν
> φέρειν δίκαιον ἀλλὰ τοῖς παθήμασιν.

Euripides can quote poetry too; in 177f he makes use of a distich from his *Aeolus* to say 'I will be brief', and at the beginning of the play, before the appearance of Agathon's slave, he makes a show of his erudition to the old man, uttering verses whose tragic style and rhythm are obvious. Yet in the three-cornered dialogue with Agathon and the old man, where he is no longer speaking *ex cathedra* but essentially as a suppliant, his style and rhythm conform to the norms of comic dialogue. The role of Agathon in *Thesmophoriazusae* is strikingly similar to that of Euripides in *Acharnians*, where Dikaiopolis comes to beg for rags. Both poets are brought on stage on the movable trolley,[13] and go back indoors on it; both respond to requests in solemn rhythm and tragic style; in both cases this tragic style is contrasted with the comic style of the character who is putting the requests to them. The

---

[13] I avoid the term *ekkyklema*, which is used in scholia of an event, not an object: ἐκκύκλημα γίνεται.

difference is that in *Thesmophoriazusae* Euripides is the asker, while in *Acharnians* he is the giver. In other words, the person we hear in each of these scenes is not a poet who speaks like a poet in order to remain true to character, but a poet who speaks as a poet only so long as he stands in a certain relationship to the other participant(s) in the scene. The language of a character in such circumstances is a function not of his personality, interests or cultural level, but of the relationship in which he is involved at the moment.[14]

All aspects of the question which we have been examining converge on the same conclusion, that in providing a character with language Aristophanes creates a compromise between convention and naturalism, neither rejecting dramatic illusion[15] altogether nor adhering to it altogether. That is much as we would have expected, because Old Comedy differs strikingly from tragedy in its attitude to dramatic illusion, both at a superficial and at a deeper level. The superficial difference appears in the fact that comic characters are accustomed to make reference to the theatre or the audience, which is absolutely excluded in tragedy.[16] The deeper difference lies in consistency and inconsistency of character. The extent to which the Greek tragic poets attached importance to consistency of character is a highly controversial question, and I am not among those who think that Tycho von Wilamowitz said the last word on it.[17] In one important respect it seems to me that tragedy attaches far more importance than comedy to consistency of character; a comic utterance can, so to speak, 'float free', attached to the preceding context but detached from what follows, in so far as it does not elicit from the other characters present the reactions which would be expected in real life. When such a joke has a purely lexical basis, the consequence of the technique is that the poet uses a dramatic character as someone possessed of the same literary perceptiveness as the poet himself. That is why Aristophanes abstains from giving each of his characters a distinctive language which would be differentiated consistently from the ordinary level of dialogue, the verbal jokes and parodies which the actors have to utter. Naturally this does not mean that Aristophanes did not create memorable persons – Philocleon alone would suffice to rebut that charge – but only that their characters develop essentially through what they say without any help from the way in which they say it.

---

[14] I do not agree with P. Händel, *Formen und Darstellungsweisen in der aristophanischen Komödie* (Heidelberg 1963), to whom (313) consistency of character seems praiseworthy in all kinds of play; to me, inconsistency seems indispensable in certain genres. Menander's technique is quite different; and on the linguistic individuality of characters in Menander see D. Del Corno, *Stud. Class. Or.* xxiv (1975) 13–48.

[15] G. M. Sifakis, *Parabasis and Animal Choruses* (London 1971) 7, denies the utility of the terms 'illusion' and 'rupture of illusion' in discussion of Greek drama; but, if an actor (e.g. Hermon) speaks *as if he were* Strepsiades, that is what I call dramatic illusion, and, if he says anything to remind us that he is an actor and not Strepsiades, that is rupture of dramatic illusion.

[16] Cf. D. M. Bain, *CQ* NS xxv (1975) 13–25.

[17] Hugh Lloyd-Jones has a good evaluation of Tycho von Wilamowitz's contribution to the study of Greek tragedy in *CQ* NS xxii (1972) 214–28. On the relation between characterization and 'theatrical effect' cf. P. E. Easterling, *Greece and Rome* xx (1973) 1–19.

26

The Skene in Aristophanes

Note. In this paper the expressions 'on stage' and 'off stage' mean 'in sight of the audience' and 'out of sight of the audience'. They do not imply that the area immediately south-south-east of the orchestra was higher than the orchestra, or that it was not.

I

No one can write an adequate commentary on a Greek play, or even edit it adequately, without producing it in his mind; that is to say, he must see in his mind's eye the exact location, movement and gesture of every character at every moment, and must hear in his mind's ear the exact tone of every word. Admittedly, we do not know so very much about the appearance of the theatre in the fifth century BC, or about the actors' costumes, or about Greek gestures; even our knowledge of the pronunciation of Greek at the relevant period is imperfect; and our ignorance of delivery and acting styles is total. Therefore, when we produce a play in our imagination we can hardly fail to import much which would be recognized as grossly erroneous if our evidence were suddenly to be increased. Yet, as so often happens in the study of the ancient world, we are confronted with a choice of risks. We can take the risk of an imaginative reconstruction which may be factually wrong but is at least reconcilable with all the evidence we have and is kept reconcilable, by modification, with whatever fresh evidence comes to light from time to time; or, alternatively, we can take the risk of missing the point of what the dramatist is saying and therefore of importing the wrong point. Even if we are not temperamentally disposed (as I am) in favour of the former risk, we are virtually forced to take it when we have committed ourselves to editing a text. The punctuation of a dramatic text is a matter for producers, not grammarians; a comma gives one instructions to the actor, a colon gives a different instruction[1] – and few editors are likely to practise *ars nesciendi* so

---

[1] This would not be true in all written languages, but let us use gratefully the system of punctuation which we have inherited in English.

pertinaciously as to refrain from giving the actors any such instructions at all.

Now, as soon as the editor begins to visualize, he becomes aware that at one point the words of the text say or imply that it is dark and at another point say or imply that it is light. Since the dramatist cannot command the sun, it seems that the audience must imagine darkness when the action requires them to do so. But, if this demand can be made upon them, what limit can be set to other demands? When a character says that he is knocking at a door, and the text implies that another character comes on stage out of the door in answer to the knock, is there really anything in the theatre which represents a door, or must the audience imagine that too?

It will not do to say that the action of the play 'needs' a door, or several doors, for no play, whether Greek or any other, actual or imaginable, *needs* anything except human beings with voices and limbs.[2] Everything else can be mimed and imagined, as in charades. The question 'What does this play need?' is answerable only with reference to the standards and expectations of the audience before which it is performed. In attempting to formulate the expectations of an ancient Athenian audience we constantly incur the danger of circular argument. We can, I think, escape this danger; but not by the assumption that the Athenian attitude to theatrical representation and our own attitude necessarily have any common ground. It is roughly true to say that a given society continues to accept any theatrical convention, no matter how great the demand made on the imagination of the audience, until someone has devised technical means of lessening this demand. As we nowadays stage plays predominantly in closed buildings, which we can darken as we wish, we are no longer willing to be told that the action of the play is taking place in the dark when we can see that the stage is brightly lit (except, of course, as an occasional *jeu d'esprit* which would lose its point if often repeated); in films, on the other hand, we commonly accept a high degree of illumination in the photography of scenes which represent action in darkness, for we are aware that the technical problem involved is intractable.

II

The question 'What objects and buildings, if any, were available to the Attic dramatist in the fifth century BC?' is answerable in part from consideration of three types of data: (1) archaeology, (2) references in non-dramatic literature,[3] and (3) rupture of dramatic illusion in comedy.

---

[2] It might perhaps be denied by Samuel Beckett that limbs are indispensable.

[3] The word σκηνοποιός, cited by Pollux vii 189, is not relevant evidence, as it need not have a theatrical reference. Pollux says τοὺς δὲ μηχανοποιοὺς καὶ σκηνοποιοὺς ἡ παλαιὰ κωμῳδία ὠνόμαζεν, and continues (190) γελωτοποιὸς κτλ . . . Ἐκπωματοποιὸς δὲ δρᾶμα Ἀλέξιδος κτλ.

1   South-south-east of the orchestra are the stone foundations of a building running roughly east to west.[4] The archaeologists tell us (and I do not argue with them) that the material and construction point to a date in the fifth century. Opposite the centre of the orchestra the stone foundation projects in a platform $c.7$ m wide by 3 m deep. The foundations on either side of this projection are slotted at regular intervals. The projection can hardly be anything but the foundation of an exit from the building, and its position indicates that its use is closely connected with the use of the orchestra; if it were anything else, e.g. the foundation of a tower or a built-out room, a more inconvenient position for it could hardly be imagined. Nowhere on the foundations of the building is there any sign of any other exit.

2   (a) Xenophon (*Cyr.* vi 1.54) refers to 'timbers as thick as those of a τραγικὴ σκηνή'. It may be that a façade of wood was built out from the stone building at Athens, and that this is the explanation of the slots; it must be remembered, however, that when Xenophon was writing the theatre at Athens was not the only place in the Greek world at which tragedies were performed, and his reference may be inappropriate to Athens.

(b) Aristotle (*Poet.* 4.14) ascribes the invention of σκηνογραφία to Sophocles. Whatever the exact meaning of σκηνογραφία is, it would not be reckless to assert that it includes some kind of representational treatment of a building for the purposes of a play.[5] Whether or not Aristotle was right in ascribing the invention of this treatment to Sophocles, at least we can infer from the fact of the ascription that representational treatment was in Aristotle's time old enough for him to regard it as belonging to the period before πολλάς μεταβολὰς μεταβαλοῦσα ἡ τραγῳδία ἐπαύσατο, ἐπεὶ ἔσχε τὴν αὑτῆς φύσιν. It is therefore reasonable to assume that the audience of Aristophanes' comedies was accustomed to representational treatment of buildings in tragedy.

This has an important implication. The treatment desired by the dramatist for one of his plays would not normally be the same as that desired by the dramatist whose plays were performed on the following day, nor would it necessarily be the same as that desired by the same dramatist for the following play of his own tetralogy. In other words, σκηνογραφία implies temporary sets. This has a further implication: if screens or panels with something painted *on* them could be set up and removed in a matter of minutes (as indeed they can), so could screens or panels with doorways *in* them.

I can see no reasonable grounds for resisting these implications. Certainly the cost is not a reasonable ground. Our primary evidence for the cost of

---

[4] Cf. W. B. Dinsmoor in *Studies Presented to David M. Robinson* (Saint Louis, Mo. 1951) 309ff.

[5] P. D. Arnott, *Greek Scenic Conventions in the Fifth Century BC* (Oxford 1962), examines, and seems rather to favour, the interpretation of σκηνογραφία as permanent decoration, no more relevant to one play than to another. But the context in which Aristotle speaks of it, and his attribution of its invention to a dramatic poet (not to a painter), make it very unlikely that he had anything of that kind in mind.

choregiai is Lys. xxi, where the speaker claims (1, 4) that a tragic choregia in 411/10 cost him 3000 drachmae and a comic choregia in 403/2 1600 drachmae. When we reflect that in the last part of the fifth century the sculptors who worked on the Erechtheum received a wage of one drachma for a day's work, and that in Ar. *Nu*. 854 Strepsiades speaks of buying a child's toy cart for one obol, it is obvious that the construction and erection of wooden screens or frameworks of wood and canvas would not appear to any choregos to threaten him with insolvency.

3 (a) The poet is said to εἰσάγειν a play or a phenomenon in a play, i.e. to 'bring it in' or, as we should say, 'put it on'. Thus in *Nu*. 546 Aristophanes says, 'I don't cheat you, the audience, εἰσάγων the same things twice or three times'; and in *Ra*. 959 'Euripides' speaks of himself as οἰκεῖα πράγματ' εἰσάγων. But also in *Frogs*, at 946, Euripides speaks of the character who appears first in a tragedy as οὐξιών; and similarly in *Pax* 744 Aristophanes, speaking of his rivals' alleged fondness for bringing beaten and weeping slaves on stage, says, οὓς ἐξῆγον κλάοντας ἀεί. Here ἐξιέναι and ἐξάγειν are used of characters coming on stage, and unless they came on stage out of a building this terminology is unintelligible.

(b) A closely related phenomenon is the use of the prefixes ἐξ and εἰς with verbs of motion in comedy where the situation which is being portrayed does not require them, e.g. *Nu*. 19: Strepsiades calls to his slave 'Bring *out* (ἔκφερε) my account-book'; *Lys*. 5: Lysistrata, impatiently awaiting the arrival of the other women, at last says 'here comes *out* (ἐξέρχεται) my κωμῆτις'; *Th*. 930: It is necessary (because of the allocation of parts) that the policeman shall go off stage for a short time, and the Prytanis tells him 'take the old man *in* (εἰσάγων) and put him in the screw-plank'; *Th*. 1007: The policeman needs a mat to lie on while he guards the old man. He says that he will bring one *out* (ʼξινίγκι). In none of these instances is 'in' or 'out' demanded by the imaginary situation; it is an accommodation of the characters' language to theatrical conditions, and would suffice in itself to prove movement into and out of a building in the theatre.

(c) At the beginning of the parabasis of *Peace* (729ff) the Chorus says, 'Let's hand over all this stuff' (*sc*. the tackle used in the rescue of the goddess) 'to our slaves for safe keeping, because there is nowhere where so many thieves creep around, up to no good, than περὶ τὰς σκηνάς.' The plural has surprised commentators; but surprise is a function of preconception, and if we approach the passage without preconceptions we see that three alternative meanings are possible:

(i) There was a complex of buildings adjoining the orchestra, and this complex was known in Aristophanes' time as αἱ σκηναί.
(ii) Wherever there was a theatre (e.g. at Peiraieus) there was a skene, and the Chorus is referring to theatres in general.
(iii) In addition to a permanent building adjoining the orchestra, there were

temporary buildings, i.e. sets for particular plays (cf. 2(b) above), and the Chorus is referring to these.

We should not let this passage of *Peace* go without a word on τοῖς ἀκολούθοις. When a comedy represents a man in a situation in which, if it belonged to real life, the man would have a slave with him, we may take it for granted that the character in the play also has a slave with him, and that the words of the text will refer to the slave's existence only if and when it is dramatically necessary or convenient. Are the ἀκόλουθοι of *Pax* 730 (i) people whom we are to imagine as the slaves of the Greek farmers whom the Chorus has represented, or (ii) slaves actually belonging to the singers and dancers who constitute the Chorus, or (iii) slaves borrowed from and by the choregos for the occasion? The rupture of dramatic illusion at the start of the parabasis suggests (ii) or (iii) rather than (i); but I suggest that in fact it does not matter, and that no one in the audience will ask himself the question. In a real Greek household, or in an outdoor activity, we should not in the least be distracted from conversation with a citizen by the comings and goings of his slaves, fetching and taking away whatever they had to; and we should not expect the Greek audience to be distracted from following the action and dialogue of a play by such familiar movements (for example, the removal of the beds between *Nu*. 90 and 125), or to ask itself 'Now, is that man meant to be a slave of Strepsiades, or is he a "scene-shifter"?'[6] I recall that in a Glyndebourne production of *The Magic Flute*, when it was necessary to be rid of the couch on which Pamina had been lying in Act II scene iii, two boys in eighteenth-century costume simply ran on and carried it away; and I would be surprised if anyone (unless he happened to be editing *Clouds* at the time) really wondered whether these boys were or were not members of Zarastro's ménage.

The question of 'scene-shifters' has a bearing on the skene, because the alternative is the trolley which we commonly (but perhaps inaccurately) designate ἐκκύκλημα.[7] I do not for a moment doubt that tragic poets made use of such a trolley – because they often had to reveal, in the course of a play, people who were dead, sick, unconscious, wounded, mad, brooding, fettered or otherwise immobilized. As this is not the case in comedy,[8] the trolley was naturally associated especially with tragedy, and that accounts for the wheeling-out of Euripides in *Acharnians* and of Agathon in *Thesmophoriazusae*.

[6] A. M. Dale, *JHS* lxxvii (1957) 206, believes that the audience would have to be improbably 'high-minded' not to be distracted by scene-shifters. This belief does not seem to me tenable with reference to any period before the invention of effective stage-curtains, and not necessary even thereafter; one would need to know, in respect of any given civilization, what audiences took for granted and what they did not.

[7] Scholiasts more often use the word as a verbal noun (e.g. ἐκκύκλημα γίνεται) than as the name of an object.

[8] The first scene of *Clouds* begins with one of two characters asleep, but that is not at all the same as revealing a sleeping character after exterior action.

As a means of revealing interior scenes in comedy, or as a means of bringing objects on stage and taking them off stage, there is little or nothing to be said for the tragic trolley; wherever the issue arises, we must ask, 'What is the easiest and the most natural way of doing this, and the way which best achieves comic effect?' If there is reason to believe that the comic effect desired is parody of tragedy, the trolley may well be the answer; but the 'limitations' of Greek theatre are a possible source of humour only if they are *unavoidable* limitations, and, in my submission, we have not as yet found any reason to believe that a uniform permanent background and a shortage of labour for the movement of objects fall in that category.[9]

(d) Heniochos fr. 5 appears to come from a prologue. The name of the play is not known. The speaker says (6ff): 'This place all round is Olympia; imagine that in seeing this skene you are looking at a θεωρικὴ σκηνή at Olympia.' We have little clue to the date of Heniochos. In the Suda he is classified as a poet of Middle Comedy. Whether by 'this skene' he means the whole of a permanent building or a temporary building, we do not know; the one important fact that emerges from the fragment is that at least in this comedy the skene referred to is not a generalized 'indoors' but a particular representation.

III

In certain plays of Aristophanes (*Acharnians*, *Clouds*, *Ecclesiazusae*) the words imply that two doors are in simultaneous use. Were there really two doors in the theatre, or only one? The hypothesis that there was only one is a logical extension of a principle which few, if any, students of Aristophanes at the present time would deny, that a door which can represent one person's house at one point in a play can represent another's house at another point. It has also been defended on the following grounds:[10]

(a) No tragedy 'needs' more than one door; and tragedy and comedy were performed in the same theatre.

(b) The construction, erection and removal of temporary sets are too difficult and expensive.

(c) (i) The trolley can be used at the central door alone;[11] (ii) interior scenes in comedy are revealed by means of the trolley; and (iii) at least in *Clouds*, an interior scene in 'Socrates' house' and an interior scene in 'Strepsiades' house' are revealed at different points in the play.

---

[9] Trygaios's rupture of dramatic illusion in *Pax* 173ff (οἴμ' ὡς δέδοικα κτλ.) is not humour at the expense of theatrical convention, but exploitation of the humorous possibilities opened up by theatrical machinery. I would draw a strong distinction.

[10] Notably Dale (205ff). But her standpoint is not entirely consistent; in suggesting (207) that in *Wasps* the 'petit-bourgeois house' cannot be 'a grand affair with paraskenia' she insists on giving the skene a representational character which her interpretation of other plays implicitly denies.

[11] Cf. Dinsmoor 326.

(d) The limitation to one door can actually enhance comic effect.

(e) *Ec*. 877–1111, which have been held to imply two doors, in fact imply one.

I accept (c)(iii), with the important reservation that the interior scene in Strepsiades' house is the scene with which *Clouds* begins, not a scene revealed in the course of the play. I am willing to accept, with slight reservations, (c)(i). I deny (b) absolutely, and in consequence deny (c)(2) and (d) as generalizations, though not unwilling to admit exceptions. (e) will be discussed in section VI. This leaves us with (a), on which three points must be made.

1   The typical tragic plot and the typical comic plot differ fundamentally. Apart from the much greater complexity and looseness of structure of the latter, tragic plots are predominantly concerned with heroic rulers who inhabit palaces. I see no good reason to accept the assumption that the Athenian theatre was built as if for tragedy alone and that comic poets were expected to make the best of it. Whatever theatrical building was done in the fifth century was done in the knowledge that both tragedies and comedies would be performed in the same theatre. When a building is constructed to meet two different purposes, one of which requires only part of what the other requires, it is normal practice and common sense to meet the purpose for which the requirements are more numerous. If, for example, a theatre were so constructed as to permit of a spectacular production of *Don Giovanni*, the production of *Così fan tutte* in the same theatre would in no way be precluded or even impaired. Many institutions are familiar with the construction of large rooms which will be used perhaps 1 per cent of the time for theatrical performances and 99 per cent of the time for lectures or assemblies; in such cases, if money permits, the theatrical use is kept in mind in designing the room.

2   In *Choephori* Orestes and Pylades arrive (653) at the outer door of the palace (ἑρκείας . . . θύρας) and are admitted as guests by Klytaimestra when the door has been opened by a slave. Aigisthos, who has been away from home, arrives and enters the palace (838–54). His death-cry is heard from within. A panic-stricken slave comes on stage and cries for the opening of the γυναικεῖοι πύλαι (878). Klytaimestra emerges from the women's quarters. Orestes and Pylades arrive on stage. All three go off stage for the killing of Klytaimestra. Then at 973 Orestes appears with the dead bodies of both Aigisthos and Klytaimestra.

Now, either the outer door of the palace and the door of the γυναικωνῖτις are represented by two different doors in the same plane; or, if there is only one door, the arrival of the frightened slave and his reference to the γυναικεῖοι πύλαι tell us that we must now imagine ourselves not, as before, outside the palace, but inside the courtyard. In the former case, so long as we think of the skene as a realistic representation, it represents something unlike any Greek house or palace.[12] In the latter case – again, so long as we think of the skene in representational terms – we have to realize that there is a change of scene (for which, indeed, the slave's words prepare us), but we lose much dramatically; for the slave, crying for the fate of Aigisthos, cannot then come out of the door through which Aigisthos has walked to his death, nor can Orestes and Pylades come out of that door, behind which we have both heard and visualized their bloody deed enacted. The slave and Orestes and Pylades must all come on stage from the wings.

Here we are in the realm of subjective disagreement on what is dramatically effective and what is not. My own preference, on grounds of dramatic effectiveness, is emphatically for two doors. I am bound to admit that if only one door was available to Aeschylus he had to manage without the dramatic effect which I would like him to have achieved. I cannot then refrain from asking the question: if only one door was available to him, would he have designed the central part of *Choephori* in the form which it has?

3   This may seem an impertinent question, and perhaps a question of a kind which it is wrong to ask – in the case of Aeschylus. It is not, I think, wrong to ask it with reference to certain scenes in Aristophanes. If we find a scene in which, after we have done our best to interpret it on alternative hypotheses, we conclude that, if only one door was available, the audience would not be amused or tantalized by words implying two doors, but confused or misled, and that comic effect would thereby be lost, then we can legitimately ask, 'Would Aristophanes have written what he did if he had only one door?', and, in my submission, we have in such a case decisive evidence for two doors.

IV.   *ACHARNIANS*

At 1097 there begins the famous scene in which Dikaiopolis and Lamachos alternately issue orders to their respective slaves to 'bring out here' this, that and the other. If only one door is available, it does not *represent* the house of Dikaiopolis or the house of Lamachos but simply serves as the point of transition from 'indoors' to 'out of doors'. Taken by itself, this is unobjectionable; my misgivings arise from what precedes the scene and, to a lesser extent, from what follows.

At 1000 a herald arrives, proclaiming the Choes. Dikaiopolis thereupon gives orders to his household to prepare an elaborate meal. The Chorus sings a song of felicitation, in the middle of which Dikaiopolis sings (1014) τὸ πῦρ ὑποσκάλευε, whereupon the Chorus: ἤκουσας ὡς μαγειρικῶς . . . αὐτῷ διακονεῖται, which implies not that Dikaiopolis and his slaves are busy with

---

[12] So Dale in *WSt* lxix (1956) 97; but, on the one-door theory, how much does the resemblance of the skene to actual houses matter? Is not argument based on the need for resemblance an attempt to have one's cake and eat it?

their cooking before our eyes but that he is *heard* giving orders indoors. If so, his appearance at 1018 with the words τίς οὑτοσί, upon the arrival of the farmer from Phyle, is comparable to the appearance of Strepsiades at *Nu*. 1221 (certainly from indoors: cf. 1212) on the approach of the creditor. After the scene with the farmer comes the antistrophe responding to 1008–17. The Chorus sings of Dikaiopolis in the third person; we hear Dikaiopolis giving an order; the Chorus sings (1041) ἤκουσας ὀρθιασμάτων; another order; then the Chorus apostrophizes Dikaiopolis (cf. *Nu*. 810–13, where it is imperative that Socrates should be off stage); and then, just before the arrival of the man from the wedding, Dikaiopolis speaks an iambic trimeter (1047): ὀπτᾶτε ταυτὶ καὶ καλῶς ξανθίζετε. This line looks like a feature very common in New Comedy, instructions given over the shoulder to people indoors as a character comes out of doors: cf. Men. *Dysk*. 206, 427, 456, 546, 874, 879. But even if Dikaiopolis were on stage continuously from 1003 (and, to my mind, ἤκουσας in 1015 and 1042 shows that he is not) it is still true that the whole passage builds up in our minds a picture of the region inside the door as *his* house; the hare (1006), thrushes (1007, 1011) and sausage (1040) for the preparation of which he gives orders are all brought to him (1106, 1110, 1119) during the scene in which everything is brought *out* (1098, 1123, 1133).

Now, when the messenger at 1071 has arrived and cried out ἰὼ πόνοι τε καὶ μάχαι καὶ Λάμαχοι, Lamachos speaks at once: τίς ἀμφὶ χαλκοφάλαρα δώματα κτυπεῖ; Where does Lamachos come from? If from the wings, why did Aristophanes choose to give him words which imply so plainly that he is being called out of his house? If from the skene, and there is only one door, it is not, I think, a misrepresentation of the facts to say that he is coming out of Dikaiopolis's kitchen, for that is what the door has come to represent, and nothing said by the messenger (contrast A. *Ch*. 877ff as interpreted on the one-door theory) prepares us for its change of representational function. I infer that there were two doors.[13]

After Lamachos and Dikaiopolis have departed, the one to war and the other to a feast, and after the Chorus has sung, one of Lamachos's attendants

---

[13] I have not yet read or heard any satisfactory interpretation of 1096 σύγκλῃε, καὶ δεῖπνόν τις ἐνσκευαζέτω, which appears to mean: 'Shut ⟨the door⟩ and let someone start preparing a dinner ⟨for packing⟩ in ⟨a hamper⟩.' 'Begin shutting up the house' would imply that Dikaiopolis is going off to the feast with his whole household, and there is nothing in the play to suggest that. If there is only one door, then (a) we have been encouraged to imagine it since 1069 as Lamachos's door, (b) in 1096 we are made to think of it as Dikaiopolis's, behind which the process of δεῖπνον ἐνσκευάζειν is to begin, and (c) in 1097 we realize that it is no longer anybody's door, but the point of transition between 'indoors' and 'on stage'. I do not see how the change of function required for 1097ff can be signalled to the audience by leaving the door open after 1072 and making Dikaiopolis say 'shut it' at 1096, when the first 'bring out . . .' order is uttered not by Dikaiopolis but by Lamachos. Given the preceding line and a half, there is something to be said for Rennie's emendation σύγκλαε, i.e. κλᾶε μετὰ τῆς Γοργόνος (the δαίμων through whom Lamachos is κακοδαίμων). Cf. κλᾶε in 1032 and Aristophanes' readiness to use rare or unattested compounds with συν-, e.g. *Eq*. 479, *Ra*. 402, *Pl*. 847; but I would keep καί rather than substitute Rennie's νυν.

arrives and delivers a messenger-speech about the wounding of his master. This speech begins with the words ὦ δμῶες οἳ κατ᾽ οἶκόν ἐστε Λαμάχου and ends ἀλλ᾽ ἄνοιγε τὴν θύραν. Lamachos then arrives, wounded, and from the other side, a moment later, Dikaiopolis, supported by two girls; presumably two slaves come out and support Lamachos, so that we have a pleasing symmetry between the happy Dikaiopolis, propped up by two girls because he is drunk, and the unhappy Lamachos, propped up by two slaves because he is hurt. It does not appear that Lamachos goes indoors, for his utterances are continuously balanced against those of Dikaiopolis throughout 1190–227, and when he says (1222) θύραζέ μ᾽ ἐξενέγκατε κτλ. he must mean not literally 'out of door' (for he is not indoors) but 'away from home'. At the end of the play he goes off in one direction, Dikaiopolis in another, the Chorus following Dikaiopolis.

This last scene can certainly be staged adequately with only one door, for Dikaiopolis does not appear from his own house, nor does he go off stage into it, nor, indeed, does he refer to it. But we may wonder why the poet appears to lay such stress on Lamachos's *house* in 1174 and (above all) 1189, when all that is needed is that slaves of Lamachos shall appear to prop their master up. The emphasis is intelligible if Dikaiopolis's house and Lamachos's house have been represented by separate doors during the preceding scene.

V.   CLOUDS

1   At 92 Strepsiades says to Pheidippides: 'Do you see that little door and little house?' He tells Pheidippides a moment later that philosophers 'live in here' (ἐνταῦθ᾽ ἐνοικοῦσ᾽, 95), and he implores Pheidippides to become one of their pupils. Pheidippides refuses; they quarrel, and Strepsiades threatens to drive Pheidippides away from home (123). Pheidippides replies,

ἀλλ᾽ οὐ περιόψεταί μ᾽ ὁ θεῖος Μεγακλέης
ἄνιππον. ἀλλ᾽ εἴσειμι, σοῦ δ᾽ οὐ φροντιῶ.

And he goes off stage, leaving Strepsiades alone. Strepsiades decides that he will go to Socrates' school himself, and, after some vacillation, he plucks up courage and knocks at the door, crying παῖ, παιδίον (132).

In this passage there is a door which consistently represents Socrates' school both before and after Pheidippides' exit. Where does Pheidippides go when he says ἀλλ᾽ εἴσειμι? Cobet observed that in two manuscripts, Canonicianus 46 and what Blaydes calls 'Mutinensis 2', we have not εἴσειμι but εἶμι. Cobet also believed that οὐ περιόψεταί μ᾽. . . ἄνιππον is not Greek. He therefore inserted a participle, giving . . . ἄνιππον ⟨ὄντ⟩. ἀλλ᾽ εἶμι κτλ. Canonicianus 46 (of which, to judge from Blaydes' apparatus, 'Mutinensis 2' – which I have not identified – is a twin) is a typical fifteenth-century manuscript of the Byzantine triad of Aristophanes, derived ultimately from the Triclinian edition and exhibiting a plentiful crop of errors which first appear in the late fourteenth or early fifteenth century. I should say from a selective collation that its chance of preserving a genuine Aristophanic reading which has slipped through the mesh of the thirty extant manuscripts datable before the middle of the fourteenth century is quite negligible. εἶμι is a non-starter unless it can be shown that οὐ περιόψεταί μ᾽ ἄνιππον is not Aristophanic Greek, and I do not think that this can be shown. In *Ach.* 55 Amphitheos exclaims περιόψεσθέ με; In *Lys.* 1019f the Chorus says οὐ σε περιόψομαι γυμνὸν ὄνθ᾽ οὕτως. οὐ περιόψεταί μ᾽ ἄνιππον occupies an intermediate place between these two constructions, exactly as *V.* 190 εἰ μή μ᾽ ἐάσεθ᾽ ἥσυχον occupies an intermediate place between *Eq.* 336 οὐκ αὖ μ᾽ ἐάσεις; and *Pax* 649 ἔα τὸν ἄνδρ᾽ . . . εἶναι κάτω.

Pheidippides, then, says 'I will go *in*'. If only one door is available, then either (i) he goes into the door which has just been described to him (and to us) as the door of the school, which he has passionately refused to enter, and a moment later Strepsiades is going to treat the same door as the door of the school, or (ii) he means 'I will go home' or 'I will go away' – in which case why does Aristophanes make him say εἴσειμι rather than ἄπειμι?

2   At 801 Strepsiades, instigated by the Chorus, declares that he will go and fetch Pheidippides and compel him to attend Socrates' school; 'and if he isn't willing to, I swear, I'll drive him out of the house'. Strepsiades then turns to Socrates and says (803), 'Just go *in* (εἰσελθών) and wait for me a moment.' The Chorus sings a stanza addressed to Socrates. Then Strepsiades and Pheidippides come on stage, Strepsiades saying (814), 'You shan't stay *here* (ἐνταυθοῖ) any longer.' Socrates is obviously off stage by this time, because when Strepsiades has eventually persuaded Pheidippides he calls out excitedly (866), 'Here, here, Socrates, come *out* (ἔξελθ᾽)!' and Socrates comes on stage.

If there is only one door, it represents at the beginning and the end of the scene the door of the school; Socrates goes through it at or immediately after 803 and emerges from it at 867. When Strepsiades and Pheidippides come on stage at 814, either (i) they come out of the same door, which now for the moment has to represent Strepsiades' house, or (ii) they come on from the wings, and when Strepsiades says, 'You shan't stay *here*!' he is saying, for our benefit, what in real life would have been said when he first started to drive Pheidippides out of his house.

There is a strong objection to (i). After Strepsiades has gone off to fetch Pheidippides the whole of the choral song is addressed to Socrates in the second person. This keeps us before – indeed, it thrusts upon us – the identification of the door which Socrates enters as the door of the school, and it maintains this identification right up to the point at which Strepsiades and Pheidippides come on stage. As for hypothesis (ii), it cannot be ruled out (and I would not rule it out, if this were the only passage on which the case for more than one door rested), but it involves one theatrical awkwardness. In the middle of his argument with his son Strepsiades says (843), 'Wait for me here a moment!' He comes on stage three lines later with a cock and a hen. From the wings – or from where we would expect him to find them, his own household?

3   At the end of the play Strepsiades determines on the physical destruction of the school. He calls to his slave (1485) to 'come out' (ἔξελθε) with a ladder and a mattock. They both go up on to the roof of the school, where the slave knocks away the tiles and Strepsiades, with a lighted torch, sets fire to the beams of the roof. Socrates and the philosophers cry in succession, 'I shall be stifled', 'I shall be burnt alive', etc.

If there is only one door, Strepsiades and his slave go up on to the roof immediately above the door out of which the ladder, the mattock and the torch have been brought. If we knew for certain that only one door was available, we should have to accept this business as forced upon the dramatist by theatrical convention; but no extra positive argument for the one-door theory can be derived from the scene. There is nothing intrinsically humorous in the double role of the door if the audience has never been accustomed to anything better; it is only after we have come to take sophisticated techniques for granted that naivety is amusing. I stress the double *role*, because, even if the philosophers appear at windows to utter their cries of distress, they must emerge from the door in time to be chased out of the theatre (1508 δίωκε βάλλε παῖε), and at that moment it is *their* door. No argument for the one-door theory can be based on the fact that it is the roof of the house which is attacked.[14] As the law of gravity has not changed since the fifth century BC, it was as imprudent then as it would be now to begin the demolition of a building anywhere but at the top; moreover, one can fire only what is inflammable, and when a house is built of stone or brick the most easily accessible inflammable portion of it is the roof-beams, which can be exposed by knocking away the tiles.

4   Immediately before calling to his slaves Strepsiades begs Hermes for forgiveness and takes the advice of Hermes on action against the philosophers. He pretends that Hermes has spoken to him, in a passage the technique of which reminds us of *Pax* 661ff, where Hermes puts a question to the silent Peace and professes to receive an answer from her. Either Strepsiades raises his hands to the sky and pretends to receive an answer which has fallen from Olympos, or there is an actual herm in sight, to which he puts his ear. The latter accords both with the passage of *Peace* and with Greek religious practice. Herms at Athens stands in doorways, and in real life the house of someone like Strepsiades would have had a herm by the door. The philosophers, on the other hand do not θεοὺς νομίζειν οὕσπερ ἡ πόλις, and a house such as theirs would not have had a herm. If there is only one door

---

[14] Dale, *JHS* lxxvii 210, comments on the 'strangeness' of attacking the roof.

throughout the play, we must 'think away' the herm whenever the door serves as a point of entry to the school, and notice it properly only when Strepsiades brings it to our attention at 1478. This would not be a serious difficulty or an unreasonable demand to make on an audience – but for its relation to a passage which immediately precedes Strepsiades' address to the herm.

One of the doctrines which Strepsiades learnt from Socrates was that Dinos is the underlying ἀνάγκη of the universe (380). Strepsiades interprets this as meaning that Dinos has overthrown Zeus just as Zeus overthrew Kronos. This is in the form in which he imparts the doctrine to Pheidippides (828), and it bounces back at him when he has implored the help of Pheidippides in the name of πατρῷος Ζεύς and Pheidippides replies (1471), 'Dinos has expelled Zeus and reigns as king'. Strepsiades replies passionately, 'He has *not* expelled him; this is something which I thought *because of this dinos*. O what a fool! I thought *you* a god – and you made of earthenware!' We have to account for the demonstrative, διὰ τουτονὶ τὸν δῖνον, and for the address to a vessel of the type called δῖνος. It is well known that οὗτος need not, and sometimes cannot, imply that the person or thing so characterized is visible in the theatre. Whether the same holds good for οὑτοσί is not certain, for the test case, *Lys*. 1168, is complicated by *double entendre*. But in the present passage the antithesis between 'Dinos has expelled Zeus' and '*this* dinos' rules out the possibility that 'this dinos' can mean 'The dinos' (in any sense) 'with which – you know what I mean – we are familiar', and the direct address to an earthenware dinos clinches the matter.

Where does the dinos come from? Van Leeuwen had the idea that Strepsiades rushed indoors and out again in mid-sentence to fetch a dinos. A more appealing idea was put forward by an ancient commentator.

The *scholia vetera* on *Clouds* exist in two main 'corpora' or 'editions'. One edition is to be found in the Venetus and, less corrupt but often abridged, in the Ravennas. The other edition is found in the Estensis (E), in the second hand of Barberinianus 126, and (generally abridged and combined with later material) in the Ambrosianus (M) and a Neapolitanus (Npl). On the whole the E-edition is fuller, more learned and more accurate than the V-edition; it was the main source of the Aldine scholia, but as this was not known in the days of Dindorf and Dübner they attributed to error or irresponsible imagination on the part of Musurus much that is old and valuable. The V-scholion on 1473 says that τουτονί is used δεικτικῶς, with reference to a μηχάνημα, namely a σφαῖρα, in the school; the author of the scholion probably has in mind 200f, where Strepsiades says, 'What's this?' and is told, 'This is astronomy.' The V-scholion continues: ἄλλως· ὡς ἀγάλματος δίνου ὄντος ἐν τῇ διατριβῇ Σωκράτους ὀστρακίνου. If this explanation were right, Strepsiades would be pointing towards, and then apostrophizing, something which is indoors and out of our sight, and for that purpose we should have to think of the skene as representing the school. The E-scholion, however, throws more light on the ancient commentator's intention. The first part of the scholion is the same as in V; but in the second part, instead of ἐν τῇ διατριβῇ we have πρὸ τῆς διατριβῆς. This has the advantage that it makes much better sense of the word ἄγαλμα. The commentator envisaged that a dinos, symbolizing the Dinos of the universe, stood outside the door of the school just as a herm stood outside the door of an ordinary Athenian house.

The hypothesis that there are two doors – one, with a herm, representing Strepsiades' house, and the other, with a dinos, representing the school – provides an explanation of 1473f which is free from difficulties of language, style and production; I know of no other hypothesis which provides this.

5   How did the dinos get there? Strepsiades at 133 knocks at the door of the school – the door which he has described as θύριον in 92 – and after a conversation with the student who has opened it he cries at 180–3, 'Open, open the door!' Immediately thereafter he exclaims at the sight of the students who are revealed by the opening. Although in the imaginary situation which the play represents he has gone indoors, a few lines later the student says to the other students (195), 'Go *in*', and when Strepsiades expostulates he explains, 'It is bad for them to be *in the open air* too long.' Strepsiades expostulates no more, and we presume that the students go in, as they have been directed. From this point on the action is imagined as taking place in the open, and when Socrates has finished the preliminary instruction of Strepsiades immediately before the parabasis they both go in through the door of the school (505–9). We have here an intricate blending of the imaginary scene and the actual situation in the theatre.

If it is suggested that the interior of the school is revealed at 183 by the extrusion of a trolley, it must be remembered that the trolley must carry at least four students (for there are two groups, each referred to in the plural [187, 191]), the objects which they leave behind them when they go in (astronomy [201], geometry [202] and a map [206] – all big enough to make a humorous point in a theatre) and the bed on which Strepsiades is told to sit at 254 (unless, of course, this is brought on by a student or slave when needed). At some stage the trolley must be withdrawn, if it is not to interfere with later entrances and exits, and there is no point in the play at which this is dramatically motivated.[15]

But there is a much easier and more natural way of producing this scene, at trivial cost. In front of one part of the skene stands a screen, composed of a wooden frame and canvas, with a door in it. This is the θύριον to which Strepsiades points[16] and at which he knocks at 132. The student who

[15] Dale 210 calls attention to 508 καταβαίνων, and suggests that Socrates and Strepsiades 'step down off the back of the eccyclema to go inside'. But κατα- is determined by the preceding and following words, εἰς τὼ χεῖρε νυν κτλ. and ὥσπερ εἰς Τροφωνίου: Strepsiades is as frightened of going *into* the school as of going *down into* the cave of Trophonios.

[16] No argument can be based on the use of the diminutive θύριον; cf. *Th*. 26, where Euripides says to his kinsman ὁρᾷς τὸ θύριον τοῦτο, referring to Agathon's door, from which Agathon will shortly be 'rolled out' (96), undoubtedly on the tragic trolley. In both *Nu*. and *Th*. the diminutive is ingratiating.

converses with him comes outside and shuts the door after him. When Strepsiades cries, 'Open the door!' at 183, the student turns round towards the screen with a sweeping gesture, and it is carried off and out of the theatre by two men who have been standing behind it, out of our sight, for precisely this purpose.[17] Its removal reveals (i) groups of students in peculiar attitudes, (ii) objects, much larger than life, which represent comic versions of scientific instruments, and (iii) another door, into a more lasting set, beside which stands a dinos on a herm-like pedestal. This door serves henceforward as the door of the school. The bed may be revealed at the same time, or brought on later. It, and all the objects other than the dinos, are carried indoors at some time or times before the parabasis by people in whose status (students, slaves of Socrates, or slaves of the choregos?) we are not interested.

VI. ECCLESIAZUSAE

At 877 we see a girl and an old woman. They are not, as is normally supposed by commentators, 'courtesans', but ordinary people, of the class which cannot afford to segregate its womenfolk all the time in a γυναικωνῖτις; we should imagine the girl as someone rather like Simaitha in Theoc. 2. The girl is waiting for her boy-friend; the old woman is pretending to have a boy-friend (933) and is determined to secure the girl's, if he comes.

The way has been prepared for this scene by the woman's revolution, which has transferred sexual initiative from men to women. When Praxagora describes (689ff) how a drunken man on his way home will be accosted by women, each saying, 'Come this way – there's a pretty girl in my house!' we miss the point if we imagine that she is speaking of prostitutes, for solicitation by, or on behalf of, prostitutes would not be a reversal of the existing social order but a continuation of it; the opposite of the state of affairs depicted by Praxagora is the customary barring of the doors against riotous drunkards. Blepyros envisages (611ff) that girls may be venal (as no doubt many were); but Praxagora clearly does not take him as referring only, or even primarily, to prostitutes, for she explains that all women will be available to all men συγκατακεῖσθαι καὶ παιδοποιεῖν, and (635ff) no one will know who are his own children. But there is a proviso, which is essential for the design of 877ff: under the new laws, no one may have intercourse with younger and more attractive women until he has satisfied the old and ugly (615ff, 700f).

The girl and the old woman use, with reference to each other, the words παρακύπτειν (884, 924) and διακύπτειν (930). διακύπτειν is used in Pax 78 of looking cautiously in through a door; παρακύπτειν is used in Th. 797 of peeping out of a window, and in Pax 982ff of peeping through the outer door

---

[17] I have seen Clouds performed in this way, in a 'shoestring' production on a floor not designed for modern theatrical requirements, and the dramatic effect was remarkable; the moving of the screen and the disclosure of the students was rather like the lifting of a big stone and the disclosure of panic-stricken woodlice.

of a house: 'Adulterous women ... παρακλίνασαι τῆς αὐλείας παρακύπτου
σιν, and if anyone notices them, they go back in, and then, if he goes away,
παρακύπτουσιν.' This peeping through doors and windows is a comparatively modest way of showing that one is willing to be pursued.

The girl and the old woman cannot be looking through the same door or
the same window. At 936 the girl says, 'I'm going away'; at 937, the old
woman says, 'So am I.' After the young man has come on stage, the old
woman says (946), 'I'll go (εἶμι) and watch what he's going to do.' Three lines
later (949) the girl speaks: 'I've cheated the old woman; she's gone, thinking
that I was staying indoors.' Now, the girl is certainly not *out* of doors, because
the young man sings (961), 'Run *down* and open this door.' It follows that the
girl and the old woman are at different *windows*;[18] and the problem which
remains is: is there one door for each of them, representing two different
houses, or only one door altogether?

This question is, I submit, answered by 989f. The young man is there trying
to escape from the old woman's clutches, and says, τηνδεδί μοι κρουστέον.
The old woman replies, ὅταν γε κρούσῃς τὴν ἐμὴν πρῶτον θύραν. In the
language of Aristophanes any word which means 'hit', 'strike' or 'knock' can
also be used as a slang word for sexual intercourse (cf. 618 ὑποκρούσει). The
two possible interpretations of 989f are therefore:

(a) τηνδεδί = 'this door'. In that case, when the old woman replies, 'Yes,
when you have knocked at my door first', the audience picks up the *double
entendre* – and this is normal Aristophanic technique. As we have seen and
heard nothing of the girl since 959, and in the meantime the old woman
has emerged from a door (976f; see below), we cannot, without mystifying
and confusing the audience, make the young man point to the door from
which the old woman has come and refer to it as a door which he regards
as not the old woman's.

(b) τηνδεδί = 'this girl', pointing to the window at which the girl had
appeared. In this case κρούειν bears its sexual meaning *only* – 'I've got to
"knock" this girl' – but in the old woman's reply we revert to the double
meaning, for she says not 'You must "knock" me first' but 'You must
knock at my door first.' As Aristophanic technique, this simply does not
ring true.

I therefore take 989f as strong evidence for two doors, and it remains to be
seen what is gained or lost by this interpretation when we look at other parts of
the scene.

1   976f. When the young man has finished singing – and his last words
(973ff) are 'Open, take me in; I suffer agonies because of you' – the old woman

---

[18] I agree with Dale (208), against Fraenkel in *Greek Poetry and Life* (Oxford 1936) 262ff, that
nothing in the language of the scene favours the supposition that the girl and the old woman are
on the roof.

speaks: οὗτος,[19] τί κόπτεις; μῶν ἐμὲ ζητεῖς;, i.e. 'You, why are you knocking? Can it be me you're looking for?' 'Of course not', says the young man (πόθεν; cf. *Ec.* 389 and *Ra.* 1455). The old woman presses the attack: καὶ τὴν θύραν γ' ἤραττες, '⟨sc. Oh, yes, you are⟩ and you bashed the door, too!' (καί . . . γε does not mean 'Oh, but . . .'). The young man's reply, ἀποθάνοιμ' ἄρα, means 'I'm damned if I did!' Cf. *Lys.* 933, where Myrrhine says 'Don't cheat me about the peace treaty!' and Kinesias replies νὴ Δί' ἀπολοίμην ἄρα, a strong declaration that he will not cheat her; cf. also the famous joke in *Ra.* 177, where the corpse refuses Dionysos's offer with the exclamation ἀναβιοίην νυν πάλιν.

Someone in this passage of dialogue is not telling the truth. If there is only one door, and the young man has knocked on it, only to be confronted by an old woman instead of the girl he expected, his denial that he knocked is a falsehood told in order to make his escape. If there are two doors, and he has knocked on the girl's door, the old woman must have darted out of her own door pretending that this, and not the girl's door, received the knock.

I wonder in fact if the young man has knocked at all. Conceivably his desire is so impatient that although he has already told the girl 'Run down and open this door' (961ff) he tries to hurry her unreasonably by knocking as well. But he does not need to knock; he has every reason to believe that in a second the girl will open the door and let him in. His visit is, after all, one of which the girl's family would be unlikely to approve; the girl has communicated with him in the age-old code of song – essentially a form of invitation which can be withdrawn, with the indignant claim that one was only singing,[20] if the wrong person answers it – and in the course of the song she has let us (but not him) know that mama is out (911ff). He is in a similar position to Delphis, invited to the house of Simaitha (Theocr. 2.101ff, 130ff),[21] or the adulterer who scratches faintly on the door (*Th.* 476ff; cf. Lys. i 14, 23). He does not want to draw any more attention to himself than is necessary; that is why he too communicates with the girl in the code of song, but a code which, thanks to a masculine lack of finesse (961ff), is more easily cracked.

Comic effect is enhanced if he is standing expectantly at the girl's door and jumps out of his skin when the old woman seizes him and pretends, with shameless determination, that he has knocked at *her* door. The more outrageous her claim, the greater his helpless bewilderment; cf. Peisetairos's treatment of Iris in *Av.* 1199ff.

2   The object of the old woman is to get the young man *into her house*; cf. the girl's words to her at 925, οὐδεὶς γὰρ ὡς σὲ πρότερον εἴσεισ' ἀντ' ἐμοῦ. The old woman says to the young man ἕπου δεῦρ' ὡς ἐμέ (1005) and δεῦρ'

---

[19] We cannot infer from the use of οὗτος anything about the distance between two characters in Aristophanes.

[20] There is deliberate grotesquerie in the employment by the old woman of a convention appropriate to those a quarter her age.

[21] Delphis's words in 118ff are a young man's brag about a purely hypothetical situation.

ἀκολουθεῖν ὡς ἐμέ (1028), and he protests (1036) that she will 'fall to pieces' ἔνδον. Now, at 1037, the girl speaks: ποῖ τοῦτον ἕλκεις; The old woman says εἰς ἐμαυτῆς εἰσάγω: but she cannot cope with the young man and the girl together, and flees, uttering threats and maledictions (1043f). The young man thanks the girl for his deliverance; but then a second old woman appears and puts the girl to flight (1049f): αὕτη σὺ ποῖ τονδὶ παραβᾶσα τὸν νόμον ἕλκεις;

If there is only one door, we cannot produce the play in such a way that (a) the first old woman is dragging the young man towards the door and (b) the girl appears at that same door and says, 'Where are you taking him?', for the old woman and the young man would be moving *towards her*. We could only produce it in such a way that (a) the old woman drags the young man parallel to the skene and (b) the girl appears at the door, runs out of it, and starts to drag him parallel to the skene in the opposite direction. This is a possible method of production, and if we knew for certain, on independent grounds, that there was only one door, it would be a necessary method. But we do not know for certain; and if we treat *Ecclesiazusae* as what it is, part of the evidence upon which we have to decide between one door or two, I see no grounds on which one door can be preferred.

27

Portrait-Masks in Aristophanes

I. THE IMPLICATIONS OF *EQ.* 230FF

The slave of Demos reassures the Sausage-seller that he will have allies in his fight to overcome the Paphlagonian: the cavalry, all good citizens, those of the audience who are δεξιοί, himself, and 'the god'. 'And', he says, 'don't be afraid':

> οὐ γάρ ἐστιν ἐξῃκασμένος·
> ὑπὸ τοῦ δέους γὰρ αὐτὸν οὐδεὶς ἤθελεν
> τῶν σκευοποιῶν εἰκάσαι. πάντως γε μὴν
> γνωσθήσεται· τὸ γὰρ θέατρον δεξιόν.

Since we have already been told, by references to hides and tanning (44 etc.) so numerous as almost to insult our δεξιότης, and also by the allegory of the 'Lakonian loaf' (54ff), that the Paphlagonian represents Kleon, it seems that we are now being told: (i) the mask worn by the actor who plays the Paphlagonian will *not* resemble the face of Kleon, and (ii) the reason for this is that the makers of theatrical properties were too afraid, and therefore unwilling, to make a likeness of Kleon.

The scholia Σ^VE on this passage assert: (i) when a character in a comedy represented a real person, it was the custom (ἔθος) to use a portrait-mask; and (ii) (ἄλλως) no one was willing to *act* the part of the Paphlagonian, and so Aristophanes acted it, μιλτώσας ἑαυτόν . . . ἢ τῇ τρυγίᾳ χρίσας ἑαυτόν.

The second part of the second scholion is highly suspect, because it implies either that an actor wore paint, not a mask, or else that the 'custom' was so binding that the only alternative to portrayal of a real character by a portrait-mask was not to have any mask at all. The idea that the actor painted his face seems to have arisen by contamination with stories about the origins of drama,[1] and I do not propose to discuss it at all. I cannot discuss the

---

[1] Cf. Pickard-Cambridge, *Dithyramb, Tragedy and Comedy*, 2nd edn (Oxford 1962) 79f. In the Hypotheses in V and E we find a different contamination; it is stated there that the mask-makers' fear was the reason why Aristophanes was himself διδάσκαλος of *Knights*.

alternative proposition without anticipating the main point of this paper. I therefore postpone consideration of why the mask-maker apparently feared something which, as the event proved, the poet, with much more reason to be afraid, was right not to fear.

It is evident that the belief that portrait-masks were customary in Aristophanic comedy was generally held in the Roman period, for statements of the belief are to be found in Σ^v on Nu. 146, in Pollux iv 143, in Aelian VH ii. 13 (where it is an article of faith rather than an item of knowledge), and in Platonius $Diff. Com.$ 13. The belief has been held ever since; it has indeed been somewhat elaborated and extended in modern times. For example, Aelian's anecdote about Socrates has been interpreted in a way which is not altogether justified by the actual text of Aelian; and Pohlenz (NGG 1952, 104) has gone so far as to to say, in defence of his own interpretation of the opening scene of $Knights$, 'Hier müssen sogar Nikias und Demosthenes vom ersten Verse an kenntlich gewesen sein ... Denkbar ist das nur so, das beide – karikierte – Porträtmasken trugen.' But of these matters, more later. The belief that portrait-masks were customary was a fair-enough inference from Eq. 230ff; it remains a fair inference; and I agree to draw it, with one reservation which may have far-reaching consequences. I would restate the proposition thus: portrait-masks were made when it was technically possible to make them. I now want to suggest certain considerations leading towards the conclusion that in many cases, including, perhaps, some cases in which poet and audience alike would most have desired a portrait, it may not have been technically possible at all.

II. THE ANALOGY OF MODERN POLITICAL CARTOONS

These considerations arise from the drawing of comparisons between the art of the ancient mask-maker for the comic stage and the art of the modern cartoonist.

Not long ago I saw a political cartoon in which two men were in a large room. One was speaking to the other, and his words were the caption beneath the cartoon. The size of the room suggested something at government level. Through the large windows one saw a cluster of onion-domes. This fact told the reader that the scene was the Kremlin. The two men were therefore members of the Russian government, and the words, on the subject of China, were such as a cartoonist might put into the mouth of a member of the Russian government. The speaker had very heavy eyebrows; by now it was easy to identify him as Brezhnev. But who was the other? One naturally thinks of Kosygin as stable-mate of Brezhnev, just as a few years ago one thought of Khrushchev and Bulganin as a pair. Probably it was Kosygin, but Podgorny was another possibility; unlike Brezhnev, with his massive eyebrows, neither Kosygin nor Podgorny has so distinctive a face that the reader, even if he is familiar with, and interested in, international politics, can be absolutely sure which the cartoonist intended. And remember: I am speaking not of a sketch by a fifth-former in a school magazine, but of a cartoonist of high standing drawing for a national newspaper.

What are the means by which a cartoonist distinguishes one individual from another? In the cartoon to which I have just referred, the feature which strikes the reader at once, before he looks at the faces or the words, is the view of the domes of the Kremlin through the window – something extraneous to the portrayal of the men themselves. Setting aside background views of this kind, we can classify individual characteristics roughly under two heads, φύσις and νόμος. In setting out the main items under these heads I shall name examples from the political scene during the period 1936–66.

(i) To φύσις we must assign the overall size and shape of the body and the features. Imposing a certain limitation for which the reason will, I hope, become apparent later, we should ask: how many eminent figures of our own day could be recognized solely from a naked silhouette, or from a series of silhouettes? De Gaulle is the only living statesman who seems to me to belong to this category; one might possibly add Ehrhard, Nasser and Kenyatta, but the list cannot be a long one.

(ii) Hair on the head and face occupies a place intermediate between τὰ κατὰ φύσιν and τὰ κατὰ νόμον. Baldness is certainly a natural phenomenon, and an important criterion of identification (e.g. Khrushchev); so is the curliness or straightness of hair, and so too is its colour. Abnormally thick eyebrows are a useful criterion; apart from Brezhnev, already mentioned, the obvious example is Chou En-lai. But the shape into which the hair is brushed, and how short it is cut, fall entirely within the province of νόμος. The tendency among adolescent males to grow the hair long is too recent – the proposition 'it is effeminate for young man to wear long hair', factually true in 1960, had become factually untrue by 1965 – to affect even the members of present governments, and the few who at an earlier date wore their hair unusually long (e.g. Lloyd George) could easily be distinguished by this fact. In an age when most people do not grow a beard, the few who do (e.g. Ho Chi Minh) are a gift to the cartoonist. Before and during the Second World War the beard was a distinctive feature of Grandi and Balbo in British cartoons, though only the most optimistic cartoonist could expect the reader to tell the difference between the two without the addition of appropriate dress. Moustaches are perhaps the most helpful of identifying features in an age when some men wear them and some do not, and they can assume so many different shapes and sizes. A cartoonist could often reasonably expect his reader to identify Hitler or Stalin by the moustache alone.

(iii) Most of the elements on which the cartoonist relies can be subsumed entirely under νόμος:

(a) Glasses: the rimless pince-nez of Himmler and Molotov; the thick hornrims of George Brown.

(b) Smoking: Wilson's pipe; Churchill's cigars (noteworthy in Britain, where continuous smoking of cigars is rare); Roosevelt's long cigarette-holder.
(c) The dress or uniform of a nation or political party: e.g. Mao Tse-tung.
(d) Local dress is sometimes helpful as a symbol, whether or not the person portrayed ever actually wears it: e.g. Johnson and Strauss.
(e) Peculiarities of dress or uniform within the conventions of one society: the wing-collars of Baldwin and Neville Chamberlain; Montgomery's pullover and black beret with two badges; the grotesqueries of Göring.

(iv) There are times when all these props fail even the most gifted and experienced cartoonist. It was noticeable, for example, how often, when the late Dr Verwoerd was caricatured – a man with regular features, conventional in hairstyle and clothing – the cartoonist added his name on the bottom of his jacket. The necessity of actually labelling the person whom he has drawn must be bitter for a cartoonist, but he really has nothing to be ashamed of. It is an obstinate fact that there are many people eminent in public life whose appearance and dress are such that, no matter how often they are photographed or filmed, no reader, however perceptive, can reasonably be expected to recognize them in caricature.

Consider now how many of these criteria which I have listed were not available to the maker of portrait-masks for Aristophanic comedy. The Greeks did not wear glasses, nor did they smoke. Since the majority of the real persons portrayed in comedy were Athenians, differences between national costumes could not be exploited, and in any case the differences of dress between Greek states were hardly comparable with those between (say) France, Persia and China in our own day.[2] But, what is more important, the Greeks did not normally shave, and this has two important consequences for caricature. First: only the few individuals who could not grow a proper beard (e.g. Kleisthenes [*Ach*. 118ff, *Th*. 571ff]) or who trimmed their beard so short as to suggest that it was not yet fully grown (possibily Agathon [*Th*. 191f, 218f] should be put in this category) could be distinguished from the majority by the presence or absence of beard or moustache. Secondly: a full growth of beard hides one of the most striking physical distinctions between individuals, the shape of the lower jaw and the chin. Cartoonists would have been greatly handicapped in the portrayal of Mussolini if all Italians at that period had worn beards.

Athenians could, of course, be bald (cf. *Pax* 771ff), they could let their hair grow long (cf. *Nu*. 348), and if they cut it they could do so in more than one way (cf. *Ach*. 849). There is, however, a reasonable probability that the citizen population of Athens was much more uniform in colour of hair and beard than that of most countries of Western Europe today. In a well-known citation

---

[2] How far individuals within the same social class in the same Greek city were recognizably different in their dress is a question on which it is hardly possible to form an opinion.

from Ion of Chios (*F. Gr. Hist.* 392F6) Sophocles is reported to have said that, whereas a painter who made Apollo's hair golden 'rather than black' would be open to criticism, a poet is at liberty to call Apollo 'golden-haired'. Sir John Beazley (*CR* lxiii [1949] 83) emended καὶ μὴ μελαίνας to καὶ μὴ ξανθὰς ἢ μελαίνας, pointing out that a vase-painter who is 'working with a full palette' (by contrast with 'the limited technique of red-figure') never portrays Apollo as dark-haired. I do not dispute the facts with Beazley (μαινοίμην γὰρ ἄν), and I am aware of the red-haired Ganymede on the red-figure krater Louvre G175 and of the red or yellow hair of some of the people painted on white-ground lekythoi; but the passage of Ion as it stands, presupposing that μέλας is the right colour for hair as such, receives some support from Pl. *R*. 420c, where it is taken for granted that μέλας is the right colour for the eyes of statues, and since in Pl. *Lys.* 217d the same person's hair is described in-differently as ξανθαί and as μέλαιναι, both as opposed to 'white', there would seem little to be gained in any case by emending Ion.[3]

It may well be objected that the analogy between a cartoon and an actor's mask is incomplete, because whereas a cartoon is static and silent we do not normally recognize an acquaintance from a 'still'; movements, gestures and, above all, the voice are major means of recognition. Now, it is quite true that recognition by movement, even at a great distance, can be extraordinarily subtle; but this is true only of people who know each other really well, and I question whether the average Attic farmer had seen Perikles or Kleon in the flesh as often as most of us see contemporary politicians on television. The idea that the Athenians were acquainted with one another as intimately as the inhabitants of a small village is not reconcilable with the manner in which the characters of a Platonic dialogue speak,[4] or with many passages in the orators. Also, recognition by movement and voice is possible only in so far as the behaviour and speech of the person recognized fall within that person's normal range. If, for example, Nikias is portrayed as a general reporting to the Assembly, well and good – his voice and stance can be mimicked directly – but, if he is portrayed as a slave howling after a beating, the actor has to imagine how Nikias would move if he were a slave and how he would howl if he were beaten. In Aristophanic comedy real people are commonly represented in unreal situations. Furthermore, mimicry of a person's voice is easier when electronic amplification frees the actor to use the full range of his voice than when his freedom is curtailed by the need to make his voice carry unaided; and at the best of times it is not particularly easy. I have seen no more talented mimicry of contemporary politicians than that of Mr John Bird on the BBC in 1965–6; but even he occasionally left me in doubt as to which member of the British cabinet he was mimicking.

[3] In Pl. *Plt*. 270e, when the passage of time was reversed, τῶν πρεσβυτέρων αἱ λευκαὶ τρίχες ἐμελαίνοντο.

[4] E.g. Pl. *Lach*. 180de: Lysimachos is a fellow-demesman of Socrates, and their fathers were friends; but he does not know enough about Socrates to realize that the Socrates of whose exciting conversation his own son has spoken is the same man.

To those difficulties we must add another which would beset the maker of portrait-masks. A mask must have eye-holes large enough to ensure that the actor can do his job without fear of fumbling or colliding. It must have a mouth-hole large enough to ensure that he can enunciate clearly. The size and shape of these apertures[5] necessarily conflict with the most important of all means of facial recognition, the set and interrelation of the eyes and mouth – facial expression, in fact. The cartoonist is absolutely free to exaggerate characteristic expressions; but imagine the difficulties which the conditions of the Athenian theatre would impose on anyone who tried to make portrait-masks of (say) Weygand or Adenauer.

I suggest that there was a very simple reason why the mask worn by the Paphlagonian in *Knights* should not resemble Kleon: that is, that there was nothing unusual about Kleon's face, and when the requirements of the apertures for eyes and mouth had been met it was impossible to make a mask such that anyone in the audience could say οὗτος ἐκεῖνος.

Now this does not mean that whenever a person happened to have regular features it was always impossible for the poet to make the audience identify a character in a play as that person. There are other aspects of the cartoonist's art, of which I have so far said nothing; symbolic allusion and the conventions created by the individual artist himself.

On one occasion in the 1930s (in what connection, I confess I have forgotten) Stanley Baldwin used the words 'My lips are sealed.' Often there-after the cartoonist David Low depicted him with a piece of sticking-plaster across his mouth. It would not have mattered, for the purposes of identification, if Low had been unable to draw Baldwin's face convincingly; the visual allusion to 'sealed lips' would have sufficed.

It also occurred to Low, about the same time, that Lord Simon, with his long neck, thin face and downy white hair, bore a certain resemblance to a plucked turkey, and in a memorable drawing of the British cabinet Low represented Simon as a turkey hanging upside-down in a butcher's shop. Simon's resemblance to a turkey was not so obvious that it would necessarily have struck anyone else; but Low created at a stroke an artistic convention which a man less fertile in new ideas could have gone on to exploit in-definitely, so that a reader familiar with his cartoons would know, years later, that in the work of that particular cartoonist a plucked turkey symbolized Simon.

Symbolism of this kind is a means by which a comic poet could have shown the audience who was represented by a character in a play even when a portrait-mask would not have sufficed.

---

[5] Note especially pls 16 and 19 in T. B. L. Webster, *Greek Theatre Production* (London 1956); pl. 16 is the famous relief from Lyme Hall, Stockport, dating from the early fourth century BC.

III.   WHY WAS THE MASK-MAKER AFRAID?

The answer to this question is, I think, intimately connected with the answer to a different question: why did Aristophanes draw attention to the fact that the Paphlagonian did not wear a portrait-mask of Kleon?

It was common in Greek politics to speak of an adversary as if his appearance, manners and voice were aesthetically objectionable; indeed, a Greek may often genuinely have experienced an unpleasant aesthetic reaction at the sight and sound of a political adversary, in a manner common today among children and not unknown among adult women (though exceedingly rare, in my experience, among adult men). Comedy adopts the same tone as politics; Kleon, who had made himself an enemy of Aristophanes by the action which he took, or threatened to take, in consequence of *Babylonians*, is treated in *V.* 1031ff as a terrifying monster of the kind we meet in folklore and archaic myth, hideous and disgusting almost beyond imagination. He has the teeth of a savage dog, and the same seething multiplicity of heads, fiery eyes and dreadful voice as Typhoeus in Hesiod (*Th.* 820ff); and, for good measure, φωκῆς ὀσμήν, Λαμίας ὄρχεις ἀπλύτους, πρωκτὸν δὲ καμήλου. Aristophanes was evidently well pleased with this assimilation of Kleon to a famous monster of mythology, for he repeated the passage in *Peace* (751ff) two years later. Certain elements in the passage are of course, foreshadowed in *Knights* itself; note especially 1017f

> σῴζεσθαί σ᾽ ἐκέλευσ᾽ ἱερὸν κύνα καρχαρόδοντα,
> ὃς πρὸ σέθεν λάσκων καὶ ὑπὲρ σοῦ δεινὰ κεκραγώς χτλ.

and 115

> ὡς μεγάλ᾽ ὁ Παφλαγὼν πέρδεται καὶ ῥέγκεται.

Now, if Kleon was in fact a man of ordinary appearance, Aristophanes had the opportunity to put on the Paphlagonian an exceptionally hideous mask, which expressed visually what he felt about Kleon, and at the same time to turn this to good comic account by pretending that, hideous as it was, it fell far short of the real Kleon – that it fell short because a portrayal of Kleon as he really was would have been too frightening even to the man who was making the mask himself! Some of us may remember how, as small children, we drew a face or a beast so horrible that we were frightened afterwards to look at what we had drawn. The Greeks, especially uneducated Greeks, were much more familiar than we are with the idea of the supernaturally frightening face; they knew the myth of the gorgon Medusa, hobgoblins lurked in the darkness of their thickets, apotropaic antefixes adorned some of their buildings, and they painted horrible faces on their shields to frighten their enemies; Dikaiopolis pretends in *Acharnians* (582) to be frightened of the face painted on the shield of Lamachos.[6]

The alternative explanation – that the mask-maker was afraid that Kleon would wreak vengeance on anyone who, even in a humble capacity, contributed to an attack on him – deprives the passage of its essentially humorous point, turns it simply into a boast by a poet about his own courage, and by implication pays an almost extravagant compliment to the power of Kleon.

IV. 'NIKIAS' AND 'DEMOSTHENES'

As mentioned above, it has sometimes been suggested that the audience's immediate identification of the two slaves at the beginning of *Knights* as Nikias and Demosthenes is necessary for the appreciation of the first scene. I have argued (*CR* NS ix [1959] 196ff) that this suggestion is unjustified, and that the humour of the scene can stand without identification of the slaves as real people. I do not wish to repeat or retract anything that I have said before on this matter, but I can amplify my argument in three respects.[7]

(i) Unless Nikias and Demosthenes were abnormal in appearance, their identity could not be established simply by portrait-masks, whether the poet wished to establish it or not. We do not know anything of significance about the build, colouring or features of Nikias or Demosthenes, nor do we know whether either of them habitually wore anything distinctive or trimmed his hair or beard in an unusual way. Therefore we do not know whether it was practicable to make a portrait-mask of either of them.

(ii) Nevertheless, it might have been possible to make the identification of Nikias and Demosthenes clear by symbolic allusion. The question whether the two slaves actually were identifiable as the two generals is not answered in the negative merely by pointing out probable impediments to the making of portrait-masks.

(iii) I drew attention to the fact that the Hypothesis of *Knights* in V and E (R has none) is tentative in its identification of one of the slaves as Demosthenes and reveals that the identification of the other slave as Nikias was a commentator's theory and not continuous tradition. In this connection I cited, as the product of a comparable theory, the assignation of speaking parts to Xanthias and Hermes in the exodos of *Clouds*. I was not at that time fully aware of the lengths to which irresponsible Hellenistic theorizing about the identification of characters could go, and I consider now that I showed insufficient disrespect for the theory in the Hypothesis of *Knights*. To encourage

---

[6] Cf. the fearful portrayal of Typhon on the shield of Hippomedon, A. *Se*. 491ff.

[7] See pp. 307–10 below. On the meaning of ἀλλ᾽ οὐκ ἔνι μοι τό θρέττε (17), I should have remarked that Σ^A Dion. Thr. 281.7, seems to classify θρεττέ (*sic*) among ἐπιρρήματα προστακτικά.

a similar disrespect in others, I offer as a parallel the treatment of the creditors in *Clouds*.

When Strepsiades is reciting his debts he says that he owes twelve mnai to Pasias (21) and three mnai to Ameinias[8] (31). At 1214 a creditor arrives with a witness. This creditor is owed twelve mnai (1224), and it is not surprising that he is called 'Pasias' in the *dramatis personae* of most manuscripts. At 1254, having failed to get his money, he says 'I will go away' (ἄπειμι), and tells Strepsiades most emphatically that he will bring a lawsuit against him. Strepsiades utters three lines – we would naturally say, as the creditor stalks off – and the next utterance (1259) is a cry of woe, to which Strepsiades responds by an exclamation of surprise and the words 'Who is this?' We can see, simply from following the text, that it is another creditor, who claims to have met with an accident while racing. Strepsiades treats him with contempt, and eventually calls for a goad and drives him away, crying (1298): ὕπαγε. τί μέλλεις; οὐκ ἐλᾷς, ὦ σαμφόρα; Σ^E *ad loc*. speaks of an interpretation which assigns the whole of this line not to Strepsiades but to 'the Witness'; Σ^{RV} assigns the last four words to 'the Witness', and the text of RV actually has not ὦ σαμφόρα but ὦ Πασία. These data prove the existence of an ancient theory that there was only one creditor all the time. Of the person who held this theory and followed it to its logical conclusions we have to say:

(a) He was indifferent to the common Aristophanic technique of showing the effect of a dramatic change in situation on a pair or series of new characters (e.g. *Ach*. 729–958, 1018–68, *Pax* 1052–121, 1197–264).

(b) He found it possible to believe that despite the first creditor's declaration 'I will go away, and I will bring a lawsuit against you' the witness remained on stage all the time and the creditor was able to reappear almost at once in a disguise which Strepsiades did not penetrate.

(c) He did not understand the point of ὦ σαμφόρα in 1298, in spite of the occurrence of the word σαμφόρας earlier in the play (122).

(d) Most important of all, he succeeded in effecting an alteration of the text, which gives us ὦ Πασία without variant in RV.

I infer from this example that the identification of characters in the hypotheses, *dramatis personae*, sigla and scholia on a play of Aristophanes should be treated on precisely the same footing as modern theories of identification. In one case they may be thoughtful and perceptive; in another case they may be reckless and obtuse. They must in every case be treated on their merits, and must never be respected simply because they originated in the ancient world.

---

[8] I have no doubt that V is right (for the wrong reason; but that is another story) in presenting Ἀμεινίᾳ, not Ἀμυνίᾳ: 'Ameinias' and 'Ameiniades' are Classical Attic names, but 'Amynias' is a Hellenistic name not recorded from Attica until the second century BC.

V. SOCRATES

Several passages in Plato and Xenophon comment on the ugliness of Socrates: his thick lips (Xen. *Smp*. 5.7), upturned nose and protruding eyes (Pl. *Tht*. 143e), all features which the Greek regarded (as we see from their vase-painting) as characteristic of a Seilenos.[9] Thus when Socrates in Xen. *Smp*. 4.19 says that Kritobulos is better-looking than he is himself, Kritobulos replies, νὴ Δί᾽ ... ἢ πάντων Σειληνῶν τῶν ἐν τοῖς σατυρικοῖς αἴσχιστος ἂν εἴην.

It is interesting that *Clouds* contains no reference to the Seilenos-like features of Socrates. Two passages were regarded in antiquity as oblique references, but neither will stand up to close scrutiny.[10]

(i) In 223 Socrates responds to Strepsiades' call by saying τί με καλεῖς, ὦ ᾽φήμερε; According to Σ^V the seilenos Marsyas addresses Olympos as ὦ τάλας ἐφάμερε in Pindar (fr. 157) and Σ suggests that Aristophanes chose the term ἐφήμερος because of Socrates' resemblance to a seilenos. On this it is sufficient to remark that the use of the term by Socrates, up in the air, to Strepsiades, down on the ground, has a humorous point of its own, and there is no need to invoke a subtle allusion to Pindar.

(ii) in 146f the flea in the experiment described by the student jumps from Chairephon's eyebrow to Socrates' head. Σ^{RV} alleges (Σ^V after a statement that portrait-masks were customary) that Chairephon had massive eyebrows and Socrates a bald head (cf. Σ^V 220). The scholion is unfortunate in two respects.

(a) As Tzetzes remarked, Chairephon does not appear in the play, so that the question of portrait-masks is irrelevant so far as he is concerned. It might be added that no other evidence on Chairephon's eyebrows is available to us, even in the material assembled by Arethas (ultimately derived from ancient works on κωμῳδούμενοι) on Pl. *Ap*. 20e.

(b) Was Socrates bald? He was believed in Hellenistic times to have been so (e.g. Luc. *Dial Mort*. 417), and we can take this as far back as Hegesandros of Delphi *ap*. Athen. 507c. Hegesandros can be dated to the middle of the second century BC;[11] the anecdote in which reference is made to Socrates' baldness involves a wry prophecy given by Socrates to Plato about how Plato would behave after Socrates' death, and, if true, describes some-

---

[9] Pl. *Smp*. 215ab should not be indiscriminately treated with these passages, because it makes a special point about a certain kind of box in which statuettes were packed.

[10] Socrates' *manner* is described (362) in terms of which Plato (*Smp*. 221b) seems to have approved. In relating τὠφθαλμὼ παραβάλλεις to ταυρηδὸν ὑποβλέψας (Pl. *Phd*. 117b) E^V displays his lack of acquaintance with bulls.

[11] Cf. Jacoby in *RE* vii 2600.

thing which can hardly have happened less than twenty years later than *Clouds*.[12]

Thanks to the story told in Aelian *VH* ii 13 the mask worn by the character Socrates in *Clouds* has become, in modern times, one of the most famous of all portrait-masks. But it is worth looking again at which Aelian actually says.

Socrates appeared in a play (περιφερομένου ἐν τῇ σκηνῇ) and his name was frequently uttered, and I would not be surprised if he was also visibly represented (οὐκ ἂν δὲ θαυμάσαιμι εἰ καὶ βλεπομένου ἐν τοῖς ὑποκριταῖς), for pretty certainly the property-makers made as close a likeness of him as possible (δῆλα γὰρ δὴ ὅτι κτλ.). The foreigners ⟨who were present⟩, not knowing the man who was being ridiculed, started talking among themselves,[13] wanting to know who this man Socrates was. Socrates, therefore, . . . in order to resolve the foreigners' perplexity, stood up and remained standing in full view throughout the course of the play. Such was the extent of his disregard (καταφρονεῖν) for comedy and for the Athenian people.

It was not, then, 'so that the audience could see his likeness to the actor'[14] that Socrates stood up, but in order to answer the question 'Who is Socrates?' He was silently saying 'I am Socrates', and we might even imagine that he implied a question of his own: 'Do I look like the sort of man who is being ridiculed in this play?' But no doubt we should restrain our imagination at this point and content ourselves with observing that the use of a portrait-mask in *Clouds* is merely incidental to Aelian's anecdote, which would remain a worthwhile anecdote if all reference to visual portraiture were cut out of it.

There is, I think, a very simple reason for the absence of any reference in the play to Socrates' face. His characteristic features – protruding eyes, a snub nose and a big mouth – being the antithesis of what was admired, were the common elements of gross caricature, as we see from humorous vase-painting and from the earliest portrayals of comic masks, notably the Stockport relief.[15] The mask-maker who wanted to produce a good caricature of Socrates for *Clouds* was faced with a difficulty of an unusual kind, and I do not know how, or whether, he surmounted it: the result of his attempt to portray a real person would resemble what he had often done before in portraying fictitious characters.

---

[12] Commentators on *Clouds* (e.g. Blaydes on 887) sometimes forget that when the play was performed in 423 Socrates was in early middle age.

[13] The text is syntactically incoherent, but the meaning is plain.

[14] As stated by Webster, *Greek Theatre Production* 60.

[15] Cf. n. 5 above.

ADDITIONAL NOTES

P. 272, on Cleon's face. I was not aware of Cratinus fr. 228 (*PCG* = 217A Edmonds), in which Cleon's eyebrows were treated as his ugliest feature. D. Welsh, *CQ* xxix (1979), first drew attention to this.

P. 275, n. 8, on the name Ἀμεινίας. I am no longer confident that V's text is right in presenting Ἀμεινίᾳ. Σ^{VE} *ad loc*. reveals a belief that Aristophanes intended a criticism of the Ameinias who was archon in 423/2 but was afraid to use his exact name, and V's Ἀμεινίᾳ may well be the result of an explanatory gloss mistaken for a correction.

28

Review of Ehrenberg,
The People of Aristophanes

V. Ehrenberg, *The People of Aristophanes*, 2nd edn (Basil Blackwell, Oxford 1952).

The first edition of this book appeared in 1943; the second edition is not only augmented by a widening of the field from which the evidence is drawn but also considerably revised. Dr Ehrenberg describes the society and economy of Athens as it was in the lifetime of Aristophanes, using as evidence primarily Aristophanes' own work and the fragments of other poets of the Old Comedy.

The book is organized in such a way as to make a sharp contrast in character between text and footnotes. The text is essentially 'popular'; I do not know if Dr Ehrenberg recoils from this word, but I use it deliberately to mean that the book can be read with understanding, interest, and profit by the intelligent Greekless reader, who will find in it a much higher level of historical learning, accuracy and judgement than is common in a 'popular' book. The footnotes are for the scholar; they give good up-to-date biblio-graphical guidance and are full of interesting and attractive interpretations of difficult passages in comedy and elsewhere. I would be reluctant to rate the main text, for the purposes of the scholar, as anything higher than an *index rerum* to Old Comedy. I do not mean that the picture presented is false; far from it; but I doubt if any scholar can escape a growing uneasiness at the curious relation between Dr Ehrenberg's conclusions and the greater part of the evidence on which he appears to base them.

The root of the trouble is the division of the evidence into two categories, one primary and the other corroborative. It seems clear from the Introduction that Dr Ehrenberg is familiar with this objection – I expect he is sick of it – and that he has met it to his own satisfaction. Not knowing all his reasons, I press the charge. The book is *not* an attempt to evaluate comedy as a historical source; apart from a highly generalized caution, Dr Ehrenberg does not tackle this important and complicated problem at all. Nor is it an elucidation of comedy by independent evidence, but exactly the reverse. There is only one situation in which a division of evidence into 'primary' and 'corroborative' is justified, and that is the existence of a category of evidence whose transmission has been different in kind from the rest and comparatively exempt from corruption. Thus, if we are interested in questions of spelling, or dates, or sums of money, we do right to take inscriptions of the period concerned as fundamental and demand that the evidence of literary sources – which, after all, we know only through papyri and manuscripts – should be consistent with them or be rejected. Again, a public document recording a political decision is in a different category from an orator's assertion, a century later, that no such decision was made. But comedy does not come into this peculiar category.

It may happen that within a given period one source is virtually the only source, and that the process of change is rapid enough to make the use of evidence from neighbouring periods perilous. But neither condition is satisfied by Dr Ehrenberg's subject. Aristophanic comedy is certainly a major source for the Athens of 430–390 BC, but with Antiphon, Andocides, the early speeches of Lysias, and the earliest of Isocrates all in the field, its importance does not amount to monopoly. Moreover, although literary, artistic, linguistic, and political changes in the Greek world occurred rapidly and drastically between the middle of the fifth century BC and the middle of the fourth, social and economic habits at middle-class and working-class level remained remarkably stable over a much longer period. Whatever the reasons – and the lack of any decisive development in means of production and communication may well be the ultimate reason – the student of authors as far apart in time and place as the early lyric poets, Isaeus and Theocritus is struck less by their differences than by the extent to which they illuminate one another. To argue from the language of Hyperides to the language of Aristophanes is often improper; to argue from the 'people of Hyperides' to the 'people of Aristophanes' is not only proper but necessary.

Old Comedy is a compound of fantasy and parody with the familiar and unheroic. Dr Ehrenberg emphasizes its historical value by laying great stress on the latter elements, but he seems to deceive himself in practice, though not in theory (37ff), in treating the element of fantasy as easily discernible and separable. There is no modern type of drama with which Old Comedy as a whole may be compared, least of all what we now know as comedy. The unheroic element is best understood by anyone who is willing to learn from the variety stage and the music-hall. Now, the music-hall comedian represents humanity as ignorant, philistine, obstinate, dirty, lazy, greedy and lecherous; God forbid that he should do otherwise; he does not show us the average man talking and acting in an average way, but a series of possibilities implicit in familiar situations, a kind of exaggerated concentrate of our lives, a myth, which is lovingly adopted by the people whom it represents and is always and inevitably – like more exalted myths – a little out of date. This relation between the comedian's myth and its living subject is the first difficulty that confronts the interpreter of Aristophanes, and Dr Ehrenberg does not face it when he uses *Lysistrata* and *Thesmophoriazusae* as firm evidence for the status of women. In the latter play the women have assembled to condemn Euripides on the grounds that the great wicked women in his tragedies have brought all their sex into disrepute. A relative of Euripides is present at this assembly, disguised as a woman, and in an effort to save the situation he argues that Euripides is justified and recites a vivid catalogue of the everyday misdeeds of women. Surely Dr Ehrenberg is wrong in using an incident in this catalogue (*Th*. 486) to suggest that the average husband was considerate (p. 197), or (p. 206) the speech as a whole to conclude that Aristophanes 'speaks mostly of the bad ways of women' and was opposed to their emancipation. The speech is a concentrated caricature of the ways of women ('My old woman . . .' in the music-hall). What else can the husband in this myth be but considerate? The average Athenian husband appears pretty odious in Lysistrata's bitter words (*Lys*. 507ff); and, again, what else is possible in the context ('My old man . . .')? A similar failure to do justice to the dramatic context appears in Dr Ehrenberg's use of *Ach*. 600 (p. 106). *Av*. 18 (p. 223) and 1567 (p. 155), *Nu*. 46ff (p. 85), *Th*. 281 (p. 105), and *V*. 579 (p. 346).

The facts that we learn from a passage in comedy rarely, if ever, emerge directly from the statements, general or particular, made by the characters; they come indirectly through an understanding of the tacit assumptions without which the joke is not a joke. The historical use of comedy appears in this respect remarkably similar to the use of oratory, which Dr Ehrenberg – wrongly, I think – underrates by comparison. The superficial case against oratory is easily made. The historian, in his attempts to discover the facts of Attic politics from the orators, easily falls into a comatose naivety which he instantly discards when his trust is solicited by contemporary politicians ('There is no shortage of . . .'), advertisers ('All the best people . . .') and acquaintances ('So I told him . . .'). It would be unplausible to say that all plain statements in the orators are false; but it would be a safer assumption than its contrary. The historian ought to discover the facts from the orators indirectly. Admissions which the speaker would have suppressed, if he could, in the interests of his own case may be taken as *prima facie* true. Again, an orator rarely says 'By *x* I understand . . .', and if he did we should doubt whether his definition was the normal one; but if he says, in contrasting two people, 'A is *x*, but B does this and that and that . . .' we can infer what the jury understood by *x*. Many arguments are patently invalid unless certain assumptions are made. Thus when the speaker of Lysias *On the Murder of Eratosthenes* says, 'I thought I heard the front door creak in the night. In the morning I thought I saw traces of make-up on my wife's face, although her brother had died less than a month before. I realize now that she let her lover in during the night', he may not be telling the truth or drawing the right inference, but his argument would make little sense to the jury unless it was abnormal for a woman to put on make-up for at least a month after the death of a near relative.

The historical use of comedy is not unlike this, but it is far harder. Both the orator and the comic poet may be said to measure what they say by the standard of credibility; but, whereas the orator is trying only to persuade us of what happened under the sun to rational beings on two legs, the comic poet is operating at a dozen different levels of the imagination. The tacit assumptions necessary to understand a joke may not be assumptions about real life at all, but assumptions within a field of convention and myth. Dr Ehrenberg seems to make no allowance for this fact at all, unless his remark on the attitude of farmers in Comedy (p. 88 n. 4) is meant to point to it. There is the further difference between oratory and comedy that in using oratory we are trying to find out what generally happened from what someone says actually happened; but the comic poet never professes to tell us directly what happened. There are times when the reader of Dr Ehrenberg's book must remind himself vigorously that comedy is a form of fiction; the slaves' conversation on desertion in *Eq*. 21ff tells us nothing of the incidence of desertion in real life (p. 186), and the wonderful creation of Lysistrata does not in the least mean that 'we may conclude . . . that Kimon's sister Elpinice and the Milesian Aspasia were not the only women in Athens who met men on their own level' (p. 206).

I doubt if there is a page in this book on which all scholars would agree that all the conclusions follow from the evidence referred to; and there are very few pages on which most scholars would not quarrel with at least one of the inferences drawn, especially inferences from fragments of lost plays. If this criticism is even half true, it may seem remarkable that as a description of Attic society the book succeeds. The reason is, I think, that Dr Ehrenberg's conclusions are founded less on the evidence he quotes than on the (often better) evidence that he does not quote; he himself is familiar with *all* the evidence relevant to his enquiry, and he is too good a historian to lose his way in it. The pity is that by elevating the evidence of comedy to a dominant status he gives himself an indefensible position to hold and misleads the reader on the peculiar difficulties of using comedy historically. The old dictum that justice should be not only done but openly done has its point for historians.

29

Review of Taillardat,
Les Images d'Aristophane

Jean Taillardat, *Les Images d'Aristophane: études de langue et de style* (Les Belles Lettres, Paris 1965) 553 pp.

This book first appeared in 1962, when it was not received for review; we now have a *deuxième tirage* in which misprints have been corrected, but random sampling has not disclosed any other changes.

Taillardat gives us a comprehensive study of figurative language in Aristophanes, classified by subject, so that the reader can quickly discover in which terms Aristophanes describes, for example, noses, pride, embezzlement, or musical composition. The discussion covers some 1600 words and phrases, a remarkable total but not quite exhaustive; I have not found, for example, any mention of κόβαλος and its derivatives (*Eq*. 270, etc.), *Nu*. 721 φρουρᾶς ᾄδων, or *Th*. 61f συγγογγύλας . . . χοανεῦσαι. Over 2000 passages of Aristophanes are mentioned, together with numerous fragments of Old and Middle Comedy, and many are discussed in detail. There is a reliable word-index and an index of the passages which are treated in detail; the latter is too selective to be really useful.

'Image' is generously defined so as to include metaphor and simile; at times, perhaps, generosity is excessive, for it is hard to say, in the light of Hes. *Th*. 459, that καταπίνειν is 'proprement *boire*' (p. 90), and the Homeric πόσιος . . . ἐξ ἔρον ἔντο should have been given great weight in discussing (p. 161) ἔρως and ἐρᾶν. Taillardat's introductory discussion (pp. 5–29) shows that he is fully alive to the problems involved in establishing the associations of words and the 'level' or 'register' to which a word belongs. His concept of 'permutants métaphoriques' (p. 17) is particularly helpful: when A and B are in some contexts almost synonymous and a derivative of A is a banal image, a similarly formed derivative of B can appear as a fresh and amusing image. He is also aware of the part played in comedy by 'plaisanteries traditionelles' (e.g. p. 88 on *Eq*. 806 στεμφύλῳ εἰς λόγον ἔλθῃ), the jokes which are moderately funny the first hundred times one hears them but lose their appeal to sophisticated people after early middle age.

No one interested in any aspect of Old Comedy can fail to profit from constant use of this book. The criticisms offered hereafter affect only a small proportion of its contents.

Taillardat deliberately (pp. 9ff) takes the scholia, Pollux, Phrynichus, Hesychius, etc., as the starting-point for the discussion of an obscure word. Sometimes this approach is profitable (e.g. p. 345, on πλύνειν), but it sometimes has to be confessed that the scholia are wrong (e.g. p. 128, on *Ach*. 1035, and p. 346 n. 6, on Pollux vii 41), and many of them which are irrelevant – usually through illegitimate transfer from one context to another (e.g. p. 316 on *Pl*. 253) – or indulge in guesswork (e.g. p. 124 n. 3 on *Pax* 789, pp. 265f on *Eq*. 755, and p. 370 on *Eq*. 1368) are not worth the space given to them. We must always ask whether the ancient commentator or lexicographer appears to have had evidence which we have not.

Since we possess only a tiny fraction of Old Comedy (to say nothing of our losses in other genres) it is a waste of time, in default of positive evidence, to assert or deny that Aristophanes invented an image. Taillardat so often recognizes this (e.g. p. 205 on *Ach*. 805f, and p. 438 on *V*. 1357) that his lapses into dogmatic assertion of Aristophanes' originality (e.g. p. 326 on *Ra*. 925, and p. 385 on *Ach*. 532) are inexplicable. Conversely, citation of Isoc. v 64 (p. 485) hardly suffices to show that *Nu*. 997 τῆς εὐκλείας ἀποθραυσθῆς 'ne fait que renouveler l'image ἐκπίπτειν ἐκ τῆς δόξης'.

It is clearly right to describe an image as 'proverbial' if it is attested earlier than Aristophanes (e.g. p. 460 on *Ec*. 943 τἀπὶ Χαριξένης ~ Cratin. 146) or if it is unintelligible on any other assumption (e.g. p. 279 on fr. 664 γαλῆν καταπέπωκεν, and p. 483 on *Eq*. 277 ἡμέτερος ὁ πυραμοῦς), just as an otherwise unattested meaning must sometimes be given to an individual word (e.g. p. 53 on *Pax* 554 εἰρήνης σαπρᾶς). There are even occasions when a later passage may indicate proverbial character (e.g. p. 48 on *Ach*. 255f γαλᾶς σοῦ μηδὲν ἧττον βδεῖν ~*Pl*. 693 βδέουσα δριμύτερον γαλῆς). But I do not understand in what sense the comparison of Socrates' school to the cave of Trophonius in *Nu*. 506ff is 'proverbial' (p. 164), and although *Av*. 186 λιμῷ Μηλίῳ *might* be called proverbial (p. 79) it was rather young for a proverb in 414. Bearing in mind the date of the parallels cited, one should reserve judgement on the proverbial status of *Lys*. 474 κινοῦσα μηδὲ κάρφος (p. 118).

It is possible to recognize elevated style from types of word and extant passages of earlier poetry, for example in *Nu*. 357 κλέος οὐρανόμηκες (p. 124). But more allowance should be made for paratragedy (e.g. p. 322 on *Ach*. 1191 κρυερὰ πάθεα, and p. 490 on *Th*. 1105f; conversely, it is hard to believe that *Pl*. 1107ff is in any sense parody [p. 349] of A. *PV* 994), for the possibility that some words which we call poetic were in general circulation in the fifth century (e.g. παλάμη, etc. [pp. 232f]), for the deliberate use of the vocabulary of other dialects (e.g. *Lys*. 93 στόλος [p. 379]), and for loanwords at colloquial level from other dialects (e.g. θωρήσσεσθαι [pp. 96f]).

Isolation of a passage from its context may give a misleading impression of its stylistic 'register'. Taillardat recognizes this (cf. pp. 160, 246ff, 253, and 352 n. 1), but he should have taken the context more fully into account in a dozen other cases. P. 34 on *Pax* 839ff: to say 'elle est enfin une interprétation comique de la croyance selon laquelle les morts deviennent des astres' hardly does justice to how the topic is introduced. P. 54 on *Ra.* 117f: the fact that Dionysus is making a journey is all-important. P. 73 on *Lys.* 992 σκυτάλη: this should not be quoted without the previous line. P. 100 on *Av.* 110f σπείρεται: seeds are important to birds. P. 142 on *Ec.* 1: the whole point and nature of 1–19 should be mentioned. P. 151 on Pl. *Smp.* 206d: physiological language is deliberately used throughout the whole passage. P. 152 on *Ra.* 45 ἀποσοβῆσαι: the point is that Dionysus hoped by his disguise to inspire fear, but Herakles cannot 'frighten away' laughter. P. 154 on Pl. *Smp.* 218a δηχθείς: this is fully intelligible only in the light of the preceding five lines. P. 177 on *Av.* 727f ὥσπερ χὠ Ζεύς: given 465–737, the simile is inevitable. P. 310 on *Ach.* 164 πορθούμενος: the Odomantians have been brought in as soldiers to overrun Boeotia (160). P. 448 on *Nu.* 923 ἐκ πηριδίου: not to be divorced from 921f.

Evidence from far beyond the context is often adduced (e.g. p. 321 on *Av.* 161 νυμφίων βίον, and p. 423 on *Pax* 645 ἐβύνουν τὸ στόμα), but should have been adduced more often. P. 39: *Ach.* 883 is parody. P. 59 on *Ra.* 191 τὴν περὶ τῶν κρεῶν: many aspects of the social situation in 406–5 are relevant if the passage is to be discussed adequately. Pp. 65ff on *Ach.* 95ff: the painting of eyes on the bows of ships is relevant. P. 77 on *Lys.* 151 δέλτα παρατετιλμέναι: it would have been prudent to look at some vase-paintings before ridiculing Wilamowitz's interpretation. P. 132 on *Pl.* 951 πανοπλίαν: dedication of the spoils of victory is important here. P. 153 on *Nu.* 620 στρεβλοῦτε: slaves were tortured. P. 159 on *Ec.* 956 ἔγκειται: the use of this word by military historians should be considered. P. 167 on *Th.* 1200: Aristophanes need not have had the famous Carian Artemisia in mind; it is not an uncommon name among Greeks from the Eastern Aegean, and very plausible for the character Euripides has assumed. P. 175 on *V.* 135 φρυαγμοσέμνακος: investigation of -ακος in Buck and Petersen's *Reverse Index* (not mentioned in Taillardat's bibliography) is rewarding. P. 180 n. 1 on *Ra.* 304 γαλήν' ὁρῶ: 'ce vers est d'Euripide' is an inadequate comment. P. 215 n. 6 on *Av.* 17 Θαρραλείδης (*sic*): there were Athenians in Aristophanes' time named Tharreleides (e.g. *SEG* xix 42b 11.5). P. 250 on *Nu.* 233 ἰκμάδα: it is more than 'possible' (n. 4) that Aristophanes is exploiting the idea of Diogenes Apolloniates. P. 267 on *Nu.* 1275 ὑγιαίνεις: to call 'you are not well' a euphemism for 'you are insane' is anachronistic; most ordinary Greeks took a sensible view of 'body' and 'mind'. P. 329 on *Nu.* 912 πάττων: Hdt. viii 120 τιήρῃ χρυσοπάστῳ shows that Aristophanes is not talking about 'saupoudrer'. P. 358 on *Eq.* 355 κασαλβίσω: Theocr. 5.116 is a closer parallel than Catullus 16.1. P. 375 on *V.* 1309 νεοπλούτῳ Φρυγί: were there no Phrygian metics at Athens? P. 388 on *Av.* 1296 Ἶβις: accusations of barbarian origin were a stock-in-trade of politicians; cf. Aeschines iii 172. P. 401, on *Eq.* 732 ἐραστής: the point here (and in Th. ii 43.1) is that lovers vie with one another to earn, by their achievements, the goodwill of the person whom they love. P. 408, 'pour beaucoup d'Athéniens ... le chef populaire n'est qu'un coquin avide de s'enrichir': it would be more accurate to say that virtually all Athens could adopt this standpoint or its opposite, according to the occasion. P. 472 on E. *Ba*. 996 γηγενῆ: see Dodds on 537ff. P. 485 on *Pl*. 1087 ἰάσεται: 'image courante' certainly; but some interesting parallels could have been assembled (including *SEG* x 98.14).

I add some miscellaneous criticisms. P. 13 on Alexis 263.1: ἐν γὰρ νομίζω τοῦτο τῶν ἀνελευθέρων εἶναι is not 'Voici qui suffit, selon moi, à distinguer les gens vulgaires'. P. 20 n. 1 on *Ach*. 321: it is hardly demonstrable that if the mixture of metaphors had been intended as humorous 'l'interlocuteur n'aurait pas manqué de la railler'. P. 33: why should Cratinus (155) have 'imagined' the πνιγεύς–οὐρανός theory to make fun of Hippon? P. 34 on *Nu*. 752: Strepsiades' desire to keep the moon in a mirror-box simply shows that he is aware that bright surfaces need to be protected from abrasion, and has no necessary connection with Empedocles. P. 38 on *V*. 193 πονηρὸς εἶ πόρρω τέχνης: why not 'you are well advanced in the art of πονηρία'? P. 47 on *Ra*. 421 ἐν τοῖς ἄνω νεκροῖσι: this is not comic use of the σῶμα–σῆμα motif, but a joke of the same kind as 177 ἀναβιοίην νυν πάλιν. P. 54 on *Ra*. 83: this does not imply that Agathon is dead, but the reverse; in 85 μακάρων is meant to suggest Μακεδόνων. P. 72 on A. *Ag*. 245 ἀταύρωτος: not 'noble', but as earthy as Pind. *N*. 10.80ff τόνδε ... στάξεν ἥρως. P. 87 on *Pax* 1308 ἐμβάλλετε: granted that the sense 'ram' is not applicable here, it should have been mentioned in n. 1. P. 97 on *Nu*. 981 κεφάλαιον τῆς ῥαφανῖδος: is ῥαφανίς always the small species which we call 'radish'? P. 103 on *Av*. 1256 τριέμβολον: possibly 'trois fois', but τρι- may be intensive. P. 105 on Schol. *Ec*. 920 λαιχάζειν: λαικάζειν is a more likely correction than λειχάζειν. Pp. 116f on fr. 47 τὴν ἀτραπὸν κατερρύην: Theocr. 1.5f ἐς τὲ καταρρεῖ ἁ χίμαρος is relevant. P. 117 on *Av*. 1681 εἰ μὴ βαδίζει γ': Bentley's βαβάζει is surely right (for εἰ μή ... γε cf. *Eq*. 186); Didymus was helpless here, as on *V*. 1309 (p. 237). P. 128 on *Ach*. 1002 ἀσκόν Κτησιφῶντος: 'rivale de' is an odd way of representing this genitive. P. 129 on fr. 377 πηνίω: Aristotle says that πηνία have passed through a larval stage, not that they are larvae. P. 166 on *Lys*. 802 μελάμπυγος: why should this be dissociated from μέλας, 'vaillant'? Both refer to sun-tan and naked exercise; cf. n. 3. P. 170 on *Nu*. 449 γλοιός: 'On ne voit pas bien le rapport, s'il existe, de γλοιός à γλοίης ou γλοιάς'; but Hsch. and *EM* (cited in n. 1) show this adequately. P. 171 on *Nu*. 451 ματιολοιχός: it is not true that 'rien n'interdit de penser que, dès les temps d'Aristophane, la langue populaire ait emprunté le mot ματτύη', for Athenaeus suggests (662f ff) careful observation of the date at which it began to appear so frequently in comedy. P. 182 on *Eq*. 437 καικίας, and p. 198 on *Ach*. 352 ὀμφακίας: *Eq*. 570 ἀμυνίας is highly relevant. P. 189 on Amphis 30.10: the suggested supplement is metrically anomalous, though not impossible. P. 257 on *Ach*. 738 Μεγαρικά τις μαχανά: the point is probably not the Megarian's lack of finesse, but a Megarian reputation at Athens for sharp practice; cf. 700–5. P. 280 on *Eq*. 1316 and *Th*. 40: *Pax* 96ff εὐφημεῖν χρή . . . καὶ τοὺς πρωκτοὺς ἐπικλῄειν is a relevant parody. P. 310 n. 2 on *Nu.* 509 κυπτάζεις: furtiveness is the link between this passage and *Pax* 731. P. 320 on Pl. Com. 169; Dobree's emendation is metrically faulty, as Kock points out. P. 323 on *V.* 1475 εἰσκεκύλικεν: the reader should be warned that this is Reiske's emendation of εἰσκεκύκληκεν. P. 361 on *Nu.* 1372 εὐθέως ἀράττω: this may well be right, but we should be warned that RV and most manuscripts have εὐθὺς ἐξαράττω. P. 365 on *Ach.* 987: the further point should be made that war leads to the destruction of vines just as a riotous guest upsets the wine. P. 369 on Petron. 37.10 *babaecalus*: why should the *Graeculi* have said *ὁ βαβαὶ καλῶς rather than ὦ κτλ? P. 432 on *Vita S.* 22: Aristophanes *may* have said κηρὸς ἐπεκαθέζετο τοῖς χείλεσιν, but it is a curious utterance. P. 460 on *Ach.* 864 οἱ σφῆκες οὐκ ἀπὸ τῶν θυρων: it is not true that 'en ce sens, σφήξ est un hapax', for Dikaiopolis comes out in the belief that the noise is made by wasps.

30

Notes on Aristophanes'
Acharnians

68–71

καὶ δῆτ' ἐτρυχόμεσθα διὰ Καϋστρίων
πεδίων ὁδοιπλανοῦντες ἐσκηνημένοι,
ἐφ' ἁρμαμαξῶν μαλθακῶς κατακείμενοι,
ἀπολλύμενοι.

Two tones are blended in the Athenian envoy's account of his mission to Persia: one is a tone of complaint, which he judges prudent in explaining the length of his absence (cf. the excuses made by Theoros, 136ff), and the other is pleasurable reminiscence, which keeps breaking through and marring the impression which he is trying to create. ἐτρυχόμεσθα and ἀπολλύμενοι belong to the first, μαλθακῶς to the second. Similarly in 73–5, having begun with ξενιζόμενοι he tries to correct the impression which this word will make by adding πρὸς βίαν; but ἄκρατον οἶνον is too much for him, and he adds (sighing at the happy memory) ἡδύν. It is this which provokes Dikaiopolis's explosion and the envoy's uneasy self-justification.

Most of us have heard people profess that an experience was full of hardship and yet betray, by the way in which they speak of it, that in fact they thoroughly enjoyed it. Rich as Aristophanic comedy is in psychological satire,[1] there is no passage sharper in observation or more felicitous in representation than *Ach*. 65–78. μαλθακῶς is crucial, and emendation[2] misses the point of the whole passage.[3]

---

[1] Cf. my note in *CR* ns ix (1959) 197.
[2] E.g. Kuster's οὐ μαλακῶς or Denys Page's μάλα κακῶς (*WSt*. lxix [1956] 116f).
[3] Another relevant consideration is Aristophanes' tendency to complete a picture when not all the details suit the argument; cf. G. J. De Vries, *Hermeneus* xxi (1949–50) 35f, on *Av*. 840 (to which we might add *Ach*. 1101).

100

| ἰαρταμαν | ἐξαρξαν ἀπίσσονα σάτρα | ΑΓ |
| | ἐξαρξας πισόναστρα | R |

Two things are obvious at once. First, Aristophanes has attempted to reproduce the most striking phonological characteristics of Old Persian, the
predominance of a vowel *a* (and perhaps also initial *ya*, which is much
commoner in Persian than initial *ια*, *ιε* or *ιο* in Greek). Secondly, the greater
part of the line is made up of three Persian words which every Greek knew, or
thought he knew: the element *arta*, so common in proper names, the name of
Xerxes, and what the Greeks no doubt assumed – quite wrongly – to be the
Persian original (actually *xšaçapāvā*) of σατράπης. As for the rest of the line,
after the fantasies discussed by Ribbeck *ad loc.* and Wackernagel's demolition
of Friedrich's more modest (but grammatically atrocious) suggestion,[4] editors
have been reluctant to look for any more Persian. But there is one question
which cannot be set aside: what determined Aristophanes' choice of syllables
to fill the gap between -ξας (-ξαν) and (ἀ)πι-? To call them random syllables
or deliberate nonsense is no answer. The King's Eye's second utterance (104)
is a perfect iambic trimeter; if, therefore, Aristophanes wrote -ξᾰς (-ξᾰν)
ἀπισσονᾱ or -ξᾰς (-ξᾰν) ᾱπισ(σ)ονᾰ, he can only have done so because he
wanted to convey or suggest some meaning which three syllables in a smooth
rhythm could not have conveyed. Or, of course, we may regard the text as a
corruption of -ξᾰς (-ξᾰν) — ◡ —and then either abandon further enquiry as
pointless or ask again: what determined his choice, and is therefore anything
meaningful of which ἀπίσσονα could be a corruption?[5]

It happens that the line resembles something which might be said by a
Persian dignitary and which might be familiar to many Greeks who knew no
other words of Persian. The following are samples (all from Darius's Behistun
inscription) of formulae which are common in Old Persian documents:[6]

DB I 28   *Kabūjiya nāma Kūrauš puça* = 'Cambyses (by) name, Cyrus's son'.
DB IV 83   *Vidafarnā nāma Vāyaspārahyā puça Pārsa* = 'Intaphernes (by) name,
           Vayaspara's son, a Persian'.
DB III 55 *Vivāna nāma Pārsa manā badaka Harauvatiyā xšaçapāvā* = 'Vivana
           (by) name, a Persian, my subject, satrap of Arachosia'.

I suggest that Aristophanes wrote:

---

[4] J. Friedrich, *IF* xxxix (1921) 93ff; J. Wackernagel, ibid. 224.
[5] Cantarella *ad loc.* suggests that 102, 'he says that the King will send you gold', should be a
translation of 100; but the point of the scene is that hopes of money from Persia are a delusion and
a waste of time – as the King's Eye himself makes plain in 104.
[6] I quote the texts from R. G. Kent, *Old Persian*, 2nd edn (New Haven, Conn. 1953).

$$\text{Ἴαρτα νᾱμᾶ} \quad \left\{ \begin{array}{l} \text{Ξαρξᾶ} \\ \text{or Ξαρξαιᾱ} \\ \text{or Ξαρξασᾱ} \end{array} \right\} \quad \text{πυσσᾱ σατρᾱ}$$

'Iarta by name, son of Xerxes, satrap.' The final syllables of *nāma* and *puça* would actually be short in Persian, but to lengthen both of them parodies the sound of Persian better.

The process of corruption is easy to see. The familiarity of ἐξαρξ- (and ἐξ- generally) was the start of the trouble; ναμ then inevitably became μάν, and the rest of the line suffered the variety of fates which befall the unintelligible at the hands of copyists.[7]

If it is objected that a man who has just been named (91, 99) as 'Pseudartabas' cannot proceed to say that his name is 'Iarta', I recall a well-worn technique of the old-fashioned English music-hall comedian. 'I will now sing you a little song entitled . . .' he says, and having given us a 'title' which is an elaborate joke in itself he goes on to sing a song which has nothing to do with the 'title' and may indeed be a well-known song with a title of its own. Similarly, the name 'Pseudartabas' is in itself a joke which expresses a certain view of Persians, but to incorporate the element ψευδ- into the Persian's own announcement would be to strike a false note and to prolong a joke beyond its natural life.

110–22

We should imagine Dikaiopolis not as simply pushing or waving the Athenian envoy away at the words ἀλλ' ἄπιθ', but as driving him right out of the orchestra, ferociously brandishing his stick. The actor who takes the part of the envoy must also be either Amphitheos or Theoros.[8] If he is Amphitheos, it is imperative to get him away before 125, for Amphitheos speaks at 129. If he is Theoros – and this is more likely, in any case, since at 55–65 the disappearance of Amphitheos and the appearance of the envoy are separated by ten lines at the most – it is less urgent to get him away before 125, for Theoros does not speak until 134; but the margin is still rather narrow, and 110 provides an excellent dramatic opportunity for enlarging it to comfortable proportions.

Dikaiopolis then advances threateningly on the King's Eye (111):

ἄγε δὴ σὺ φράσον ἐμοὶ σαφῶς πρὸς τουτονί.

What is τουτονί, before which (in respect for which, in fear of which, with which in mind) the Persian is to tell the truth? At least we can get more help from the context here than we get in *Nu.* 1146f

---

[7] The textual transmission of Plautus *Poen.* 930–1027 is rich in parallels.

[8] *Ach.* 1–203 require four actors plus one extra (who speaks no real Greek) for the King's Eye.

ἀλλὰ τουτονὶ πρῶτον λαβέ·
χρὴ γὰρ ἐπιθαυμάζειν τι τὸν διδάσκαλον

where the scholiast guesses (with 689 in mind) that Strepsiades brings a sack (θύλακος) of meal. The context in *Acharnians* suggests that Dikaiopolis's 'this' is his stick, with which the Persian will be bloodied if he lies or prevaricates. βακτηρία, however, is feminine; it follows that Dikaiopolis has what the audience would think of as a σκίπων,[9] or alternatively, that there existed in colloquial Attic another masculine word for 'stick' of which we know nothing.[10]

Menacingly, Dikaiopolis raises his stick and shouts at the King's Eye (113),

βασιλεὺς ὁ μέγας ἡμῖν ἀποπέμψει χρυσίον;

The Persian and his two eunuchs (see below) naturally shrink from this alarming and incomprehensible assailant, and try to placate him (as one does in such circumstances) by vehement gestures of negation. Dikaiopolis takes this as the answer to his question, and asks (114),

ἄλλως ἄρ' ἐξαπατώμεθ' ὑπὸ τῶν πρέσβεων;

This time the three men nod vigorously, still hoping to placate him – for, as they can see, their previous negation only seemed to make him angrier – but having no idea what he is talking about. He seizes on this (115):

Ἑλληνικόν γ' ἐπένευσαν ἄνδρες οὑτοιί,
κοὐκ ἔσθ' ὅπως οὐχ εἰσὶν ἐνθένδ' αὐτόθεν.

'They gave a *Greek* nod!', 'they nodded *in Greek*!' The joke is not that a Greek nod differs from a Persian nod,[11] but of the same type as 'he can sign his name in four languages!' Dikaiopolis is taking the line 'I don't believe in Persians!' and now affects to think that the Persians (including the King's Eye himself,[12] as the relation between 116 and 117 makes perfectly plain) are Athenians in disguise. He thus embarks on a type of joke favoured by bullies in all ages – deliberate misunderstanding, pressed relentlessly and noisily until the victim is put to flight or reduced to tears and helpless anger (cf. Peisetairos's treatment of Iris in *Av.* 1199ff). Approaching one of the two attendants, he pulls away the clothing with which the lower half of the man's

---

[9] Cf. Pollux x 131, where σκίπων is among things which προσήκουσι γεωργοῖς.

[10] As we knew nothing of [β]αθρόθυμα and [ἐπιβ]λήτιον (neither is mentioned by Pollux) until the discovery of the *tabulae poletarum* of 414/13 (*SEG* xiii 16.33, 12.219ff; cf. W. K. Pritchett, *Hesperia* xxv [1956] 247, 309f).

[11] The scholiast *ad loc.*, in saying that it does, is probably reproducing an invention of someone who failed to see the joke; but, even if he is right, he is irrelevant.

[12] This is overlooked in the interpretation of the scene by V. Gordziejew, *Eos* xxxix (1938) 463.

face, in Persian fashion, is covered,[13] revealing a beardless mask. Until that is done, the audience does not know that these two attendants are eunuchs, and, if strict logic mattered (as it does not), Dikaiopolis could not know either; but, in order that the joke should have its full impact, it is important both that it should not be prematurely disclosed (i.e. at 94) and also that when it does come the audience should be left in no doubt of its nature. Dikaiopolis declares that one of the eunuchs is Kleisthenes, and a little later he will declare the other to be Straton (117f, 122). These two men are ridiculed as beardless in *Eq*. 1373f

> Δη. οὐδ' ἀγοράσει γ' ἀγένειος οὐδεὶς ἐν ἀγορᾷ.
> Αλ. ποῦ δῆτα Κλεισθένης ἀγοράσει καὶ Στράτων;

We do not know the name of Kleisthenes' father. ὁ Σιβυρτίου (118) is probably a specimen of that type of joke in which a man is ridiculed not by a nickname or a perversion of his own name or of his demotic but by an imaginary patronymic; 1131, where Lamachos (actually son of Xenophanes) is called τὸν Γοργάσου, is a clear case, and there is an affinity between this practice and the convention by which serious poets characterize supernatural beings or forces by inventing a parentage for them, e.g. Alkaios fr. 327L-P, where Eros is the child of Iris and Zephyros. The only Sibyrtios known to us from the fifth century had a παλαίστρα when Alkibiades was a boy (Antiphon fr. 68 [Thalheim] = Plu. *Alc*. 3); 'Kleisthenes son of Sibyrtios' may be sarcasm.[14]

Dikaiopolis mocks 'Kleisthenes' with two parodies: the first (119) adapts a verse of Euripides, emphasizing Kleisthenes' hairlessness, and the second (120f) a verse of Archilochos (fr. 83D³).

> ὦ θερμόβουλον πρῶκτον ἐξυρημένε,
> τοιόνδε δ' ὦ πίθηκε τόν πώγων' ἔχων . . .

If the verse of Archilochos is taken from a fable which, like some later fables (e.g. Aesop 38 and 39 [Chambry]), culminated in the discomfiture of an ape,[15] we might expect τοιόνδε . . . ἔχων to be indignant: 'with such a . . ., nevertheless . . .!' (cf. Babrios 130.10). But in Dikaiopolis's adaptation indignation would seem to have a point only if the eunuchs were wearing the masks of ordinary bearded Greeks: 'with a (*sc*. great) beard like that, you've dared to come dressed up as a *eunuch*?' Since, however, he is pretending that the eunuchs are notoriously *beardless* Athenians, either (i), whatever the original

---

[13] Cf. H. Müller-Strübing, *Aristophanes und die historische Kritik* (Leipzig 1873) 692. Persian swathing of the face is the point of the joke about ἄσκωμα in 97.

[14] So Elmsley *ad loc.*

[15] I deliberately put this cautiously, being chary of reconstructions of Archilochos. Those who prefer something less cautious may find it in S. Luria, *Philologus* lxxxv (1930) 1ff. O. Immisch, *SHAW* 1930/1, 3ff, and F. Lasserre, *Les Épodes d'Archiloque* (Paris 1950) 128ff.

context in Archilochos, he is not asking an indignant question but uttering a triumphant exclamation, plucking the eunuch's beardless chin as he does so: 'It's because you have the kind of beard that you have that you've come dressed up as a eunuch!'; or (ii) the words are a mock-indignant question (cf. above on ὁ Σιβυρτίου), making fun of Kleisthenes' beardlessness by pretending that Kleisthenes, of all people, could never pass himself off as a eunuch (cf. a recurrent element in popular humour, the pretence that one is terrified of a very small and inoffensive man). Linguistically (ii) is preferable, for Dikaiopolis's words – especially after the reproach implied in θερμόβουλον – sound more like indignation than anything else (cf. *V.* 1043f). But (i) makes the humour less complicated, and a writer who quotes or parodies another is under no obligation to retain the point or implications of the original passage (cf. Mimnermos fr. 2.8 ~ *H* 451).

I have not been able to take seriously the idea which has commended itself to many editors, that Aristophanes intends us actually to imagine the Persians as disguised Athenians.[16] The sentiment underlying the scene is not that advocates of dealings with Persia are ingenious and elaborate frauds, but that Persians are useless, gibbering decadents, fit only to be mocked and bullied by honest Athenians.

158

τίς τῶν Ὀδομάντων τὸ πέος ἀποτεθρίακεν;

The asking of a question which affects to misunderstand the situation is one of the oldest and most widespread forms of malicious humour; cf. on 115f above, and *Nu*. 1266f

> Στ. τί δαί σε Τληπόλεμός ποτ᾽ εἴργασται κακόν;
> Δα. μὴ σκῶπτε ὦ μ᾽ τᾶν. . . .

If, therefore, Aristophanes means us to imagine the Odomantians as coming fresh from amatory exercises, the question 'who has pushed back their foreskins?' is a feeble joke precisely because it admits of a correct answer. If, on the other hand, they are represented as circumcised, it is a real joke. To this interpretation it has long been objected, first, that Thracians did not practise circumcision, and, secondly, that the Athenians must have known that. Both statements are true (cf. Hdt. ii 104.2), but neither is a cogent objection. The Greeks, familiar with circumcision as a practice characteristic of Egypt and Syria, found it so amusing[17] that they exploited it for humorous

---

[16] On this view, an Athenian disguised as a Persian for the purpose of deceiving the Assembly says (104), 'you *won't* get gold!'

[17] Cf. the artist's treatment of Egyptians in an Attic red-figure pelike (Athens 9683, illustrated in *Imago* 1961, pl. 47) which depicts the triumph of Herakles over Busiris.

purposes in general. The type of leather phallos to which Aristophanes refers derogatorily in *Nu*. 537ff must have represented a circumcised penis, for otherwise it could not have been simultaneously 'hanging down' and 'red at the end'.[18] It should also be noted that Odysseus on a well-known Kabeirion vase is circumcised;[19] not because the vase-painter really believed that he was, but simply as an element of caricature, like a pot-belly and a snub nose (cf. *Pl.* 266f).

In the case of the Odomantians Aristophanes used an established humorous device to emphasize their barbarous character, and neither he nor his audience was troubled by ethnological pedantry.[20]

271–5

> πολλῷ γάρ ἐσθ᾽ ἥδιον, ὦ Φαλῆς Φαλῆς,
> κλέπτουσαν εὑρόνθ᾽ ὡρικὴν ὑληφόρον,
> τὴν Στρυμοδώρου Θρᾷτταν ἐκ τοῦ φελλέως,
> μέσην λαβόντ᾽, ἄραντα, κατα–
> βαλόντα καταγιγαρτίσαι.

Dikaiopolis's way with a thief is precisely the way attributed in later times to Priapos, the ungovernably salacious protector of crops and fruit;[21] and, like Priapos and for the same reason, he is not wholly displeased that there should be thieves.[22] The incident which he envisages as typical of a happy rustic life perhaps reflects a conventional assumption that a thief, slave or free, is fair game for the appetites of the offended farmer. In Theocr. 5.116ff after the two rustics, Lakon and Komatas, have cursed in turn the creatures which spoil or steal crops and fruit – locusts, cicadas, foxes and beetles – Komatas says,

> ἦ οὐ μέμνασ᾽, ὅκ᾽ ἐγώ τυ κατήλασα, καὶ τὺ σεσαρὼς
> εὖ ποτεκιγκλίζευ καὶ τᾶς δρυὸς εἴχεο τήνας;

and Lakon retorts,

> τοῦτο μὲν οὐ μέμναμ᾽· ὅκα μάν ποκα τεῖδέ τυ δήσας
> Εὐμάρας ἐκάθηρε, καλῶς μάλα τοῦτό γ᾽ ἴσαμι.

---

[18] Reference to vase-painting depicting comic phalloi with long foreskins cannot disprove anatomical facts, nor does it even pose a problem. In *Clouds* Aristophanes is speaking of particular humorous devices which had been exploited (by himself, among others) on various occasions, but it does not follow that all of them were of universal application.

[19] Illustrated in L. Breitholtz, *Die dorische Farce im griechischen Mutterland* (Stockholm 1960) figs 21–2.

[20] Others were; the scholiast on 156 records a view that the Odomantians were Jews.

[21] Cf. *Anth. Plan.* 236 (attributed to Leonidas of Taras); *Carmina Priapea* (Bücheler) 13, 22, 35, al.; H. Herter, *De Priapo* (Giessen 1932) 16f, 209f; R. Lullies, *RE* xxii, col. 1927.

[22] Cf. *Carmina Priapea* 5 and 38.

Were not perhaps Lakon's fate at the hands of Komatas and Komatas's thrashing by Eumaras[23] both penalties for thieving?

344–6

ἐκσέσεισται χαμᾶζ· οὐχ ὁρᾷς σειόμενον;
ἀλλὰ μή μοι πρόφασιν, ἀλλὰ κατάθου τὸ βέλος,
ὡς ὅδε γε σειστὸς ἅμα τῇ στροφῇ γίγνεται.

Given the first line, in which the chorus call attention to the way in which the cloak of each man is shaken so that the stones collected as missiles fall out of it, the last line seems extraordinarily feeble: 'for this (i.e. this cloak) is becoming shaken (σειστός) as it is whirled round' (or, 'as I whirl round'). It has a point, however, if σειστός meant in Attic what it means in Hellenistic and Byzantine Greek,[24] 'pendant' or (as a neuter plural or masculine singular noun) 'feminine ornaments'. After saying οὐχ ὁρᾷς σειόμενον; the chorus gyrate and make their cloaks, held by a fastening at the neck, fly out and come to rest hanging down, in front or behind, like useless pendants.

For a word of similar historical distribution cf. ὕων, 'pigsty', found in a Hellenistic papyrus and a virtually certain restoration of [Υ]ΟΝ in *SEG* xiii 16.39 (414/13), but nowhere to be found in literature and not mentioned by Pollux.

348

ὀλίγου τ᾽ ἀπέθανον ἄνθρακες Παρνάσ (σ) ιοι

It is unfortunate that Coulon in his apparatus criticus cites Meisterhans, *Grammatik der attischen Inschriften*, 3rd edn (Berlin 1900) 98, in support of the emendation Παρνήσσιοι. Meisterhans is speaking of Parnassos, not Parnes, and refers to *CIA* ii 609 (= *IG* ii² 1285.25), where we find Ἀπόλλωνος Παρνησσίου. This line of *Acharnians* provides our only example of an objective formed from Πάρνης. It may be corrupt, for the expected form is Παρνήθιοι, which Bentley conjectured here and LSJ adopted; but it is not certainly corrupt. Since Parnes was not a deme, Aristophanes may have had to coin an adjective; and, since the λάρκος containing the ἄνθρακες is consistently personified in 331–51, he may have wished to coin a word resembling a demotic in form. He may then have recalled the demotic which

---

[23] I agree with Gow *ad loc.* that ἐκάθηρε is not obscene (note δήσας). I have been tempted to interpret *V.* 449–51, where Philokleon reproaches his own slave for ingratitude, as obscene, but there are linguistic, physiological and sociological objections to such an interpretation; also, the passage is funnier 'clean' than 'dirty', like *Nu.* 55, where some editors see obscenity.

[24] Cf. LSJ and Du Cange, *s.v.*

most intimate geographical connection with Parnes, and invented Παρνάσιοι on the analogy of the equally unexpected Φυλή/Φυλᾶσιοι (1028).[25]

377–8 AND 501–2

αὐτός τ᾽ ἐμαυτὸν ὑπὸ Κλέωνος ἅπαθον
ἐπίσταμαι διὰ τὴν πέρυσι κωμῳδίαν.

ἐγὼ δὲ λέξω δεινὰ μέν, δίκαια δέ·
οὐ γάρ με νῦν γε διαβαλεῖ Κλέων. . . .

Whether it was Kallistratos or Aristophanes or both whom Kleon attacked in 426 – and on that question I have no fresh evidence to offer, except the observation that he is most likely to have attacked both – it is remarkable to hear a character in the play using the first person singular in referring not to what had happened to himself in the course of the play but to what had happened to the author or producer. But it is not in the least necessary to interpret 'I', as 'I, Kallistratos', or 'I, Aristophanes'; it is 'I, the comic hero' or – looking at the same person from a slightly different standpoint – 'I, the comic protagonist'. Without wishing either to revive the view[26] that Aristophanic comedy evolved from a comedy of 'stock types' or to exaggerate such community of character as there may be between various Aristophanic 'heroes' (cf. on 1018ff below), I would draw attention to the fact that in one type of Aristophanic comedy, exemplified by *Acharnians*, *Peace*, *Birds* and *Lysistrata*, the play revolves around a single 'hero', who has the right to speak for Comedy. Aristophanes treats Dikaiopolis as if were an annual visitor to Athens who got into trouble on the last occasion on which he attempted to δίκαια λέγειν.

446

εὐδαιμονοίης· Τηλέφῳ δ᾽ ἁγὼ φρονῶ.

εὐδαιμονοίης is the traditional response of the ingratiating beggar to generosity: 'God bless you, sir!' (cf. 457). The second half of the line is direct quotation from *Telephus* (fr. 707), where the dative was syntactically appropriate. Absence of syntactical adjustment between quotation and context is unusual, but in Aristophanes' line the dative was perhaps felt as natural and intelligible. Cf. Dem. xxiii 50, 'ἄν τις τύπτῃ τινά' φησιν (*sc*. the law, or its maker) . . . 'τὰ ψευδῆ'. προσέθηκεν . . . πανταχοῦ τὴν πρόφασιν βεβαιοῦσαν

[25] Ἀναγυροῦς/Ἀναγυρᾶσιοι (fr. 6 Dem.) is also unexpected.
[26] Decisively criticized by Breitholtz 83ff.

τὸ πρᾶγμ' εὑρήσομεν. ἀλλ' οὐ σοί[27] (i.e. in the case of the decree which you have proposed), ἀλλ' ἁπλῶς, 'ἄν τις ἀποκτείνῃ . . .'.

530–1

ἐντεῦθεν ὀργῇ Περικλέης οὑλύμπιος
ἤστραπτ', ἐβρόντα, ξυνεκύκα τὴν Ἑλλάδα.

Cicero took this passage as evidence for Perikles' rhetorical technique and for its effect on his audience, *Or*. 29 'qui si tenui genere uteretur, numquam ab Aristophane poeta fulgere tonare permiscere Graeciam dictus esset'. Plutarch (*Per*. 8.5) similarly treated it, together with *Com. Adesp*. 10 δεινὸν κεραυνὸν ἐν γλώσσῃ φέρειν, as supporting the view that Perikles' rhetorical style was the reason why the comic poets called him 'Zeus' or 'Olympian' (e.g. Cratin. fr. 240); cf. Luc. *Dem. Enc*. 20. This interpretation, however, is an error engendered by the characteristic preoccupation of later antiquity with rhetoric. Aristophanes' point is that Perikles reacted to the Megarian transgression as Zeus reacts with thunder and lightning, his supernatural weapons (cf. *Π* 384ff, where Zeus rains furiously when men are unjust); the fact that Perikles had been called 'Olympian' provided him with the obvious metaphor. I would also suggest that the author of *Com. Adesp*. 10 referred not to Perikles' manner of speaking but to the political power which he wielded by means of his persuasive and authoritative speeches, and that the metaphor was again prompted by the established nickname. The joke with which Aristophanes continues (532ff) is a joke not against Perikles' rhetoric but against the language of decrees.[28]

731–2

ἀλλ' ὦ πονηρὰ κόριχ' ἀθλίω πατρός,
ἄμβατε ποττὰν μάδδαν, αἴ χ' εὕρητέ πα.

Aristophanes' Megarian completely ignores initial and intervocalic digamma; we could explain 783 ποττὰν ματέρ' εἰκασθήσεται on the grounds that Aristophanes, not being a philologist, might not have known how a Megarian would pronounce εἰκάζειν if he pronounced it at all, but this explanation will not serve for 742 εἴξεῖτ' οἴκαδις and 782 πέντ' ἐτῶν.[29] Direct epigraphic evidence for the dialect of Megara in the fifth century is negligible; and before drawing

---

[27] σοί SYF: σύ A: παρά σοι (*sic*) S[8.1.]F[γρ.]

[28] Of the kind found (e.g.) in *Athenian Tribute Lists*, D17.21ff: οὐκ ἀποστήσομαι ἀπὸ τοῦ δήμου τοῦ Ἀθηναίων οὔτε τέχνῃ οὔτε μηχανῇ οὐδεμιᾷ οὐδ' ἔπει οὐδὲ ἔργῳ οὐδὲ τῷ ἀφισταμένῳ πείσομαι . . . .

[29] 783 σάφ' ἴσθι is not metrically guaranteed.

the conclusion, from the other West Greek dialects (including those of Megarian colonies), that Aristophanes is an untrustworthy witness we should reflect on three considerations:

(i) In dialectology the genealogical model is a concise way of summarising hypotheses about the changes in the distribution of alternative forms *up to* a given time, but it never provides a complete explanation of their distribution *at* a given time. There are always phenomena of which the geographical distribution is at variance with their putative history. So far from being surprised if there proved to be phenomena shared in 425 BC by Megara, Boeotia and Attica but not by the territories adjoining that area, we should be surprised if there were not (cf. on 868 below).

(ii) Since every dialect of every language is in process of change at any given moment, no dialect is ever wholly consistent. Inconsistency in the literary representation of a dialect is therefore not necessarily the product of carelessness on the part of the writer.

(iii) Initial digamma is a conspicuous and constantly recurring difference of pronunciation between Greek dialects, precisely the kind of difference which a writer exploiting a dialect for comic effect would emphasize. The Spartans in *Lysistrata* pronounce it: 155 παρᾶϊδῶν (παρενιδών codd.), 1096 τὸ ἔσθος.[30]

I infer that initial and intervocalic digamma had perished from the dialect of Megara by 425.[31] Postconsonantal digamma poses a more complicated problem. The Megarian says κᾱλός (765, 766, 788) and μόνος (794); the Boeotian says ξένος (867, 884) and κόρᾱν (883, but that is Aeschylean parody); and the Spartans in *Lysistrata* say κᾱλός (180, 1148, 1243). It simply will not do to discount the evidence of Aristophanes on the grounds that he is a comedian, for it is just because he is a comedian that we expect him to exaggerate dialect (cf. on 775 below), not to tone it down by depriving some of the commonest words in Greek of what his audience would recognize as non-Attic pronunciation. Again, I infer without hesitation or surprise that the pronunciations κᾱλός, ξένος, μόνος were the norm throughout much of the Greek mainland.

At the same time the Megarian endearment κόριχον retained a long first syllable, as 731 shows. However Aristophanes spelt the word, he intended the actor to say κούριχ', possibly κώριχ' or conceivably κόρριχ' (cf. ὄρρος < ὄρϜος in DGE 732, from the Megarian colony Heraclea Pontica).[32]

---

[30] The Boeotian says nothing in which the presence of absence of initial digamma can be metrically guaranteed; cf. on 911 below.

[31] SGDI 3045 (= DGE 165g), cited by Elliott (219), is in the dialect of Selinus, not of the Megarid, and in any case belongs to the beginning of the fifth century (T. J. Dunbabin, *The Western Greeks* [Oxford 1948] 417f).

[32] Cf. however H. Jacobsohn, *Hermes* xliv (1909) 84f, who offers good reasons for thinking that the language of this inscription is barbarized.

775

τὸ δέ νιν εἴμεναι τίνος δοκεῖς;

Epigraphically, the infinitival ending -μεναι and the infinitive ἔμμεναι are attested only in Lesbos, and εἴμεναι nowhere; in Boeotia and the eastern Peloponnese we find only εἶμεν and ἦμεν (cf. 741, 771). ἔμ(μ)εναι does however belong to the language of epic, and is freely used by fifth-century poets, e.g. Parm. frr. 6.1, 8.38, Euenos fr. 9.1. This time there is no excuse to be made for Aristophanes; he is concocting a bizarre form and for the moment equating a particular non-Attic dialect with the non-Attic in general. In somewhat the same manner the composers of epitaphs were apt to treat all that was alien as necessarily poetic, putting side by side forms which belong neither to the same local dialect nor to the same genre of poetry.[33] This is the simplest explanation, too, of the strange vocative Στρεψίαδες in the old rustic's amateurish enkomion, *Nu*. 1206.[34]

832–3

Δι.   καὶ χαῖρε πόλλ'.
Με.   ἀλλ' ἀμὶν οὐκ ἐπιχώριον.
Δι.   πολυπραγμοσύνη νυν ἐς κεφαλὴν τράποιτ' ἐμοί.

νυν, which most commonly accompanies an imperative, is found with an optative in *V*. 758f μή νυν ἔτ' ἐγὼ ... Κλέωνα λάβοιμι. In many passages it has the sense 'then', 'if that is so', e.g. *Eq*. 1107, *Nu*. 189, 506, 742; the closest parallel to *Ach*. 832f is 1018f

Δι.   ὦ Ἡράκλεις, τίς οὑτοσί;
Γε.   ἀνὴρ κακοδαίμων.
Δι.   κατὰ σεαυτόν νυν τρέπου.

(cf. *Nu*. 1262f).

The joke, which has often been thought forced or obscure,[35] turns upon the fact that in the latter part of the fifth century πολυπραγμοσύνη or πολλὰ πράττειν, in the sense 'interference with the internal affairs and interrelations of other states', was a well-known reproach against Athens and a boast of the

---

[33] E.g. Peek, *Griechische Versinschriften* i 161 (Athens, sixth century, elegiacs) μητρὸς ἐφημοσύνᾳ; cf. ibid. 902 (Paphos, third century, elegiacs).

[34] Strepsiades feels that to make a composition truly poetic it is essential to use eccentric accidence. For a more subtle explanation (too subtle, to my mind) cf. B. Marzullo, *Maia* vi 91953) 99ff.

[35] Cf. Page 123f.

Athenians themselves; cf. E. *Su*. 576, Th. vi 87.2f.[36] When the Megarian declines to 'rejoice' (cf. 176) on the grounds that rejoicing is no part of the Megarian way of life (cf. Th. iv 17.2 ἐπιχώριον ὂν ἡμῖν . . . μὴ πολλοῖς χρῆσθαι), Dikaiopolis apologizes gracefully for his interference with other people's ἐπιχώρια. The curse which he calls upon himself is harmless enough; he will not be the loser if χαῖρε comes home to roost.

868

Θείβαθε γὰρ φύσαντες ἐξόπισθέ μου. . . .

Elmsley's Θείβαθε (-θι codd.) not only suits the sense but supports and is supported by a desirable emendation of 911 (see below). The substitution of θε (on the analogy of πρόσθε(ν) etc.) for the ablative noun-suffix θεν is an admirable example of a phenomenon which has a coherent geographical distribution in conflict with the genealogical relationship of the dialects in which it appears (cf. 731 above). We find it in the Boeotian Pindar[37] (*P*. 4.102 ἀντρόθε γάρ; *N*. 7.70 πάτραθε Σώγενες; *I*. 3.17 ματρόθε Λαβδαχίδαισι); in Attica from the middle of the fourth century;[38] and in Eretria from the beginning of the third (*IG* xii. (9) 248A 4, 7, 11; 249B III 377, 425).

905f

νεὶ τὼ σιώ,
λάβοιμι μεντᾶν κέρδος. . . .

Dialect in Greek texts has suffered two opposite processes of corruption in transmission: banalization, i.e. the changing of unfamiliar to familiar forms, and misplaced pedantry, the exaggeration of the unfamiliar.[39] In general, the earlier the copy of the text we have, the freer it is from banalization. Exaggeration and distortion, on the other hand, begin with the author himself (cf. on 775 above), though his motives are different from those of Hellenistic scholars. Some distortions of this kind can be detected metrically and removed;[40] where there is no metrical check, we must often be content to leave

---

[36] Isoc. vii 80, viii 26, 30, 58, 108 are also interesting in this connection; cf. V. Ehrenberg, *JHS* lxvii (1947) 46ff on the concept of πολυπραγμοσύνη.

[37] Let him, for once, draw upon his native speech.

[38] Cf. Meisterhans 146. Ἀλωπεκῆθε should not be cited in this connection from the early fifth century ostrakon *IG* i² 908; the illustration in *IG* I Suppl. 192 shows that the writer had almost no room left for ΦE and none at all for N.

[39] A good example of the operation of both processes is provided by the fate of Alkman fr. 41 (Page) in the MSS of Plu., *Lyc*. 21.6 and *De Alex. Fort*. 2, where we are offered the variants κιθαρίσδην, κιθαρίσδειν, κιθαρίζειν, κιθαρίδδειν, κιθαρίδδεν.

[40] E.g. Pindar *O*. 2.76 ἐχέμεν (CN); *P*. 3.46 νούσους (BGH); *N*. 6.53 καββάς (BD).

the question open (the sporadic appearance of -ζ > -δδ- in the Megarian scene, on which the manuscript evidence is conflicting, is a case in point) but the attribution of νεὶ τὼ σιώ to a Boeotian poses a problem which we must not shirk.

θ > σ is a purely Lakonian phenomenon, fully exploited in *Lysistrata*; ναὶ τὼ σιώ is a prominent Spartan oath (ten times in *Lysistrata*, and cf. *Pax* 214). The oath itself occurs in other dialects (though the two gods are not the same everywhere), but an Athenian writer would no more put it into the mouth of a Boeotian in the form σιώ than a London writer would put 'Och, by gum!' instead of 'Eh, by gum!' into the mouth of a comic Lancashire man. I infer therefore that σιώ is a distortion in transmission caused by the familiarity of the Spartan oath; εἴμεναι in 775 is quite different, since it would be associated by the audience with the unfamiliar element in poetic language and not exclusively with a particular nationality.

910f

τῶδ' ἐμὰ
Θείβαθεν, ἴττω Δεύς.

The epigraphic evidence for the maintenance of initial digamma in Boeotia is very strong. A Boeotian would have said Ϝίττω Δεὺς. Since this expression was the hallmark of the Boeotian (cf. Pl. *Phd*. 62a *Ep*. 7.345a), as ναὶ τὼ σιώ was of the Spartan (cf. above), to modify it in pronunciation (however one chose to write it in Attic spelling) would be disastrous, as if we were to make our comic Lancashire man say 'Oh, by gum!' Read, therefore, Θείβαθε (cf. on 868 above) and interpret ἴττω as Ϝίττω.

1018ff

The farmer from Phyle, like Dikaiopolis himself (509ff), has suffered losses through the war, but there is to be no peace for him; Dikaiopolis mocks him brutally and drives him away, without deigning to offer any rational excuse for what is, even by Greek standards, heartless behaviour. Nor does the chorus suggest any excuse in their only comment on the scene (1037ff).

ἀνὴρ ἐφηύρηκέν τι ταῖς
σπονδαῖσιν ἡδύ, κοὐκ ἔοι-
κεν οὐδενὶ μεταδώσειν.

Dikaiopolis explains his later generosity to the young bride by saying (1062), ὁτιὴ γυνή 'στι τοῦ πολέμου τ' οὐκ ἀξία[41]

from which it is open to us to infer that he regards the farmer, together with all adult Athenian males except himself, as deserving the suffering which the war inflicts, because they made it needlessly and refuse to make peace; rather as Hesiod (*Op*. 396ff) declares that he will give no more to Perses, for Perses has only himself to blame for poverty and misfortune. This reason, however, is not made explicit in the scene with the farmer, and we should interpret Dikaiopolis's attitude not in the light of what he subsequently says to someone else but in the light of the kind of character which he has already been shown to possess. Two different elements exist in that character. When he argues (309ff, 513ff) that the Spartans, in making war, were only behaving as men must be expected to behave, he is explicitly defending his own peace treaty, but he also necessarily implies that a real peace would be to Athens' advantage. This element, however, is submerged, as well as being disguised by Euripidean parody. The dominant element in Dikaiopolis is a selfishness so pure that it exists only in fictional characters; he is the real hero of popular comedy, through whom the spectator vicariously escapes from duties and discomforts and commitments and takes refuge in a world of fantasy – a world provided, of course, by a supernatural agent (in this case, Amphitheos) and made up of food and drink and sex. This fantastic selfishness is fully savoured when it is denied to an equal, but it may be granted, with lordly caprice, to an inferior, e.g. a woman or a child.

The contrast between Dikaiopolis's selfishness and the benevolent international conscience of Trygaios in *Peace* is striking, but lest we draw too hasty conclusions about the development of Aristophanes' own conscience we must remember that *Peace*, composed at a time when the Athenians had turned their minds to peace and performed just before the treaty was formally ratified, was a response, not a stimulus, to popular sentiment. It is *Lysistrata*, not *Acharnians* or *Peace*, which poses the really worthwhile questions about Aristophanes' personal convictions and their relation to the sentiments of his contemporaries.

1065f

ὅταν στρατιώτας καταλέγωσι, τουτῳὶ
νύκτωρ ἀλειφέτω τὸ πέος τοῦ νυμφίου.

Frequently a passage which is overtly non-sexual has covert sexual associations (e.g. 994–9). In the present case the situation is reversed; an overtly

---

[41] 'And does not deserve (*sc*. the sufferings inflicted by) war.' Blaydes' emendation αἰτία was influenced by Bentley's αἴτιος for ἄξιος in 633, but should not have been; the corruption αἴτιος > ἄξιος in 633 was not visual, but arose from familiarity with the poet's self-praise in parabases elsewhere, e.g. *Eq*. 509 (νῦν δ' ἄξιός ἐσθ' ὁ ποιητής), *Pax* 738, *Nu*. 525.

sexual passage has covert non-sexual associations. Most Greeks in the fifth century failed to draw a firm distinction between magic and pharmacy; spells were supplementary (e.g. Pl. *Chrm*. 155e) or alternative (e.g. Pl. *R*. 426b) to draughts and ointments.[42] Thus in telling the bride to take a course of action which will naturally tempt the bridegroom to stay at home and disobey the call-up Dikaiopolis models his instructions on those of a magician or quack-doctor selling an ointment (to be applied νύκτωρ, for the hour is important in magic, and many such practices belong to the dark) which will keep the young man safe from the dangers of being called up.

1154f

> ὅς γ' ἐμὲ τὸν τλήμονα Λήναια χορη-
> γῶν ἀπέλυσ' ἄδειπνον.

ἐμέ means 'me, the comic choreutes'. The point is, therefore: 'Antimachos, choregos for a comedy at the Lenaia, did not entertain the chorus adequately' (cf. 886). It does not follow that the men who danced in that chorus were the same as those who danced in *Acharnians*; they speak for comic choreutai in general, just as Demosthenes says to a jury, 'you allowed Meidias to secure the disenfranchisement of Straton' (xxi 91), 'the other trierarchs escorted you when you sailed back from Styra' (xxi 167), 'you made Charidemos a citizen' (xxiii 187), 'you know the law, for you made it' (xlii 18), identifying in each case a particular jury with juries in general and with the whole Athenian people from which juries were drawn (cf. also on 377f above). Still less does it follow[43] that Aristophanes competed at the Lenaia of 427/6.

1180–8

> καὶ τῆς κεφαλῆς κατέαγε περὶ λίθῳ πεσών,
> καὶ Γόργον' ἐξήγειρεν ἐκ τῆς ἀσπίδος.
> πτίλον δὲ τὸ μέγα κομπολακύθου πεσὸν
> πρὸς ταῖς πέτραισι δεινὸν ἐξηύδα μέλος·
> 'ὦ κλεινὸν ὄμμα, νῦν πανύστατόν σ' ἰδὼν
> λείπω, φάος γε τοὐμόν· οὐκέτ' εἰμ' ἐγώ'.
> τοσαῦτα λέξας εἰς ὑδρορρόαν πεσὼν
> ἀνίσταταί τε καὶ ξυναντᾷ δραπέταις
> λῃστὰς ἐλαύνων καὶ κατασπέρχων δορί.

---

[42] This remained true for many times and places. Cato *RR* 83 and 160, considered in relation to the surrounding material, bring home to us the uncertainty of the boundaries between cookery, pharmacy, magic and cult.

[43] As is inferred by C. F. Russo, *Aristofane autore di teatro* (Florence 1962) 26ff.

The last three lines of this passage have been severely criticized for their incoherence,[44] but they can in fact be made splendidly theatrical and comic if the messenger works himself into a frenzy of emotion and mimes each phrase with grotesque exaggeration. If such a style was characteristic of actors playing messenger roles – or of one well-known actor in Aristophanes' time – we are provided not simply with a means of making an apparent intolerable passage theatrically tolerable but with a positive reason why Aristophanes should have given 1186–8 the form and content which they have.[45]

The difficulty of 1181, which has found few defenders, is, I believe, illusory. That the messenger, in describing how an undignified disaster befell Lamachos, should adapt a line which Lamachos himself used (574) in a blustering mood is in keeping with the Aristophanic trick of turning a man's own words against him (cf. *Nu*. 1053 ~ 225 and *Th*. 51 ~ 43). The words mean just what they say, and exemplify an idea which often enters into popular humorous narrative and has been exploited ad nauseam by cartoon films: the idea that a shock brings to life statues, paintings or corpses (cf. *Ra*. 170ff).

The real difficulty lies in 1182, πεσόν at the end of the line, coming so soon after πεσών at the end of 1180, strikes a discordant note in a passage where colour and variety of vocabulary are wanted; both πτίλον τὸ μέγα and κομπολακύθου are frigid reminiscences of jokes which had a point in their original contexts (587 and 589) but here have none,[46] and though, according to the manuscripts, it is the feather which falls and utters a valediction to its master,[47] it is Lamachos whom any hearer will want to take as the subject of τοσαῦτα λέξας κτλ.[48] Just conceivably the incoherence of τοσαῦτα λέξας is all part of the fun; but it is one of four separate counts against 1182, of which not more than two can be met by emendation of πεσόν.

The interpolation of a patchwork line is not unparalleled, even in this play. 803, which does not scan, makes no sense dramatically, and is absent from the Suda's quotation of the passage (though there was a line between 802 and 804 in the Berlin papyrus), was probably generated from a gloss, and between *Nu*. 907 and 908 the Ravennas has incorporated a scholion divided into three units resembling short verses. I suggest the possibility that at 1182 Aristophanes wrote words meaning 'And seeing his feather crushed . . .' and used for 'his feather' an expression (e.g. στρουθῶν ἄωτον) which was glossed by words drawn from 587–9; the gloss ousted the original line.

---

[44] Cf. esp. Page 126.

[45] It is possible that the incoherence itself is meant to be humorous, without any parody of tragic composition or tragic action; cf. Eduard Fraenkel, *Beobachtungen zu Aristophanes* (Rome 1962) 41, comparing *Ra*. 1331ff.

[46] Cf. Page, *loc. cit.*; this criticism has not been properly met by defenders of 1182.

[47] Cf. Fraenkel 38.

[48] A. M. Dale, *BICS* viii (1961) 148, suggests that the feather (thoroughly personified by now, and so masculine in gender) is the subject; a suggestion which I would accept if 1182 were not suspect on other grounds.

1207f

Λα. στυγερὸς ἐγώ, μογερὸς ἐγώ.
Δι. τί με σὺ κυνεῖς; τί με σὺ δάκνεις;

If Dikaiopolis's words meant '*why* do you kiss me?' they would indeed be absurd;[49] but utterances in the form of questions are not all questions. τί φῄς, for example, is not an enquiry; it expresses surprise, horror, or indignation at what has just been said. Similarly, when the girl in the pseudo-Theokritean *Oaristus* says to Daphnis (27.49),

τί ῥέζεις, σατυρίσκε; τί δ' ἔνδοθεν ἄψαο μαζῶν;

she is not being so silly as to ask him *why* he has put his hand to her breasts; she is expressing real or affected fear or indignation at his having done so. Dikaiopolis is talking the universal language of flirtation; having told his two girls to kiss him (1200f), he teases them by affecting delighted surprise ('kissing me, eh?') when they renew the game on their own initiative.

ADDITIONAL NOTES

P. 289, on the line of pseudo-Persian. M. L. West, *CR* NS xviii (1968) 5ff, is right, I think, in associating πισσ- with the satrap whose name the Greeks transcribed as Πισσούθνης, rather than with *puça* 'son'. I am surprised, however, that he under-estimates the impression which the frequency of long *a* in Persian would have made on Greek ears; of the first 100 syllables of col. I of Darius's Behistun inscription, 34 contain *ā*, and of the first 100 syllables of *Acharnians*, only 2.

P. 295, on σειστός. I should also have cited στρεπτός; but E. K. Borthwick, *Mnemosyne* 1967, 409ff, pointing out that σείειν is the normal word used of casting dice, makes the attractive suggestion that, as the chorus whirls round, the stones they had been carrying in their cloaks fly out like dice from the shaker.

P. 297, on 731f. See also R. T. Elliott's edition of the play (Oxford 1914) 164, 219.

P. 299, on πολυπραγμοσύνη. In *Ra*. 228 the frogs call Dionysos πολλὰ πράττων because he has expressed a vehemently adverse opinion of their constant κοὰξ κοάξ. A touchy government may similarly accuse foreign journalists of 'interference' when all that they have done is express their opinions.

P. 299, on εἴμεναι. I should have mentioned the puzzling ἀλεξέμεναι of Th. v 77.3, in the text of a treaty between Sparta and Argos. It may be an epicism perpetrated by an ancient editor; if it is not, then εἴμεναι and ἀλεξέμεναι support one another.

P. 302, on Dikaiopolis's selfishness. D. M. MacDowell, *Greece and Rome* xxx (1983) 159f, observes that in the fourth century a real Derketes of Phyle is attested on inscriptions. The farmer in the play may well be intended to represent an earlier member of the

---

[49] They are strongly condemned by Page (124f), who conjectures τί μ' οὐ κυνεῖς etc. But, even if emendation were required, this would strike a false note; for the optimum contrast with the fate of Lamachos, we want Dikaiopolis to be εὖ πάσχων, not importunately saying 'come on, kiss me!'

family; and, if a Derketes of Phyle contemporary with Aristophanes was an enthusiastic supporter of the war, we can see why Dikaiopolis does not treat him as one of its unhappy anonymous victims.

P. 304, on the messenger's speech. See now A. H. Sommerstein, *CQ* N.S. xxviii (1978) 390–5.

31
Aristophanes, *Knights* 11–20

The two slaves who have been conversing in lines 1–9 intone line 10 together. It is therefore impossible to decide which of the two speakers distinguishable in 1–9 speaks 11–12, and we are free to call him 'A'.

A poses the question 'surely we ought to be thinking of a plan?', and B, who has no ready answer, says (13),

$$\tau i\varsigma \; o\tilde{v}v \; \gamma \acute{\epsilon}vo\iota\tau' \; \ddot{\alpha}v; \; \lambda \acute{\epsilon}\gamma \epsilon \; \sigma \acute{v}$$

inviting A to speak.[1] Now, A has no answer either, but he does not want to betray this. He conceals his impotence by courtesy (13–14)

$$\sigma \grave{v} \; \mu \grave{\epsilon}v \; o\tilde{v}v \; \mu o\iota \; \lambda \acute{\epsilon}\gamma \epsilon,$$
$$\tilde{\iota}v\alpha \; \mu \grave{\eta} \; \mu \acute{\alpha}\chi \omega \mu \alpha \iota.$$

'No, *you* say – I don't want to quarrel about it.' B outdoes him in courtesy, and in doing so makes it plain even to the densest spectator that neither slave has an idea and neither is willing to admit the fact (14–15)

$$\mu \grave{\alpha} \; \tau \grave{o}v \; {}'A\pi \acute{o}\lambda\lambda\omega \; {}'\gamma \grave{\omega} \; \mu \grave{\epsilon}v \; o\mathring{v}.$$
$$\mathring{\alpha}\lambda\lambda' \; \epsilon \mathring{\iota}\pi \grave{\epsilon} \; \theta \alpha \varrho \varrho \tilde{\omega}v, \; \epsilon \mathring{\iota}\tau \alpha \; \kappa \mathring{\alpha}\gamma \grave{\omega} \; \sigma o\grave{\iota} \; \varphi \varrho \acute{\alpha}\sigma\omega.$$

'Oh, no, no, not I! Come, on, don't hesitate, tell me, and then I'll tell you mine!' This is gentle satire upon the 'after you!' game which we sometimes play when we want to conceal our ignorance. There is more of this type of satire in Aristophanes than is sometimes seen; two obvious examples are the creditor of *Nu.* 1214–21 trying to talk down his own embarrassment, and the young man of *Pl.* 1076–9 pretending to renounce magnanimously what he is in fact glad to get rid of.

Impasse. Silence. Then a guilty, dangerous thought strikes both of them,

---

[1] Vahlen, *Opuscula* ii (Leipzig 1908) 271ff, says all that need be said in defence of the manuscripts' assignation of λέγε σύ to the same speaker as τίς οὖν γένοιτ' ἄν;

and one of them – let us call him A, since B spoke last, but it could still be B – voices his feelings by quoting the line with which Phaedra in E. *Hp*. 345 expresses her agonized reluctance to speak (16):

$$\pi\tilde{\omega}\varsigma \,\, \tilde{\alpha}\nu \,\, \sigma\acute{\upsilon} \,\, \mu o\iota \,\, \lambda\acute{\epsilon}\xi\epsilon\iota\alpha\varsigma \,\, \dot{\alpha}\mu\grave{\epsilon} \,\, \chi\varrho\grave{\eta} \,\, \lambda\acute{\epsilon}\gamma\epsilon\iota\nu;$$

'If only *you* would say what it is for *me* to say!' B knows what A is thinking; he is thinking the same himself; but he confesses his own reluctance (17):

$$\dot{\alpha}\lambda\lambda' \,\, o\dot{\upsilon}\kappa \,\, \check{\epsilon}\nu\iota \,\, \mu o\iota \,\, \tau\grave{o} \,\, \theta\varrho\acute{\epsilon}\tau\tau\epsilon.$$

'Oh, but τὸ θρέττε isn't in me!' This enigmatic word is explained in a muddled Scholion simultaneously as 'confidence' and οὐδὲ τὸ τυχὸν ἔχω περὶ τούτων εἰπεῖν.[2] Its formal affinities are, on the one hand, with θρεττανελό in *Pl*. 290, 296, an imitation of a musical instrument, and, on the other hand, with the war-cries παῖε, βάλλε, etc. The former has no relevance here, and the latter offer some slight support to what is in any case a reasonable guess. B's point is: 'I haven't quite the dash (the drive, guts, the face) to say it outright.' Then he wonders how to put the ugly idea in elegant obscurity (17–18):

$$\pi\tilde{\omega}\varsigma \,\, \tilde{\alpha}\nu \,\, o\check{\upsilon}\nu \,\, \pi o\tau\epsilon$$
$$\epsilon\check{\iota}\pi o\iota\mu' \,\, \tilde{\alpha}\nu \,\, \alpha\dot{\upsilon}\tau\grave{o} \,\, \delta\tilde{\eta}\tau\alpha \,\, \kappa o\mu\psi\epsilon\upsilon\varrho\iota\pi\iota\kappa\tilde{\omega}\varsigma;$$

The 'guilty thoughts' humour of 16–18 has now gone far enough, and needs to be broken off; this is done by making the mention of Euripides provoke from A the familiar joke about vegetables (19), and in 20, which makes the suggestion of desertion plainly, the way is cleared for the next joke.

In this interpretation I have kept the order of lines and the distribution between speakers exactly as they are in the manuscripts. So do Neil (with a little hesitation), Rogers (with a mistranslation of 14), and Erbse, none of whom, however, seems to me to see where the humour of the passage lies. Various transpositions have been favoured by the majority. Sauppe, with the approval of Vahlen and van Leeuwen, transposed 15 and 16 in order to make ἀλλ' οὐκ ἔνι μοι τὸ θρέττε answer ἀλλ' εἰπὲ θαρρῶν; a frivolous reason for transposition. Herbert Richards,[3] followed by Coulon, put 16 after 18, on the ground that the quotation from Euripides should follow πῶς ἂν οὖν ... κομψευριπικῶς. It is, however, pointless for one and the same speaker, after wondering how he can 'say it', i.e. put his plan forward, in Euripidean fashion, to quote a line which throws the whole proceedings back to the previous stage by expressing a wish that he did not have to speak at all.

[2] Pohlenz, *NAWG* (Ph.-hist.) 1952, 106f, translates 'Ich habe nicht die geringste Ahnung, was du meinst', comparing such expressions as *Ach*. 1035 οὐδ' ἂν στριβιλίκιγξ. Erbse, *Eranos*, lii (1954) 103, points out that the definite article differentiates τὸ θρέττε from those expressions. [See now p. 274 (above), n. 7.]

[3] *Aristophanes and Others* (London 1909) 13.

Moreover, there is no dramatic objection to allowing the Euripidean line to pass without comment while the explicit mention of Euripides provokes a horrified reaction. Aristophanes several times in this play puts into the mouth of a speaker a tragic line appropriate in sense to the comic situation, and by that very fact humorous in its own right, without making any other speaker comment on its tragic character, e.g. 813 (composite), 1240, 1244 (almost certainly tragic), 1302 (adapted?).

These are comparatively trivial considerations. A much more powerful influence upon editors and critics is the long-standing identification of the two slaves with Demosthenes and Nicias.[4] The speaker of 40–72 is 'Demosthenes' since he complains in 45–57 that he made the 'Laconian loaf' which the Paphlagonian stole and served up to Demos – a thin disguise for the parts played by Demosthenes and Cleon in the reduction of Sphacteria. This identification has meant that the speakers of 11–20 are regarded not as A and B but as 'Demosthenes' and 'Nicias', and that the text must be so ordered that neither of the two says anything out of character; in particular, the words ἵνα μὴ μάχωμαι must be spoken by 'Nicias'. It has been assumed that the identity of the slaves is made plain to the audience by portrait-masks; Pohlenz goes so far as to say that this is essential for the understanding of the humour of the scene.

Now, if I am right in supposing that a brief silence falls after line 15, and that 16 may or may not be spoken by the same person as 15, the identification of the speakers in 11–15 is freed from any necessary relation to the distribution of lines from 16 onwards. There is, however, a bigger issue at stake. In the manuscript tradition of Aristophanes the *sigla personarum* sometimes represent the firm adoption of what was in origin a tentative conjecture. So the Old Man of *Th.*, a kinsman of Euripides, nowhere named in the text of the play, becomes 'Mnesilochus', since that was the name of Euripides' father-in-law (*Vita E*. 5). So too the First Creditor of *Nu*. 1214ff becomes 'Pasias' (cf. 21), the Scholar of 1505 'Chaerephon', and a speaking part is found for the statue of Hermes in 1478ff. It is therefore not surprising that the slaves of *Knights* are Δημ(οσθένης) and Νικ(ίας). The Hypotheses, by contrast, speak with exemplary caution. Neither Hypothesis hesitates over the identification of the Paphlagonian, but Hypothesis i offers no identification of his ὁμόδουλοι, while Hypothesis ii says ἔοικεν ὁ προλογίζων εἶναι Δημοσθένης and λέγουσι δὲ τῶν οἰκετῶν τὸν μὲν εἶναι Δημοσθένην τὸν δὲ Νικίαν, ἵνα ὦσι δημηγόροι οἱ δύο.

These last words illuminate the part played in the identification by conceptions of dramatic symmetry. It is dramatically desirable, given that the Paphlagonian is Cleon, that the two other slaves should consistently represent real individuals. It is certain that *if* the speaker of 40–72 consistently represents any real individual, he represents Demosthenes. It then becomes doubly desirable that the remaining slave should consistently represent a real

---

[4] Especially in K. F. Hermann, *Progymnasmata ad Aristophanis Equites* (Marburg 1835).

individual. There is room for difference of opinion on the extent to which Aristophanes would have acquiesced in our demands for symmetry and for consistency; but if my scepticism on this general issue is misplaced, let me still plead for caution on three points of a more particular character:

(i) If the second slave represents a real person, Nicias is not necessarily the best candidate. We have been influenced by Thucydides' selection, emphasis, and portrayal of the events of 425; so had the Hellenistic scholars; Aristophanes had not.

(ii) If the slave is Nicias, he is not necessarily invested with the character which the Sicilian Expedition, several years after *Knights*, revealed in Nicias.

(iii) In the whole of the opening dialogue of *Knights* there is no passge which requires for the appreciation of its humour any knowledge of the character of any real person.

Index

II. GREEK WORDS AND PHRASES

III. GENERAL